THE WORLD CUP

1930 - 1990

Sixty Glorious Years of Soccer's Premier Event

THE WORLD CUP

1930 - 1990

Sixty Glorious Years of
Soccer's Premier Event

Jack Rollin

Facts On File
New York • Oxford

Facts on File, Inc.
460 Park Avenue South
New York NY 10016

Library of Congress Cataloging-in-Publication Data
Rollin, Jack
    World Cup Soccer/Jack Rollin
     p.   cm.
    Includes index
    ISBN 0-8160-2523-1
    1. World Cup (Soccer) — — History. 2. Soccer — — Records. I. Title
GV943.49.R65 1990
796.334'668 — — dc20

Facts on File books are available at special discounts when purchased in bulk quantities for businesses, associations, institutions or sales promotions. Please call our Special Sales Department in New York at 212/683-2244 (dial 800/322-8755 except in NY, AK or HI).

Black and white illustrations courtesy of ALLSPORT except where stated.

Text design design by Sports Editions Limited, 3 Greenlea Park, Prince George's Road, London SW19 2JD, England

Typeset in Kabel by Sports Editions Limited

Printed and bound in Great Britain by The Bath Press, Bath

10 9 8 7 6 5 4 3 2 1

Acknowledgements

The author would like to acknowledge the following sources:
World Cup (Brian Glanville and Jerry Weinstein) 1958
World Cup Digest (Jack Rollin) 1966
England's World Cup Triumph (Jack Rollin) 1966
A-Z of World Soccer (Norman S. Barrett) 1973
FIFA Technical Study 1970, 1974
Armada Book of the World Cup (Gordon Jeffrey) 1974
Official FIFA Report, World Cup Argentina 1978
Complete World Cup Guide (Jack Rollin) 1982
FIFA News
Don Aldridge

CONTENTS

How it all began 6

The Competitions
Uruguay 1930 8
Italy 1934 12
France 1938 16
Brazil 1950 20
Switzerland 1954 24
Sweden 1958 29
Chile 1962 36
England 1966 42
Mexico 1970 50
West Germany 1974 58
Argentina 1978 68
Spain 1982 76
Mexico 1986 86
Italy 1990 96

21 World Cup All-Time Greats 105
Banks 106
Beckenbauer 108
Charlton 110
Cruyff 112
Dalglish 114
Didi 116
Facchetti 118
Fontaine 120
Hidegkuti 122
Krol 124
Lineker 126
Maradona 128
Moore 130
Muller 132
Pele 134
Platini 136
Santos 138
Schiaffino 140
Walter 142

Zico 144
Zoff 146

The 1990 Finalists' World Cup pedigree 148
Austria 150
Czechoslovakia 151
Italy 152
USA 153
Cameroon 154
Argentina 155
USSR 156
Rumania 157
Costa Rica 158
Brazil 159
Scotland 160
Sweden 161
West Germany 162
Colombia 163
United Arab Emirates 164
Yugoslavia 165
Belgium 166
Spain 167
Uruguay 168
South Korea 169
Egypt 170
England 171
Holland 172
Republic of Ireland 173

World Cup Records 174

World Cup Trivia 178

FIFA Affiliated countries 184

Looking ahead: USA 1994 186

Index 188

HOW IT ALL BEGAN

The idea of a World Cup first emerged in 1904 when FIFA was formed, but it was not until 1930 that it became reality and the tournament has since matured into the symbol of world soccer supremacy. In the 60 years that have followed, both the membership of FIFA and the competition itself have grown in stature. Long-forgotten has been the simple idea of a knock-out tournament; the World Cup has become a business operation, with television and sponsorship considerations taking precedence over all other aspects.

But it began modestly enough. The Federation Internationale de Football Association (FIFA) was founded on 21 May 1904 in Paris by representatives of seven European countries: France, Belgium, Denmark, the Netherlands, Spain, Sweden and Switzerland. Included in the statutes of what was to become the governing body of world football was a clause to the effect that FIFA alone would have the right to organise a world championship.

Membership gradually increased. Germany joined shortly afterwards; Austria, England and Italy the following year. By the end of the First World War, there were 25 countries affiliated including Scotland and Wales, admitted in 1910, and Northern Ireland a year later, plus Argentina, Brazil and Chile as well as the USA from the Americas.

In 1921 Jules Rimet, a French lawyer, became President of FIFA and the possibility of a World Cup came closer, though it took years of lengthy persuasion on his part to convince others to accept the concept. His efforts were assisted in a practical way by Uruguay coming over from South America to win the Olympic Games football tournaments in Europe in 1924 and 1928. In May 1929 it was agreed that a World Cup competition would be held the following year.

FIFA's membership then stood at 41, though England, Northern Ireland, Wales and Scotland had left the organisation for a second time and were ineligible for the inaugural competition. The four had originally withdrawn after refusing to be associated with either Austria, Germany or Hungary (members of the axis nations in the First World War) and they quit for a second time over broken time-payments to amateurs.

Although there had not been universal approval among the members, FIFA's meeting in 1926 had brought a strong plea from Henri Delaunay, secretary of the French Federation, that an international football tournament at the highest level could no longer be confined to the Olympics because of professionalism. At the 1928 Congress however, the proposals put forward by Delaunay were carried with over 80 percent of the members in favour of the project.

Six countries — Italy, Holland, Hungary, Sweden, Spain and Uruguay — applied to stage the finals. But Sweden had even voted against the idea! Uruguay was the obvious choice. They had proved their playing ability with two Olympic gold medals, the country was celebrating its independence centenary in 1930 and they promised to underwrite the costs of the competing countries.

It was only then that enthusiasm began to wane. Few European countries could afford to send a team to South America, since the players would be away from home for at least two months, travelling to and from the venue by boat. Had it not been for the intervention of Rimet himself, France would not have entered, and neither would Belgium but for their FIFA representative Rudolphe Seeldrayers. Rumania and Yugoslavia were the only other European acceptors. King Carol of Rumania actually picked his team and succeeded in obtaining time off

Jules Rimet, the man who gave his name to the first World Cup trophy. A Frenchman, he was President of FIFA from 1921 to 1954. (POPPERFOTO)

work for the players who were chosen to undertake the journey.

All four European teams travelled together and South America dominated the overall entry. Uruguay had also guaranteed a new ground and work on the Centenario Stadium in Montevideo was started in February. It remained unfinished at the beginning of the tournament on 13 July, despite day and night construction, because of intermittent heavy rain. Opening matches were played either at the Pocitos or Parque Central stadia until the main stadium was available.

The trophy which was presented to the winners of the World Cup was a gold cup designed by Abel Lafleur, a French sculptor; appropriately it was named after Jules Rimet himself. After Brazil's three successes in 1958, 1962 and 1970 they were allowed to retain it. It was replaced by the FIFA World Cup, designed by the Italian sculptor Silvio Gazamiga, made of solid gold 36 cm high and insured for £1.8 million.

FIFA's membership now stands at 166 countries, distributed in six Confederations and there is a waiting list of other nations eager to join the world-wide organisation. The World Cup every four years has to attempt to satisfy the clamour of all of them to have a reasonable chance of progressing to the final stage. The increase from 16 to 24 teams in the final tournament has eased the problem but by no means solved it.

It would be naive to pretend that the finalists represent all of the most outstanding of contemporary teams. The system does not allow for this eventuality. Indeed it would be difficult to conceive of a tournament on a world-wide scale that could improve on the present one, without alienating a huge chunk of the member nations. But it remains the game's pinnacle and a target for all the countries to aim at.

Lorenzo
Fernandez, Pedro
Cea and Hector
Scarone celebrate
Uruguay's World
Cup victory in
Montevideo.
(HULTON DEUTSCH)

URUGUAY

1930

Uruguay proved to be worthy champions and despite the disappointment of the the small European entry, this first tournament was a success with only one serious reservation: the bitterness between the supporters of the two finalists, Uruguay and Argentina. The repercussions of this reverberated back from Montevideo to Buenos Aires across the River Plate and resulted in the Argentine FA severing connections with the hosts.

The first hint of trouble came two days after the competition had started on July 13, when the Uruguayan crowd supported the French team against Argentina. Argentine supporters had arrived in ten boats and were searched for weapons both at the docks and before entering the ground. All the visiting teams were guarded by soldiers with fixed bayonets!

Argentina's delegation almost returned home as a result of this incident, in a match which ended in a bizarre manner. Referee Almeida Rego blew for time a full five minutes too early, as France appeared likely to score an equaliser. The crowd invaded the pitch and after protests from the French, the remaining minutes were then completed.

Controversy followed Argentina. The Bolivian referee Ulysses Saucedo awarded five penalties in their game with Mexico and police had to step in to stop fighting between players in the fracas with Chile, instigated by Argentine centre-half Luisito Monti, a belligerent if commanding figure.

The United States team, nicknamed the 'shot-putters' by the French, included five ex-Scottish professionals and an Englishman. They won their group well and were fancied in the semi-final with Argentina. But they lost one player with a broken leg after ten minutes, their goalkeeper was badly injured by half-time and another received a kick in the mouth. They lost 6-1.

Uruguay reached the final without being over-extended. They also had a 6-1 semi-final win, over Yugoslavia. Their strength was built around the half-back line of Jose Andrade, Lorenzo Fernandez and Alvaro Gestido, known as 'la costilla metallica' — the iron curtain. The nucleus of the side which had won the 1924 and 1928 Olympics was formidable.

Although Pablo Dorado scored for Uruguay after 12 minutes, Argentina led 2-1 at half-time through goals by Peucelle and Stabile, the latter effort claimed as off-side by the Uruguayans. After the break, the home crowd saw Uruguay's territorial domination and slight technical superiority turned into goals. Pedro Cea scored an opportunist equaliser and Iriarte made it 3-2. In the dying moments Castro put a truer finish on the score with a splendid long-range drive.

Though the game had been played in a good spirit, in Buenos Aires the locals took it badly. There were public demonstrations and anti-Uruguayan outbursts in the press. It proved that national prestige meant as much as the game itself.

Jose Leandro Andrade, Uruguay's outstanding right-half in their 1924 and 1928 Olympic winning teams and in their successful 1930 World Cup side.

The two captains, Nasazzi (left) of
Uruguay and Ferreyra (right) of
Argentina, shake hands before the
1930 final in Montevideo, watched
by Belgian referee Langenus.
(HULTON DEUTSCH)

Final Tournament URUGUAY
GROUP 1

13.7.30 France (3) 4, Mexico (0) 1 MONTEVIDEO
France: Thepot, Mattler, Capelle, Villaplane, Pinel, Chantrel, Liberati, Delfour, Maschinot (2), Laurent (1), Langiller (1)
Mexico: Bonfiglio, Gutierrez R, Rosas M, Rosas F, Sanchez, Amezcua, Perez, Carreno (1), Mejia, Ruiz, Lopez
Referee: Lombardi (Uruguay)

15.7.30 Argentina (0) 1, France (0) 0 MONTEVIDEO
Argentina: Bossio, Della Torre, Muttis, Suarez, Monti (1), Evaristo J, Perinetti, Varallo, Ferreyra, Gierro, Evaristo M
France: Thepot, Mattler, Capelle, Villaplane, Pinel, Chantrel, Liberati, Delfour, Maschinot, Laurent, Langiller
Referee: Rego (Brazil)

16.7.30 Chile (1) 3, Mexico (0) 0 MONTEVIDEO
Chile: Cortes, Morales, Porier, Torres A, Saavedra, Helgueta, Ojeda, Subiabre (2), Villalobos, Vidal (1), Scheuerberger
Mexico: Sota, Gutierrez R, Rosas M, Rosas F, Sanchez, Amezcua, Perez, Carreno, Ruiz, Gayon, Lopez
Referee: Christophe (Belgium)

19.7.30 Chile (0) 1, France (0) 0 MONTEVIDEO
Chile: Cortes, Ciaparro, Morales, Torres A, Saavedra, Torres C, Ojeda, Subiabre (1), Villalobos, Vidal, Scheuerberger
France: Thepot, Mattler, Capelle, Chantrel, Delmer, Villaplane, Liberati, Delfour, Pinel, Veinante, Langiller
Referee: Tejada (Uruguay)

19.7.30 Argentina (3) 6, Mexico (1) 3 MONTEVIDEO
Argentina: Bossio, Della Torre, Paternoster, Cividini, Zumelzu (2 pens), Orlandini, Peucelle, Varallo (1), Stabile (3), Demaria, Spadaro
Mexico: Bonfiglio, Gutierrez R, Gutierrez F, Rosas M (2 pens), Sanchez, Rodriguez, Rosas F, Lopez (1), Gayon, Carreno, Olivares
Referee: Saucedo (Bolivia)

22.7.30 Argentina (2) 3, Chile (1) 1 MONTEVIDEO
Argentina: Bossio, Della Torre, Paternoster, Evaristo J, Monti, Orlandini, Peucelle, Varallo, Stabile (2), Ferreyra, Evaristo M (1)
Chile: Cortes, Ciaparro, Morales, Torres A, Saavedra, Torres C, Avellane, Subiabre (1), Villalobos, Vidal, Aquilera
Referee: Langenus (Belgium)

	P	W	D	L	F	A	Pts
Argentina	3	3	0	0	10	4	6
Chile	3	2	0	1	5	3	4
France	3	1	0	2	4	3	2
Mexico	3	0	0	3	4	13	0

GROUP 2

14.7.30 Yugoslavia (2) 2, Brazil (0) 1 MONTEVIDEO
Yugoslavia: Jaksic, Ivkovic, Mihailovic, Arsenijevic, Stefanovic, Dokic, Tirnanic (1), Marjanovic (1), Beck, Vujadinovic, Sekulic
Brazil: Joel, Brilhante, Italia, Hermogenes, Fausto, Fernando, Poly, Nilo, Araken, Preguinho (1), Moderato
Referee: Tejada (Uruguay)

17.7.30 Yugoslavia (0) 4, Bolivia (0) 0 MONTEVIDEO
Yugoslavia: Jaksic, Ivkovic, Mihailovic, Arsenijevic, Stefanovic, Dokic, Tirnanic, Marjanovic (1), Beck (2), Vujadinovic (1), Najdanovic
Bolivia: Bermudez, Durandal, Ciavarria, Argote, Lara, Valderrama, Gomez, Bustamante, Mendez, Alborta, Fernandez
Referee: Mateucci (Mexico)

20.7.30 Brazil (1) 4, Bolivia (0) 0 MONTEVIDEO
Brazil: Velloso, Ze Luiz, Italia, Hermogenes, Fausto, Fernando, Benedito, Russinho, Leite, Preguinho (2), Moderato (2)
Bolivia: Bermudez, Durandal, Ciavarria, Sainz, Lara, Valderrama, Ortiz, Bustamante, Mendez, Alborta, Fernandez
Referee: Balway (France)

	P	W	D	L	F	A	Pts
Yugoslavia	2	2	0	0	6	1	4
Brazil	2	1	0	1	5	2	2
Bolivia	2	0	0	2	0	8	0

GROUP 3

14.7.30 Rumania (1) 3, Peru (0) 1 MONTEVIDEO
Rumania: Lapusneanu, Steiner, Burger, Rafinski, Vogl, Fieraru, Covaci, Desu, Wetzer, Staucin (2), Barbu (1)
Peru: Valdiviso, De Las Casas, Soria, Galindo, Garcia, Valle, Flores, Villanueva, Denegri, Neira, Souza (1)
Referee: Warken (Chile)

18.7.30 Uruguay (0) 1, Peru (0) 0 MONTEVIDEO
Uruguay: Ballesteros, Nasazzi, Tejera, Andrade, Fernandez, Gestido, Urdinaran, Castro (1), Petrone, Cea, Iriarte
Peru: Pardon, De Las Casas, Maquillon, Denegri, Galindo, Astengo, Lavalle, Flores, Villanueva, Neira, Souza
Referee: Langenus (Belgium)

21.7.30 Uruguay (3) 4, Rumania (0) 0 MONTEVIDEO
Uruguay: Ballesteros, Nasazzi, Mascheroni, Andrade, Fernandez, Gestido, Dorado (1), Scarone (1), Anselmo (1), Cea (1), Iriarte
Rumania: Lapusneanu, Burger, Tacu, Robi, Vogl, Fieraru, Covaci, Desu, Wetzer, Rafinski, Barbu
Referee: Rego (Brazil)

	P	W	D	L	F	A	Pts
Uruguay	2	2	0	0	5	0	4
Rumania	2	1	0	1	3	5	2
Peru	2	0	0	2	1	4	0

GROUP 4

13.7.30 USA (2) 3, Belgium (0) 0 MONTEVIDEO
USA: Douglas, Wood, Moorhouse, Gallacher, Tracey, Brown, Gonzalvez, Florie, Patenaude (1), Auld, McGhee (2)
Belgium: Badjou, Nouwens, Hoydonckx, Braine, Hellemans, Declercq, Diddens, Moeschal, Adams, Voorhoof, Versijp
Referee: Macias (Argentina)

17.7.30 USA (2) 3, Paraguay (0) 0 MONTEVIDEO
USA: Douglas, Wood, Moorhouse, Gallacher, Tracey, Brown, Gonzalvez, Florie (1), Patenaude (2), Auld, McGhee
Paraguay: Denis, Olmedo, Miracca, Etcheverrey, Diaz, Aguirre, Nessi, Dominquez, Gonzales, Gaceres, Pena
Referee: Macias (Argentina)

20.7.30 Paraguay (1) 1, Belgium (0) 0 MONTEVIDEO
Paraguay: Benitez P, Olmedo, Flores, Benitez S, Diaz, Garcete, Nessi, Romero, Gonzales, Gaceres, Pena (1)
Belgium: Badjou, Dedeken, Hoydonckx, Braine, Hellemans, Moeschal, Versijp, Delbeke, Adams, Nouwens, Diddens
Referee: Vallarino (Uruguay)

	P	W	D	L	F	A	Pts
USA	2	2	0	0	6	0	4
Paraguay	2	1	0	1	1	3	2
Belgium	2	0	0	2	0	4	0

SEMI FINALS

26.7.30 Argentina (1) 6, USA (0) 1 MONTEVIDEO
Argentina: Botasso, Della Torre, Paternoster, Evaristo J, Monti (2), Orlandini, Peucelle, Scopelli (2), Stabile (2), Ferreyra, Evaristo M
USA: Douglas, Wood, Moorhouse, Gallacher, Tracey, Brown (1), Gonzalvez, Florie, Patenaude, Auld, McGhee
Referee: Langenus (Belgium)

27.7.30 Uruguay (3) 6, Yugoslavia (1) 1 MONTEVIDEO
Uruguay: Ballesteros, Nasazzi, Mascheroni, Andrade, Fernandez, Gestido, Dorado, Scarone, Anselmo (2), Cea (3), Iriarte (1)
Yugoslavia: Jaksic, Ivkovic, Mihailovic, Arsenijevic, Stefanovic, Dokic, Tirnanic, Marjanovic, Beck, Vujadinovic, Sekulic (1)
Referee: Rego (Brazil)

FINAL

30.7.30 Uruguay (1) 4, Argentina (2) 2 MONTEVIDEO
Uruguay: Ballesteros, Nasazzi, Mascheroni, Andrade, Gestido, Fernandez, Dorado (1), Scarone, Castro (1), Cea (1), Iriarte (1)
Argentina: Botasso, Della Torre, Paternoster, Evaristo J, Monti, Suarez, Peucelle (1), Varallo, Stabile (1), Ferreyra, Evaristo M
Referee: Langenus (Belgium)

The Italian team
raise their arms in
the fascist salute
prior to the 1934
final against
Czechoslovakia.
(HULTON DEUTSCH)

ITALY

1934

Apart from the doubtful political aspect, Italy was a good choice as the host nation. Dictator Mussolini was determined to make as much capital out of the competition as possible, but it had needed eight meetings of FIFA to agree to the Italian venue.

Thirty-two countries originally entered and were geographically grouped in 12 sections of a qualifying tournament. England, still outside FIFA, and Uruguay, piqued by the lack of interest in their own series and worried by domestic matters, did not enter. Even Italy had to play a qualifying game, against Greece.

The 16 finalists were paired in a knock-out round, eight seeded against weaker opposition, the matches held in eight different cities. Italy were the favourites, largely because it was agreed that Austria's 'wunderteam' was over-the-hill. The Italian manager Vittorio Pozzo was shrewd and had a talented team. He had succeeded in blending the natural strength and team work he had so admired when he had visited England, with the individual ability of the Latins.

Two factors stood out — the individual performances of several players and the increase of violence on the field as national pride and international disagreement came to the fore.

Czechoslovakia had a resourceful and adept goalkeeper in Frantisek Planicka, and Spain a custodian of equal ability in the legendary Ricardo Zamora. The latter played in what was then the most disgraceful of all World Cup matches, Italy's violent clash with Spain in Florence. The result was a 1-1 draw, but when the replay took place the following day, seven injured Spaniards and four Italians were non-starters!

Italy won the replay 1-0 and had a similar result in the semi-final against Austria, the goal being scrambled in off a post by the Argentine-born Enrico Guaita, one of three

from that country of Italian parentage, including Monti from the 1930 final. The Italians' star forward was Giuseppe Meazza, but in the final the Czechs' neat, short-passing game surprised the hosts. The stadium in Rome was not full, but Mussolini was among the 55,000. Twenty minutes from the end of an undistinguished match, the crowd was stunned when Puc put Czechoslovakia ahead following a corner, much to the delight of visiting supporters who had travelled to Rome from Prague by road and rail.

Possibly through over-eagerness the Czechs then missed two further chances, one hitting a post. The Italians switched their forwards in a desperate bid to save the game. Eight minutes from time the Argentine Raimondo Orsi hit a swerving shot of speculative origin to equalise.

Only in extra time did the Italians display the tactical skill and strategy for which they were renowned and Angelo Schiavio scored the winner. For the Italian regime, it represented everything they had hoped for.

Qualifying Tournament

32 entries

Argentina, Austria, Belgium, Brazil, Bulgaria, Chile, Cuba, Czechoslovakia, Egypt, Estonia, France, Germany, Greece, Haiti, Holland, Hungary, Rep of Ireland, Italy, Lithuania, Luxembourg, Mexico, Palestine, Peru, Poland, Portugal, Rumania, Spain, Sweden, Switzerland, Turkey, USA, Yugoslavia

A preliminary qualification round in ten regional groups had been prepared. This was adapted according to the entries and increased to twelve groups. Each group produced one qualifier with the exception of groups 8, 10, 11 and 12 where the first two progressed. However there were one or two complications.

In Group 10, Switzerland qualified after successfully protesting that Rumania had fielded an ineligible player against them. Rumania's qualification was thus under threat. Meanwhile in Group 1, Cuba had won two and drawn one of three games in Haiti and went on to play three games in Mexico which they lost. Since the USA had not played, it was agreed that an extra qualifying game would be completed between them and Mexico. At the same time there would be a possibility that the USA could compete in the finals in any case, because of the likely loss of a qualifier from Group 10. So the extra game was arranged in Rome, three days before the final tournament began. But Rumania appealed against the decision involving their alleged ineligible player and found it upheld in their favour. They were then awarded a place in the finals. The USA and Mexico played off for another place.

Many of the preliminary groups had seeded teams in them. Italy in Group 7 needed to play just one home game with Greece to qualify, presumably so as not to risk them losing over two matches and thus not appearing in their own tournament!

In Group 8, Austria merely had to play Bulgaria at home while their opponents were forced to play Hungary home and away. Moreover, though the Bulgaria v Hungary scores cancelled each other out, the 6-1 defeat in Vienna put Bulgaria out of the finals.

In Groups 10 and 11, each of the three teams had one home game; in Group 12 Germany and France each played away in Luxembourg. In Group 5, Sweden played Estonia at home and Lithuania away, while in Group 9 Poland, having lost at home to Czechoslovakia, withdrew before the return match. In Group 11, Belgium qualified on goal average over the Republic of Ireland.

Group 1 (USA, Cuba, Mexico, Haiti)
Haiti v Cuba 1 - 3, 1 - 1, 0 - 6
Mexico v Cuba 3 - 2, 5 - 0, 4 - 1
Extra qualifying match (in Rome): USA v Mexico 4 - 2
USA qualified

Group 2 (Brazil, Peru)
Brazil qualified (Peru withdrew)

Group 3 (Argentina, Chile)
Chile qualified (Argentina withdrew)

Group 4 (Egypt, Palestine; Turkey withdrew)
Egypt v Palestine 7 - 1, 4 - 1
Egypt qualified

Group 5 (Sweden, Estonia, Lithuania)
Sweden v Estonia 6 - 2; Lithuania v Sweden 0 - 2
Sweden qualified

Group 6 (Spain, Portugal)
Spain v Portugal 9 - 0, 2 - 1
Spain qualified

Group 7 (Italy, Greece)
Italy v Greece 4 - 0
Italy qualified

Group 8 (Austria, Hungary, Bulgaria)
Bulgaria v Hungary 1 - 4; Austria v Bulgaria 6 - 1; Hungary v Bulgaria 4 - 1
Austria and Hungary qualified

Group 9 (Czechoslovakia, Poland)
Poland v Czechoslovakia 1 - 2. Poland withdrew before return match.
Czechoslovakia qualified.

Group 10 (Yugoslavia, Switzerland, Rumania)
Yugoslavia v Switzerland 2 - 2; Switzerland v Rumania 2 - 2; Rumania v Yugoslavia 2 - 1
Switzerland and Rumania qualified

Group 11 (Holland, Belgium, Rep of Ireland)
Rep of Ireland v Belgium 4 - 4; Holland v Rep of Ireland 5 - 2; Belgium v Holland 2 - 4
Holland and Belgium qualified (Belgium on goal average)

Group 12 (Germany, France, Luxembourg)
Luxembourg v Germany 1 - 9; Luxembourg v France 1 - 6
Germany and France qualified

Final Tournament ITALY
Preliminary round
27.5.34 Italy (3) 7, USA (0) 1 ROME
Italy: Combi, Rosetta, Allemandi, Pizzioli, Monti, Bertolini, Guaita, Meazza (1), Schiavio (3), Ferrari (1), Orsi (2)
USA: Hjulian, Czerkiewicz, Moorhouse, Pietras, Gonzalvez, Florie, Ryan, Nilson, Donelli (1), Dick, MacLean
Referee: Mercet (Switzerland)

27.5.34 Czechoslovakia (0) 2, Rumania (1) 1 TRIESTE
Czechoslovakia: Planicka, Zenizek, Ctyroky, Kostalek, Cambal, Krcil, Junek, Silny, Sobotka, Nejedly (1), Puc (1)
Rumannia: Zambori, Vogl, Albu, Deheleanu, Cotormani, Moravet, Bindea, Covaci, Sepi, Bodola, Dobai (1)
Referee: Langenus (Belgium)

27.5.34 Spain (3) 3, Brazil (0) 1 GENOA
Spain: Zamora, Ciriaco, Quincoces, Cilaurren, Muquerza, Marculeta, Lafuente, Iraragorri (1 pen), Langara (2), Lecue, Gorostiza
Brazil: Pedrosa, Sylvio, Luz, Tinoco, Martim, Armandinho, Canalli, Luizinho, Waldemar, Patesko, Leonidas (1)
Referee: Birlem (Germany)

27.5.34 Switzerland (2) 3, Holland (1) 2 MILAN
Switzerland: Sechehaye, Minelli, Weiler II, Guinchard, Jaccard, Hufschmid, Von Kanel, Passello, Kielholz (2), Abegglen (1), Bossi
Netherlands: Van der Meulen, Weber, Van Run, Pellikaan, Anderiesen, Van Heel, Wels, Vente (1), Bakhuijs, Smit (1), Van Nellen
Referee: Eklind (Sweden)

27.5.34 Sweden (1) 3, Argentina (1) 2 BOLOGNA
Sweden: Rydberg, Axelsson, Andersson S, Carlsson, Rosen, Andersson E, Dunker, Gustavsson, Jonasson (2), Keller, Kroon (1)
Argentina: Freschi, Pedevilla, Belis (1), Nehin, Sosa-Ubrieta, Lopez, Rua, Wilde, De Vincenzi, Galateo (1), Iraneta
Referee: Braun (Austria)

27.5.34 Germany (1) 5, Belgium (2) 2 FLORENCE
Germany: Kress, Haringer, Schwartz, Janes, Szepan, Zielinski, Lehner, Hohmann, Conen (3), Siffling, Kobierski (2)
Belgium: Van De Weyer, Smellinckx, Joachim, Peeraer, Welkenhuyzen, Klaessens, Devries, Voorhoof (2), Capelle, Gimmonprez, Herremans
Referee: Mattea (Italy)

27.5.34 Austria (1) 3, France (1) 2 (aet, 1 - 1 at 90 mins) TURIN
Austria: Platzer, Cisar, Sesta, Wagner, Smistik, Urbanek, Zischek, Bican (1), Sindelar (1), Schall (1), Viertel
France: Thepot, Mairesse, Mattler, Delfour, Verriest (1 pen), Llense, Keller, Alcazar, Nicolas (1), Rio, Aston
Referee: Van Moorsel (Netherlands)

27.5.34 Hungary (2) 4, Egypt (2) 2 NAPLES
Hungary: Szabo A, Futo, Sternberg, Palotas, Szucs, Lazar, Markos, Vincze (1), Teleki (1), Toldi (2), Szabo F
Egypt: Moustafa Kemal, Ali Caf, Hamitu, El Far, Refaat, Rayab, Latif, Fawzi (2), Muktar, Masoud Kemal, Hassan
Referee: Barlassina (Italy)

QUARTER FINALS
31.5.34 Germany (0) 2, Sweden (0) 1 MILAN
Germany: Kress, Haringer, Busch, Gramlich, Szepan, Zielinski, Lehner, Hohmann (2), Conen, Siffling, Kobierski

Sweden: Rydberg, Axelsson, Andersson S, Carlsson, Rosen, Andersson E, Dunker (1), Gustavsson, Jonasson, Keller, Kroon
Referee: Barlassina (Italy)

31.5.34 Czechoslovakia (1) 3, Switzerland (1) 2 TURIN
Czechoslovakia: Planicka, Zenizek, Ctyroky, Kostalek, Cambal, Krcil, Junek, Svoboda (1), Sobotka (1), Nejedly (1), Puc
Switzerland: Sechehaye, Minelli, Weiler II, Guinchard, Jaccard, Hufschmid, Von Kanel, Jaeggi IV, Kielholz (1), Abegglen III (1), Jack
Referee: Beranek (Austria)

31.5.34 Austria (1) 2, Hungary (0) 1 BOLOGNA
Austria: Platzer, Cisar, Sesta, Wagner, Smistik, Urbanek, Zischek (1), Bican, Sindelar, Horvath (1), Viertel
Hungary: Szabo A, Vago, Sternberg, Palotas, Szucs, Szalay, Markos, Avar, Sarosi (1 pen), Toldi, Kemeny
Referee: Mattea (Italy)

31.5.34 Italy (0) 1, Spain (0) 1 (aet, 1 - 1 at 90 mins) FLORENCE
Italy: Combi, Monzeglio, Allemandi, Pizziolo, Monti, Castellazzi, Guaita, Meazza, Schiavio, Ferrari (1), Orsi
Spain: Zamora, Ciriaco, Quincoces, Cillaurren, Muquerza, Lecue, Lafuente, Iraragorri, Langara, Regueiro (1), Gorostiza
Referee: Baert (Belgium)

Quarter Final replay
1.6.34 Italy (1) 1, Spain (0) 0 FLORENCE
Italy: Combi, Monzeglio, Allemandi, Ferraris IV, Monti, Bertolini, Guaita, Meazza (1), Borel II, Demaria, Orsi
Spain: Nogues, Zabalo, Quincoces, Cillaurren, Muquerza, Lecue, Ventolra, Regueiro, Campanal, Chacha, Bosch
Referee: Mercet (Switzerland)

SEMI FINALS
3.6.34 Czechoslovakia (1) 3, Germany (0) 1 ROME
Czechoslovakia: Planicka, Ctyroky, Burger, Kostalek, Kambal, Krcil (1), Junek, Svoboda, Sobotka, Nejedly (2), Puc
Germany: Kress, Busch, Haringer, Zielinski, Szepan, Bender, Lehner, Conen, Noack (1), Kobierski
Referee: Barlassina (Italy)

3.6.34 Italy (1) 1, Austria (0) 0 MILAN
Italy: Combi, Monzeglio, Allemandi, Ferraris IV, Monti, Bertolini, Guaita (1), Meazza, Schiavio, Ferrari, Orsi
Austria: Platzer, Cisar, Sesta, Wagner, Smistik, Urbanek, Zischek, Bican, Sindelar, Schall, Viertal
Referee: Carraro (Italy)

Match for third place
6.6.34 Germany (3) 3, Austria (1) 2 NAPLES
Germany: Jakob, Janes, Busch, Zielinski, Munzenberg, Bender, Lehner (2), Siffling, Conen (1), Szepan, Heidemann
Austria: Platzer, Cisar, Sesta (1), Wagner, Smistik, Urbanek, Zischek, Braun, Bican, Horvath (1), Viertel
Referee: Carraro (Italy)

FINAL
10.6.34 Italy (0) 2, Czechoslovakia (0) 1 (aet, 1-1 at 90 mins) ROME
Italy: Combi, Monzeglio, Allemandi, Ferraris IV, Monti, Bertolini, Guaita, Meazza, Schiavio (1), Ferrari, Orsi (1)
Czechoslovakia: Planicka, Zenizek, Ctyroky, Kostalek, Cambal, Krcil, Junek, Svoboda, Sobotka, Nejedly (1), Puc (1)
Referee: Eklind (Sweden)

Pozzo brandishes the Jules Rimet trophy after Italy's second successive World Cup victory, surrounded by delighted players and officials. (HULTON DEUTSCH)

16

FRANCE
1938

The Italians retained the World Cup four years after staging the tournament, overcoming Hungary in an entertaining final, while the war clouds were gathering in Europe. The sound of hostilities had already been heard in two of the countries who qualified and the atmosphere was charged with apprehension.

As a gesture to FIFA President Jules Rimet, it had been agreed to hold the 1938 competition in France. There was a record entry of 36 but of this number, Austria found themselves overrun by Germany after qualifying and Spain was embroiled in a civil war. The 1930 finalists Uruguay and Argentina did not enter, the former because of continuing domestic problems, the latter after withdrawing a late application for entry. England received an invitation to compete, but again declined. As holders, Italy were exempted from the qualifying competition.

In the Preliminary Round, Austria's withdrawal gave Sweden a walk-over in the knock-out system retained from the previous series. The highest scoring match involved Brazil and Poland, the Brazilians winning 6-5 after extra time. Both sides had an ace marksman who scored four times: Brazil's Leonidas da Silva and Poland's Ernest Willimowski.

Italy, with only two survivors from 1934 — the captain Meazza and Ferrari — but several members of their 1936 Olympic Games gold medal side, struggled to beat Norway 2-1 after the extra period. Czechoslovakia, who had been Italy's final victims four years earlier, were involved in a second round battle with Brazil in Bordeaux. Brazil had Procopio and Machado sent off along with the Czechs' Riha. Czechoslovakia also lost Nejedly with a broken leg and goalkeeper Planicka with a broken arm. The sides were level 1-1 after extra time. The teams showed 15 changes for the replay which passed

Italy's cultured right-back Alfredo Foni executes an overhead kick to clear his lines in the 1938 final against Hungary. (HULTON DEUTSCH)

off without incident, with Brazil winning 2-1.

The Brazilians were so confident they left out Leonidas and Tim for the semi-final with Italy in Marseilles, in order to save them for the final. But Colaussi put the Italians ahead and when Domingos da Guia pulled down Italy's crack centre-forward Silvio Piola, Meazza scored from the spot in a 2-1 win.

In the other semi-final, Hungary cleverly cut off the supply to Sweden's Gustav Wetterstrom, who had scored four times against Cuba, and won easily 5-1. But in the final, Italy swept aside the delicate Hungarians.

Colaussi scored after six minutes, but Hungary's persistence with short-passing produced an equaliser. Back came Italy with more goals from Colaussi and Piola before half-time. Afterwards, the Hungarians gained a hold in midfield and made it 3-2, before Piola drove in another ten minutes from the end.

Then Meazza's fascist salute said it all.

Qualifying Tournament

36 entries

Europe (25): Austria, Belgium, Bulgaria, Czechoslovakia, Egypt, Estonia, Finland, France, Germany, Greece, Holland, Hungary, Republic of Ireland, Italy, Latvia, Lithuania, Luxembourg, Norway, Palestine, Poland, Portugal, Rumania, Sweden, Switzerland, Yugoslavia

North and Central America (5): Costa Rica, Cuba, Mexico, El Salvador, USA

South America (4): Argentina, Brazil, Colombia, Surinam

Asia (2): Dutch East Indies, Japan

Spain had also entered but because of the civil war could not compete. Argentina's entry was late, but accepted — then they withdrew! For the first time both holders (Italy) and hosts (France) were exempted from the qualifying competition.

Europe had eight groups, each producing one qualifier with the exception of groups 1, 2 and 8 where the first two progressed. Final places in France were to be distributed as follows: Europe (11 + France, Italy), North and Central America (1), South America (1), Asia (1).

In Group 2 there was a sub-division of two teams playing against each other in the four-team section. In Group 4 Switzerland and Portugal met in one match played in a neutral country, while in Group 5, Hungary played the winners of Palestine v Greece in one game. In Group 1 teams played each other just once.

Austria, who also met the winners of Latvia and Lithuania in one match and qualified, were drawn to play Sweden in the finals in Lyons on 5 June, but on 12 April the organisers were informed that Germany's annexation of Austria had left the country without an independent team which reduced the number of finalists to 15.

Group 1 (Germany, Sweden, Estonia, Finland)
Sweden v Finland 4 - 0; Sweden v Estonia 7 - 2; Finland v Germany 0 - 2; Finland v Estonia 0 - 1; Germany v Estonia 4 -1; Germany v Sweden 5 - 0
Germany and Sweden qualified

Group 2 (Poland, Norway, Yugoslavia, Rep of Ireland)
Poland v Yugoslavia 4 - 0; Yugoslavia v Poland 1 - 0;
Norway v Rep of Ireland 3 - 2; Rep of Ireland v Norway 3 - 3
Poland and Norway qualified

Group 3 (Rumania, Egypt)
Rumania qualified (Egypt withdrew)

Group 4 (Switzerland, Portugal)
Switzerland v Portugal 2 - 1 (in Milan)
Switzerland qualified

Group 5 (Hungary, Greece, Palestine)
Palestine v Greece 1 - 3; Greece v Palestine 1 - 0
Hungary v Greece 11 - 1
Hungary qualified

Group 6 (Czechoslovakia, Bulgaria)
Bulgaria v Czechoslovakia 1 - 1, 0 - 6
Czechoslovakia qualified

Group 7 (Austria, Latvia, Lithuania)
Latvia v Lithuania 4 - 2; Lithuania v Latvia 1 - 5;
Austria v Latvia 2 - 1
Austria qualified

Group 8 (Belgium, Holland, Luxembourg)
Holland v Luxembourg 4 - 0; Luxembourg v Belgium 2 - 3;
Belgium v Holland 1-1
Holland and Belgium qualified

Group 9 (Dutch East Indies, Japan)
Dutch East Indies qualified (Japan withdrew)

Group 10 (Brazil, Argentina)
Brazil qualified (Argentina withdrew)

Group 11 (USA)
USA withdrew

Group 12 (Colombia, Costa Rica, Cuba, Mexico, El Salvador, Surinam)
All teams except Cuba withdrew
Cuba qualified

Final Tournament FRANCE

Preliminary round

4.6.38 Switzerland (1) 1, Germany (1) 1 (aet, 1-1 at 90 mins) PARIS
Switzerland: Huber, Minelli, Lehmann, Springer, Vernati, Lortscher, Amado, Walaschek, Bickel, Abegglen III (1), Aeby
Germany: Raftl, Janes, Schmaus, Kupfer, Mock, Ritzinger, Lehner, Gellesch, Gauchel (1), Hahnemann, Pesser
Referee: Langenus (Belgium)

4.6.38 Hungary (4) 6, Dutch East Indies (0) 0 REIMS
Hungary: Hada, Koranyi, Biro, Lazar, Turai, Balogh, Sas, Zsengeller (2), Sarosi (2), Toldi (1), Kohut (1)
Dutch East Indies: Mo Heng, Hu Kon, Samuels, Nawir, Meng, Anwar, Hang Djin, Soedarmadji, Sommers, Pattiwael, Taihutti
Referee: Conrie (France)

5.6.38 France (2) 3, Belgium (1) 1 PARIS
France: Dilorto, Cazenave, Mattler, Bastien, Jordan, Diagne, Aston, Nicolas (2), Delfour, Vienante (1), Heisserer
Belgium: Badjou, Paverick, Sayes, Van Alphen, Stynen, De Winter, Van de Wouwer, Voorhoof, Isemborghs (1), Braine, Byle
Referee: Wuthrich (Switzerland)

5.6.38 Brazil (2) 6, Poland (1) 5 (aet, 4 - 4 at 90 mins) STRASBOURG
Brazil: Batatais, Domingos, Machado, Procopio, Martim, Afonsinho, Lopes, Romeu (1), Leonidas (4), Peracio (1), Hercules
Poland: Madesjski, Szcepaniak, Galecki, Gora, Nyc, Dytko, Piece L, Piontek (1), Szerfke, Willimowski (4), Wodarz
Referee: Eklind (Sweden)

5.6.38 Czechoslovakia (0) 3, Holland (0) 0 (aet, 0 - 0 at 90 mins) LE HAVRE
Czechoslovakia: Planicka, Burger, Dauick, Kostalek (1), Boucek (1), Kopecky, Riha, Simunek, Zeman, Nejedly (1), Puc
Holland: Van Male, Weber, Caldenhove, Paauwe, Anderiesen, Van Heel, Wels, Van de Veen, Smit, Vente, De Harder
Referee: Leclerq (France)

5.6.38 Italy (1) 2, Norway (0) 1 (aet, 1 - 1 at 90 mins) MARSEILLES
Italy: Olivieri, Monzeglio, Rava, Serantoni, Andreolo, Locatelli, Pasinati, Meazza, Piola (1), Ferrari, Ferraris II
Norway: Johansen H, Johannesen R, Holmsen, Henriksen, Eriksen, Homberg, Frantzen, Kvammen, Brunyldsen, Isaksen, Brustad (1)
Referee: Beranek (Austria)

5.6.38 Cuba (1) 3, Rumania (1) 3 (aet, 2-2 at 90 mins) TOULOUSE
Cuba: Carvajales, Barquin, Chorens, Arias, Rodriguez, Bergas, Maquina (1), Fernandez, Sosorro, Tunes, Sosa (1)
Rumania: Pavlovici, Burger, Chiroiu, Vintila, Rasinaru, Rafinski, Bindea, Covaci (1), Baratki (1), Bodola, Dobai (1)
Referee: Scarpi (Italy)

Replays

9.6.38 Switzerland (1) 4, Germany (2) 2 PARIS
Switzerland: Huber, Minelli, Lehmann, Springer, Vernati, Lortscher (o. g.), Amado, Abegglen III (2), Bickel (1), Walaschek (1), Aeby
Germany: Raftl, Janes, Streitle, Kupfer, Goldbrunner, Skoumal, Lehner, Stroh, Hahnemann (1), Szepan, Neumer
Referee: Eklind (Sweden)

9.6.38 Cuba (1) 2, Rumania (1) 1 TOULOUSE
Cuba: Ayra, Barquin, Chorens, Arias, Rodriguez, Berges, Maquina (1), Fernandez, Socorro (1), Tunas, Sosa
Rumania: Sadowski, Burger, Felecan, Barbulescu, Racinaru, Rafinski, Bogden, Moldoveanu, Baratki, Pranzler, Dobai (1)
Referee: Birlem (Germany)

QUARTER FINALS

12.6.38 Sweden (4) 8, Cuba (0) 0 ANTIBES
Sweden: Abrahamsson, Eriksson, Kallgren, Almgren, Jacobsson, Svanstrom, Wetterstrom (4), Keller (1), Andersson H (1), Jonasson (1), Nyberg (1)
Cuba: Carvajales, Barquin, Chorens, Arias, Rodriguez, Berges, Ferrer, Fernandez, Socorro, Tunas, Alonzo
Referee: Krist (Czechoslovakia)

12.6.38 Hungary (1) 2, Switzerland (0) 0 LILLE
Hungary: Szabo, Koranyi, Biro, Szalay, Turai, Lazar, Sas, Vincze, Sarosi, Zsengeller (2), Kohut
Switzerland: Huber, Stelzer, Lehmann, Springer, Vernati, Lortscher, Amado, Walashek, Bickel, Abegglen III, Grassi
Referee: Barlasina (Italy)

12.6.38 Italy (1) 3, France (1) 1 PARIS
Italy: Olivieri, Foni, Rava, Serantoni, Andreolo, Locatelli, Biavati, Meazza, Piola (2), Ferrari, Colaussi (1)
France: Dilorto, Cazenave, Mattler, Bastien, Jordan, Diagne, Aston, Heisserer (1), Nicolas, Delfour, Veinante
Referee: Baert (Belgium)

12.6.38 Brazil (1) 1, Czechoslovakia (1) 1 (aet, 1 - 1 at 90 mins) BORDEAUX
Brazil: Walter, Domingos, Machado, Procopio, Martim, Afonsinho, Lopes, Romeu, Leonidas (1), Peracio, Hercules
Czechoslovakia: Planicka, Burger, Daucik, Kostalek, Boucek, Kopecky, Riha, Simunek, Ludl, Nejedly (1 pen), Puc
Referee: Hertzka (Hungary)

Replay

14.6.38 Brazil (0) 2, Czechoslovakia (1) 1 BORDEAUX
Brazil: Walter, Jau, Nariz, Brito, Brandao, Argemiro, Roberto (1), Luizinho, Leonidas, Tim, Patesko
Czechoslovakia: Burkert, Burger, Daucik, Kostalek, Boucek, Ludl, Horak, Senecky, Kreutz, Kopecky (1), Rulc
Referee: Capdeville (France)

SEMI FINALS

16.6.38 Italy (0) 2, Brazil (0) 1 MARSEILLES
Italy: Olivieri, Foni, Rava, Serantoni, Andreolo, Locatelli, Biavati, Meazza (1 pen), Piola, Ferrari, Colaussi (1)
Brazil: Walter, Domingos, Machado, Procopio, Martim, Afonsinho, Lopes, Luizinho, Peracio, Romeu (1), Patesko
Referee: Wuthrich (Switzerland)

16.6.38 Hungary (3) 5, Sweden (1) 1 PARIS
Hungary: Szabo, Koranyi, Biro, Szalay, Turai, Lazar, Sas, Zsengeller (3), Sarosi (1), Toldi, Titkos (1)
Sweden: Abrahamsson, Eriksson, Kallgren, Almgren, Jacobsson, Svanstrom, Wetterstrom, Keller, Andersson H, Jonasson, Nyberg (1)
Referee: Leclerq (France)

Match for third place

19.6.38 Brazil (1) 4, Sweden (2) 2 BORDEAUX
Brazil: Batatais, Domingos, Machado, Procopio, Brandao, Afonsinho, Roberto, Romeu (1), Leonidas (2) Peracio (1), Patesko
Sweden: Abrahamsson, Eriksson, Nilsson, Almgren, Linderholm, Svanstrom, Persson, Andersson H, Jonasson (1), Andersson A, Nyberg (1)
Referee: Langenus (Belgium)

FINAL

19.6.38 Italy (3) 4, Hungary (1) 2 PARIS
Italy: Olivieri, Foni, Rava, Serantoni, Andreolo, Locatelli, Biavati, Meazza, Piola (2), Ferrari, Colaussi (2)
Hungary: Szabo, Polgar, Biro, Szalay, Szucs, Lazar, Sas, Vincze, Sarosi (1), Zsengeller, Titkos (1)
Referee: Capdeville (France)

Second World War

Zurich, the headquarters of FIFA in neutral Switzerland, managed to keep its office open throughout the war under Dr Ivo Schricker. Although the 1940 Congress planned for Luxembourg was postponed indefinitely, some meetings of the continental members of the executive committee were held. Resources were non-existent and without a full complement attending , no resolutions were passed, although in 1941 Germany put forward the idea that charging by players challenging for the ball should be made legal...

Italy had won the World Cup in 1938, and the Jules Rimet Trophy itself was the subject of considerable wartime mystery. Most of the sports officials in the Italian government were by definition Mussolini supporters, including the brothers Francesco and Giovanni Mauro, secretary Ottorino Barassi and the Head of Italian Sport, Consule-Generale Giorgio Vaccaro.

Yet all of them put sport above politics and for security decided not to trust each other too much. Thus General Vaccaro and Giovanni Mauro smuggled the trophy from the safe of the Italian bank in Rome. But Dr Barassi, fearing the Nazis would still confiscate the gold statuette, decided to find a safer hiding place for it. Thus the World Cup spent most of the war in a shoe box under his bed!

BRAZIL
1950

Brazil was chosen as the venue for the fourth World Cup. The entire South American continent had been unaffected by the ravages of war but overall only 31 teams entered including the British associations for the first time,all four having rejoined FIFA in 1946.

The Home Championship was used as part of the qualification, with two places guaranteed in the finals. But when England beat Scotland 1-0 at Hampden Park to win the title, the Scots carried out their threat not to go to Brazil unless they were champions.

Travel requirements in this vast country called upon teams to make enormous journeys. France, originally eliminated, were invited to take part when Turkey withdrew, but declined on learning their tour itinerary. India withdrew when informed by FIFA that they would not be allowed to play barefooted! Thus only 13 teams competed in the finals, the competition unsatisfactorily split in four groups — Uruguay had just one opponent in their section — plus a final pool with no knock-out matches at all.

Brazil, firm favourites, won their group, dropping only one point — to Switzerland in Sao Paulo, when they purposely included many local players. One of their goals looked suspect; the ball appeared to have gone out of play before being crossed. By the final pool the Brazilians were showing irresistible form, their individual brilliance dove-tailing as a team in a relaxed, but masterful manner.

(Main photo) England's most humiliating moment: USA centre-forward Larry Gaetjens beats Bert Williams with the only goal of the game in Belo Horizonte, 13 June 1950. (GSL) **(Inset) Barbosa, the Brazilian goalkeeper, scrambles the ball away from the feet of Hans Jeppson, Sweden's centre-forward. It was one of few anxious moments for Brazil who won this final pool game 7-1.**(JR)

Sweden became the overall 'giant-killers' beating Italy 3-2. Coached by George Raynor, it was an ironic triumph for the Swedes who had lost many of their 1948 Olympic stars to Italian clubs. Yet the real shock was England losing to the hotch-potch USA. This humiliating defeat was sealed after 37 minutes; left-half Walter Bahr crossed into the goalmouth, goalkeeper Bert Williams failed to gather cleanly and the oncoming Larry Gaetjens deflected the ball in with his head. England had been unimpressive in beating Chile 2-0, but it was a scintillating performance compared with this shattering shambles.

In the final pool Ademir scored four as Brazil slaughtered Sweden 7-1; Uruguay, after taking eight goals off Bolivia, were held 2-2 by Spain who had topped England's group. The firecrackers were already heralding a Brazilian success. A samba 'Brazil the Victors' was recorded. Spain were crushed 6-1 by the rampant Brazilians. Uruguay's 3-2 win over Sweden left Brazil needing a point for the title.

Brazil were 10-1 on favourites and put Uruguay's well-organised defence under constant pressure. When Friaca gave them the lead just after the interval, Brazil looked safe. However, with nothing to lose Uruguay made every pass count. Spurred on by the industrious Rodriguez Andrade and fine distribution by Obdulio Varela, they took control. Slender schemer Juan Schiaffino hit Chico Ghiggia's cross first time for the equaliser and 11 minutes from time, Ghiggia drove in low for the winner inside Barbosa's near post.

Qualifying Tournament

32 entries

Europe and Near East (19): Austria, Belgium, England, Finland, France, Northern Ireland, Replic of Ireland, Israel, Italy, Luxembourg, Portugal, Scotland, Spain, Sweden, Switzerland, Syria, Turkey, Wales, Yugoslavia

South America (8): Argentina, Bolivia, Brazil, Chile, Ecuador, Paraguay, Peru, Uruguay

North and Central America (3): Cuba, Mexico, USA

Asia (3): Burma, India, Philippines

Europe and the Near East had six groups. In four of these one seeded team met the winners of another tie. In another, the Home International Championship was used to determine the first British entry into the World Cup. Two representatives were guaranteed final places from this group, one each from the other five.

There were two groups from South America, each with two final places plus one representative from North and Central America and Asia. Final places in Brazil were to be distributed as follows: Europe and Near East (7 + Italy), South America (4 + Brazil), North and Central America (2), Asia (I).

The knock-out principle was abandoned completely for the finals. For the first time the winners of four groups were required to play in a final section. There were four seeded teams: Brazil as hosts, Italy as holders, England as the British champions and Argentina representing South America. But withdrawals ruined these arrangements.

Europe

Group 1 (Austria, Turkey, Syria)

Turkey v Syria 7 - 0

Austria withdrew; Syria refused to play the return game with Turkey, who withdrew. Portugal were offered a place in finals but declined.

Group 2 (Yugoslavia, Israel, France)

Yugoslavia v Israel 6 - 0; Israel v Yugoslavia 2 - 5; France v Yugoslavia 1 - 1; Yugoslavia v France 1 - 1

Play-off (in Florence): Yugoslavia v France 3 - 2

Yugoslavia qualified

Group 3 (Switzerland, Luxembourg, Belgium)

Belgium withdrew

Switzerland v Luxembourg 5 - 2, 3 - 2

Switzerland qualified

Group 4 (Sweden, Rep of Ireland, Finland)

Sweden v Rep of Ireland 3 - 1; Rep of Ireland v Finland 3 - 0; Finland v Rep of Ireland 1 - 1; Rep of Ireland v Sweden 1 - 3

Sweden qualified

Group 5 (England, Scotland, Northern Ireland, Wales)

Northern Ireland v Scotland 2 - 8; Wales v England 1 - 4; Scotland v Wales 2 - 0; England v Northern Ireland 9 - 2; Wales v Northern Ireland 0 - 0; Scotland v England 0 - 1

	P	W	D	L	F	A	Pts
England	3	3	0	0	14	3	6
Scotland	3	2	0	1	10	3	4
Wales	3	0	1	2	1	6	1
Northern Ireland	3	0	1	2	4	17	1

England qualified with Scotland, who refused a final place as did France, who were invited to replace them

Group 6 (Spain, Portugal)

Spain v Portugal 5 - 1, 2 - 2

Spain qualified

South America

Group 7 (Chile, Bolivia, Argentina)

Chile and Bolivia qualified (Argentina withdrew)

Group 8 (Uruguay, Paraguay, Ecuador and Peru)

Uruguay and Paraguay qualified (Ecuador and Peru withdrew)

Asia

Group 9 (Burma, India, Philippines)

All withdrew

North and Central America

Group 10 (USA, Mexico, Cuba) (In Mexico City)

USA v Mexico 0 - 6; Mexico v USA 6 - 2; Cuba v USA 1 - 1; USA v Cuba 5 - 2; Cuba v Mexico 0 - 3; Mexico v Cuba 2 - 0

	P	W	D	L	F	A	Pts
Mexico	4	4	0	0	17	2	8
USA	4	1	1	2	8	15	3
Cuba	4	0	1	3	3	11	1

USA and Mexico qualified

Final Tournament BRAZIL
GROUP 1

24.6.50 Brazil (1) 4 , Mexico (0) 0 RIO DE JANEIRO

Brazil: Barbosa, Augusto, Juvenal, Ely, Danilo, Bigode, Maneca, Ademir (2), Baltazar (1), Jair (1), Friaca

Mexico: Carbajal, Zetter, Montemajor, Ruiz, Ochoa, Roca, Septien, Ortiz, Casarin, Perez, Velasquez

Referee: Reader (England)

25.6.50 Yugoslavia (3) 3, Switzerland (0) 0 BELO HORIZONTE

Yugoslavia: Mrkusic, Horvat, Stankovic, Cajkovski I, Jovanovic, Djajic, Ognanov (1), Mitic, Tomasevic (2), Bobek, Vukas

Switzerland: Stuber, Lusenti, Quinche, Bocquet, Eggimann, Neury, Bickel, Antenen, Tamini, Bader, Fatton

Referee: Galeati (Italy)

28.6.50 Brazil (2) 2, Switzerland (1) 2 SAO PAULO
Brazil: Barbosa, Augusto, Juvenal, Bauer, Rui, Noronha, Alfredo II (1), Maneca, Baltazar (1), Ademir, Friaca
Switzerland: Stuber, Neury, Bocquet, Lusenti, Eggimann, Quinche, Tamini, Bickel, Friedlander, Bader, Fatton (2)
Referee: Azon (Spain)

28.6.50 Yugoslavia (2) 4, Mexico (0) 1 PORTO ALEGRE
Yugoslavia: Mrkusic, Horvat, Stankovic, Cajkovski I, Jovanovic, Djajic, Mihailovic, Mitic, Tomasevic (1), Bobek (1), Cajovski II (2)
Mexico: Carbajal, Gutierrez, Ruiz, Gomez, Ochoa, Ortiz, Flores, Naranjo, Casarin (1), Perez, Velasquez
Referee: Leafe (England)

1.7.50 Brazil (1) 2, Yugoslavia (0) 0 RIO DE JANEIRO
Brazil: Barbosa, Augusto, Juvenal, Bauer, Danilo, Bigode, Maneca, Zizinho (1), Ademir (1), Jair, Chico
Yugoslavia: Mrkusic, Horvat, Brokela, Cajkovski I, Jovanovic, Djajic, Vukas, Mitic, Tomasevic, Bobek, Cajkovski II
Referee: Griffiths (Wales)

2.7.50 Switerland (2) 2, Mexico (0) 1 PORTO ALEGRE
Switzerland: Hug, Neury, Bocquet, Lusenti, Eggimann, Quinche, Tamini, Antenen, Freidlander, Bader (1), Fatton (1)
Mexico: Carbajal, Gutierrez, Gomez, Roca, Ortiz, Guevara, Flores, Ochoa, Casarin, Borbolla, Velasquez (1)
Referee: Eklind (Sweden)

	P	W	D	L	F	A	Pts
Brazil	3	2	1	0	8	2	5
Yugoslavia	3	2	0	1	7	3	4
Switzerland	3	1	1	1	4	6	3
Mexico	3	0	0	3	2	10	0

GROUP 2
24.6.50 England (1) 2, Chile (0) 0 RIO DE JANEIRO
England: Williams, Ramsey, Aston, Wright, Hughes, Dickinson, Finney, Mortensen (1), Bentley, Mannion (1), Mullen
Chile: Livingstone, Farias, Roldon, Alvarez, Busquets, Carvalho, Prieto, Cremaschi, Robledo, Munoz, Diaz
Referee: Van de Meer (Netherlands)

25.6.50 Spain (0) 3, USA (1) 1 CURITIBA
Spain: Eizaguirre, Antunez, Alonso, Gonzalvo III, Gonazalvo II, Puchades, Basora (2), Hernandez, Zarra (1), Igoa, Gainza
USA: Borghi, Keough, Marca, McIlvenny, Colombo, Bahr, Craddock, Souza J (1), Gaetjens, Pariani, Valentini
Referee: Viana (Brazil)

29.6.50 USA (1) 1 England (0) 0 BELO HORIZONTE
USA: Borghi, Keough, Marca, McIlvenny, Colombo, Bahr, Wallace, Pariani, Gaetjens (1), Souza J, Souza E
England: Williams, Ramsey, Aston, Wright, Hughes, Dickinson, Finney, Mortensen, Bentley, Mannion, Mullen
Referee: Dattilo (Italy)

29.6.50 Spain (2) 2, Chile (0) 0 RIO DE JANEIRO
Spain: Ramallets, Alonso, Parra, Gonzalvo III, Gonzalvo II, Puchades, Basora (1), Igoa, Zarra (1), Panizo, Gainza
Chile: Livingstone, Farias, Roldon, Alvarez, Busqueta, Carvalho, Prieto, Cremaschi, Robledo, Munoz, Diaz
Referee: De Gama (Brazil)

2.7.50 Spain (0) 1, England (0) 0 RIO DE JANEIRO
Spain: Ramallets, Alonso, Parra, Gonzalvo III, Gonazalvo II, Puchades, Basora, Igoa, Zarra (1), Panizo, Gainza
England: Williams, Ramsey, Eckersley, Wright, Hughes, Dickinson, Matthews, Mortensen, Milburn, Baily, Finney
Referee: Galeati (Italy)

2.7.50 Chile (2) 5, USA (0) 2 RECIFE
Chile: Livingstone, Machuca, Roldon, Alvarez, Busquets, Farias, Munoz, Cremaschi (3), Robledo (1), Prieto (1), Ibanez
USA: Borghi, Keough, Marca, McIlvenny, Colombo, Bahr, Wallace, Pariani (1), Gaetjens, Souza J (1 pen), Souza E
Referee: Gardelli (Brazil)

	P	W	D	L	F	A	Pts
Spain	3	3	0	0	6	1	6
England	3	1	0	2	2	2	2
Chile	3	1	0	2	5	6	2
USA	3	1	0	2	4	8	2

GROUP 3
25.6.50 Sweden (2) 3, Italy (1) 2 SAO PAULO
Sweden: Svensson, Samuelsson, Nilsson E, Andersson (1), Nordahl K, Gaerd, Sundqvist, Palmer, Jeppson (2), Skoglund, Nilsson S
Italy: Sentimenti IV, Giovannini, Furiassi, Annovazzi, Parola, Magli, Muccinelli (1), Boniperti, Capello, Campatelli, Carapellese (1)
Referee: Lutz (Switerland)

29.6.50 Sweden (2) 2, Paraguay (0) 2 CURITIBA
Sweden: Svensson, Samuelsson, Nilsson E, Andersson, Nordahl K, Gaerd, Jonsson, Palmer, Jeppson, Skoglund, Sundqvist (1)
Paraguay: Vargas, Gonzalito, Cespedes, Gavilan, Lequizamon, Cantero, Avalos, Lopez A (1), Saquir, Lopez F (1), Unzain
Referee: Mitchell (Scotland)

2.7.50 Italy (1) 2, Paraguay (0) 0 SAO PAULO
Italy: Moro, Blason, Furiassi, Fattori, Remondini, Mari, Muccinelli (1), Amadei, Capello, Carapellese (1)
Paraguay: Vargas, Gonzales, Cespedes, Gavilan, Lequizamon, Cantero, Avalos, Loprez A, Saquir, Lopez F, Unzain
Referee: Ellis (England)

	P	W	D	L	F	A	Pts
Sweden	2	1	1	0	5	4	3
Italy	2	1	0	1	4	3	2
Paraguay	2	0	1	1	2	4	1

GROUP 4
2.7.50 Uruguay (4) 8, Bolivia (0) 0 BELO HORIZONTE
Uruguay: Maspoli, Gonzales M, Tejera, Gonzales J, Varela, Andrade, Ghiggia (1), Perez, Miquez (2), Schiaffino (4), Vidal (1)
Bolivia: Gutierrez I, Acha, Bustamante, Greco, Valencia, Ferrel, Algranez, Ugarte, Caparelli, Gutierrez II, Maldonado
Referee: Reader (England)

FINAL POOL
9.7.50 Brazil (3) 7, Sweden (0) 1 RIO DE JANEIRO
Brazil: Barbosa, Augusto, Juvenal, Bauer, Danilo, Bigode, Maneca (1), Zizinho, Ademir (4), Jair, Chico (2)
Sweden: Svensson, Samuelsson, Nilsson E, Andersson (1 pen), Nordahl K, Gaerd, Sundqvist, Palmer, Jeppson, Skoglund, Nilsson S
Referee: Ellis (England)

9.7.50 Uruguay (1) 2, Spain (2) 2 SAO PAULO
Uruguay: Maspoli, Gonzales M, Tejera, Gonzales J, Varela (1), Andrade, Ghiggia (1), Perez, Miquez, Schiaffino, Vidal
Spain: Ramallets, Alonso, Gonzalvo II, Gonzalvo III, Parra, Puchades, Basora 2, Igoa, Zarra, Molowny, Gainza
Referee: Griffiths (Wales)

13.7.50 Brazil (3) 6, Spain (0) 1 RIO DE JANEIRO
Brazil: Barbosa, Augusto, Juvenal, Bauer, Danilo, Bigode, Friaca, Zizinho (1), Ademir (2), Jair (1), Chico (2)
Spain: Ramallets, Alonso, Gonzalvo II, Gonzalvo III, Parra, Puchades, Basora, Igoa, Zarra, Panizo, Gainza
Referee: Leafe (England)

13.7.50 Uruguay (1) 3, Sweden (2) 2 SAO PAULO
Uruguay: Paz, Gonzales M, Tejera, Gambetta, Varela, Andrade, Ghiggia, Perez (1), Miquez, Schiaffino (2), Vidal
Sweden: Svensson, Samuelsson, Nilsson E, Andersson, Johansson, Gaerd, Sunqvist, Palmer (1), Jeppson (1), Jonsson, Nilsson S
Referee: Galeati (Italy)

16.7.50 Sweden (2) 3, Spain (0) 1 SAO PAULO
Sweden: Svensson, Samuelsson, Nilsson E, Andersson, Johansson, Gaerd, Jonsson, Mellberg (1), Rydell, Palmer (1), Sundqvist (1)
Spain: Eizaguirre, Alonso, Asensi, Silva, Parra, Puchades, Basora, Hernandez, Zarra (1), Paniza, Juncosa
Referee: Van de Meer (Netherlands)

16.7.50 Uruguay (0) 2, Brazil (0) 1 RIO DE JANEIRO
Uruguay: Maspoli, Gonzales M, Tejera, Gambetta, Varela, Andrade, Ghiggia (1), Perez, Miquez, Schiaffino (1), Moran
Brazil: Barbosa, Augusto, Juvenal, Bauer, Danilo, Bogode, Friaca (1), Zizinho, Ademir, Jair, Chico
Referee: Reader (England)

	P	W	D	L	F	A	Pts
Uruguay	3	2	1	0	7	5	5
Brazil	3	2	0	1	14	4	4
Sweden	3	1	0	2	6	11	2
Spain	3	0	1	2	4	11	1

SWITZERLAND

1954

The tournament in Switzerland produced another beaten favourite in the final, the most disgraceful scenes in the history of the competition and the finest exhibition of World Cup football. By coincidence, Hungary were involved in all three.

Yet it was West Germany, only re-admitted by FIFA four years earlier, following banishment after the Second World War, who upset the form book in an eccentrically-organised tournament. There were two seeded teams in each of the four groups and they did not play each other. The unseeded Germans cheekily exploited the system to their advantage.

Although designed to reduce the risk of shock results, the scheme back-fired in Group 2. Hungary swamped the luckless South Koreans 9-0 and West Germany beat seeded Turkey 4-1. Gambling that they could defeat the Turks in a play-off if level on points, the German team manager, Sepp Herberger, cunningly fielded six reserves against Hungary. As it was, the Hungarians won 8-3. However Ferenc Puskas suffered a badly injured ankle.

Goalscoring generally reached new heights as a result of positive ideas, at least half a dozen teams possessing players of outstanding ability, the peculiarities of the system and some weak competitors.

(Main photo) Before the match deteriorated into the 'Battle of Berne', both Hungary and Brazil played some delightful football. Left to right: Castilho (Brazil's goalkeeper, on one knee); Hungary's Nandor Hidegkuti; Didi and Bauer (6), both of Brazil. (HULTON DEUTSCH)
(Inset, above) Stanley Matthews (7) watches Uruguay's Roque Maspoli punch clear from England centre-forward Nat Lofthouse. (POPPERFOTO)
(Inset, below) Maspoli is on all fours as Tom Finney (second from left) and the sprawling Lofthouse try to force the ball home. Uruguay's Andrade is far left. England lost 4-2 in Basle, but gave an improved performance. (POPPERFOTO)

The Germans duly won their play-off, beating Turkey 7-2 and there were other surprise unseatings of seeds. In Group 1, France lost to Yugoslavia and in Group 4, Italy were forced to play-off with Switzerland and found themselves beaten 4-1. England improved after an error-ridden 4-4 draw with Belgium to beat the Swiss 2-0 on one of the few hot days.

Scotland were trounced 7-0 by Uruguay and then lost by the only goal of the game to Austria. Brazil, after a comfortable win over Mexico, were held by the Yugoslavs and found themselves drawn against Hungary in the quarter-finals.

They met in what became known as the infamously belligerent Battle of Berne. A hotly disputed penalty which put the Hungarians 3-1 ahead really ignited an already smouldering match. English referee Arthur Ellis sent off the Brazilian Nilton Santos and Hungary's Joszef Boszik for fighting and later dismissed a second Brazilian, Humberto. Hungary eventually won 4-2 but fights continued in the dressing-room afterwards.

The goals flowed freely in Lausanne. Switzerland scored five against Austria, but still lost. They were 3-0 up in 20 minutes but went in at half-time losing 5-4. They also missed a penalty and were beaten 7-5. The Germans clinically disposed of Yugoslavia, and Uruguay beat a much improved England side 4-2.

In the semi-final at Lausanne played in torrential rain, Hungary and Uruguay put on a classic. The anticipated blood bath did not materialise and the ring of coal-scuttle helmeted soldiers surrounding the pitch proved unnecessary. Hungary won 4-2 in extra time, Sandor Kocsis heading two superbly taken goals to finish off the gallant South Americans, who thus suffered their first ever defeat in the World Cup.

The West German machine was now operating in top gear and ran through the erratic but attractive Austrians, the brothers Walter scoring twice each in a 6-1 win which drove them into the final and another meeting with Hungary.

Hungary's manager Gustav Sebes gambled on bringing back Puskas, declared fit after a morning test. It rained heavily again but the Hungarians seemed home and dry, especially when Puskas pounced on a deflection after six minutes and Zoltan Czibor capitalised on a defensive mistake two minutes later.

Creditably the Germans refused to be rattled. They swung the ball about cleverly, using their fast raiding wingers to good effect, and aided by the slippery conditions they put the Hungarians out of their stride. They were helped considerably by a goal scored one minute after Hungary's second, Max Morlock netting from another deflection. On 18 minutes they were level, Helmut Rahn driving in a left-wing corner when Gyula Grosics failed to clear.

Hungary came back to hit the woodwork twice, but Toni Turek was inspired in the German goal and eventually his team counter-attacked. Six minutes from time a defensive error enabled Rahn to plant his second goal, only for Puskas to immediately equalise, the effort ruled out by English referee Bill Ling after Welsh linesman Mervyn Griffiths controversially waved offside. Germany won 3-2 on merit, but Hungary were probably the finest team in Europe. Moreover, it provided a memorable final.

Qualifying Tournament

38 entries

Europe and Near East (28): Austria, Belgium, Bulgaria, Czechoslovakia, Egypt, England, Finland, France, West Germany, Greece, Hungary, Republic of Ireland, Northern Ireland, Israel, Italy, Luxembourg, Norway, Poland, Portugal, Rumania, Saar, Scotland, Spain, Sweden, Switzerland, Turkey, Wales, Yugoslavia

North and Central America (3): Haiti, Mexico, USA

South America (4): Brazil, Chile, Paraguay, Uruguay

Asia (3): China, Japan, South Korea

In addition to the misguided system that produced two seeded teams in each group of four for the finals, these 'seeds' were determined before the qualifying tournament. Thus when Spain, one of the seeded teams, were eliminated by Turkey, the victors automatically became the 'seed'. It was to have far-reaching consequences as the tournament unfolded. Again the Home International Championship produced two places. Final places in Switzerland were to be distributed as follows: Europe and Near East (11 + Switzerland), North and Central America (1), South America (1 + Uruguay), Asia (1)

Europe

Group 1 (West Germany, Saar, Norway)

Norway v Saar 2 -3 ; Saar v Norway 0 - 0; West Germany v Saar 3 - 0; Saar v West Germany 1 -3 ; Norway v West Germany 1 - 1; West Germany v Norway 5 - 1

	P	W	D	L	F	A	Pts
West Germany	4	3	1	0	12	3	7
Saar	4	1	1	2	4	8	3
Norway	4	0	2	2	4	9	2

West Germany qualified

Group 2 (Belgium, Sweden, Finland)

Finland v Belgium 2 - 4; Belgium v Finland 2 - 2; Sweden v Belgium 2 - 3; Belgium v Sweden 2 - 0; Finland v Sweden 3 - 3; Sweden v Finland 4 - 0

	P	W	D	L	F	A	Pts
Belgium	4	3	1	0	11	6	7
Sweden	4	1	1	2	9	8	3
Finland	4	0	2	2	7	13	2

Belgium qualified

Group 3 (England, Scotland, Northern Ireland, Wales)

Northern Ireland v Scotland 1 - 3; Wales v England 1 - 4; Scotland v Wales 3 - 3; England v Northern Ireland 3 - 1; Wales v Northern Ireland 1 - 2; Scotland v England 2 - 4

	P	W	D	L	F	A	Pts
England	3	3	0	0	11	4	6
Scotland	3	1	1	1	8	8	3
Northern Ireland	3	1	0	2	4	7	2
Wales	3	0	1	2	5	9	1

England and Scotland qualified

Group 4 (France, Rep of Ireland, Luxembourg)

Luxembourg v France 1 - 6; France v Luxembourg 8 - 0; Rep of Ireland v Luxembourg 4 - 0; Luxembourg v Rep of Ireland 0 - 1; Rep of Ireland v France 3 - 5; France v Rep of Ireland 1 - 0

	P	W	D	L	F	A	Pts
France	4	4	0	0	20	4	8
Rep of Ireland	4	2	0	2	8	6	4
Luxembourg	4	0	0	4	1	19	0

France qualified

Group 5 (Austria, Portugal)
Austria v Portugal 9 - 1, 0 - 0
Austria qualified

Group 6 (Turkey, Spain)
Spain v Turkey 4 - 1, 0 - 1
Play-off (in Rome): Turkey v Spain 2 - 2 (Turkey won toss up)
Turkey qualified

Group 7 (Hungary, Poland)
Hungary qualified (Poland withdrew)

Group 8 (Czechoslovakia, Rumania, Bulgaria)
Czechoslovakia v Rumania 2 - 0; Rumania v Czechoslovakia 0 - 1; Bulgaria v Czechoslovakia 1 - 2; Czechoslovakia v Bulgaria 0 - 0; Rumania v Bulgaria 3 - 1; Bulgaria v Rumania 1 - 2

	P	W	D	L	F	A	Pts
Czechoslovakia	4	3	1	0	5	1	7
Rumania	4	2	0	2	5	5	4
Bulgaria	4	0	1	3	3	7	1

Czechoslovakia qualified

Group 9 (Italy, Egypt)
Egypt v Italy 1 - 2, 1 - 5
Italy qualified

Group 10 (Yugoslavia, Greece, Israel)
Israel v Yugoslavia 0 - 1; Yugoslavia v Israel 1 - 0; Yugoslavia v Greece 1 - 0; Greece v Yugoslavia 0 - 1; Israel v Greece 0 - 2; Greece v Israel 1 - 0

	P	W	D	L	F	A	Pts
Yugoslavia	4	4	0	0	4	0	8
Greece	4	2	0	2	3	2	4
Israel	4	0	0	4	0	5	0

Yugoslavia qualified

North and Central America
Group 11 (Mexico, USA, Haiti)
Mexico v Haiti 8 - 0; Haiti v Mexico 0 - 4; Mexico v USA 3 - 1; USA v Mexico 0 - 4; USA V Haiti 3 - 0; Haiti v USA 2 - 3

	P	W	D	L	F	A	Pts
Mexico	4	4	0	0	19	1	8
USA	4	2	0	2	7	9	4
Haiti	4	0	0	4	2	18	0

Mexico qualified

South America
Group 12 (Brazil, Paraguay, Chile)
Paraguay v Chile 4 - 0; Chile v Paraguay 1 - 3; Chile v Brazil 0 - 2; Brazil v Chile 1 - 0; Brazil v Paraguay 4 - 1; Paraguay v Brazil 0 - 1

	P	W	D	L	F	A	Pts
Brazil	4	4	0	0	8	1	8
Paraguay	4	2	0	2	8	6	4
Chile	4	0	0	4	1	10	0

Brazil qualified

Asia
Group 13 (South Korea, Japan, China)
China withdrew

Japan v South Korea (in Tokyo) 1 - 5, 2 - 2
South Korea qualified

Final Tournament SWITZERLAND
GROUP 1
16.6.54 Yugoslavia (1) 1, France (0) 0 LAUSANNE
Yugoslavia: Beara, Stankovic, Crnkovic, Cajkovski, Horvat, Boskov, Milutinovic (1), Mitic, Vukas, Bobek, Zebec
France: Remetter, Gianessi, Kaelbel, Penverne, Jonquet, Marcel, Kopa, Glovacki, Strappe, Dereuddre, Vincent
Referee: Griffiths (Wales)

16.6.54 Brazil (4) 5, Mexico (0) 0 GENEVA
Brazil: Castilho, Santos D, Santos N, Brandaozinho, Pinheiro, Bauer, Julinho (1), Didi (1), Baltazar (1), Pinga (2), Rodriguez
Mexico: Mota, Lopez, Gomez, Cardenas, Romo, Avalos, Torres, Naranjo, Lamadrid, Balcazar, Arellano
Referee: Wyssling (Switzerland)

19.6.54 France (1) 3, Mexico (0) 2 GENEVA
France: Remetter, Gianessi, Marche, Marcel, Kaelbel, Mahjoub, Kopa (1 pen), Dereuddre, Strappe, Ben Tifour, Vincent (1)
Mexico: Carbajal, Lopez, Romo, Cardenas (o. g.), Avalos, Martinez, Torres, Naranjo (1), Lamadrid, Balcazar (1), Arellano
Referee: Asensi (Spain)

19.6.54 Brazil (0) 1, Yugoslavia (0) 0 (aet, 1 - 1 at 90 mins) LAUSANNE
Brazil: Castilho, Santos D, Santos N, Brandaozinho, Pinheiro, Bauer, Julinho, Didi (1), Baltazar, Pinga, Rodriguez
Yugoslavia: Beara, Stankovic, Crnkovic, Cajkovski, Horvat, Boskov, Milutinovic, Mitic, Zebec (1), Vukas, Dvornik
Referee: Faultless (Scotland)

	P	W	D	L	F	A	Pts
Brazil	2	1	1	0	6	1	3
Yugoslavia	2	1	1	1	2	1	3
France	2	1	0	1	3	3	2
Mexico	2	0	0	2	2	8	0

GROUP 2
17.6.54 Hungary (4) 9, South Korea (0) 0 ZURICH
Hungary: Grosics, Buzanszky, Lantos (1), Bozsik, Lorant, Szojka, Budai, Kocsis (3), Palotas (2), Puskas (2), Czibor (1)
South Korea: Hong, Kyu Park, Kang, Min, Yae Seung Park, Chu, Chung, Kap Park, Sung, Woo, Yung Keun Choi
Referee: Vincenti (France)

17.6.54 West Germany (1) 4, Turkey (1) 1 BERNE
West Germany: Turek, Laband, Kohlmeyer, Eckel, Posipal, Mai, Klodt (1), Morlock (1), Walter O (1), Walter F, Schafer (1)
Turkey: Turgay, Ridvan, Basri, Mustafa, Cetin, Rober, Erol, Suat (1), Feridun, Burhan, Lefter
Referee: Da Costa (Portugal)

20.6.54 Hungary (3) 8, West Germany (1) 3 BASLE
Hungary: Grosics, Buzanszky, Lantos, Bozsik, Lorant, Zakarias, Toth (1), Kocsis (4), Hidegkuti (2), Puskas (1), Czibor
West Germany: Kwaitkowski, Bauer, Kohlmeyer, Posipal, Liebrich, Mebus, Rahn (1), Eckel, Walter F, Pfaff (1), Hermann (1)
Referee: Ling (England)

20.6.54 Turkey (4) 7, South Korea (0) 0 GENEVA
Turkey: Turgay, Ridvan, Basri, Mustafa, Cetin, Rober, Erol (1), Suat (2), Necmettin, Lefter (1), Burhan (3)
South Korea: Hong, Kyu Park, Kang, Han, Chong Kap Lee, Kim, Yung Keun Choi, Soo Nam Lee, Gi Choo Lee, Woo, Chung
Referee: Marino (Uruguay)

	P	W	D	L	F	A	Pts
Hungary	2	2	0	0	17	3	4
West Germany	2	1	0	1	7	9	2
Turkey	2	1	0	1	8	4	2
South Korea	2	0	0	2	0	16	0

Play off for 2nd place
23.6.54 West Germany (3) 7, Turkey (1) 2 ZURICH
West Germany: Turek, Laband, Bauer, Eckel, Posipal, Mai, Klodt, Morlock (3), Walter O (1), Walter F (1), Schafer (2)
Turkey: Sukru, Ridvan, Basri, Naci, Cetin, Rober, Erol, Mustafa (1), Necmettin, Coskun, Lefter (1)
Referee: Vincenti (France)

GROUP 3
16.6.54 Austria (1) 1, Scotland (0) 0 ZURICH
Austria: Schmied, Hanappi, Barschandt, Ocwirk, Happel, Koller, Korner R, Schleger, Dienst, Probst (1), Korner A
Scotland: Martin, Cunningham, Aird, Docherty, Davidson, Cowie, McKenzie, Fernie, Mochan, Brown, Ormond
Referee: Franken (Belgium)

16.6.54 Uruguay (0) 2, Czechoslovakia (0) 0 BERNE
Uruguay: Maspoli, Santamaria, Martinez, Andrade, Varela, Cruz, Abbadie, Ambrois, Miquez (1), Schiaffino (1),Borges
Czechoslovakia: Reimann, Safranek, Novak, Trnka, Hledlik, Hertl, Hlavacek, Hemele, Kacany, Pazicky, Peser
Referee: Ellis (England)

19.6.54 Austria (4) 5, Czechoslovakia (0) 0 ZURICH
Austria: Schmied, Hanappi, Barschandt, Ocwirk, Happel, Koller, Korner R, Wagner, Stojaspal (2), Probst (3), Korner A
Czechoslovakia: Stacho, Safranek, Novak, Trnka, Pluskal, Hertl, Hlavacek, Hemele, Kacany, Pazicky, Krauss
Referee: Stafanovic (Yugoslavia)

19.6.54 Uruguay (2) 7, Scotland (0) 0 BASLE
Uruguay: Maspoli, Santamaria, Martinez, Andrade, Varela, Cruz, Abbadie (2), Ambrois, Miquez (2), Schiaffino, Borges (3)
Scotland: Martin, Cunningham, Aird, Docherty, Davidson, Cowie, McKenzie, Fernie, Mochan, Brown, Ormond
Referee: Orlandini (Italy)

	P	W	D	L	F	A	Pts
Uruguay	2	2	0	0	9	0	4
Austria	2	2	0	0	6	0	4
Czechoslovakia	2	0	0	2	0	7	0
Scotland	2	0	0	2	0	8	0

GROUP 4
17. 6. 54 England (2) 4, Belgium (1) 4 (aet, 3 - 3 at 90 mins) BASLE
England: Merrick, Staniforth, Byrne, Wright, Owen, Dickinson (o.g), Matthews, Broadis, Lofthouse (2), Taylor, Finney
Belgium: Gernaey, Dries, Van Brandt, Huysmans, Carre, Mees, Van den Bosch P, Houf, Coppens (1), Anoul (2), Mermans
Referee: Schmetzer (West Germany)

17.6.54 Switzerland (1) 2, Italy (1) 1 LAUSANNE
Switzerland: Parlier, Neury, Kernen, Fluckiger, Bocquet, Casali I, Ballaman (1), Vonlanthen, Hugi II (1), Meier, Fatton
Italy: Ghezzi, Vincenzi, Giacomazzi, Neri, Tognon, Nesti, Muccinelli, Boniperti (1), Galli, Pandolfini, Lorenz
Referee: Viana (Brazil)

20.6.54 England (1) 2, Switzerland (0) 0 BERNE
England: Merrick, Staniforth, Byrne, McGarry, Wright, Dickinson, Finney, Broadis, Wilshaw (1), Taylor, Mullen (1)
Switzerland: Parlier, Neury, Kernen, Eggimann, Bocquet, Bigler, Antenen, Vonlanthen, Meier, Ballaman, Fatton
Referee: Zsolt (Hungary)

26.6.54 Italy (1) 4, Belgium (0) 1 LUGANO
Italy: Ghezzi, Magnini, Giacomazzi, Neri, Tognon, Nesti, Frignani (1), Cappello, Galli (1), Pandolfini (1 pen), Lorenzi (1)
Belgium: Gernaey, Dries, Van Brandt, Huysmans, Carre, Mees, Mermans, Van den Bosch H, Coppens, Anoul (1), Van Den Bosch P
Referee: Steiner (Austria)

	P	W	D	L	F	A	Pts
England	2	1	1	0	6	4	3
Switzerland	2	1	0	1	2	3	2
Italy	2	1	0	1	5	3	2
Belgium	2	0	1	1	5	8	1

Play off for 2nd place
23.6.54 Switzerland (1) 4, Italy (0) 1 BASLE
Switzerland: Parlier, Neury, Kernen, Eggimann, Bocquet, Casali, Antenen, Vonlanthen, Hugi II (2), Ballaman (1), Fatton (1)
Italy: Viola, Magnini, Giacomazzi, Mari, Tognon, Nesti (1), Muccinelli, Pandolfini, Lorenzi, Segato, Frignani
Referee: Griffiths (Wales)

QUARTER FINALS
26.6.54 Austria (5) 7, Switzerland (4) 5 LAUSANNE
Austria: Schmied, Hanappi (o. g.), Barschandt, Ocwirk (1), Happel, Koller, Korner R, Wagner (3), Stojaspal, Probst (1), Korner A (2)
Switzerland: Parlier, Neury, Kernen, Eggimann, Bocquet, Casali, Antenen, Vonlanthen, Hugi II (2), Ballaman (2), Fatton
Referee: Faultless (Scotland)

26.6.54 Uruguay (2) 4, England (1) 2 BASLE
Uruguay: Maspoli, Santamaria, Martinez, Andrade, Varela (1), Cruz, Abbadie, Ambrois, Miquez (1), Schiaffino (1), Borges (1)
England: Merrick, Staniforth, Byrne, McGarry, Wright, Dickinson, Matthews, Broadis, Lofthouse (1), Wilshaw, Finney (1)
Referee: Steiner (Austria)

27.6.54 West Germany (1) 2, Yugoslavia (0) 0 GENEVA
West Germany: Turek, Laband, Kohlmeyer, Eckel, Liebrich, Mai, Rahn (1), Morlock, Walter O, Walter F, Schafer
Yugoslavia: Beara, Stankovic, Crnkovic, Cajkovski, Horvat (o. g.), Boskov, Milutinovic, Mitic, Vukas, Bobek, Zebec
Referee: Zsolt (Hungary)

27.6.54 Hungary (2) 4, Brazil (1) 2 BERNE
Hungary: Grosics, Buzanszky, Lantos (1 pen), Bozsik, Lorant, Zakarias, Toth M, Kocsis (2), Hidegkuti (1), Czibor, Toth J
Brazil: Castilho, Santos D (1 pen), Santos N, Brandaozinho, Pinheiro, Bauer, Julinho (1), Didi, Indio, Humberto, Maurinho
Referee: Ellis (England)

SEMI FINALS
30.6.54 West Germany (1) 6, Austria (0) 1 BASLE
West Germany: Turek, Posipal, Kohlmeyer, Eckel, Liebrich, Mai, Rahn, Morlock (1), Walter O (2), Walter F (2 pens), Schafer (1)
Austria: Zeman, Hanappi, Schleger, Ocwirk, Happel, Koller, Korner R, Wagner, Stojaspal, Probst (1), Korner A
Referee: Orlandini (Italy)

30.6.54 Hungary (1) 4, Uruguay (0) 2 (aet, 2 - 2 at 90 mins) LAUSANNE
Hungary: Grosics, Buzanszky, Lantos, Bozsik, Lorant, Zakarias, Budai, Kocsis (2), Palotas, Hidegkuti (1), Czibor (1)
Uruguay: Maspoli, Santamaria, Martinez, Andrade, Carballo, Cruz, Souto, Ambrois, Schiaffino, Hohberg (2), Borges
Referee: Griffiths (Wales)

Match for third place
3.7.54 Austria (1) 3, Uruguay (1) 1 ZURICH
Austria: Schmied, Hanappi, Barschandt, Ocwirk (1), Kollmann, Koller, Korner R, Wagner, Dienst, Stojaspal (1 pen), Probst
Uruguay: Maspoli, Santamaria, Martinez, Andrade, Carballo, Cruz (o. g.), Abbadie, Hohberg (1), Mendez, Schiaffino, Borges
Referee: Wyssling (Switzerland)

FINAL
4.7.54 West Germany (2) 3, Hungary (2) 2 BERNE
West Germany: Turek, Posipal, Kohlmeyer, Eckel, Liebrich, Mai, Rahn (2), Morlock (1), Walter O, Walter F, Schafer
Hungary: Grosics, Buzanszky, Lantos, Bozsik, Lorant, Zakarias, Czibor (1) Kocsis, Hidegkuti, Puskas (1), Toth J
Referee: Ling (England)

SWEDEN

1958

Though England, Northern Ireland, Scotland and Wales all reached the finals in Sweden, it was George Raynor, the English-born manager of the host nation, who almost achieved the impossible with a team packed with ageing exiles brought back from Italy.

Against any country other than Brazil, who had been perfecting a 4-2-4 system, the Swedes might have succeeded. But by stealing the ball, rather than tackling for it, and plundering opposing defences, the Brazilians emerged as the first team to win the competition outside their own continent.

It was the most truly representative series staged to date, 46 of the 53 original entries played in 89 qualifying games, watched by four million spectators. For the first time, no team other than the host nation and holders had a bye to the finals and when no opponent could be found for politically isolated Israel, Wales made the most of their second-chance ballot success as promising runners-up in the preliminary round.

Though Scotland again disappointed, Wales, Northern Ireland and England — despite the Munich air disaster the previous February in which they lost Roger Byrne, Duncan Edwards and Tommy Taylor — were not disgraced. There were several other pleasing features about the competition. In the cooler atmosphere of Scandinavia, there was a refreshing absence of some of the unpleasantness which had marred earlier tournaments.

The French tandem of Just Fontaine (with 13 goals, the leading marksman) and Raymond Kopa impressed, but was overshadowed by a Brazilian trio: a teenage prodigy called Pele, a devastating right-winger in Garrincha, and Didi, an inside-forward of rare delicacy.

There were four groups, with each comprising a team from South America, Eastern Europe, Britain and Western Europe. Teams level on points had to play-off. Northern Ireland, under the shrewd guidance of manager Peter Doherty, had problems finding a suitable centre-forward but showed typical spirit and considerable skill until hit hard by injuries. They defeated Czechoslovakia 2-1 in a play-off to go through with West Germany, who had drawn 2-2 with the Irish.

Yugoslavia went through on merit in Group 2 after beating the talented French 3-2 while in Group 3, Wales edged out Hungary 2-1 in a play-off, the beaten finalists of four years earlier clearly over-the-hill as a team. But in Group 4 England put up a splendid performance against Brazil, drawing 0-0 thanks chiefly to some superb handling by goalkeeper Colin McDonald. Alas, forward weaknesses proved costly when the USSR beat them by the only goal in a play-off.

With the system requiring so many play-offs, it was 48 hours and further action for the victors. Gallant Wales defended magnificently against Brazil and only went down by a single goal. Had John Charles been fit to play in the game, it might have been even more interesting. But Northern Ireland, ravaged by injuries, conceded four goals to the ebullient French.

The USSR became the third play-off winner to lose; Sweden scoring twice in the second half to eliminate them. The other successful quarter-final side was West Germany, who needed all their guile to overcome Yugoslavia in Malmo, which they did with a first-half Helmut Rahn goal.

The Brazilians took full advantage of an injury to a key French defender in the semi-final, when the score was still 1-1, to win 5-2 in a match of free-flowing attack at both ends. In the other game, Sweden, spurred on by a growing enthusiasm from their followers, beat West Germany 3-1 but it was a close run thing.

(Above) England inside-forward Johnny Haynes finds his attempt at goal blocked by Brazilian goalkeeper Gylmar.

Brazil's talented squad spent most of the 1958 tournament scoring goals and enjoying the aftermath. Here Vava is injured scoring against the USSR (left) but is prevented from falling to the ground by his colleagues.

The Germans took the lead, and when Nils Liedholm, 36, started the move which led to Sweden's equaliser, he clearly handled the ball. In the second half, the German left-back Juskowiak, who had been tormented by Kurt Hamrin on the Swedish right-wing, was sent off for retaliation. Gunnar Gren, 37, and Hamrin added further goals for Sweden.

In the final it rained and appeared to give the hosts a better chance. Indeed they went ahead when the intrepid Liedholm contrived an opening for himself after only four minutes. Undeterred, Brazil kept their heads as well as they had lost them in 1954 and, playing with even more style than the 1950 side, were soon in control. It took them just three minutes to draw level. Garrincha, the 'Little Bird' flying on the wing who had only been put into the side following a deputation of players to coach Vicente Feola, destroyed Sweden's left flank.

His acceleration and swerving runs led to crosses and Vava supplied the finish, equalising then putting Brazil ahead. After the break Pele, memorably, and Zagalo made it 4-1 before Sweden, shut down on the wings, managed a goal through Agne Simonsson. But Pele had the last word with a header to make it 5-2. It had been a remarkable triumph for instinctive innovation in a 4-2-4 formation which was to be adapted elsewhere as the shield of the unskilled.

French forward Raymond Kopa leaps high in the air (left) but Brazilian goalkeeper Gylmar fists the ball away from danger. Injury-hit France lost this semi-final 5-2.

(Below) England held Brazil to a goalless draw in Gothenburg, thanks to some splendid goalkeeping by Colin McDonald, seen here gathering the ball safely. (AP)

Qualifying Tournament

53 entries

Europe (29): Austria, Belgium, Bulgaria, Czechoslovakia, Denmark, England, Finland, France, East Germany, West Germany, Greece, Holland, Hungary, Iceland, Rep of Ireland, Northern Ireland, Italy, Luxembourg, Norway, Poland, Portugal, Rumania, Scotland, Spain, Sweden, Switzerland, USSR, Wales, Yugoslavia

South America (9): Argentina, Bolivia, Brazil, Chile, Colombia, Paraguay, Peru, Uruguay, Venezuela

North and Central America (6): Canada, Costa Rica, Curacao, Guatemala, Mexico, USA

Asia/Africa (9): China, Cyprus, Egypt, Indonesia, Israel, Sudan, Syria, Taiwan, Turkey

This qualifying competition proved to be the most satisfactory to date, with the exception of the Asia/Africa group. The original plan there was for the winners of the four groups to meet for one place in the finals. Only two groups actually managed to record games. The others were beset by withdrawals caused by politics. Thus Israel were left without an opponent. FIFA decided that as no other country apart from the hosts and holders had failed to play at least two matches in order to reach the finals, Israel would have to meet one of the originally eliminated teams. This was achieved by a lottery.

Final places in Sweden were to be distributed as follows: Europe (9 + West Germany, Sweden); South America (3), North and Central America (1), Asia/Africa (1).

Europe

Group 1 (England, Rep of Ireland, Denmark)

Rep of Ireland v Denmark 2 - 1; England v Denmark 5 - 2; England v Rep of Ireland 5 - 1; Denmark v England 1 - 4; Rep of Ireland v England 1 - 1; Denmark v Rep of Ireland 0 - 2

	P	W	D	L	F	A	Pts
England	4	3	1	0	15	5	7
Rep of Ireland	4	2	1	1	6	7	5
Denmark	4	0	0	4	4	13	0

England qualified

Group 2 (France, Belgium, Iceland)

France v Belgium 6 - 3; France v Iceland 8 - 0; Belgium v Iceland 8 - 3; Iceland v France 1 - 5; Iceland v Belgium 2 - 5; Belgium v France 0 - 0

	P	W	D	L	F	A	Pts
France	4	3	1	0	19	4	7
Belgium	4	2	1	1	16	11	5
Iceland	4	0	0	4	6	26	0

France qualified

Group 3 (Hungary, Bulgaria, Norway)
Norway v Bulgaria 1 -2 ; Norway v Hungary 2 - 1, Hungary v Bulgaria 4 - 1;
Bulgaria v Hungary 1 - 2; Bulgaria v Norway 7 - 0; Hungary v Norway 5 - 0

	P	W	D	L	F	A	Pts
Hungary	4	3	0	1	12	4	6
Bulgaria	4	2	0	2	11	7	4
Norway	4	1	0	3	3	15	2

Hungary qualified

Group 4 (Czechoslovakia, Wales, East Germany)
Wales v Czechoslovakia 1 - 0; East Germany v Wales 2 - 1; Czechoslovakia
v Wales 2 - 0;East Germany v Czechoslovakia 1 - 4

	P	W	D	L	F	A	Pts
Czechoslovakia	4	3	0	1	9	3	6
Wales	4	2	0	2	6	5	4
East Germany	4	1	0	3	5	12	2

Czechoslovakia qualified

Group 5 (Austria, Holland, Luxembourg)
Austria v Luxembourg 7 - 0; Holland v Luxembourg 4 - 1;
Austria v Holland 3 - 2; Luxembourg v Holland (in Rotterdam) 2 -5;
Holland v Austria 1 - 1; Luxembourg v Austria 0 - 3

	P	W	D	L	F	A	Pts
Austria	4	3	1	0	14	3	7
Holland	4	2	1	1	12	7	5
Luxembourg	4	0	0	4	3	19	0

Austria qualified

Group 6 (USSR, Poland, Finland)
USSR v Poland 3 - 0; Finland v Poland 1 - 3; USSR v Finland 2 - 1;
Finland v USSR 0 - 10; Poland v USSR 2 - 1; Poland v Finland 4 - 0

	P	W	D	L	F	A	Pts
USSR	4	3	0	1	16	3	6
Poland	4	3	0	1	9	5	6
Finland	4	0	0	4	2	19	0

Play-off (in Leipzig): USSR v Poland 2 - 0
USSR qualified

Group 7 (Yugoslavia, Rumania, Greece)
Greece v Yugoslavia 0 - 0; Greece v Rumania 1 - 2; Rumania v Yugoslavia
1 - 1; Rumania v Greece 3 - 0; Yugoslavia v Greece 4 - 1
Yugoslavia v Rumania 2 - 0

	P	W	D	L	F	A	Pts
Yugoslavia	4	2	2	0	7	2	6
Rumania	4	2	1	1	6	4	5
Greece	4	0	1	3	2	9	1

Yugoslavia qualified

Group 8 (Northern Ireland, Italy, Portugal)
Portugal v Northern Ireland 1 - 1; Italy v Northern Ireland 1 - 0; Northern
Ireland v Portugal 3 - 0; Portugal v Italy 3 - 0; Italy v Portugal 3 - 0;
Northern Ireland v Italy 2 - 1

	P	W	D	L	F	A	Pts
Northern Ireland	4	2	1	1	6	3	5
Italy	4	2	0	2	5	5	4
Portugal	4	1	1	2	4	7	2

Northern Ireland qualified

Group 9 (Scotland, Spain, Switzerland)
Spain v Switzerland 2 - 2; Scotland v Spain 4 - 2; Switzerland v Scotland;
1 - 2; Spain v Scotland 4 -1 ; Scotland v Switzerland 3 - 2
Switzerland v Spain 1 - 4

	P	W	D	L	F	A	Pts
Scotland	4	3	0	1	10	9	6
Spain	4	2	1	1	12	8	5
Switzerland	4	0	1	3	6	11	1

Scotland qualified

South America
Group 1 (Brazil, Peru, Venezuela)
Venezuela withdrew
Peru v Brazil 1 - 1, 0 - 1
Brazil qualified

Group 2 (Argentina, Bolivia, Chile)
Chile v Bolivia 2 - 1; Bolivia v Chile 3 - 0; Bolivia v Argentina 2-0;
Chile v Argentina 0 - 2; Argentina v Chile 4 - 0; Argentina v Bolivia 4 - 0

	P	W	D	L	F	A	Pts
Argentina	4	3	0	1	10	2	6
Bolivia	4	2	0	2	6	6	4
Chile	4	1	0	3	2	10	2

Argentina qualified

Group 3 (Paraguay, Uruguay, Colombia)
Colombia v Uruguay 1 - 1; Colombia v Paraguay 2 - 3; Uruguay v Colombia
1 - 0; Paraguay v Colombia 3 - 0; Paraguay v Uruguay 5 - 0;
Uruguay v Paraguay 2 - 0

	P	W	D	L	F	A	Pts
Paraguay	4	3	0	1	11	4	6
Uruguay	4	2	1	1	4	6	5
Colombia	4	0	1	3	3	8	1

Paraguay qualified

North and Central America
Sub-Group 1 (Costa Rica, Curacao, Guatemala)
Guatemala v Costa Rica 2 - 6; Costa Rica v Guatemala 3 - 1 (match
abandoned, awarded to Costa Rica); Costa Rica v Curacao 4 - 0;
Guatemala v Curacao 1 - 3; Curacao v Costa Rica 1 - 2; Curacao
v Guatemala not played

	P	W	D	L	F	A	Pts
Costa Rica	4	4	0	0	15	4	8
Curacao	3	1	0	2	4	7	2
Guatemala	3	0	0	3	4	12	0

Sub-Group 2 (Mexico, Canada, USA)
Mexico v USA 6 - 0; USA V Mexico 2 - 7; Canada v USA 5 - 1; Mexico
v Canada 3 - 0; Canada v Mexico 0 - 2 (in Mexico City); USA v Canada 2 - 3

	P	W	D	L	F	A	Pts
Mexico	4	4	0	0	18	2	8
Canada	4	2	0	2	8	8	4
USA	4	0	0	4	5	21	0

Final round
Mexico v Costa Rica 2 - 0, 1 - 1
Mexico qualified

Asia/Africa
Sub-Group 1 (Indonesia, China, Taiwan)
Taiwan withdrew
Indonesia v China 2 - 0, 3 - 4
Play-off (in Rangoon): Indonesia v China 0 - 0
(Indonesia won on scoring more goals in previous matches)

Sub-Group 2 (Israel, Turkey)
Turkey withdrew

Sub-group 3 (Egypt, Cyprus)
Cyprus withdrew

Sub-Group 4 (Sudan, Syria)
Sudan v Syria 1 - 0, 1 - 1

Second round
Israel walked over (Indonesia withdrew); Sudan walked over
(Egypt withdrew)

Final round
Israel walked over (Sudan withdrew); Wales won draw among all second-
placed teams to play Israel, Belgium and Uruguay declined
Israel v Wales 0 - 2, 0 - 2
Wales qualified

Final Tournament SWEDEN
GROUP 1
8.6.58 West Germany (2) 3, Argentina (1) 1 MALMO
West Germany: Herkenrath, Stollenwerk, Juskowiak, Eckel, Erhardt, Szymaniak, Rahn (2), Walter F, Seeler (1), Schmidt, Schafer
Argentina: Carrizo, Dellacha, Vairo, Lombardo, Rossi, Varacka, Corbatta (1), Prado, Menendez, Rojas, Cruz
Referee: Leafe (England)

8.6.58 Northern Ireland (1) 1, Czechoslovakia (0) 0 HALMSTAD
Northern Ireland: Gregg, Keith, McMichael, Blanchflower, Cunningham, Peacock, Bingham, Cush (1), Dougan, McIlroy, McParland
Czechoslovakia: Dolejsi, Mraz, Novak, Pluskal, Cadek, Masopust, Hovorka, Dvorak, Borovicka, Hertl, Krauss
Referee: Seipelt (Austria)

11.6.58 West Germany (0) 2, Czechoslovakia (2) 2 HALSINGBORG
West Germany: Herkenrath, Stollenwerk, Juskowiak, Schnellinger, Erhardt, Szymaniak, Rahn (1), Walter F, Seeler, Schafer (1), Klodt
Czechoslovakia: Dolejsi, Mraz, Novak, Pluskal, Popluhar, Masopust, Hovorka, Dvorak (1 pen), Molnar, Farajsl, Zikan (1)
Referee: Ellis (England)

11.6.58 Argentina (1) 3, Northern Ireland (1) 1 HALMSTAD
Argentina: Carrizo, Dellacha, Vairo, Lombardo, Rossi, Varacka, Corbatta (1 pen), Avio (1), Menendez (1), Labruna, Boggio
Northern Ireland: Gregg, Keith, McMichael, Blanchflower, Cunningham, Peacock, Bingham, Cush, Coyle, McIlroy, McParland (1)
Referee: Ahlner (Sweden)

15.6.58 West Germany (1) 2, Northern Ireland (1) 2 MALMO
West Germany: Herkenrath, Stollenwerk, Juskowiak, Eckel, Erhardt, Szymaniak, Rahn (1), Walter F, Seeler (1), Schafer, Klodt
Northern Ireland: Gregg, Keith, McMichael, Blanchflower, Cunningham, Peacock, Bingham, Cush, Casey, McIlroy, McParland (2)
Referee: Campos (Portugal)

15.6.58 Czechoslovakia (3) 6, Argentina (0) 1 HALSINGBORG
Czechoslovakia: Dolejsi, Mraz, Novak, Dvorak (1), Popluhar, Masopust, Hovorka (1), Borovicka, Molnar, Farajsl (2), Zikan (2)
Argentina: Carrizo, Dellacha, Vairo, Lombardo, Rossi, Varacka, Corbatta (1), Avio, Menendez, Labruna, Cruz
Referee: Ellis (England)

	P	W	D	L	F	A	Pts
West Germany	3	1	2	0	7	5	4
Northern Ireland	3	1	1	1	4	5	3
Czechoslovakia	3	1	1	1	8	4	3
Argentina	3	1	0	2	5	10	2

Play off for 2nd place
17.6.58 Northern Ireland (1) 2, Czechoslovakia (1) 1 (aet, 1 - 1 at 90 mins) MALMO
Northern Ireland: Uprichard, Keith, McMichael, Blanchflower, Cunningham, Peacock, Bingham, Cush, Scott, McIlroy, McParland (2)
Czechoslovakia: Dolejsi, Mraz, Novak, Bubernik, Popluhar, Masopust, Dvorak, Molnar, Farajsl, Borovicka, Zikan (1)
Referee: Guigue (France)

GROUP 2
8.6.58 Yugoslavia (1) 1, Scotland (0) 1 VASTERAS
Yugoslavia: Beara, Sijakovic, Crnkovic, Krstic, Zebec, Boskov, Petakovic (1), Veselinovic, Milutinovic, Sekularac, Rajkov
Scotland: Younger, Caldow, Hewie, Turnball, Evans, Cowie, Leggat, Murray (1), Mudie, Collins, Imlach
Referee: Wyssling (Switzerland)

8.6.58 France (2) 7, Paraguay (2) 3 NORRKOPING
France: Remetter, Kaelbel, Lerond, Penverne, Jonquet, Marcel, Wisnieski (1), Fontaine (3), Kopa (1), Piantoni (1), Vincent (1)
Paraguay: Mageregger, Miranda, Arevalo, Villalba, Lezcano, Achucarro, Aguero, Parodi, Romero (1), Re, Amarilla (2, 1 pen)
Referee: Gardeazabal (Spain)

11.6.58 Paraguay (2) 3, Scotland (1) 2 NORRKOPING
Paraguay: Aguilar, Arevalo, Echague, Villalba, Lezcano, Achucarro, Aguero (1), Parodi, Romero (1), Re (1), Amarilla
Scotland: Younger, Parker, Caldow, Turnball, Evans, Cowie, Leggat, Collins (1), Mudie (1), Robertson, Fernie
Referee: Orlandini (Italy)

11.6.58 Yugoslavia (1) 3, France (1) 2 VASTERAS
Yugoslavia: Beara, Tomic, Crnkovic, Krstic, Zebec, Boskov, Petakovic (1), Veselinovic (2), Milutinovic, Sekularac, Rajkov
France: Remetter, Kaelbel, Marche, Penverne, Jonquet, Lerond, Wisnieski, Fontaine, Kopa, Piantoni, Vincent
Referee: Griffiths (Wales)

15.6.58 France (2) 2, Scotland (0) 1 OREBRO
France: Abbes, Kaelbel, Lerond, Penverne, Jonquet, Marcel, Wisnieski, Fontaine (1), Kopa (1), Piantoni, Vincent
Scotland: Brown, Caldow, Hewie, Turnball, Evans, Mackay, Collins, Murray, Mudie, Baird (1), Imlach
Referee: Brozzi (Argentina)

15.6.58 Paraguay (1) 3, Yugoslavia (2) 3 ESKISTUNA
Paraguay: Aguilar, Arevalo, Echague, Villalba, Lezcano, Achucarro, Aguero (1), Parodi, Romero (1), Re, Amarilla
Yugoslavia: Beara, Tomic, Crnkovic, Krstic, Zebec, Boskov, Petakovic, Veselinovic (1), Ogjanovi (2), Sekularac, Rajkov
Referee: Macko (Czechoslovakia)

	P	W	D	L	F	A	Pts
France	3	2	0	1	11	7	4
Yugoslavia	3	1	2	0	7	6	4
Paraguay	3	1	1	1	9	12	3
Scotland	3	0	1	2	4	6	1

GROUP 3
8.6.58 Sweden (1) 3, Mexico (0) 0 STOCKHOLM
Sweden: Svensson, Bergmark, Axbom, Liedholm (1 pen), Gustavsson, Parling, Hamrin, Mellberg, Simonsson (2), Gren, Skoglund
Mexico: Carbajal, Del Muro, Villegas, Portugal, Romo, Flores, Hernandez, Reyes, Calderon, Gutierrez, Sesma
Referee: Latyschev (USSR)

8.6.58 Hungary (1) 1, Wales (1) 1 SANDVIKEN
Hungary: Grosics, Matrai, Sarosi, Bozsik (1), Sipos, Berendi, Sandor, Hidegkuti, Tichy, Bundzsak, Fenyvesi
Wales: Kelsey, Williams, Hopkins, Sullivan, Charles M, Bowen, Webster, Medwin, Charles J (1), Allchurch, Jones
Referee: Codesal (Uruguay)

11.6.58 Mexico (1) 1, Wales (1) 1 STOCKHOLM
Mexico: Carbajal, Del Muro, Gutierrez, Cardenas, Romo, Flores, Belmonte (1), Reyes, Blanco, Gonzalez, Sesma
Wales: Kelsey, Williams, Hopkins, Baker, Charles M, Bowen, Webster, Medwin, Charles J, Allchurch (1), Jones
Referee: Lemesic (Yugoslavia)

12.6.58 Sweden (2) 2, Hungary (0) 1 STOCKHOLM
Sweden: Svensson, Bergmark, Axbom, Liedholm, Gustavsson, Parling, Hamrin (2), Mellberg, Simonsson, Gren, Skoglund
Hungary: Grosics, Matrai, Sarosi, Szojka, Sipos, Berendi, Sandor, Bundzsak, Bozsik, Tichy (1), Fenyvesi
Referee: Mowat (Scotland)

15.6.58 Sweden (0) 0, Wales (0) 0 STOCKHOLM
Sweden: Svensson, Bergmark, Axbom, Borjesson, Gustavsson, Parling, Berndtsson, Selmosson, Kallgren, Lofgren, Skoglund
Wales: Kelsey, Williams, Hopkins, Sullivan, Charles M, Bowen, Vernon, Hewitt, Charles J, Allchurch, Jones
Referee: Van Nuffel (Belgium)

15.6.58 Hungary (1) 4, Mexico (0) 0 SANDVIKEN
Hungary: Ilku, Matrai, Sarosi, Szojka, Sipos, Kotasz, Budai, Bencsics, Hidegkuti, Tichy, Sandor (1)
Mexico: Carbajal, Del Muro, Gutierrez, Cardenas, Sepulveda, Flores, Belmonte, Reyes, Blanco, Gonzalez (o. g.), Sesma
Referee: Eriksson (Finland)

	P	W	D	L	F	A	Pts
Sweden	3	2	1	0	5	1	5
Wales	3	0	3	0	2	2	3
Hungary	3	1	1	1	6	3	3
Mexico	3	0	1	2	1	8	1

Play off for 2nd place
17.6.58 Wales (0) 2, Hungary (1) 1 STOCKHOLM
Wales: Kelsey, Williams, Hopkins, Sullivan, Charles M, Bowen, Medwin (1), Hewitt, Charles J, Allchurch (1), Jones
Hungary: Grosics, Matrai, Sarosi, Bozsik, Sipos, Kostasz, Budai, Bencsics, Tichy (1), Bundzsak, Fenyvesi
Referee: Latyschev (USSR)

GROUP 4
8.6.58 USSR (1) 2, England (0) 2 GOTHENBURG
USSR: Yashin, Kessarov, Kusnezov, Voinov, Krischevsky, Zarev, Ivanov A, Ivanov V (1), Simonian (1), Salnikov, Iljin
England: McDonald, Howe, Banks, Clamp, Wright, Slater, Douglas, Robson, Kevan (1), Haynes, Finney (1 pen)
Referee: Zsolt (Hungary)

8.6.58 Brazil (1) 3, Austria (0) 0 UDEVALLA
Brazil: Gylmar, De Sordi, Santos N (1), Dino, Bellini, Orlando, Joel, Didi, Mazzola (2), Dida, Zagalo
Austria: Szanwald, Halla, Svoboda, Hanappi, Happel, Koller, Horak, Senekowitsch, Buzek, Korner A, Schleger
Referee: Guigue (France)

11.6.58 Brazil (0) 0, England (0) 0 GOTHENBURG
Brazil: Gylmar, De Sordi, Santos N, Dino, Bellini, Orlando, Joel, Didi, Mazzola, Vava, Zagalo
England: McDonald, Howe, Banks, Clamp, Wright, Slater, Douglas, Robson, Kevan, Haynes, A'Court
Referee: Dusch (West Germany)

11.6.58 USSR (1) 2, Austria (0) 0 BORAS
USSR: Yashin, Kessarov, Kusnezov, Voinov, Krischevsky, Zarev, Ivanov A, Ivanov V (1), Simonian, Salnikov, Iljin (1)
Austria: Schmied, Kozliczek E, Svoboda, Hanappi, Stotz, Koller, Horak, Kozliczek P, Buzek, Korner A, Senekowitsch
Referee: Jorgensen (Denmark)

15.6.58 Brazil (1) 2, USSR (0) 0 GOTHENBURG
Brazil: Gylmar, De Sordi, Santos N, Zito, Bellini, Orlando, Garrincha, Didi, Vava (2), Pele, Zagalo
USSR: Yashin, Kessarov, Kusnezov, Voinov, Krischevsky, Zarev, Ivanov A, Ivanov V, Simonjan, Netto, Iljin
Referee: Guigue (France)

15.6.58 England (0) 2, Austria (1) 2 BORAS
England: McDonald, Howe, Banks, Clamp, Wright, Slater, Douglas, Robson, Kevan (1), Haynes (1), A'Court
Austria: Szanwald, Kollmann, Svoboda, Hanappi, Happel, Koller (1), Kozliczek E, Kozliczek P, Buzek, Korner A (1), Senekowitsch
Referee: Asmussen (Denmark)

	P	W	D	L	F	A	Pts
Brazil	3	2	1	0	5	0	5
USSR	3	1	1	1	4	4	3
England	3	0	3	0	4	4	3
Austria	3	0	1	2	2	7	1

Play off for 2nd place
17.6.58 USSR (0) 1, England (0) 0 GOTHENBURG
USSR: Yashin, Kessarov, Kusnezov, Voinov, Krischevsky, Zarev, Apuchtin, Ivanov V, Simonian, Falin, Iljin (1)
England: McDonald, Howe, Banks, Clayton, Wright, Slater, Brabrook, Broadbent, Kevan, Haynes, A'Court
Referee: Dusch (West Germany)

QUARTER FINALS
19.6.58 West Germany (1) 1, Yugoslavia (0) 0 MALMO
West Germany: Herkenrath, Stollenwerk, Juskowiak, Eckel, Erhardt, Szymaniak, Rahn (1), Walter F, Seeler, Schmidt, Schafer
Yugoslavia: Krivokuca, Sijakovic, Crnkovic, Boskov, Zebec, Krstic, Petakovic, Ogjanovic, Milutinovic, Veselinovic, Rajkov
Referee: Wyssling (Switzerland)

19.6.58 France (1) 4, Northern Ireland (0) 0 NORRKOPING
France: Abbes, Kaelbel, Lerond, Penverne, Jonquet, Marcel, Wisnieski (1), Fontaine (2), Kopa, Piantoni (1), Vincent
Northern Ireland: Gregg, Keith, McMichael, Blanchflower, Cunningham, Cush, Bingham, Casey, Scott, McIlroy, McParland
Referee: Gardeazabal (Spain)

19.6.58 Sweden (0) 2, USSR (0) 0 STOCKHOLM
Sweden: Svensson, Bergmark, Axbom, Borjesson, Gustavsson, Parling, Hamrin, Gren, Simonsson, Liedholm, Skoglund
USSR: Yashin, Kessarov, Kuznezov, Voinov, Krischevsky, Zarev, Ivanov A, Ivanov V, Simonian, Salnikov, Iljin
Referee: Leafe (England)

19.6.58 Brazil (0) 1, Wales (0) 0 GOTHENBURG
Brazil: Gylmar, De Sordi, Santos N, Zito, Bellini, Orlando, Garrincha, Didi, Mazzola, Pele (1), Zagalo
Wales: Kelsey, Williams, Hopkins, Sullivan, Charles M, Bowen, Medwin, Hewitt, Webster, Allchurch, Jones
Referee: Seipelt (Austria)

SEMI FINALS
24.6.58 Sweden (1) 3, West Germany (1) 1 GOTHENBURG
Sweden: Svensson, Bergmark, Axbom, Borjesson, Gustavsson, Parling, Hamrin (1), Gren (1), Simonsson, Liedholm, Skoglund (1)
West Germany: Herkenrath, Stollenwerk, Juskowiak, Eckel, Erhardt, Szymaniak, Rahn, Walter F, Seeler, Schafer (1), Cieslarczyk
Referee: Zsolt (Hungary)

24.6.58 Brazil (2) 5, France (1) 2 STOCKHOLM
Brazil: Gylmar, De Sordi, Santos N, Zito, Bellini, Orlando, Garrincha, Didi (1), Vava (1), Pele (3), Zagalo
France: Abbes, Kaelbel, Lerond, Penverne, Jonquet, Marcel, Wisnieski, Fontaine (1), Kopa, Piantoni (1), Vincent
Referee: Griffiths (Wales)

Match for third place
28.6.58 France (3) 6, West Germany (1) 3 GOTHENBURG
France: Abbes, Kaelbel, Lerond, Penverne, Lafond, Marcel, Wisnieski, Douis (1), Kopa (1 pen), Fontaine (4), Vincent
West Germany: Kwiatkowski, Stollenwerk, Erhardt, Schnellinger, Wewers, Szymaniak, Rahn (1), Sturm, Kelbassa, Schafer (1), Cieslarczyk (1)
Referee: Brozzi (Argentina)

FINAL
29.6.58 Brazil (2) 5, Sweden (1) 2 STOCKHOLM
Brazil: Gylmar, Santos D, Santos N, Zito, Bellini, Orlando, Garrincha, Didi, Vava (2), Pele (2), Zagalo (1)
Sweden: Svensson, Bergmark, Axbom, Borjesson, Gustavsson, Parling, Hamrin, Gren, Simonsson (1), Liedholm (1), Skoglund
Referee: Guigue (France)

35

CHILE
1962

Chile held the tournament despite being devastated by earthquakes a year previously. A new stadium in Santiago had been completed in December, another more modest ground was located at the coastal town of Vina del Mar, while Rancagua and Arica completed the four sites. However, apart from Chile's matches, which were the best attended of all, only Brazil's group attracted crowds of more than four figures. High admission charges did not help.

Brazil retained their title in a singularly uninspired series, stifled by defensive-minded football and pockmarked by some of the crudest, if effective tactics ever seen in international competition. The opening matches produced some serious injuries, several as the result of reckless tackling. An appeal for restraint by FIFA to the competing nations and Yugoslavia's withdrawal from the tournament of a player sent off after being involved with a Russian who suffered a broken leg, did not altogether restore calm.

Chile, who surprised and surpassed themselves, ultimately taking third place, were unfortunately involved in the debacle which became known as the 'Battle of Santiago'. Italy's Ferrini was sent off by English referee Ken Aston for a foul. Then Chile's outside-left Leonel Sanchez, son of a professional boxer, broke the nose of the Italian Humberto Maschio with a flawless left hook clearly seen by television and film audiences, but missed by the linesman standing only feet away. Italian defender Mario David was not so lucky to escape, as his retaliatory kick at Sanchez ended in dismissal, though years later Sanchez admitted he had not been touched.

Garrincha of Brazil caused England endless problems. Here Ray Wilson manages to get a toe to the ball on the edge of the penalty area. (POPPERFOTO)

While the Italians had failed to stamp the right kind of authority on the matches themselves, their *catenaccio* defensive system led to others copying this negative trend. Even Brazil did not operate as smoothly as before, despite retaining nine of their 1958 side; they used a more cautious 4-3-3 pattern, with winger Zagalo dropping back.

Goal difference counted in the group games and merely added to the safety-first measures employed. However, there were the usual shocks. Uruguay and the physical Argentines were eliminated after being expected to do well. England overcame Argentina 3-1 after losing 2-1 to Hungary, and a goalless draw with Bulgaria saw them reach the last eight.

The USSR and Yugoslavia had come through in Group 1, though the normally efficient Lev Yashin had a nightmare game in goal against Colombia in a 4-4 draw which stunned the Russians. Unbeaten West Germany and Chile progressed in Group 2 while Brazil and Czechoslovakia, who shared a goalless draw in Group 3, also reached the quarter-finals. But it was to be Pele's last appearance in the tournament after suffering a pulled muscle.

In Santiago, Yugoslavia's single-goal victory over West Germany was clinched by Radakovic with four minutes remaining. It buried the memory of two quarter-final defeats in previous tournaments against the Germans. England had to bow to Brazil, or rather Garrincha, who was behind all three goals in their 3-1 win.

Czechoslovakia owed much to their half-back line of Pluskal, Popluhar and Masopust and the goalkeeping of Schroif in the 1-0 win over Hungary, whose 6-1 group win over Bulgaria had given Florian Albert the only hat-trick of the tournament. Then in the other quarter-final, Russia's Yashin had another poor day which allowed Sanchez and Eladio Rojas to score for a now rampant Chile in a 2-1 win.

This brought the Chileans a semi-final with Brazil and inevitable trouble. One player from each side was sent off, but Garrincha was given permission to play in the final after Brazil's 4-2 win. He and Vava had each scored twice. In the all-Eastern bloc game between Czechoslovakia and Yugoslavia, the Czechs' finishing was clinical in a 3-1 success, though their opponents had enjoyed more of the play.

There was some consolation for Chile as they took third place, much to the delight of the local supporters, with a 1-0 win over Yugoslavia. But considerable interest surrounded the final in which the Brazilians were again parading their 'Pele-substitute' Amarildo, whose two goals on his first appearance in the tournament had beaten Spain 2-1.

Yet it was the Czechs who opened the scoring, Scherer splitting the Brazilian defence for Masopust to run in. Brazil equalised through Amarildo who squeezed the ball inside Schroif's near post from a ludicrously acute angle. Amarildo centred for Zito to head Brazil into a second-half lead, and 13 minutes from the end, Schroif erred again. He flapped at a high cross and allowed Vava to slot in the third Brazilian goal.

For Brazil it was a worthy victory, without the flamboyance achieved in Sweden. But it was the least remembered of the World Cups and did not bode well for the future, as the game withdrew into itself defensively, faced with the fear of defeat.

Qualifying Tournament

56 entries

Eastern Hemisphere (Africa, Asia, Europe) (39): Africa — Egypt, Ethiopia, Ghana, Morocco, Nigeria, Sudan, Tunisia; Asia — Indonesia, Japan, South Korea; Europe — Belgium, Bulgaria, Cyprus, Czechoslovakia, England, Finland, France, East Germany, West Germany, Greece, Holland, Hungary, Republic of Ireland, Northern Ireland, Israel, Italy, Luxembourg, Norway, Poland, Portugal, Rumania, Scotland, Spain, Sweden, Switzerland, Turkey, USSR, Wales, Yugoslavia

Western Hemisphere (North, Central and South America) (17): North — Canada, Mexico, USA; Central — Costa Rica, Guatemala, Honduras, Netherlands Antilles, Surinam;

South America — Argentina, Bolivia, Brazil, Chile, Colombia, Ecuador, Paraguay, Peru, Uruguay.

Ten groups in Europe included provision for play-offs against the winners from sub-groups of Asia, Africa and the Near East. With hosts and holders from South America, that continent was awarded places in the final tournament for just over half its entry of nine. The original scheme was for the final competition to be held in nine different towns and cities, but ultimately only four were used.

Final places in Chile were to be distributed as follows: Europe (10)*, South America (3 + Brazil, Chile), North/Central America (1), Asia/Africa (0)*.

*Play-off between Yugoslavia and South Korea gave Europe a further final place.

Europe/Africa/Asia
Group 1 (Switzerland, Sweden, Belgium)
Sweden v Belgium 2 - 0; Belgium v Switzerland 2 - 4; Switzerland v Belgium 2 - 1; Sweden v Switzerland 4 - 0; Belgium v Sweden 0 -2 ; Switzerland v Sweden 3 - 2

	P	W	D	L	F	A	Pts
Sweden	4	3	0	1	10	3	6
Switzerland	4	3	0	1	9	9	6
Belgium	4	0	0	4	3	10	0

Play-off (in Berlin): Switzerland v Sweden 2 - 1
Switzerland qualified

Group 2 (Bulgaria, France, Finland)
Finland v France 1 - 2; France v Bulgaria 3 - 0; Finland v Bulgaria 0 - 2; France v Finland 5 - 1; Bulgaria v Finland 3 - 1; Bulgaria v France 1 - 0

	P	W	D	L	F	A	Pts
Bulgaria	4	3	0	1	6	4	6
France	4	3	0	1	10	3	6
Finland	4	0	0	4	3	12	0

Play-off (in Milan): Bulgaria v France 1 - 0
Bulgaria qualified

Group 3 (West Germany, Northern Ireland, Greece)
Northern Ireland v West Germany 3 - 4; Greece v West Germany 0 -3 ; Greece v Northern Ireland 2 - 1; West Germany v Northern Ireland 2 - 1; Northern Ireland v Greece 2 - 0; West Germany v Greece 2 - 1

	P	W	D	L	F	A	Pts
West Germany	4	4	0	0	11	5	5
Northern Ireland	4	1	0	3	7	8	2
Greece	4	1	0	3	3	8	2

West Germany qualified

Group 4 (Hungary, Holland, East Germany)
Hungary v East Germany 2 - 0; Holland v Hungary 0 - 3; East Germany v Holland 1 - 1; East Germany v Hungary 2 - 3; Hungary v Holland 3 - 3; Holland v East Germany not played

	P	W	D	L	F	A	Pts
Hungary	4	3	1	0	11	5	7
Holland	3	0	2	1	4	7	2
East Germany	3	0	1	2	3	6	1

Hungary qualified

Group 5 (USSR, Turkey, Norway)
Norway v Turkey 0 - 1; USSR v Turkey 1 - 0; USSR v Norway 5 - 2; Norway v USSR 0 - 3; Turkey v Norway 2 - 1; Turkey v USSR 1 - 2

	P	W	D	L	F	A	Pts
USSR	4	4	0	0	11	3	8
Turkey	4	2	0	2	4	4	4
Norway	4	0	0	4	3	11	0

USSR qualified

Group 6 (England, Portugal, Luxembourg)
Luxembourg v England 0 - 9; Portugal v Luxembourg 6 - 0; Portugal v England 1 - 1; England v Luxembourg 4 - 1; Luxembourg v Portugal 4 - 2; England v Portugal 2 - 0

	P	W	D	L	F	A	Pts
England	4	3	1	0	16	2	7
Portugal	4	1	1	2	9	7	3
Luxembourg	4	1	0	3	5	21	2

England qualified

Group 7
Sub-Group A (Cyprus, Israel, Ethiopia)

First Round
Cyprus v Israel 1 - 1, 1 - 6

Second Round
Israel v Ethiopia (in Tel Aviv) 1 - 0, 3 - 2

Sub-Group B (Italy, Rumania)
Rumania withdrew

Israel v Italy 2 - 4, 0 - 6
Italy qualified

Group 8 (Czechoslovakia, Scotland, Rep of Ireland)
Scotland v Rep of Ireland 4 - 1; Rep of Ireland v Scotland 0 - 3; Czechoslovakia v Scotland 4 - 0; Scotland v Czechoslovakia 3 - 2; Rep of Ireland v Czechoslovakia 1 - 3; Czechoslovakia v Rep of Ireland 7 - 1

	P	W	D	L	F	A	Pts
Czechoslovakia	4	3	0	1	16	5	6
Scotland	4	3	0	1	10	7	6
Rep of Ireland	4	0	0	4	3	17	0

Play-off (in Brussels): Czechoslovakia v Scotland 4 - 2
Czechoslovakia qualified

Group 9 (Spain, Wales)
Wales v Spain 1 - 2, 1 - 1

Sub-Group 1 (Sudan and Egypt)
Both withdrew

Sub-Group 2 (Morocco, Tunisia)
Morocco v Tunisia 2 - 1, 1 - 2
Play-off (in Palermo): Morocco v Tunisia 1 - 1
(Morocco won on toss-up)

Sub-Group 3 (Ghana, Nigeria)
Ghana v Nigeria 4 - 1, 2 - 2

Sub-Group final
Ghana v Morocco 0 - 0, 0 - 1

Group final
Morocco v Spain 0 - 1, 2 - 3
Spain qualified

Group 10 (Yugoslavia, Poland)
Yugoslavia v Poland 2 - 1, 1 - 1

Sub-Group 1 (South Korea, Indonesia, Japan)
Indonesia withdrew
South Korea v Japan 2 - 1, 2 - 0

Group final
Yugoslavia v South Korea 5 - 1, 3 - 1
Yugoslavia qualified

South America
Group 11 (Argentina, Ecuador)
Ecuador v Argentina 3 - 6, 0 - 5
Argentina qualified

Group 12 (Uruguay, Bolivia)
Bolivia v Uruguay 1 - 1, 1 - 2
Uruguay qualified

Group 13 (Colombia, Peru)
Colombia v Peru 1 - 0, 1 - 1
Colombia qualified

Group 14 (Paraguay)
Play-off with North and Central American group winners

North and Central America
Sub-Group 1 (USA, Canada, Mexico)
Canada withdrew
USA v Mexico 3 - 3, 0 - 3

Sub-Group 2 (Costa Rica, Guatemala, Honduras)
Costa Rica v Guatemala 3 - 2; Guatemala v Costa Rica 4 -4; Honduras v Costa Rica 2 - 1; Costa Rica v Honduras 5 - 0; Honduras v Guatemala 1 - 1; Guatemala v Honduras 0 - 2 (abandoned)

	P	W	D	L	F	A	Pts
Costa Rica	4	2	1	1	13	8	5
Honduras	3	1	1	1	3	7	3
Guatemala	3	0	2	1	7	8	2

Play-off (in Guatemala): Honduras v Costa Rica 0 - 1

Sub-Group 3 (Surinam, Netherlands Antilles)
Surinam v Netherlands Antilles 1 - 2, 0 - 0

Final round

Costa Rica v Mexico 1 - 0; Costa Rica v Netherlands Antilles 6 - 0; Mexico v Netherlands Antilles 7 - 0; Mexico v Costa Rica 4 - 1; Netherlands Antilles v Costa Rica 2 - 0; Netherlands Antilles v Mexico 0 - 0

	P	W	D	L	F	A	Pts
Mexico	4	2	1	1	11	2	5
Costa Rica	4	2	0	2	8	6	4
N'lands/Antilles	4	1	1	2	2	13	3

Mexico v Paraguay 1 - 0, 0 - 0
Mexico qualified

Final Tournament CHILE
GROUP 1

30.5.62 Uruguay (0) 2, Colombia (1) 1 ARICA
Uruguay: Sosa, Troche, Alvarez E W, Mendez, Goncalvez, Alvarez E, Cubilla (1), Rocha, Langon, Sasia (1), Perez
Colombia: Sanchez C, Gonzalez J, Lopez, Echeverri, Zuluaga (1), Silva, Aceros, Coll, Klinger, Gamboa, Arias
Referee: Dorogi (Hungary)

31.5.62 USSR (0) 2, Yugoslavia (0) 0 ARICA
USSR: Yashin, Dubinski, Maslonkin, Ostrovsky, Voronin, Netto, Metreveli, Ivanov V (1), Ponedelnik (1), Kanevski, Meschki
Yugoslavia: Soskic, Durkovic, Jusufi, Matus, Markovic, Popovic, Mujic, Sekularac, Jerkovic, Galic, Skoblar
Referee: Dusch (West Germany)

2.6.62 Yugoslavia (2) 3, Uruguay (1) 1 ARICA
Yugoslavia: Soskic, Durkovic, Radakovic, Markovic, Jusufi, Popovic, Melic, Sekularac, Jerkovic (1), Galic (1), Skoblar (1)
Uruguay: Sosa, Troche, Alvarez E W, Mendez, Goncalvez, Alvarez E, Rocha, Bergara, Cabrera (1), Sasia, Perez
Referee: Galba (Czechoslovakia)

3.6.62 USSR (3) 4, Colombia (1) 4 ARICA
USSR: Yashin, Tschokeli, Ostrovsky, Voronin, Maslonkin, Netto, Chislenko (1), Ivanov V (2), Ponedelnik (1), Kanevski, Meschki
Colombia: Sanchez C, Alzate, Gonzalez J, Echeverri, Lopez, Serrano, Aceros (1), Coll (1), Klinger (1), Rada (1), Gonzalez H
Referee Filho (Brazil)

6.6.62 USSR (1) 2, Uruguay (0) 1 ARICA
USSR: Yashin, Tschokeli, Voronin, Netto, Ostrovsky, Maslonkin, Chislenko, Ivanov V (1), Ponedelnik, Mamykin (1), Chusainov
Uruguay: Sosa, Mendez, Alvarez E W, Goncalvez, Alvarez E, Troche, Cubilla, Cortes, Cabrera, Sasia (1), Perez
Referee: Jonni (Italy)

7.6.62 Yugoslavia (2) 5, Colombia (0) 0 ARICA
Yugoslavia: Soskic, Durkovic, Jusufi, Radakovic, Markovic, Popovic, Ankovic, Sekularc, Jerkovic (3), Galic (1), Melic (1)
Colombia: Sanchez C, Alzate, Gonzalez J, Echeverri, Lopez, Serrano, Aceros, Coll, Klinger, Rada, Gonzalez H
Referee: Robles (Chile)

	P	W	D	L	F	A	Pts
USSR	3	2	1	0	8	5	5
Yugoslavia	3	2	0	1	8	3	4
Uruguay	3	1	0	2	4	6	2
Colombia	3	0	1	2	5	11	1

GROUP 2

30.5.62 Chile (1) 3, Switzerland (1) 1 SANTIAGO
Chile: Escuti, Eyzaguirre, Sanchez R, Navarro, Contreras, Rojas, Ramirez (1), Toro, Landa, Fouilloux, Sanchez L (2)
Switzerland: Elsener, Grobety, Morf, Weber, Schneiter, Tacchella, Antenen, Allemann, Wuthrich (1), Eschmann, Pottier
Referee: Aston (England)

31.5.62 West Germany (0) 0, Italy (0) 0 SANTIAGO
West Germany: Fahrian, Nowak, Schnellinger, Schulz, Erhardt, Szymaniak, Sturm, Haller, Seeler, Brulls, Schafer
Italy: Buffon, Losi, Robotti, Salvadore, Maldini, Radice, Ferrini, Rivera, Altafini, Sivori, Menichelli
Referee: Davidson (Scotland)

2.6.62 Chile (0) 2, Italy (0) 0 SANTIAGO
Chile: Escuti, Eyzaguirre, Sanchez R, Navarro, Contreras, Rojas, Ramirez (1), Toro (1), Landa, Fouilloux, Sanchez L
Italy: Mattrel, David, Robotti, Salvadore, Janich, Tumburus, Mora, Maschio, Altafini, Ferrini, Menichelli
Referee: Aston (England)

3.6.62 West Germany (1) 2, Switzerland (0) 1 SANTIAGO
West Germany: Fahrian, Nowak, Schnellinger, Schulz, Erhardt, Szymaniak, Koslowski, Haller, Seeler (1), Schafer, Brulls (1)
Switzerland: Elsener, Schneiter (1), Tacchella, Grobety, Wuthrich, Weber, Antenen, Vonlanthen, Eschmann, Allemann, Durr
Referee: Horn (Netherlands)

6.6.62 West Germany (1) 2, Chile (0) 0 SANTIAGO
West Germany: Fahrian, Nowak, Schnellinger, Schulz, Erhardt, Giesemann, Kraus, Szymaniak, Seeler (1 pen), Seeler (1), Schafer, Brulls
Chile: Escuti, Eyzaguirre, Navarro, Contreras, Sanchez R, Rojas, Moreno, Tobar, Landa, Sanchez L, Ramirez
Referee: Davidson (Scotland)

7.6.62 Italy (1) 3, Switzerland (0) 0 SANTIAGO
Italy: Buffon, Losi, Radice, Salvadore, Maldini, Robotti, Mora (1), Bulgarelli (1), Sormani, Sivori, Pascutti (1)
Switzerland: Elsener, Schneiter, Tacchella, Groberty, Meier, Weber, Antenen, Vonlanthen, Wuthrich, Allemann, Durr
Referee: Latyschev (USSR)

	P	W	D	L	F	A	Pts
West Germany	3	2	1	0	4	1	5
Chile	3	2	0	1	5	3	4
Italy	3	1	1	1	3	2	3
Switzerland	3	0	0	3	2	8	0

GROUP 3

30.5.62 Brazil (0) 2, Mexico (0) 0 VINA DEL MAR
Brazil: Gylmar, Santos D, Santos N, Zito, Mauro, Zozimo, Garrincha, Didi, Vava, Pele (1), Zagalo (1)
Mexico: Carbajal, Del Muro, Villegas, Cardenas, Sepulveda, Najera, Del Aguila, Reyes, Hernandez H, Jasso, Diaz
Referee: Dienst (Switzerland)

31.5.62 Czechoslovakia (0) 1, Spain (0) 0 VINA DEL MAR
Czechoslovakia: Schroif, Lala, Novak, Pluskal, Popluhar, Masopust, Stibranyi (1), Scherer, Kvasnak, Adamec, Jelinek
Spain: Carmelo, Rivilla, Reija, Segarra, Santamaria, Garay, Del Sol, Puskas, Martinez, Suarez, Gento
Referee: Steiner (Austria)

2.6.62 Brazil (0) 0, Czechoslovakia (0) 0 VINA DEL MAR
Brazil: Gylmar, Santos D, Santos N, Zito, Mauro, Zozimo, Garrincha, Didi, Vava, Pele, Zagalo
Czechoslovakia: Schroif, Lala, Novak, Pluskal, Popluhar, Masopust, Stibranyi, Scherer, Kvasnak, Adamec, Jelinek
Referee: Schwinte (France)

3.6.62 Spain (0) 1, Mexico (0) 0 VINA DEL MAR
Spain: Carmelo, Rodriguez, Gracia, Verges, Santamaria, Pachin, Del Sol, Peiro (1), Puskas, Suarez, Gento
Mexico: Carbajal, Del Muro, Jauregui, Cardenas, Sepulveda, Jasso, Najera, Del Aguila, Reyes, Hernandez H, Diaz
Referee: Tesanic (Yugoslavia)

6.6.62 Brazil (0) 2, Spain (1) 1 VINA DEL MAR
Brazil: Gylmar, Santos D, Santos N, Zito, Mauro, Zozimo, Garrincha, Didi, Vava, Amarildo (2), Zagalo
Spain: Araquistain, Rodriguez, Gracia, Verges, Echeverria, Pachin, Collar, Adelardo (1), Puskas, Peiro, Gento
Referee: Bustamante (Chile)

7.6.62 Mexico (2) 3, Czechoslovakia (1) 1 VINA DEL MAR
Mexico: Carbajal, Del Muro, Sepulveda, Jauregui, Cardenas, Najera, Del Aguila (1), Hernandez A, Hernandez H (1 pen), Reyes, Diaz (1)
Czechoslovakia: Schroif, Lala, Novak, Pluskal, Popluhar, Masopust, Stibranyi, Scherer, Kvasnak, Adamec, Masek (1)
Referee: Dienst (Switzerland)

	P	W	D	L	F	A	Pts
Brazil	3	2	1	0	4	1	5
Czechoslovakia	3	1	1	1	2	3	3
Mexico	3	1	0	2	3	4	2
Spain	3	1	0	2	2	3	2

GROUP 4

30.5.62 Argentina (1) 1, Bulgaria (0) 0 RANCAGUA
Argentina: Roma, Navarro, Marzolini, Sainz, Sacchi, Paez, Facundo (1), Rossi, Pagani, Sanfilippo, Belen
Bulgaria: Naidenov, Rakarov, Dimitrov, Kitov, Kostov D, Rovatchev, Diev, Velitschkov, Iljev, Yakimov, Kolev
Referee: Gardeazabal (Spain)

31.5.62 Hungary (1) 2, England (0) 1 RANCAGUA
Hungary: Grosics, Matrai, Meszoly, Sarosi, Solymosi, Sipos, Sandor, Rakosi, Tichy (1), Albert (1), Fenyvesi
England: Springett, Armfield, Wilson, Moore, Norman, Flowers (1 pen), Douglas, Greaves, Hitchens, Haynes, Charlton R
Referee: Horn (Netherlands)

2.6.62 England (2) 3, Argentina (0) 1 RANCAGUA
England: Springett, Armfield, Wilson, Moore, Norman, Flowers (1 pen), Douglas, Greaves (1), Peacock, Haynes, Charlton R (1)
Argentina: Roma, Cap, Marzolini, Sacchi, Navarro, Paez, Oleniak, Rattin, Sosa, Sanfilippo (1), Belen
Referee: Latyschev (USSR)

3.6.62 Hungary (4) 6, Bulgaria (0) 1 RANCAGUA
Hungary: Ilku, Matrai, Sarosi, Solymosi (1), Meszoly, Sipos, Sandor, Gorocs, Albert (3), Tichy (2), Fenyvesi
Bulgaria: Naidenov, Rakarov, Kitov, Kostov D, Dimitrov, Kovatchev, Sokolov (1), Velitschkov, Asparoukhov, Kolev, Dermendjiev
Referee: Gardeazabal (Spain)

6.6.62 Hungary (0) 0, Argentina (0) 0 RANCAGUA
Hungary: Grosics, Matrai, Sarosi, Solymosi, Meszoly, Sipos, Kuharszky, Gorocs, Monostori, Tichy, Rakosi
Argentina: Dominguez, Sainz, Marzolini, Delgado, Cap, Sacchi, Facundo, Pando, Pagani, Oleniak, Gonzalez
Referee: Yakasaki (Peru)

7.6.62 England (0) 0, Bulgaria (0) 0 RANCAGUA
England: Springett, Armfield, Wilson, Moore, Norman, Flowers, Douglas, Greaves, Peacock, Haynes, Charlton R
Bulgaria: Naidenov, Pentshev, Jetchev, Kostov D, Dimitrov, Kovatchev, Kostov A, Velitschkov, Sokolov, Kolev, Dermendjiev
Referee: Blavier (Belgium)

	P	W	D	L	F	A	Pts
Hungary	3	2	1	0	8	2	5
England	3	1	1	1	4	3	3
Argentina	3	1	1	1	2	3	3
Bulgaria	3	0	1	2	1	7	1

QUARTER FINALS

10.6.62 Yugoslavia (0) 1, West Germany (0) 0 SANTIAGO
Yugoslavia: Soskic, Durkovic, Jusufi, Radakovic (1), Markovic, Popovic, Kovacevic, Sekularac, Jerkovic, Galic, Skoblar
West Germany: Fahrian, Nowak, Schnellinger, Schulz, Erhardt, Giesemann, Brulls, Haller, Seeler, Szymaniak, Schafer
Referee: Yamasaki (Peru)

10.6.62 Chile (2) 2, USSR (1) 1 ARICA
Chile: Escuti, Eyzaguirre, Navarro, Contreras, Sanchez R, Rojas (1), Ramirez, Toro, Landa, Tobar, Sanchez L (1)
USSR: Yashin, Tschokeli, Ostrovsky, Voronin, Maslonkin, Netto, Chislenko (1), Ivanov, Ponedelnik, Mamykin, Meschki
Referee: Horn (Netherlands)

10.6.62 Brazil (1) 3, England (1) 1 VINA DEL MAR
Brazil: Gylmar, Santos D, Santos N, Zito, Mauro, Zozimo, Garrincha (2), Didi, Vava (1), Amarildo, Zagalo
England: Springett, Armfield, Wilson, Moore, Norman, Flowers, Douglas, Greaves, Hitchens (1), Haynes, Charlton R
Referee: Schwinte (France)

10.6.62 Czechoslovakia (1) 1, Hungary (0) 0 RANCAGUA
Czechoslovakia: Schroif, Lala, Novak, Pluskal, Popluhar, Masopust, Pospichal, Scherer (1), Kadraba, Kvasnak, Jelinek
Hungary: Grosics, Matrai, Sarosi, Solymosi, Meszoly, Sipos, Sandor, Rakosi, Tichy, Albert, Fenyvesi
Referee: Latyschev (USSR)

SEMI FINALS

13.6.62 Czechoslovakia (0) 3, Yugoslavia (0) 1 VINA DEL MAR
Czechoslovakia: Schroif, Lala, Novak, Pluskal, Popluhar, Masopust, Pospichal, Scherer (2, 1 pen), Kvasnak, Kadraba (1), Jelinek
Yugoslavia: Soskic, Durkovic, Jusufi, Radakovic, Markovic, Popovic, Sijakovic, Sekularac, Jerkovic (1), Galic, Skoblar
Referee: Dienst (Switzerland)

13.6.62 Brazil (2) 4, Chile (1) 2 SANTIAGO
Brazil: Gylmar, Santos D, Santos N, Zito, Mauro, Zozimo, Garrincha (2), Didi, Vava (2), Amarildo, Zagalo
Chile: Escuti, Eyzaguirre, Rodriguez, Contreras, Sanchez R, Rojas, Ramirez, Toro (1), Landa, Tobar, Sanchez L (1 pen)
Referee: Yamasaki (Peru)

Match for third place

16.6.62 Chile (0) 1, Yugoslavia (0) 0 SANTIAGO
Chile: Godoy, Eyzaguirre, Rodriguez, Cruz, Sanchez R, Rojas (1), Ramirez, Toro, Campos, Tobar, Sanchez L
Yugoslavia: Soskic, Durkovic, Svinjarevic, Radakovic, Markovic, Popovic, Kovacevic, Sekularac, Jerkovic, Galic, Skoblar
Referee: Gardeazabal (Spain)

FINAL

17.6.62 Brazil (1) 3, Czechoslovakia (1) 1 SANTIAGO
Brazil: Gylmar, Santos D, Santos N, Zito (1), Mauro, Zozimo, Garrincha, Didi, Vava (1), Amarildo (1), Zagalo
Czechoslovakia: Schroif, Tichy, Novak, Pluskal, Popluhar, Masopust (1), Pospichal, Scherer, Kadraba, Kvasnak, Jelinek
Referee: Latyschev (USSR)

ENGLAND

1966

Alf Ramsey's wingless Wembley wonders deserved their extra-time win over West Germany, who had prolonged their agony with a dramatic last-minute equaliser, but Geoff Hurst's hat-trick was a controversial treble for England. The first was a header from a free-kick quickly taken while Dienst, the referee, was admonishing an opponent; the second hit the bar and came down so fast that the official had to consult his Russian linesman, Bakhramov, who was badly positioned 10 yards from the goal-line; the third, in the dying minutes, came with three spectators running inside the opposite touchline.

In a tournament of cynical tackling, with players apparently fouling in rotation, five men were sent off: two Argentines, two Uruguayans and a Russian. Four of the dismissals were against the often provocative West Germans; the other culprit, Argentine captain Antonio Rattin, was sent off by a German referee for 'violence of the tongue'.

Yet England showed only flashes in their group games, being easily contained by a defensive Uruguay and beating a poor Mexican side and an injury-hit French team, both by two clear goals. In Group 2, Argentina and West Germany also settled for no goals to ensure that the top two places would not be unrealistic.

However, Group 3 appeared to be the strongest overall. Hungary and Portugal had looked attractive in pre-World Cup games, Bulgaria were tough and Brazil still had Pele; moreover a fit Pele. But he was singled out for roughing-up treatment in the opening game with Bulgaria. Brazil won by two free-kicks, one from Garrincha, who had lost his speed, the other from Pele.

Martin Peters (16) scores England's second goal in the 1966 final against West Germany. (POPPERFOTO)

The Portuguese combination of Mario Coluna's midfield scheming, the giant Jose Torres up front and the athleticism of Eusebio proved too much for Hungary, for whom goalkeeping appeared a lost art. But the Mighty Magyars did better against a Brazil lacking Pele, who had suffered a right knee injury against Bulgaria. Facing elimination, the ten-man Brazilian selection committee brought in nine new players against Portugal, then watched 'old-boy' Pele, not quite fit, get kicked out of the cup. Vicente had him limping after half an hour, Morais finished him off just before the interval.

Still, the real shock came in Group 4, where the unknown North Koreans humiliated Italy. Reduced by injury to ten men after 35 minutes, the Italians fell behind to a goal from Pak Doo Ik just three minutes before half-time and never recovered. The North Koreans progressed behind the USSR, who topped the section.

In the quarter-final at Wembley, Argentina's spoiling tactics upset referee Rudolf Kreitlein more than the England players. His notebook was beginning to curl up at the edges in the sun. Someone had to go. Captain Rattin argued over every decision and once too often; Kreitlein ordered him off. Unfortunately it took eight minutes to persuade him to leave. Incredibly Argentina dominated the game, until tiring. Then in the 78th minute, Hurst headed in at the near post from Peters' cross.

(Top left) Eusebio climbs above a North Korean defender during Portugal's 5-3 quarter-final win over the Asians who shocked an unsuspecting western world in 1966. (POPPERFOTO)

(Top right) The most controversial goal in a World Cup final. Geoff Hurst's shot hits the bar and bounces behind the German goalkeeper Hans Tilkowski.
(Main photo) Both sides appeal, and some look towards the Russian linesman Bakhramov; his verdict was that the ball had crossed the line and the referee awarded a goal.

44

(Left) West Germany's Uwe Seeler appears pole-axed by this tackle from the Uruguayan defender Manicera. The Germans won 4-0 in a controversial game at Hillsborough, Sheffield.

(HULTON DEUTSCH)

At Hillsborough there was more grief for the South American continent. Uruguay hit the bar against West Germany and then had a strong claim for a penalty, when Karl-Heinz Schnellinger handled under the crossbar, turned down by English referee Jim Finney. The West Germans, sensing they could provoke the Uruguayans into retaliation, achieved their objective. Four goals down at the end with nine men said it all for Uruguay.

At Roker Park, had the goalkeepers changed places, Hungary would probably have beaten the Russians, but the sensation was reserved for Goodison Park where the Koreans had the audacity to score three times before Portugal and Eusebio woke up. Eusebio eventually scored four himself including two penalties and the Portuguese won 5-3.

England had played all their games at Wembley and — surprise, surprise — they also met Portugal there in the semi-final. The Portuguese had apparently decided beforehand to atone for their previous sins, leaving out their hatchet men. However there was much speculation that England's more-than-combative midfield player Nobby Stiles would be taking care of Eusebio.

Reality was something else. Eusebio was insignificant, there was scarcely an infringement and England appeared to coast through with a Charlton effort from a rebound and another driven in just inside the penalty area. Eusebio did manage to convert a penalty for Banks' first back-breaking effort.

The war of attrition which masqueraded as the other semi-final between heavyweights West Germany and the USSR at Goodison Park, finally went to the West Germans by the same 2-1 scoreline, the Russians having Igor Chislenko sent off and another handicapped by injury.

For the final, the Germans rightly or wrongly decided to allow Franz Beckenbauer to shadow Charlton. But they led after Helmut Haller snapped up Ray Wilson's one error of the tournament in the 12th minute. Seven minutes later England were level, Bobby Moore's free-kick being headed in by Hurst. But it was not until the 78th minute that England regained the lead, Peters stabbing the ball in following a corner and a blocked shot from Hurst.

In the dying seconds Wolfgang Weber equalised. A dubious free-kick bounced agonisingly around, hit a defender, was prodded at by Siggi Held, appeared to be handled by Schnellinger and was finally knocked over the line by Weber. Extra time gave England the victory their preparation, dedication, spirit and teamwork had deserved.

Qualifying Tournament

71 entries

Europe (32): Albania, Austria, Belgium, Bulgaria, Cyprus, Czechoslovakia, Denmark, England, Finland, France, East Germany, West Germany, Greece, Holland, Hungary, Republic of Ireland, Northern Ireland, Israel, Italy, Luxembourg, Norway, Poland, Portugal, Rumania, Scotland, Spain, Sweden, Switzerland, Turkey, USSR, Wales, Yugoslavia

South America (10): Argentina, Bolivia, Brazil, Chile, Colombia, Ecuador, Paraguay, Peru, Uruguay, Venezuela

North, Central America and Caribbean (9): Costa Rica, Cuba, Honduras, Jamaica, Mexico, Netherlands Antilles, Surinam, Trinidad, USA

Africa, Asia, Australia (20): Algeria, Australia, Cameroon, Egypt, Ethiopia, Gabon, Ghana, Guinea, Liberia, Libya, Mali, Morocco, Nigeria, North Korea, Senegal, South Africa, South Korea, Sudan, Syria, Tunisia.

The mass withdrawal of all 16 African countries plus the suspension of South Africa by FIFA for violating anti-discrimination codes in the FIFA charter, left only three teams in the sprawling Africa, Asia and Australia zone. A tournament in Cambodia was boycotted by South Korea on the pretext that they preferred to concentrate on the 1968 Olympics, leaving only North Korea and Australia to contest a place in the finals.

In Europe, the draw was made geographically group by group, but with only one team from a particular region in each section. This was not entirely satisfactory though, as there were five groups of four teams and another three of three but only two teams in Group 9 following the withdrawal of Syria. Israel were included in Group 1.

Final places in England were to be distributed as follows: Europe (9 + England), South America (3 + Brazil), North/Central America and Caribbean (1), Asia (1). For the first time since holders and hosts had been exempted to the finals, Brazil and England were offically drawn in the qualifying stages but given a group of their own without opposition.

Europe

Group 1 (Bulgaria, Belgium, Israel)

Belgium v Israel 1 - 0; Bulgaria v Israel 4 - 0; Bulgaria v Belgium 3 - 0; Belgium v Bulgaria 5 - 0; Israel v Belgium 0 - 5; Israel v Bulgaria 1 - 2

	P	W	D	L	F	A	Pts
Belgium	4	3	0	1	11	3	6
Bulgaria	4	3	0	1	9	6	6
Israel	4	0	0	4	1	12	0

Play-off (in Florence): Bulgaria v Belgium 2 - 1

Bulgaria qualified

Group 2 (West Germany, Sweden, Cyprus)

West Germany v Sweden 1 - 1; West Germany v Cyprus 5 - 0; Sweden v Cyprus 3 - 0; Sweden v West Germany 1 - 2; Cyprus v Sweden 0 - 5; Cyprus v West Germany 0 - 6

	P	W	D	L	F	A	Pts
West Germany	4	3	1	0	14	2	7
Sweden	4	2	1	1	10	3	5
Cyprus	4	0	0	4	0	19	0

West Germany qualified

Group 3 (France, Norway, Yugoslavia, Luxembourg)

Yugoslavia v Luxembourg 3 - 1; Luxembourg v France 0 - 2; Luxembourg v Norway 0 - 2; France v Norway 1 - 0; Yugoslavia v France 1 - 0; Norway v Luxembourg 4 - 2; Norway v Yugoslavia 3 - 0; Norway v France 0 - 1; Luxembourg v Yugoslavia 2 - 5; France v Yugoslavia 1 - 0; France v Luxembourg 4 - 1; Yugoslavia v Norway 1 - 1

	P	W	D	L	F	A	Pts
France	6	5	0	1	9	2	10
Norway	6	3	1	2	10	5	7
Yugoslavia	6	3	1	2	10	8	7
Luxembourg	6	0	0	6	6	20	0

France qualified

Group 4 (Portugal, Czechoslovakia, Rumania, Turkey)

Portugal v Turkey 5 - 1; Turkey v Portugal 0 - 1; Czechoslovakia v Portugal 0 - 1; Rumania v Turkey 3 - 0; Rumania v Czechoslovakia 1 - 0; Portugal v Rumania 2 - 1; Czechoslovakia v Rumania 3 - 1; Turkey v Czechoslovakia 0 - 6; Turkey v Rumania 2 - 1; Portugal v Czechoslovakia 0 - 0; Czechoslovakia v Turkey 3 - 1; Rumania v Portugal 2 - 0

	P	W	D	L	F	A	Pts
Portugal	6	4	1	1	9	4	9
Czechoslovakia	6	3	1	2	12	4	7
Rumania	6	3	0	3	9	7	6
Turkey	6	1	0	5	4	19	2

Portugal qualified

Group 5 (Switzerland, Northern Ireland, Holland, Albania)

Holland v Albania, 2- 0; Northern Ireland v Switzerland 1 - 0;Albania v Holland 0 - 2; Switzerland v Northern Ireland 2 -1; Northern Ireland v Holland 2 - 1; Holland v Northern Ireland 0 - 0; Albania v Switzerland 0 - 2; Switzerland v Albania 1 - 0; Northern Ireland v Albania 4 - 1; Holland v Switzerland 0 - 0; Switzerland v Holland 2 - 1; Albania v Northern Ireland 1 - 1

	P	W	D	L	F	A	Pts
Switzerland	6	4	1	1	7	3	9
Northern Ireland	6	3	2	1	9	5	8
Holland	6	2	2	2	6	4	6
Albania	6	0	1	5	2	12	1

Switzerland qualified

Group 6 (Hungary, East Germany, Austria)

Austria v East Germany 1 - 1; East Germany v Hungary 1 - 1; Austria v Hungary 0 - 1; Hungary v Austria 3 - 0; Hungary v East Germany 3 - 2; East Germany v Austria 1 - 0

	P	W	D	L	F	A	Pts
Hungary	4	3	1	0	8	3	7
East Germany	4	1	2	1	5	5	4
Austria	4	0	1	3	1	6	1

Hungary qualified

Group 7 (USSR, Wales, Greece, Denmark)

Denmark v Wales 1 - 0; Greece v Denmark 4 - 2; Greece v Wales 2 - 0; Wales v Greece 4 - 1; USSR v Greece 3 - 1; USSR v Wales 2 - 1; USSR v Denmark 6 - 0; Greece v USSR 1 - 4; Denmark v USSR 1 - 3; Denmark v Greece 1 - 1; Wales v USSR 2 - 1; Wales v Denmark 4 - 2

	P	W	D	L	F	A	Pts
USSR	6	5	0	1	19	6	10
Wales	6	3	0	3	11	9	6
Greece	6	2	1	3	10	14	5
Denmark	6	1	1	4	7	18	3

USSR qualified

Group 8 (Italy, Scotland, Poland, Finland)

Scotland v Finland 3 - 1; Italy v Finland 6 - 1; Poland v Italy 0 - 0; Poland v Scotland 1 - 1; Finland v Scotland 1 - 2; Finland v Italy 0 - 2; Finland v Poland 2 - 0; Scotland v Poland 1 - 2; Poland v Finland 7 - 0; Italy v Poland 6 - 1; Scotland v Italy 1 - 0; Italy v Scotland 3 - 0

	P	W	D	L	F	A	Pts
Italy	6	4	1	1	17	3	9
Scotland	6	3	1	2	8	8	7
Poland	6	2	2	2	11	10	6
Finland	6	1	0	5	5	20	2

Italy qualified

Group 9 (Spain, Rep of Ireland, Syria (withdrew))

Rep of Ireland v Spain 1 - 0; Spain v Rep of Ireland 4 - 1
Play-off (in Paris): Spain v Rep of Ireland 1 - 0
Spain qualified

Group 10 (England)

England qualified

South America

Group 11 (Uruguay, Peru, Venezuela)

Peru v Venezuela 1 - 0; Uruguay v Venezuela 5 - 0; Venezuela v Uruguay 1 - 3; Venezuela v Peru 3 - 6; Peru v Uruguay 0 - 1; Uruguay v Peru 2 - 1

	P	W	D	L	F	A	Pts
Uruguay	4	4	0	0	11	2	8
Peru	4	2	0	2	8	6	4
Venezuela	4	0	0	4	4	15	0

Uruguay qualified

Group 12 (Chile, Ecuador, Colombia)

Colombia v Ecuador 0 - 1; Ecuador v Colombia 2 - 0; Chile v Colombia 7 - 2; Colombia v Chile 2 - 0; Ecuador v Chile 2 - 2; Chile v Ecuador 3 - 1

	P	W	D	L	F	A	Pts
Chile	4	2	1	1	12	7	5
Ecuador	4	2	1	1	6	5	5
Colombia	4	1	0	3	4	10	2

Play-off (in Lima): Chile v Ecuador 2 - 1
Chile qualified

Group 13 (Argentina, Paraguay, Bolivia)

Paraguay v Bolivia 2 - 0; Argentina v Paraguay 3 - 0; Paraguay v Argentina 0 - 0; Argentina v Bolivia 4 - 1; Bolivia v Paraguay 2 - 1; Bolivia v Argentina 1 - 2

	P	W	D	L	F	A	Pts
Argentina	4	3	1	0	9	2	7
Paraguay	4	1	1	2	3	5	3
Bolivia	4	1	0	3	4	9	2

Argentina qualified

Group 14 (Brazil)

Brazil qualified

North and Central America

Group 15

Sub-Group 1 (Jamaica, Netherlands Antilles, Cuba)

Jamaica v Cuba 1 - 0; Cuba v Netherlands Antilles 1 - 1; Jamaica v Netherlands Antilles 2 - 0; Netherlands Antilles v Cuba 1 - 0; Netherlands Antilles v Jamaica 0 - 0; Cuba v Jamaica 2 - 1

	P	W	D	L	F	A	Pts
Jamaica	4	2	1	1	4	2	5
Netherlands Antilles	4	1	2	1	2	3	4
Cuba	4	1	1	2	3	4	3

Sub-Group 2 (Costa Rica, Surinam, Trinidad)

Trinidad v Surinam 4 - 1; Costa Rica v Surinam 1 - 0; Costa Rica v Trinidad 4 - 0; Surinam v Costa Rica 1 - 3; Trinidad v Costa Rica, 0 - I; Surinam v Trinidad 6 - 1

	P	W	D	L	F	A	Pts
Costa Rica	4	4	0	0	9	1	8
Surinam	4	1	0	3	8	9	2
Trinidad	4	1	0	3	5	12	2

Sub-Group 3 (Mexico, USA, Honduras)

Honduras v Mexico 0 - 1; Mexico v Honduras 3 - 0; USA v Mexico 2 - 2; Mexico v USA 2 - 0; Honduras v USA 0 - 1; USA v Honduras 1 - 1

	P	W	D	L	F	A	Pts
Mexico	4	3	1	0	8	2	7
USA	4	1	2	1	4	5	4
Honduras	4	0	1	3	1	6	1

Final round

Costa Rica v Mexico 0 - 0; Jamaica v Mexico 2 - 3; Mexico v Jamaica 8 - 0; Costa Rica v Jamaica 7 - 0; Mexico v Costa Rica 2 - 0; Jamaica v Costa Rica 1 -1

	P	W	D	L	F	A	Pts
Mexico	4	3	1	0	12	2	7
Costa Rica	4	1	2	1	8	2	4
Jamaica	4	0	1	3	3	19	1

Mexico qualified

Asia/Africa

Group 16 (Australia, North Korea, South Korea)

(In Cambodia)
South Korea withdrew
North Korea v Australia 6 - 1, 3 - 1
North Korea qualified

Final Tournament ENGLAND
GROUP 1
11.7.66 England (0) 0, Uruguay (0) 0 WEMBLEY
England: Banks, Cohen, Wilson, Stiles, Charlton J, Moore, Ball, Greaves, Hunt, Charlton R, Connelly
Uruguay: Mazurkiewicz, Troche, Manicera, Ubinas, Goncalvez, Caetano, Cortes, Viera, Silva, Rocha, Perez
Referee: Zsolt (Hungary)

13.7.66 France (0) 1, Mexico (0) 1 WEMBLEY
France: Aubour, Djorkaeff, Artelesa, Budzinski, De Michele, Bonnel, Bosquier, Combin, Herbin, Gondet, Hausser (1)
Mexico: Calderon, Chaires, Nunez, Hernandez, Pena, Mercado, Diaz, Reyes, Fragoso, Padilla, Borja (1)
Referee: Ashkenasi (Israel)

15.7.66 Uruguay (2) 2, France (1) 1 WHITE CITY
Uruguay: Mazurkiewicz, Troche, Manicera, Ubinas, Goncalvez, Caetano, Cortes (1), Viera, Sasia, Rocha (1), Perez
France: Aubour, Djorkaeff, Artelesa, Budzinski, Bosquier, Bonnel, Simon, Herbet, De Bourgoing (1 pen), Gondet, Hausser
Referee: Galba (Czechoslovakia)

16.7.66 England (1) 2, Mexico (0) 0 WEMBLEY
England: Banks: Cohen, Wilson, Stiles, Charlton J, Moore, Paine, Greaves, Hunt (1), Charlton R (1), Peters
Mexico: Calderon, Chaires, Pena, Del Muro, Juaregui, Diaz, Padilla, Borja, Nunez, Reyes, Hernandez
Referee: Lo Bello (Italy)

19.7.66 Uruguay (0) 0, Mexico (0) 0 WEMBLEY
Uruguay: Mazurkiewicz, Troche, Manicera, Ubinas, Goncalvez, Caetano, Cortes, Viera, Sasia, Rocha, Perez
Mexico: Carbajal, Chaires, Pena, Nunez, Hernandez, Diaz, Mercado, Reyes, Cisneros, Borja, Padilla
Referee: Loow (Sweden)

20.7.66 England (1) 2, France (0) 0 WEMBLEY
England: Banks, Cohen, Wilson, Stiles, Charlton J, Moore, Callaghan, Greaves, Hunt (2), Charlton R, Peters
France: Aubour, Djorkaeff, Artelesa, Budzinski, Bosquier, Bonnel, Simon, Herbet, Gondet, Herbin, Hausser
Referee: Yamasaki (Peru)

	P	W	D	L	F	A	Pts
England	3	2	1	0	4	0	5
Uruguay	3	1	2	0	2	1	4
Mexico	3	0	2	1	1	3	2
France	3	0	1	2	2	5	1

GROUP 2
12.7.66 West Germany (3) 5, Switzerland (0) 0 HILLSBOROUGH
West Germany: Tilkowski, Hottges, Weber, Schulz, Schnellinger, Beckenbauer (2), Haller (2, 1 pen), Brulls, Seeler, Overath, Held (1)
Switzerland: Elsener, Grobety, Schneiter, Tacchella, Fuhrer, Bani, Durr, Odermatt, Kunzli, Hosp, Schindelholz
Referee: Phillips (Scotland)

13.7.66 Argentina (0) 2, Spain (0) 1 VILLA PARK
Argentina: Roma, Ferreiro, Perfumo, Albrecht, Marzolini, Solari, Rattin, Gonzalez, Artime (2), Onega, Mas
Spain: Iribar, Sanchis, Gallego, Zoco, Eladio, Pirri (1), Suarez, Del Sol, Ufarte, Peiro, Gento
Referee: Rumentschev (Bulgaria)

15.7.66 Spain (0) 2, Switzerland (1) 1 HILLSBOROUGH
Spain: Iribar, Sanchis (1), Gallego, Zoco, Reija, Pirri, Del Sol, Amancio (1), Peiro, Suarez, Gento
Switzerland: Elsener, Fuhrer, Brodmann, Leimgruber, Stierli, Bani, Armbruster, Gottardi, Hosp, Kuhn, Quentin (1)
Referee: Bakhramov (USSR)

16.7.66 West Germany (0) 0, Argentina (0) 0 VILLA PARK
West Germany: Tilkowski, Hottges, Weber, Schulz, Schnellinger, Beckenbauer, Haller, Brulls, Seeler, Overath, Held
Argentina: Roma, Ferreiro, Perfumo, Albrecht, Mazolini, Solari, Rattin, Gonzalez, Artime, Onega, Mas
Referee: Zecevic (Yugoslavia)

19.7.66 Argentina (0) 2, Switzerland (0) 0 HILLSBOROUGH
Argentina: Roma, Ferreiro, Perfumo, Calics, Marzolini, Solari, Rattin, Gonzalez, Artime (1), Onega (1), Mas
Switzerland: Eichmann, Fuhrer, Bani, Brodmann, Stierli, Armbruster, Kuhn, Gottardi, Kunzli, Hosp, Quentin
Referee: Campos (Portugal)

20.7.66 West Germany (1) 2, Spain (1) 1 VILLA PARK
West Germany: Tilkowski, Hottges, Weber, Schulz, Schnellinger, Beckenbauer, Overath, Kramer, Seeler (1), Held, Emmerich (1)
Spain: Iribar, Sanchis, Gallego, Zoco, Reija, Glaria, Fuste (1), Amancio, Adelardo, Marcelino, Lapetra
Referee: Marques (Brazil)

	P	W	D	L	F	A	Pts
West Germany	3	2	1	0	7	1	5
Argentina	3	2	1	0	4	1	5
Spain	3	1	0	2	4	5	2
Switzerland	3	0	0	3	1	9	0

GROUP 3
12.7.66 Brazil (1) 2, Bulgaria (0) 0 GOODISON PARK
Brazil: Gylmar, Santos D, Bellini, Altair, Paulo Henrique, Denilson, Lima, Garrincha (1), Alcindo, Pele (1), Jairzinho
Bulgaria: Naidenov, Chalamanov, Penev, Vutzov, Gaganelov, Kitov, Jetchev, Dermendjiev, Asparoukhov, Yakimov, Kolev
Referee: Tschenscher (West Germany)

13.7.66 Portugal (1) 3, Hungary (0) 1 OLD TRAFFORD
Portugal: Carvalho, Morais, Baptista, Vicente, Hilairo, Graca, Coluna, Jose Augusto (2), Eusebio, Torres (1), Simoes
Hungary: Szentmihalyi, Kaposzta, Matrai, Meszoly, Sovari, Nagy I, Sipos, Bene (1), Albert, Farkas, Rakosi
Referee: Callaghan (Wales)

15.7.66 Hungary (1) 3, Brazil (1) 1 GOODISON PARK
Hungary: Gelei, Matrai, Kaposzta, Meszoly (1 pen), Sipos, Szepesi, Mathesz, Rakosi, Bene (1), Albert, Farkas (1)
Brazil: Gylmar, Santos D, Bellini, Altair, Paulo Henrique, Gerson, Lima, Garrincha, Alcindo, Tostao (1), Jairzinho
Referee: Dagnall (England)

16.7 66 Portugal (2) 3, Bulgaria (0) 0 OLD TRAFFORD
Portugal: Pereira, Festa, Germano, Vicente, Hilario, Graca, Coluna, Jose Augusto, Eusebio (1), Torres (1), Simoes
Bulgaria: Naidenov, Chalamanov, Vutzov (o. g.), Gaganelov, Penev, Jetchev, Yakimov, Dermendjiev, Jekov, Asparoukhov, Kostov
Referee: Codesal (Uruguay)

17.7.66 Portugal (2) 3, Brazil (0) 1 GOODISON PARK
Portugal: Pereira, Morais, Baptista, Vicente, Hilairo, Graca, Coluna, Jose Augusto, Eusebio (2), Torres, Simoes (1)
Brazil: Manga, Fidelis, Brito, Orlando, Rildo (1), Denilson, Lima, Jairzinho, Silva, Pele, Parana
Referee: McCabe (England)

20.7.66 Hungary (2) 3, Bulgaria (1) 1 OLD TRAFFORD
Hungary: Gelei, Matrai, Kaposzta, Meszoly (1), Sipos, Szepesi, Mathesz, Rakosi, Bene (1), Albert, Farkas
Bulgaria: Simeonov, Penev, Largov, Vutzov, Gaganelov, Jetchev, Davidov (o. g.), Yakimov, Asparoukhov (1), Kolev, Kostov
Referee: Goicoechea (Argentina)

	P	W	D	L	F	A	Pts
Portugal	3	3	0	0	9	2	6
Hungary	3	2	0	1	7	5	4
Brazil	3	1	0	2	4	6	2
Bulgaria	3	0	0	3	1	8	0

GROUP 4
12.7.66 USSR (2) 3, North Korea (0) 0 AYRESOME PARK
USSR: Kavazashvili, Ponomarev, Shesternev, Khurtsilava, Ostrovsky, Sabo, Sichinava, Chislenko, Banischevski (1), Khusainov, Malofeyev (2)
North Korea: Chan Myung, Li Sup, Yung Kyoo, Bong Chil, Zoong Sun, Seung Hwi, Bong Zin, Doo Ik, Ryong Woon, Seung Il, Seung Zin
Referee: Gardeazabal (Spain)

13.7.66 Italy (1) 2, Chile (0) 0 ROKER PARK
Italy: Albertosi, Burgnich, Rosato, Salvadore, Facchetti, Bulgarelli, Lodetti, Perani, Mazzola (1), Rivera, Barison (1)
Chile: Olivares, Eyzaguirre, Cruz, Figueroa, Villanueva, Prieto, Marcos, Fouilloux, Araya, Tobar, Sanchez L
Referee: Dienst (Switzerland)

13.7.66 North Korea (0) 1, Chile (1) 1 AYRESOME PARK
North Korea: Chan Myung, Li Sup, Yung Kyoo, Zoong Sun, Yoon Kyung, Seung Zin (1), Seung Hwi, Bong Zin, Doo Ik, Dong Woon, Seung Il
Chile: Olivares, Valentini, Cruz, Figueroa, Villanueva, Prieto, Marcos (1 pen), Araya, Landa, Fouilloux, Sanchez L
Referee: Kandil (Egypt)

16.7.66 USSR (0) 1, Italy (0) 0 ROKER PARK
USSR: Yashin, Ponomarev, Shesternev, Khurtsilava, Danilov, Sabo, Voronin, Chislenko (1), Malofeyev, Banischevski, Khusainov
Italy: Albertosi, Burgnich, Rosato, Salvadore, Facchetti, Lodetti, Leoncini, Meroni, Mazzola, Bulgarelli, Pascutti
Referee: Kreitlein (West Germany)

19.7.66 North Korea (1) 1, Italy (0) 0 AYRESOME PARK
North Korea: Chang Myung, Zoong Sun, Yung Kyoo, Yung Won, Yoon Kyung, Seung Hwi, Bong Zin, Doo Ik (1), Seung Zin, Bong Hwan, Seung Kook
Italy: Albertosi, Landini, Guarneri, Janich, Facchetti, Bulgarelli, Fogli, Perani, Mazzola, Rivera, Barison
Referee: Schwinte (France)

20.7.66 USSR (1) 2, Chile (1) 1 ROKER PARK
USSR: Kavazashvili, Getmanov, Shesternev, Kornejev, Ostrovsky, Voronin, Afonin, Metreveli, Serebrannikov, Markarov, Porkujan (2)
Chile: Olivares, Valentini, Cruz, Figueroa, Villanueva, Marcos (1), Prieto, Araya, Landa, Yavar, Sanchez L
Referee: Adair (Northern Ireland)

	P	W	D	L	F	A	Pts
USSR	3	3	0	0	6	1	6
North Korea	3	1	1	1	2	4	3
Italy	3	1	0	2	2	2	2
Chile	3	0	1	2	2	5	1

QUARTER FINALS
23.7.66 England (0) 1, Argentina (0) 0 WEMBLEY
England: Banks, Cohen, Wilson, Stiles, Charlton J, Moore, Ball, Hunt, Hurst (1), Charlton R, Peters
Argentina: Roma, Ferreiro, Perfumo, Albrecht, Marzolini, Solari, Rattin, Gonzalez, Artime, Onega, Mas
Referee: Kreitlein (West Germany)

23.7.66 West Germany (1) 4, Uruguay (0) 0 HILLSBOROUGH
West Germany: Tilkowski, Hottges, Weber, Schulz, Schnellinger, Haller (2), Beckenbauer (1), Overath, Seeler (1), Emmerich, Held
Uruguay: Mazurkiewicz, Troche, Ubinas, Caetano, Manicera, Rocha, Goncalvez, Salva, Cortes, Silva, Perez
Referee: Finney (England)

23.7.66 Portugal (2) 5, North Korea (3) 3 GOODISON PARK
Portugal: Pereira, Morais, Baptista, Vicente, Hilario, Graca, Coluna, Jose Augusto (1), Eusebio (4, 2 pens), Torres, Simoes
North Korea: Chan Myung, Zoong Sun, Yung Kyoo, Yung Won, Yoon Kyung, Seung Zin, Seung Hwi, Bong Zin, Doo Ik, Dong Woon (1), Seung Kook (2)
Referee: Ashkenasi (Israel)

23.7.66 USSR (1) 2, Hungary (0) 1 ROKER PARK
USSR: Yashin, Ponomarev, Shesternev, Danilov, Voronin, Sabo, Khusainov, Chislenko (1), Banischevski, Malofeyev, Porkujan (1)
Hungary: Gelei, Kaposzta, Matrai, Meszoly, Szepesi, Nagy I, Sipos, Bene (1), Albert, Farkas, Rakosi
Referee: Gardeazabal (Spain)

SEMI FINALS
25.7.66 West Germany (1) 2, USSR (0) 1 GOODISON PARK
West Germany: Tilkowski, Lutz, Weber, Schulz, Schnellinger, Beckenbauer (1), Overath, Seeler, Haller (1), Held, Emmerich
USSR: Yashin, Ponomarev, Shesternev, Danilov, Voronin, Sabo, Khusainov, Chislenko, Banischevski, Malofeyev, Porkujan (1)
Referee: Lo Bello (Italy)

26.7.66 England (1) 2, Portugal (0) 1 WEMBLEY
England: Banks, Cohen, Wilson, Stiles, Charlton J, Moore, Ball, Hunt, Hurst, Charlton R (2), Peters
Portugal: Pereira, Festa, Baptista, Jose Carlos, Hilario, Graca, Coluna, Jose Augusto, Eusebio (1 pen), Torres, Simoes
Referee: Schwinte (France)

Match for third place
28.7.66 Portugal (1) 2, USSR (1) 1 WEMBLEY
Portugal: Pereira, Festa, Baptista, Jose Carlos, Hilario, Graca, Coluna, Jose Augusto, Eusebio (1 pen), Torres (1), Simoes
USSR: Yashin, Ponomarev, Korneev, Khurtsilava, Danilov, Voronin, Sichinava, Serebrannikov, Banischevski, Malofeyev (1), Metreveli
Referee: Dagnall (England)

FINAL
30.7.66 England (1) 4, West Germany (1) 2 (aet, 2-2 at 90 mins) WEMBLEY
England: Banks, Cohen, Wilson, Stiles, Charlton J, Moore, Ball, Hunt, Hurst (3), Charlton R, Peters (1)
West Germany: Tilkowski, Hottges, Weber (1), Schulz, Schnellinger, Haller (1), Beckenbauer, Overath, Seeler, Emmerich, Held
Referee: Dienst (Switzerland)

MEXICO

1970

Pele powers in a header to put Brazil 1-0 up against Italy in the 1970 final in Mexico City. Brazil won 4-1 in a masterly display of individual skill and flair.

Fears that the choice of Mexico as the venue would produce untold problems relating to heat and altitude as well as fan the flames of violence on the field were dispelled. Skill, thought and officials who threatened to use the the red and yellow disciplinary cards to advantage, contributed to a memorable tournament.

Its winners were Brazil, easily the most gifted team, if possessing certain weaknesses. As usual, their off-the-field preparations were faultless. A meticulous four months' training was rewarded with a vintage victory. They succeeded not only through this single-minded devotion to detail, but because of outstanding performances by several brilliant individuals, whose ability overcame the shortcomings of colleagues.

Brazil had even had a change of manager after the qualifying stage, Joao Saldanha giving way to Zagalo who had collected two winners medals as a player. He inherited a goalkeeper in Felix who was shaky, and had to struggle to keep his four-man zonal defence operating the system at all, when they were not giving the ball away.

But moving foward, either in swift counter-attacks or with breathtaking passing movements, simply transformed Brazil into a flexible, potent striking force. There was the deceptively languid Gerson controlling the midfield; the industry of Clodoaldo; the explosive dead-ball shooting of Rivelino; Jairzinho's penetration on the flank and the unselfishness of Tostao, forbidden to head the ball because of an operation for a detached retina. Above all there was Pele, restored to full vigour and at the peak of his illustrious career.

A rash of yellow cards in the opening goalless draw between Mexico and the USSR set the pattern for improved behaviour and the competition did not produce one dismissal. These two teams progressed to

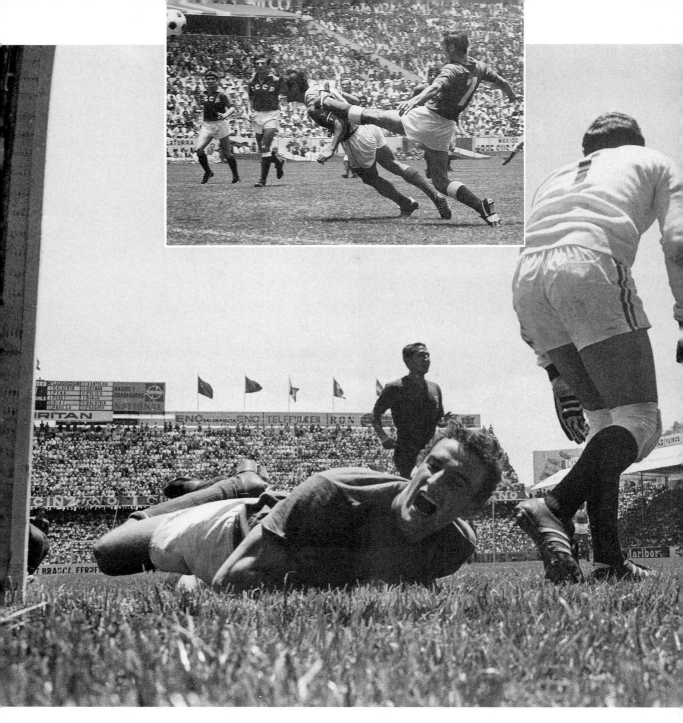

the quarter-finals as did Italy and Uruguay in Group 2, though neither impressed. Italy scored only one goal, an error by the Swedish goalkeeper.

Group 3 was well contested with Brazil winning all three games, though runners-up England pressed them fiercely in Guadalajara. The only goal came from an unselfish pass from Pele for the onrushing Jairzinho, but England still moved on. Yet the most entertaining group was the one in which West Germany and Peru emerged in front of Bulgaria and Morocco.

The Germans paired the veteran Uwe Seeler with the lethal poacher Gerd Muller and with substitutes allowed for the first time in the competition, switched wingers to telling effect during the games. Overall, some imaginative free-kicks added to the spectators' delight and the cavalier approach of Peru was another pleasing aspect.

In the quarter-finals, Uruguay survived a gruelling extra-time encounter with the USSR to emerge 1-0 winners in Mexico City, but it was the other three matches that had the drama and the goals.

England met West Germany in Leon, a repeat of the 1966 World Cup final at Wembley. Again it went to extra time, but with an entirely different narrative. Alan Mullery from six yards and Martin Peters running in at the far post had given England a deserved half-time lead. But in the 57th minute, Helmut Schoen the West Germany manager put on Grabowski as a fresh winger to run at a tiring defence. Beckenbauer rounded Mullery and reduced the scoreline to 2-1. Ramsey replied by taking off Charlton and bringing on Colin Bell.

Nine minutes from the end Seeler scored with a back header from an acute angle to force extra time. Inevitably, with the Germans once more underestimated but on top, it was Muller who stole in to hook the winner from close range. Ramsey's always cautious approach had proved his downfall.

The Guadalajara meeting between Brazil and Peru provided another feast of fast, entertaining fare, Brazil winning 4-2, while in Toluca, Italy hit the hosts Mexico with three goals in a 12-minute spell in the second half to win 4-1.

But the real heart-stopping affair was the semi-final involving the Italians and Germans in Mexico City. Roberto Boninsegna scored for Italy after eight minutes and they held the lead until the last minute when Schnellinger equalised with a volley. The Germans were handicapped, with Beckenbauer bravely playing on despite a dislocated shoulder, as they had used both substitutes.

Both teams were exhausted and it was a question of which side made more mistakes. Muller forced one over the line, Burgnich equalised. Riva restored Italy's lead only for Muller to head the Germans level at 3-3. Equality lasted only two minutes. Gianni Rivera drove in the winner in the 112th minute.

(Top left) The opening game in any World Cup tournament invariably ends in a goalless draw. 1970 was no exception. Horatio Lopez (Mexico) has his head menaced by USSR forward Gennadi Logofet (7).

(Left) Down but not out: Luigi Riva shouts in delight after scoring Italy's fourth goal against Mexico. Italy won their quarter-final tie 4-1.

(Below) Contrasting moods: Roberto Boninsegna (20) leaps for joy, Muller (13) despairs as Italy score against the Germans.

In the other semi-final in Guadalajara, Uruguay gave a fine account of themselves in the first half against Brazil, taking the lead through a half-hit angled shot from Luis Cubilla that made Felix look vulnerable. But Clodoaldo equalised right on half-time and in the second half it was all Brazil, though they did not score again until the 76th minute through Jairzinho and then in the last minute through Rivelino.

Thus the *catenaccio* of Italy faced Brazil's improvisation in the final and it stayed goalless only until the 17th minute when a teasing cross from Rivelino was headed powerfully in by Pele. Sheer carelessness gave Boninsegna an equaliser 20 minutes later and it was not until the 65th minute that Brazil regained the lead. Gerson's strong, long-range, left-foot drive finally broke down Italian resistance and Pele again laid on goals for Jairzinho six minutes later and for Carlos Alberto with three minutes remaining. Brazil had won the Jules Rimet Trophy for the third time and were allowed to keep it. But it was the end of an era.

Qualifying Tournament

70 entries

Europe (30): Austria, Belgium, Bulgaria, Cyprus, Czechoslovakia, Denmark, England, Finland, France, East Germany, West Germany, Greece, Holland, Hungary, Republic of Ireland, Northern Ireland, Italy, Luxembourg, Norway, Poland, Portugal, Rumania, Scotland, Spain, Sweden, Switzerland, Turkey, USSR, Wales, Yugoslavia

South America (10): Argentina, Bolivia, Brazil, Chile, Colombia, Ecuador, Paraguay, Peru, Uruguay, Venezuela

Concacaf (12): Bermuda, Canada, Costa Rica, Guatemala, Haiti, Honduras, Jamaica, Netherlands Antilles, El Salvador, Surinam, Trinidad, USA

Asia/Oceania (7): Australia, Israel, Japan, New Zealand, North Korea, Rhodesia, South Korea

Africa (11): Algeria, Cameroon, Ethiopia, Ghana, Libya, Morocco, Nigeria, Senegal, Sudan, Tunisia, Zambia

Finding a niche in the World Cup qualifying stages was becoming a problem politically for Israel. They were moved into the Asia/Oceania zone only to discover North Korea unwilling to meet them. Moreover although Rhodesia's entry had been accepted, they had a government which was not recognised; it was impossible for other countries to travel to Rhodesia or receive a team from that country. However Australia finally agreed to meet them on neutral territory over two matches in Mozambique.

Again England as holders and Mexico as hosts were included in the qualifying draw without having to play; again given a group of their own.

Final places in Mexico were to be distributed as follows:

Europe (8 + England), South America (3), Concacaf (1 + Mexico), Asia/Oceania (1), Africa (1)

Europe

Group 1 (Rumania, Greece, Switzerland, Portugal)

Switzerland v Greece 1 - 0; Portugal v Rumania 3 - 0; Rumania v Switzerland 2 - 0; Greece v Portugal 4 - 2; Portugal v Switzerland 0 - 2; Greece v Rumania 2 - 2; Portugal v Greece 2 - 2; Switzerland v Rumania 0 - 1; Rumania v Portugal 1 - 0; Greece v Switzerland 4 - 1; Switzerland v Portugal 1 - 1; Rumania v Greece 1 - 1

	P	W	D	L	F	A	Pts
Rumania	6	3	2	1	7	6	8
Greece	6	2	3	1	13	9	7
Switzerland	6	2	1	3	5	8	5
Portugal	6	1	2	3	8	10	4

Rumania qualified

Group 2 (Hungary, Czechoslovakia, Denmark, Rep of Ireland)

Denmark v Czechoslovakia 0 - 3; Czechoslovakia v Denmark 1 - 0; Rep of Ireland v Czechoslovakia 1 - 2; Hungary v Czechoslovakia 2 - 0; Rep of Ireland v Denmark 1 - 1 (after abandoned game after 51 minutes at 1 - 1 due to fog); Rep of Ireland v Hungary 1 - 2; Denmark v Hungary 3 - 2; Czechoslovakia v Hungary 3 - 3; Czechoslovakia v Rep of Ireland 3 - 0; Denmark v Rep of Ireland 2 - 0; Hungary v Denmark 3 - 0; Hungary v Rep of Ireland 4 - 0

	P	W	D	L	F	A	Pts
Hungary	6	4	1	1	16	7	9
Czechoslovakia	6	4	1	1	12	6	9
Denmark	6	2	1	3	6	10	5
Rep of Ireland	6	0	1	5	3	14	1

Play-off (in Marseilles): Czechoslovakia v Hungary 4 - 1
Czechoslovakia qualified

Group 3 (Italy, East Germany, Wales)

Wales v Italy 0 - 1; East Germany v Italy 2 - 2; East Germany v Wales 2 - 1; Wales v East Germany 1 - 3; Italy v Wales 4 - 1; Italy v East Germany 3 - 0

	P	W	D	L	F	A	Pts
Italy	4	3	1	0	10	3	7
East Germany	4	2	1	1	7	5	5
Wales	4	0	0	4	3	10	0

Italy qualified

Group 4 (USSR, Northern Ireland, Turkey)

Northern Ireland v Turkey 4 - 1; Turkey v Northern Ireland 0 - 3; Northern Ireland v USSR 0 - 0; USSR v Turkey 3 - 0; USSR v Northern Ireland 2 - 0; Turkey v USSR 1 - 3

	P	W	D	L	F	A	Pts
USSR	4	3	1	0	8	1	7
Northern Ireland	4	2	1	1	7	3	5
Turkey	4	0	0	4	2	13	0

USSR qualified

Group 5 (Sweden, France, Norway)

Sweden v Norway 5 - 0; France v Norway 0 - 1; Norway v Sweden 2 - 5; Norway v France 1 - 3; Sweden v France 2 - 0; France v Sweden 3 - 0

	P	W	D	L	F	A	Pts
Sweden	4	3	0	1	12	5	6
France	4	2	0	2	6	4	4
Norway	4	1	0	3	4	13	2

Sweden qualified

Group 6 (Belgium, Yugoslavia, Spain, Finland)

Finland v Belgium 1 - 2; Yugoslavia v Finland 9 - 1; Belgium v Finland 6 - 1; Belgium v Yugoslavia 3 - 0; Yugoslavia v Spain 0 - 0; Spain v Belgium 1 - 1; Belgium v Spain 2 - 1; Finland v Yugoslavia 1 - 5; Finland v Spain 2 - 0; Spain v Finland 6 - 0; Yugoslavia v Belgium 4 - 0

	P	W	D	L	F	A	Pts
Belgium	6	4	1	1	14	8	9
Yugoslavia	6	3	1	2	19	7	7
Spain	6	2	2	2	10	6	6
Finland	6	1	0	5	6	28	2

Belgium qualified

Group 7 (West Germany, Scotland, Austria, Cyprus)

Austria v Cyprus 7 - 1; Austria v West Germany 0 - 2; Scotland v Austria 2 - 1; Cyprus v West Germany 0 - 1; Cyprus v Scotland 0 - 5; Scotland v West Germany 1 - 1; West Germany v Austria 1 - 2; West Germany v Cyprus 12 - 0; West Germany v Scotland 3 - 2; Austria v Scotland 2 - 0

	P	W	D	L	F	A	Pts
West Germany	6	5	1	0	20	3	11
Scotland	6	3	1	2	18	7	7
Austria	6	3	0	3	12	7	6
Cyprus	6	0	0	6	2	35	0

West Germany qualified

Group 8 (Bulgaria, Poland, Holland, Luxembourg)

Luxembourg v Holland 0 - 2; Bulgaria v Holland 2 - 0; Holland v Luxembourg 4 - 0; Poland v Luxembourg 8 - 1; Bulgaria v Luxembourg 2 - 1; Holland v Poland 1 - 0; Bulgaria v Poland 4 - 1; Poland v Holland 2 - 1; Luxembourg v Poland 1 - 5; Holland v Bulgaria 1 - 1; Poland v Bulgaria 3 - 0; Luxembourg v Bulgaria 1 - 3

	P	W	D	L	F	A	Pts
Bulgaria	6	4	1	1	12	7	9
Poland	6	4	0	2	19	8	8
Holland	6	3	1	2	9	5	7
Luxembourg	6	0	0	6	4	24	0

Bulgaria qualified

Group 9 (England)

England qualified as holders

South America
Group 10 (Peru, Bolivia, Argentina)

Bolivia v Argentina 3 - 1; Peru v Argentina 1 - 0; Bolivia v Peru 2 - 1; Peru v Bolivia 3 - 0; Argentina v Bolivia 1 - 0; Argentina v Peru 2 - 2

	P	W	D	L	F	A	Pts
Peru	4	2	1	1	7	4	5
Bolivia	4	2	0	2	5	6	4
Argentina	4	1	1	2	4	6	3

Peru qualified

Group 11(Brazil, Paraguay, Colombia, Venezuela)

Colombia v Venezuela 3 - 0; Venezuela v Colombia 1 - 1; Colombia v Brazil 0 - 2; Venezuela v Paraguay 0 - 2; Colombia v Paraguay 0 - 1; Venezuela v Brazil 0 - 5; Paraguay v Brazil 0 - 3; Brazil v Colombia 6 - 2; Paraguay v Venezuela 1 - 0; Brazil v Venezuela 6 - 0; Paraguay v Colombia 2 - 1; Brazil v Paraguay 1 - 0

	P	W	D	L	F	A	Pts
Brazil	6	6	0	0	23	2	12
Paraguay	6	4	0	2	6	5	8
Colombia	6	1	1	4	7	12	3
Venezuela	6	0	1	5	1	18	1

Brazil qualified

Group 12 (Uruguay, Chile, Ecuador)

Ecuador v Uruguay 0 - 2; Chile v Uruguay 0 - 0; Uruguay v Ecuador 1 - 0; Chile v Ecuador 4 - 1; Ecuador v Chile 1 - 1; Uruguay v Chile 2 - 0

	P	W	D	L	F	A	Pts
Uruguay	4	3	1	0	5	0	7
Chile	4	1	2	1	5	4	4
Ecuador	4	0	1	3	2	8	1

Uruguay qualified

Concacaf
Group 13 (Honduras, Costa Rica, Jamaica, Haiti, Guatemala, Trinidad, El Salvador, Surinam, Netherlands Antilles, USA, Canada, Bermuda)

Sub-Group A

Costa Rica v Jamaica 3 - 0; Jamaica v Costa Rica 1 - 3; Honduras v Jamaica 3 - 1; Jamaica v Honduras 0 - 2; Honduras v Costa Rica 1 - 0; Costa Rica v Honduras 1 - 1

	P	W	D	L	F	A	Pts
Honduras	4	3	1	0	7	2	7
Costa Rica	4	2	1	1	7	3	5
Jamaica	4	0	0	4	2	11	0

Sub-Group B

Guatemala v Trinidad 4 - 0; Trinidad v Guatemala 0 - 0; Trinidad v Haiti 0 - 4; Haiti v Trinidad 2 - 4; Haiti v Guatemala 2 - 0; Guatemala v Haiti 1 - 1

	P	W	D	L	F	A	Pts
Haiti	4	2	1	1	9	5	5
Guatemala	4	1	2	1	5	3	4
Trinidad	4	1	1	2	4	10	3

Sub-Group C

Surinam v Netherlands Antilles 6 - 0; El Salvador v Surinam 6 - 0; Netherlands Antilles v Surinam 2 - 0; El Salvador v Netherlands Antilles 1 - 0; Netherlands Antilles v El Salvador 1 - 2; Surinam v El Salvador 4 - 1

	P	W	D	L	F	A	Pts
El Salvador	4	3	0	1	10	5	6
Surinam	4	2	0	2	10	9	4
N'lands/ Antilles	4	1	0	3	3	9	2

Sub-Group D

Canada v Bermuda 4 - 0; Canada v USA 4 - 2; Bermuda v Canada 0 - 0; USA v Canada 1 - 0; USA v Bermuda 6 - 2; Bermuda v USA 0 - 2

	P	W	D	L	F	A	Pts
USA	4	3	0	1	11	6	6
Canada	4	2	1	1	8	3	5
Bermuda	4	0	1	3	2	12	1

2nd Round

Haiti v USA 2 - 0, 1 - 0; Honduras v El Salvador 1 - 0, 0 - 3
Play-off (in Mexico City): El Salvador v Honduras 3 - 2

3rd Round

Haiti v El Salvador 1 - 2, 3 - 0
Play-off (in Kingston): El Salvador v Haiti 1 - 0
El Salvador qualified

Group 14 (Mexico)

Mexico qualified as hosts

Oceania
Group 15 (Australia, South Korea, Japan, Rhodesia, Israel, New Zealand)
Sub-Group A (in Seoul)

Australia v Japan 3 - 1; South Korea v Japan 2 - 2; Australia v South Korea 2 - 1; Japan v Australia 1 - 1; South Korea v Japan 2 - 0; South Korea v Australia 1 - 1

	P	W	D	L	F	A	Pts
Australia	4	2	2	0	7	4	6
South Korea	4	1	2	1	6	5	4
Japan	4	0	2	2	4	8	2

Sub-Group B (in Tel Aviv)

North Korea eliminated for refusing to play Israel
Israel v New Zealand 4 - 0, 2 - 0

2nd Round (in Lourenco Marques)

Australia v Rhodesia 1 - 1, 0 - 0
Play-off: Australia v Rhodesia 3 - 1

Final Round

Israel v Australia 1 - 0, 1 - 1
Israel qualified

Africa
Group 16 (Algeria, Tunisia, Nigeria, Cameroon, Ghana (bye), Morocco, Senegal, Libya, Ethiopia, Zambia, Sudan)

Morocco v Senegal 1 - 0, 1 - 2; Play-off (in Las Palmas): Morocco v Senegal 2 - 0; Algeria v Tunisia 1 - 2, 0 - 0; Libya v Ethiopia 2 - 0, 1 - 5; Zambia v Sudan 4 - 2, 2 - 4 (Sudan winners by scoring more goals in second match); Nigeria v Cameroon 1 - 1, 3 - 2

2nd Round

Tunisia v Morocco 0 - 0, 0 - 0; Play-off: Morocco v Tunisia 2 - 2 (Morocco won on toss of coin); Ethiopia v Sudan 1 - 1, 1 - 3; Nigeria v Ghana 2 - 1, 1 - 1

Final Round

Nigeria v Sudan 2 - 2; Morocco v Nigeria 2 - 1; Sudan v Nigeria 3 - 3; Sudan v Morocco 0 - 0; Morocco v Sudan 3 - 0; Nigeria v Morocco 2 - 0

	P	W	D	L	F	A	Pts
Morocco	4	2	1	1	5	3	5
Nigeria	4	1	2	1	8	7	4
Sudan	4	0	3	1	5	8	3

Morocco qualified

Final Tournament MEXICO
GROUP 1
31.5.70 Mexico (0) 0, USSR (0) 0 MEXICO CITY
Mexico: Calderon, Pena, Perez, Hernandez, Lopez, Vantolra, Guzman, Pulido, Velarde (Manguia), Valdivia, Fragoso
USSR: Kavazashvili, Kaplichny Lovchev, Logofet, Shesternev, Asatiani, Muntian, Serebrannikov (Puzach), Nodia (Khmelnitski) Byshovets, Evryushikhin
Referee: Tchenscher (West Germany)

3.6.70 Belgium (1) 3, El Salvador (0) 0 MEXICO CITY
Belgium: Piot, Heylens, Thissen, Dewalque, Dockx, Semmeling (Polleunis), Van Moer (2), Devrindt, Van Himst, Puis, Lambert (1 pen)
El Salvador: Magana, Rivas, Mariona, Osorio, Quintanilla, Rodriguez Lindo (Sermeno), Vasquez, Martinez, Cabezas, Aparicio, Manzano (Mendes C)
Referee: Radulescu (Rumania)

6.6.70 USSR (1) 4, Belgium (0) 1 MEXICO CITY
USSR: Kavazashvili, Dzodzuashvili (Kiselev), Afonin, Shesternev, Khurtsilava, Kaplichny (Lovchev), Asatiani (1), Muntian, Byshovets (2), Evryushikhin, Khmelnitski (1)
Belgium: Piot, Heylens, Thissen, Dewalque, Jeck, Dockx, Semmeling, Van Moer, Van Himst, Puis, Lambert (1)
Referee: Scheurer (Switzerland)

7.6.70 Mexico (1) 4, El Salvador (0) 0 MEXICO CITY
Mexico: Calderon, Vantolra, Pena, Guzman, Perez, Gonzalez, Munguia, Valdivia (2), Borja (Lopez then Basaguren (1)), Fragoso (1), Padilla
El Salvador: Magana, Rivas, Mariona, Osorio, Mendez C (Monge), Quintanilla, Rodriguez Lindo, Vasquez, Martinez, Cabezas, Aparicio (Mendez S)
Referee: Kandil (Egypt)

10.6.70 USSR (0) 2, El Salvador (0) 0 MEXICO CITY
USSR: Kavazashvili, Dzodzuashvili, Khurtsilava, Shesternev, Afonin, Kiselev (Asatiani), Serebrannikov, Muntian, Pusach (Evryushikhin), Byshovets (2), Khmelnitski
El Salvador: Magana, Rivas, Mariona, Castro, Osorio, Vasquez, Portillo, Cabezas (Aparicio), Rodriguez Lindo (Sermeno), Mendez S, Monge
Referee: Hormazabal (Chile)

11.6.70 Mexico (1) 1, Belgium (0) 0 MEXICO CITY
Mexico: Calderon, Vantolra, Guzman, Pena (1 pen), Perez, Pulido, Gonzalez, Munguia, Padilla, Valdivia (Basaguren), Fragosa
Belgium: Piot, Heylens, Thissen, Dewalque, Jeck, Dockx, Semmeling, Van Moer, Van Himst, Puis, Polleunis (Devrindt)
Referee: Coerezza (Argentina)

	P	W	D	L	F	A	Pts
USSR	3	2	1	0	6	1	5
Mexico	3	2	1	0	5	0	5
Belgium	3	1	0	2	4	5	2
El Salvador	3	0	0	3	0	9	0

GROUP 2
2.6.70 Uruguay (1) 2, Israel (0) 0 PUEBLA
Uruguay: Mazurkiewicz, Ubinas, Ancheta, Matosas, Mujica (1), Montero Castillo, Rocha (Cortes), Maneiro (1), Cubilla, Esparrago, Losado
Israel: Vissoker, Schwager, Rosen, Rosenthal, Primo, Spiegel, Shum, Spiegler, Talbi (Bar), Faygenbaum, Rom (Vollach)
Referee: Davidson (Scotland)

3.6.70 Italy (1) 1, Sweden (0) 0 TOLUCA
Italy: Albertosi, Burgnich, Facchetti, Cera, Niccolai (Rosato), Bertini, Riva, Domenghini, Mazzola, Di Sisti, Boninsegna
Sweden: Hellstrom, Axelsson, Nordqvist, Grip, Svensson, Bo Larsson (Nicklasson), Eriksson (Ejderstedt), Kindvall, Grahn, Cronqvist, Olsson
Referee: Taylor (England)

6.6.70 Uruguay (0) 0, Italy (0) 0 PUEBLA
Uruguay: Mazurkiewicz, Ancheta, Matosas, Ubinas, Montero Castillo, Mujica, Cubilla, Esparrago, Maneiro, Bareno (Zubia), Cortes
Italy: Albertosi, Burgnich, Facchetti, Cera, Rosato, Bertini, Riva, Domenghini (Furino), Mazzola, De Sisti, Boninsenga
Referee: Glockner (East Germany)

7.6.70 Sweden (0) 1, Israel (0) 1 TOLUCA
Sweden: Larsson S G, Selander, Axelsson, Olsson, Grip, Svensson, Bo Larsson, Nordahl, Kindvall, Persson (Palsson), Turesson (1)
Israel: Vissoker, Bar, Schwager, Rosen, Rosenthal, Primo, Spiegel, Vollach (Schuruk), Spiegler (1), Faygenbaum, Shum
Referee: Tarekegn (Ethiopia)

10.6.70 Sweden (0) 1, Uruguay (0) 0 PUEBLA
Sweden: Larsson S G, Selander, Axelsson, Nordqvist, Grip, Svensson, Bo Larsson, Eriksson, Kindvall (Turesson), Persson, Nicklasson (Grahn (1))
Uruguay: Mazurkiewicz, Ancheta, Matosas, Ubinas, Montero Castillo, Mujica, Esparrago (Fontes), Maneiro, Zubia, Cortes, Losada
Referee: Landauer (USA)

11.6.70 Italy (0) 0, Israel (0) 0 TOLUCA
Italy: Albertosi, Burgnich, Facchetti, Cera, Rosato, Bertini, Riva, Domenghini (Rivera), Mazzola, De Sisti, Boninsegna
Israel: Vissoker, Bar, Bello, Primo, Rosen, Rosenthal, Shum, Spiegel, Faygenbaum (Rom), Spiegler, Schwager
Referee: De Moraes (Brazil)

	P	W	D	L	F	A	Pts
Italy	3	1	2	0	1	0	4
Uruguay	3	1	1	1	2	1	3
Sweden	3	1	1	1	2	2	3
Israel	3	0	2	1	1	3	2

GROUP 3
2.6.70 England (0) 1, Rumania (0) 0 GUADALAJARA
England: Banks, Newton (Wright), Cooper, Mullery, Labone, Moore, Lee (Osgood), Ball, Hurst (1), Charlton R, Peters
Rumania: Adamache, Satmareanu, Lupescu, Dinu, Mocanu, Dumitru, Tataru (Neagu) Nunweiler, Dembrovschi, Dumitrache, Lucescu
Referee: Loraux (Belgium)

3.6.70 Brazil (1) 4, Czechoslovakia (1) 1 GUADALAJARA
Brazil: Felix, Carlos Alberto, Brito, Piazza, Everaldo, Clodoaldo, Gerson (Paulo Cesar), Rivelino (1), Jairzinho (2), Tostao, Pele (1)
Czechoslovakia: Viktor, Dobias, Migas, Horvath, Hagara, Kuna, Hrdlicka (Kvasnak), Vesely F (Vesely B), Petras (1), Adamec, Jokl
Referee: Barreto (Uruguay)

6.6.70 Rumania (0) 2, Czechoslovakia (1) 1 GUADALAJARA
Rumania: Adamache, Satmareanu, Dinu, Lupescu, Mocanu, Dumitru (Ghergeli), Nunweiler, Dembrovschi, Neagu (1), Dumitrache (1 pen), Lucescu (Tataru)
Czechoslovakia: Vencel, Dobias, Migas, Horvath, Zlocha, Kuna, Kvasnak, Vesely B, Jurkanin (Adamec), Petras (1), Jokl (Vesely F)
Referee: De Leo (Mexico)

7.6.70 Brazil (1) 1, England (0) 0 GUADALAJARA
Brazil: Felix, Carlos Alberto, Brito, Piazza, Everaldo, Clodoaldo, Paulo Cesar, Rivelino, Jairzinho (1), Tostao (Roberto), Pele
England: Banks, Wright, Cooper, Mullery, Labone, Moore, Lee (Bell), Ball, Charlton R (Astle), Hurst, Peters
Referee: Klein (Israel)

10.6.70 Brazil (2) 3, Rumania (1) 2 GUADALAJARA
Brazil: Felix, Carlos Alberto, Brito, Fontana, Everaldo (Marco Antonio), Clodoaldo (Edu), Piazza, Paulo Cesar, Jairzinho (1), Tostao, Pele (2)
Rumania: Adamache (Raducanu), Satmareanu, Lupescu, Dinu, Mocanu, Dumitru, Nunweiler, Dembrovschi (1), Lucescu, Neagu, Dumitrache (1) (Tataru)
Referee: Marshall (Austria)

11.6.70 England (0) 1, Czechoslovakia (0) 0 GUADALAJARA
England: Banks, Newton, Cooper, Mullery, Charlton J, Moore, Bell, Clarke (1 pen), Astle (Osgood), Charlton R (Ball), Peters
Czechoslovakia: Viktor, Dobias, Hrivnak, Migas, Hagara, Pollak, Kuna, Vesely F, Petras, Adamec, Capkovic (Jokl)
Referee: Machin (France)

	P	W	D	L	F	A	Pts
Brazil	3	3	0	0	8	3	6
England	3	2	0	1	2	1	4
Rumania	3	1	0	2	4	5	2
Czechoslovakia	3	0	0	3	2	7	0

GROUP 4

2.6.70 Peru (0) 3, Bulgaria (1) 2 LEON
Peru: Rubinos, Campos (Gonzalez J), De la Torre, Chumpitaz (1), Fuentes, Mifflin, Challe, Baylon (Sotil), Leon, Cubillas (1), Gallardo (1)
Bulgaria: Simeonov, Chalamanov, Dimitrov, Davidov, Aladjov, Penev, Bonev (1) (Asparoukhov), Yakimov, Popov (Marachliev), Jekov, Dermendjiev (1)
Referee: Sbardella (Italy)

3.6.70 West Germany (0) 2, Morocco (1) 1 LEON
West Germany: Maier, Vogts, Schulz, Fichtel, Hottges (Lohr), Haller (Grabowski), Beckenbauer, Overath, Seeler (1), Muller (1), Held
Morocco: Allal, Abdallah, Boujemaa, Khannoussi, Slimani, Maaroufi, Bamous (Faras), El Filali, Said, Ghazouani (Khyati), Houmane (1)
Referee: Van Ravens (Netherlands)

6.6.70 Peru (0) 3, Morocco (0) 0 LEON
Peru: Rubinos, Gonzales P, De la Torre, Chumpitaz, Fuentes, Mifflin, Challe (1), Sotil, Leon, Cubillas (2), Gallardo (Ramirez)
Morocco: Allal, Abdallah, Boujemaa (Fadili), Khannoussi, Slimani, Maaroufi, Bamous, El Filali, Said (Alaoui), Ghazouani, Houmane
Referee: Bakhramov (USSR)

7.6.70 West Germany (2) 5, Bulgaria (1) 2 LEON
West Germany: Maier, Vogts, Fichtel, Schnellinger, Hottges, Seeler (1), Beckenbauer (Weber), Overath, Libuda (1), Muller (3, 1 pen), Lohr (Grabowski)
Bulgaria: Simeonov, Gaidarski, Jetchev, Nikodimov (1), Gaganelov (Chalamanov), Penev, Bonev, Kolev (1), Marachliev, Asparoukhov, Dermendiev (Mitkov)
Referee: De Mendibil (Spain)

10.6.70 West Germany (3) 3, Peru (1) 1 LEON
West Germany: Maier, Vogts, Fichtel, Schnellinger, Hottges (Patzke), Seeler, Beckenbauer, Overath, Libuda (Grabowski), Muller (3), Lohr
Peru: Rubinos, Gonzales P, De la Torre, Chumpitaz, Fuentes, Mifflin, Challe (Cruzado), Sotil, Leon (Ramirez), Cubillas (1), Gallardo
Referee: Aguilar (Mexico)

11.6.70 Bulgaria (1) 1, Morocco (0) 1 LEON
Bulgaria: Yordanov, Chalamanov, Penev (Dimitrov), Jetchev (1), Gaidarski, Kolev, Nikodimov, Yakimov (Bonev), Popov, Asparoukhov, Mitkov
Morocco: Hazzaz, Fadili, Slimani, Khannoussi, Boujemaa, Maaroufi, Bamous (Choukri), El Filali, Said, Alaoui (Faras), Ghazouani (1)
Referee: Saldanha (Portugal)

	P	W	D	L	F	A	Pts
West Germany	3	3	0	0	10	4	6
Peru	3	2	0	1	7	5	4
Bulgaria	3	0	1	2	5	9	1
Morocco	3	0	1	2	2	6	1

QUARTER FINALS

14.6.70 Uruguay (0) 1, USSR (0) 0 (aet, 0 - 0 at 90 mins) MEXICO CITY
Uruguay: Mazurkiewicz, Ancheta, Matosas, Ubinas, Montero Castillo, Mujica, Cubilla, Maneiro, Morales (Gomez), Fontes (Esparrago (1)), Cortes
USSR: Kavazashvili, Dzodzuashvili, Afonin, Shesternev, Khurtsilava (Logofet), Kaplichny, Asatiani (Kiselev), Muntian, Byshovets, Evryushikhin, Khmelnitzki
Referee: Van Ravens (Netherlands)

14.6.70 Italy (1) 4, Mexico (1) 1 TOLUCA
Italy: Albertosi, Burgnich, Facchetti, Cera, Rosato, Bertini, Riva (2), Domenghini (1) (Gori), Mazzola (Rivera (1)), De Sisti, Boninsegna
Mexico: Calderon, Vantolra, Guzman, Pena, Perez, Pulido, Gonzalez (1) (Borja), Munguia (Diaz), Padilla, Valdivia, Fragoso
Referee: Scheurer (Switzerland)

14.6.70 Brazil (2) 4, Peru (1) 2 GUADALAJARA
Brazil: Felix, Carlos Alberto, Brito, Piazza, Marco Antonio, Clodoaldo, Gerson (Paulo Cesar), Rivelino (1), Jairzinho (1) (Roberto), Tostao (2), Pele
Peru: Rubinos, Campos, Fernandez, Chumpitaz, Fuentes, Challe, Mifflin, Baylon (Sotil), Leon (Reyes), Cubillas (1), Gallardo (1)
Referee: Loraux (Belgium)

14.6.70 West Germany (0) 3, England (2) 2 (aet, 2 - 2 at 90 mins) LEON
West Germany: Maier, Vogts, Fichtel, Schnellinger, Hottges (Schulz), Seeler (1), Beckenbauer (1), Overath, Libuda (Grabowski), Muller (1), Lohr
England: Bonetti, Newton, Cooper, Mullery (1), Labone, Moore, Lee, Ball, Hurst, Charlton R (Bell), Peters (1) (Hunter)
Referee: Coerezza (Argentina)

SEMI FINALS

17.6.70 Italy (1) 4, West Germany (0) 3 (aet, 1 - 1 at 90 mins) MEXICO CITY
Italy: Albertosi, Burgnich (1), Facchetti, Cera, Rosato (Poletti), Bertini, Riva (1), Domenghini, Mazzora (Rivera (1)), De Sisti, Boninsegna (1)
West Germany: Maier, Vogts, Schnellinger (1), Schulz, Patzke (Held), Beckenbauer, Overath, Grabowski, Seeler, Muller (2), Lohr (Libuda)
Referee: Yamasaki (Peru)

17.6.70 Brazil (1) 3, Uruguay (1) 1 GUADALAJARA
Brazil: Felix, Carlos Alberto, Brito, Piazza, Everaldo, Clodoaldo (1), Gerson, Rivelino (1), Jairzinho (1), Tostao, Pele
Uruguay: Mazurkiewicz, Ubinas, Ancheta, Matosas, Mujica, Montero Castillo, Maneiro (Esparrago), Cortes, Cubilla (1), Fontes, Morales
Referee: De Mendibil (Spain)

Match for third place

20.6.70 West Germany (1) 1, Uruguay (0) 0 MEXICO CITY
West Germany: Wolter, Patzke, Weber, Schnellinger (Lorenz), Fichtel, Vogts, Overath (1), Libuda (Lohr), Seeler, Muller, Held
Uruguay: Mazurkiewicz, Ubinas, Ancheta, Matosas, Mujica, Montero Castillo, Maneiro (Sandoval), Cortes, Cubilla, Fontes (Esparrago), Morales
Referee: Sbardella (Italy)

FINAL

21.6.70 Brazil (1) 4, Italy (1) 1 MEXICO CITY
Brazil: Felix, Carlos Alberto (1), Brito, Piazza, Everaldo, Clodoaldo, Gerson (1), Rivelino, Jairzinho (1), Tostao, Pele (1)
Italy: Albertosi, Burgnich, Facchetti, Cera, Rosato, Bertini (Juliano), Riva, Domenghini, Mazzola, De Sisti, Boninsegna (1) (Rivera)
Referee: Glockner (East Germany)

WEST GERMANY

1974

FIFA's technical study of the tournament in West Germany revealed that the two teams which consistently produced the highest ratio of penetrating attacks were the finalists, West Germany and Holland. But attacks are one factor, scoring goals another. Of the three goals registered in the final, two came from the penalty spot and the Dutch concept of 'total football' was let down by poor finishing.

Even in the single goal defeat by East Germany, the West Germans had 23 attempts at scoring, 15 of them from inside the penalty area. Holland's highlight, in what proved to be a goalless draw, was when they mounted 61 penetrating attacks against Sweden and had 36 shots, again 15 of them from inside the area.

Goalscoring actually reached a new low. This was never better illustrated than when a lack of goals cost unbeaten Scotland a place in the second round and saw Italy eliminated on goal difference. In Group 1, six games produced nine goals, five of them conceded by Australia. Group 2 did have 16, but all but two were at the expense of Zaire! Holland did not concede a goal to an opponent until the final apart from an own goal, while Haiti also let in 14 in three games.

Instead of a quarter-final knock-out round, the eight qualifiers from the four groups were split into two further sections of four, causing some jockeying for positions. For example the last game in Group 1, which pitted the two halves of Germany against each other, saw the West Germans unconcerned over the outcome and preferring to avoid Holland in the second stage. Jurgen Sparwasser's 77th-minute goal settled it for the East.

Sweden and West Germany provided a thriller in the rain when they met in the second round. Swedish keeper Ronnie Hellstrom keeps out a shot from Gerd Muller (dark shirt).

Billy Bremner (4, dark shirt) holds his head after missing from close range against Brazil, to the despair of team-mate David Hay and the relief of Brazil's Rivelino (10).

(Far right) Holland faced their toughest opposition on the way to the final in Group 3, when Sweden held them 0-0 in Dortmund. Dutch goalkeeper Jongbloed (8) dives to thwart an attempt on goal.

Certainly the system did not encourage goalscoring but Yugoslavia succeeded in scoring nine against Zaire, who had a player sent off, one of five dismissed in the finals, though there were 84 cautioned.

For practically the entire tournament it rained. In this there was a good omen for West Germany, who had prevailed in similar circumstances 20 years earlier. But they had their problems off the field, with scarcely secret differences between manager Helmut Schoen and captain Franz Beckenbauer over team selection. Schoen persisted with wingers and discovered a fine powerhouse in Rainer Bonhof during the competition.

Brazil were rugged without a vestige of the flair of former days. Even so they finished fourth. Jairzinho led the attack virtually on his own. Zagalo could have had Pele had he asked him to play, but seemed not to relish the prospect of the 'Black Pearl' gaining the accolade of a Brazilian victory.

Poland, who had deprived England of a place in the finals, had their strongest squad of all time. Their last match for a place in the final was against West Germany in Frankfurt. The kick-off was delayed half an hour while groundsmen attempted to remove gallons of rainwater from the pitch. Polish goalkeeper Jan Tomaszewski saved a penalty from Uli Hoeness, his second such stop in the finals, but it was Gerd Muller who scooped up the only goal in the second half. Grzegorz Lato, top scorer in the tournament with seven goals, had missed two first-half chances in a game which rose above the conditions.

Chile, who had qualified when the USSR refused to play a return game in Santiago for political reasons, were held to a goalless draw in a Group 1 game by Australia. The Aussies had a player shown two yellow cards but he was allowed to continue, until a linesman drew the referee's attention to the situation and he was sent off.

(Left) Joe Jordan (9, white shirt) celebrates a late equaliser for Scotland against Yugoslavia in Frankfurt, but it was not enough to prevent the Scots' elimination from the tournament.

Torrential rain in Frankfurt (below) almost caused West Germany's game with Poland to be postponed. Uli Hoeness (white shirt) loses out to the grounded Jerzy Gorgon of Poland.

When Yugoslavia were awarded a free-kick against Zaire, one of the Zaire defenders rushed out of the defensive wall and booted the ball into touch! He received a swift red card for his indiscretion. Scotland held Brazil without undue difficulty, in another of the five scoreless matches in the opening phase, and then managed a 1-1 draw with Yugoslavia. This left the Brazilians with the task of scoring at least three times against Zaire. They only just managed it, thanks to the African goalkeeper being beaten on his near post by an angled drive from substitute Valdomiro.

But in the second stage, the Brazilians were well beaten by Holland, whose goals from Johan Neeskens and Johan Cruyff, who had covered more ground than almost any player in the tournament, emphasised their mobility and strength. It was enough to put the Dutch into the final against the hosts West Germany.

There had never been a penalty awarded in a previous final. Inside half an hour there were two. Holland kicked off and were awarded the first within a minute of play, without a German touching the ball. Cruyff was brought down inside the area and Neeskens hit the spot kick straight at goal while goalkeeper Sepp Maier was diving to his right.

Jack Taylor the English referee had shown immense courage in this award, but there were critics of his next decision when Wim Jansen was adjudged to have clipped the legs of Bernd Holzenbein in the 26th minute. But up stepped Paul Breitner to level the scores. Two minutes from the break, Bonhof raided on the right and pulled the ball back. It fell slightly behind Muller, who checked, turned and scored.

It was a crushing blow for the Dutch who had dominated much of the play. In fact Cruyff was so incensed that he argued with Taylor as the players went off for half-time. Holland huffed and puffed in the second half but the Germans held firm to win the cup, the new FIFA World Cup.

Qualifying Tournament
99 entries
Europe (33): Albania, Austria, Belgium, Bulgaria, Cyprus, Czechoslovakia, Denmark, England, Finland, France, East Germany, West Germany, Greece, Holland, Hungary, Iceland, Republic of Ireland, Northern Ireland, Italy, Luxembourg, Malta, Norway, Poland, Portugal, Rumania, Scotland, Spain, Sweden, Switzerland, Turkey, USSR, Wales, Yugoslavia
Africa (23): Algeria, Cameroon, Congo, Dahomey, Egypt, Ethiopia, Gabon, Ghana, Guinea, Ivory Coast, Kenya, Lesotho, Madagascar, Mauritius, Morocco, Nigeria, Senegal, Sierra Leone, Sudan, Tanzania, Tunisia, Zaire, Zambia
Concacaf (14): Antigua, Canada, Costa Rica, Guatemala, Haiti, Honduras, Jamaica, Mexico, Netherlands Antilles, Puerto Rico, El Salvador, Surinam, Trinidad/Tobago, USA
South America (10): Argentina, Bolivia, Brazil, Chile, Colombia, Ecuador, Paraguay, Peru, Uruguay, Venezuela
Asia (17): Hong Kong, India, Indonesia, Iran, Iraq, Israel, Japan, North Korea, South Korea, Kuwait, Malaysia, Philippines, Sri Lanka, Syria, Thailand, United Arab Emirates, South Vietnam
Oceania (2): Australia, New Zealand
Seven countries withdrew before the qualifying tournament began: Gabon, India, Jamaica, Madagascar, Philippines, Sri Lanka, Venezuela.

The final qualifying tie between the winners of Europe Group 9 and South America Group 3 was not completed. The USSR and Chile had drawn 0 - 0 in Moscow but the Soviets refused to play the return in the National Stadium in Santiago because it had been used to house prisoners when the military overthrew the elected government. In the African Zone, Nigeria's home game with Ghana was abandoned following crowd disturbances with Ghana leading 3 - 2. Ghana were declared winners 2 - 0. Zaire had already qualified for the finals when Morocco refused to play their home game as a protest against the refereeing of the match in Zaire. In Europe's Group 3, Iceland played 'home' games in Belgium and Holland.

Final places in West Germany were to be distributed as follows: Europe (8 + West Germany)*, South America (3 + Brazil)*, Concacaf (1), Africa (1), Asia/Oceania (1).
*Play-off between USSR and Chile gave South America a further final place.

Europe
Group 1 (Austria, Sweden, Hungary, Malta)
Malta v Hungary 0 - 2; Austria v Malta 4 - 0; Hungary v Malta 3 - 0; Sweden v Hungary 0 - 0; Austria v Sweden 2 - 0; Sweden v Malta 7 - 0; Austria v Hungary 2 - 2; Malta v Austria 0 - 2; Hungary v Austria 2 - 2; Sweden v Austria 3 - 2; Hungary v Sweden 3 - 3; Malta v Sweden 1 - 2

	P	W	D	L	F	A	Pts
Sweden	6	3	2	1	15	8	8
Austria	6	3	2	1	14	7	8
Hungary	6	2	4	0	12	7	8
Malta	6	0	0	6	1	20	0

Play-off: Austria v Sweden (in Gelsenkirchen) 1 - 2
Sweden qualified

Group 2 (Italy, Turkey, Switzerland, Luxembourg)
Luxembourg v Italy 0 - 4; Switzerland v Italy 0 - 0; Luxembourg v Turkey 2 - 0; Turkey v Luxembourg 3 - 0; Italy v Turkey 0 - 0; Turkey v Italy 0 - 1; Italy v Luxembourg 5 - 0; Luxembourg v Switzerland 0 - 1; Switzerland v Turkey 0 - 0; Switzerland v Luxembourg 1 - 0; Italy v Switzerland 2 - 0; Turkey v Switzerland 2 - 0

	P	W	D	L	F	A	Pts
Italy	6	4	2	0	12	0	10
Turkey	6	2	2	2	5	3	6
Switzerland	6	2	2	2	2	4	6
Luxembourg	6	1	0	5	2	14	2

Italy qualified

Group 3 (Holland, Belgium, Norway, Iceland)
Belgium v Iceland 4 - 0; Iceland v Belgium 0 - 4; Norway v Iceland 4 - 1; Norway v Belgium 0 - 2; Holland v Norway 9 - 0; Belgium v Holland 0 - 0; Iceland v Norway 0 - 4; Iceland v Holland 0 - 5; Holland v Iceland 8 - 1; Norway v Holland 1 - 2; Belgium v Norway 2 - 0; Holland v Belgium 0 - 0

	P	W	D	L	F	A	Pts
Holland	6	4	2	0	24	2	10
Belgium	6	4	2	0	12	0	10
Norway	6	2	0	4	9	16	4
Iceland	6	0	0	6	2	29	0

Holland qualified

Group 4 (East Germany, Rumania, Finland, Albania)
Finland v Albania 1 - 0; Finland v Rumania 1 - 1; East Germany v Finland 5 - 0; Rumania v Albania 2 - 0; East Germany v Albania 1 - 4; Rumania v East Germany 1 - 0; Finland v East Germany 1 - 5; East Germany v Rumania 2 - 0; Albania v Finland 1 - 0; Rumania v Finland 9 - 0; Albania v East Germany 1 - 4

	P	W	D	L	F	A	Pts
East Germany	6	5	0	1	18	3	10
Rumania	6	4	1	1	17	4	9
Finland	6	1	1	4	3	21	3
Albania	6	1	0	5	3	13	2

East Germany qualified

Group 5 (Poland, England, Wales)

Wales v England 0 - 1; England v Wales 1 - 1; Wales v Poland 2 - 0; Poland v England 2 - 0; Poland v Wales 3 - 0; England v Poland 1 - 1

	P	W	D	L	F	A	Pts
Poland	4	2	1	1	6	3	5
England	4	1	2	1	3	4	4
Wales	4	1	1	2	3	5	3

Poland qualified

Group 6 (Bulgaria, Portugal, Northern Ireland, Cyprus)

Portugal v Cyprus 4 - 0; Cyprus v Portugal 0 - 1; Bulgaria v Northern Ireland 3 - 0; Cyprus v Bulgaria 0 - 4; Cyprus v Northern Ireland 1 - 0; Northern Ireland v Portugal 1 - 1; Bulgaria v Portugal 2 - 1; Northern Ireland v Cyprus 3 - 0 (at Fulham); Northern Ireland v Bulgaria 0 - 0; Portugal v Bulgaria 2 - 2; Portugal v Northern Ireland 1 - 1; Bulgaria v Cyprus 2 - 0

	P	W	D	L	F	A	Pts
Bulgaria	6	4	2	0	13	3	10
Portugal	6	2	3	1	10	6	7
Northern Ireland	6	1	3	2	5	6	5
Cyprus	6	1	0	5	1	14	2

Bulgaria qualified

Group 7 (Spain, Yugoslavia, Greece)

Spain v Yugoslavia 2 - 2; Yugoslavia v Greece 1 - 0; Greece v Spain 2 - 3; Spain v Greece 3 - 1; Yugoslavia v Spain 0 - 0; Greece v Yugoslavia 2 - 4

	P	W	D	L	F	A	Pts
Spain	4	2	2	0	8	5	6
Yugoslavia	4	2	2	0	7	4	6
Greece	4	0	0	4	5	11	0

Play-off: Spain v Yugoslavia (in Frankfurt) 0 - 1

Yugoslavia qualified

Group 8 (Scotland, Czechoslovakia, Denmark)

Denmark v Scotland 1 - 4; Scotland v Denmark 2 - 0; Denmark v Czechoslovakia 1 - 1; Czechoslovakia v Denmark 6 - 0; Scotland v Czechoslovakia 2 - 1; Czechoslovakia v Scotland 1 - 0

	P	W	D	L	F	A	Pts
Scotland	4	3	0	1	8	3	6
Czechoslovakia	4	2	1	1	9	3	5
Denmark	4	0	1	3	2	13	1

Scotland qualified

Group 9 (USSR, Rep of Ireland, France)

France v USSR 1 - 0; Rep of Ireland v USSR 1 - 2; Rep of Ireland v France 2 - 1; USSR v Rep of Ireland 1 - 0; France v Rep of Ireland 1 - 1; USSR v France 2 - 0

	P	W	D	L	F	A	Pts
USSR	4	3	0	1	5	2	6
Rep of Ireland	4	1	1	2	4	5	3
France	4	1	1	2	3	5	3

Play-off with South American Group 3 winners

USSR v Chile 0 - 0

USSR disqualified by FIFA for refusing to play return leg in Santiago.

Chile qualified

South America

Group 1 (Uruguay, Colombia, Ecuador)

Colombia v Ecuador 1 - 1; Colombia v Uruguay 0 - 0; Ecuador v Colombia 1 - 1; Ecuador v Uruguay 1 - 2; Uruguay v Colombia 0 - 1; Uruguay v Ecuador 4 - 0

	P	W	D	L	F	A	Pts
Uruguay	4	2	1	1	6	2	5
Colombia	4	1	3	0	3	2	5
Ecuador	4	0	2	2	3	8	2

Uruguay qualified

Group 2 (Argentina, Paraguay, Bolivia)

Bolivia v Paraguay 1 - 2; Argentina v Bolivia 4 - 0; Paraguay v Argentina 1 - 1; Bolivia v Argentina 0 - 1; Paraguay v Bolivia 4 - 0; Argentina v Paraguay 3 - 1

	P	W	D	L	F	A	Pts
Argentina	4	3	1	0	9	2	7
Paraguay	4	2	1	1	8	5	5
Bolivia	4	0	0	4	1	11	0

Argentina qualified

Group 3 (Chile, Peru, Venezuela)

Venezuela withdrew

Peru v Chile 2 - 0; Chile v Peru 2 - 0

Play-off (in Montevideo): Chile v Peru 2 - 1

Concacaf

Preliminary Round

Group 1

Canada v USA 3 - 2; Canada v Mexico 0 - 1; USA v Canada 2 - 2; Mexico v USA 3 - 1; Mexico v Canada 2 - 1; USA v Mexico 1 - 2

	P	W	D	L	F	A	Pts
Mexico	4	4	0	0	8	3	8
Canada	4	1	1	2	6	7	3
USA	4	0	1	3	6	10	1

Group 2

Guatemala v El Salvador 1 - 0, 1 - 0

Group 3

Honduras v Costa Rica 2 - 1, 3 - 3

Group 4

Netherlands Antilles v Jamaica (withdrew)

Group 5

Haiti v Puerto Rico 7 - 0, 5 - 0

Group 6

Surinam v Trinidad 1 - 2; Trinidad v Surinam 1 - 1; Surinam v Antigua 3 - 1; Antigua v Surinam 0 - 6; Trinidad v Antigua 11 - 1; Antigua v Trinidad 1 - 2

	P	W	D	L	F	A	Pts
T'dad/Tobago	4	3	1	0	16	4	7
Surinam	4	2	1	1	11	4	5
Antigua	4	0	0	4	3	22	0

Final Round (in Haiti)

Honduras v Trinidad 2 - 1; Mexico v Guatemala 0 - 0; Haiti v Netherlands Antilles 3 - 0; Mexico v Honduras 1 - 1; Haiti v Trinidad 2 - 1; Guatemala v Netherlands Antilles 2 - 2; Haiti v Honduras 1 - 0; Mexico v Netherlands Antilles 8 - 0; Trinidad v Guatemala 1 - 0; Netherlands Antilles v Honduras 2 - 2; Haiti v Guatemala 2 - 1; Trinidad v Mexico 4 - 0; Honduras v Guatemala 1 - 1; Trinidad v Netherlands Antilles 4 - 0; Mexico v Haiti 1 - 0

	P	W	D	L	F	A	Pts
Haiti	5	4	0	1	8	3	8
T'dad/Tobago	5	3	0	2	11	4	6
Mexico	5	2	2	1	10	5	6
Honduras	5	1	3	1	6	6	5
Guatemala	5	0	3	2	4	6	3
N'lands/Antilles	5	0	2	3	4	19	2

Haiti qualified

Africa

1st Round

Morocco v Senegal 0 - 0, 2 - 1; Algeria v Guinea 1 - 0, 1 - 5; Egypt v Tunisia 2 - 1, 0 - 2; Sierra Leone v Ivory Coast 0 - 1, 0 - 2; Kenya v Sudan 2 - 0, 0 - 1; Mauritius v Madagascar (withdrew); Ethiopia v Tanzania 0 - 0, 1 - 1; Play-off: Ethiopia v Tanzania 3 - 0; Lesotho v Zambia 0 - 0, 1 - 6; Nigeria v Congo 2 - 1, 1 - 1; Dahomey v Ghana 0 - 5, 1 - 5; Togo v Zaire 0 - 0, 0 - 4; Cameroon v Gabon (withdrew)

2nd Round

Kenya v Mauritius 3 - 1, 2 - 2; Guinea v Morocco 1 - 1, 0 - 2; Tunisia v Ivory Coast 1 - 1, 1 - 2; Ethiopia v Zambia 0 - 0, 2 - 4: Nigeria v Ghana 2 - 3 (abandoned), 0 - 0 (Nigeria disqualified from competition by FIFA Disciplinary Committee); Cameroon v Zaire 0 - 1, 1 - 0; Play-off: Zaire v Cameroon 2 - 0

3rd Round

Ivory Coast v Morocco 1 - 1, 1 - 4; Zambia v Kenya 2 - 0, 2 - 2; Ghana v Zaire 1 - 0, 1 - 4

Final Round
Zambia v Morocco 4 - 0; Zambia v Zaire 0 - 2; Zaire v Zambia 2 - 1;
Morocco v Zambia 2 - 0; Zaire v Morocco 3 - 0;
Morocco (withdrew) v Zaire (awarded game 2 - 0)

	P	W	D	L	F	A	Pts
Zaire	4	4	0	0	9	1	8
Zambia	4	1	0	3	5	6	2
Morocco	4	1	0	3	2	9	2

Zaire qualified

Asia/ Oceana
Preliminary Round (to determine Group composition)
South Vietnam v Thailand 1 - 0; Israel v Japan 2 - 1; Hong Kong v Malaysia
1 - 0; South Korea bye

Group A (in Seoul)
Sub-Group 1
Hong Kong v South Vietnam 1 - 0; Hong Kong v Japan 1 - 0;
Japan v South Vietnam 4 - 0

	P	W	D	L	F	A	Pts
Hong Kong	2	2	0	0	2	0	4
Japan	2	1	0	1	4	1	2
South Vietnam	2	0	0	2	0	5	0

Sub-Group 2
Israel v Malaysia 3 - 0; Israel v Thailand 6 - 0; Israel v South Korea 0 - 0;
South Korea v Thailand 4 - 0; South Korea v Malaysia 0 - 0;
Malaysia v Thailand 2 - 0

	P	W	D	L	F	A	Pts
Israel	3	2	1	0	9	0	5
South Korea	3	1	2	0	4	0	4
Malaysia	3	1	1	1	2	3	3
Thailand	3	0	0	3	0	12	0

Semi-finals
South Korea v Hong Kong 3 - 1; Israel v Japan 1 - 0

Final
South Korea v Israel 1 - 0

Group B
Sub-Group 1 (in Australia)
New Zealand v Australia 1 - 1; Indonesia v New Zealand 1 - 1; Australia
v Iraq 3 - 1; Iraq v New Zealand 2 - 0; Australia v Indonesia 2 - 1; Iraq
v Indonesia 1 - 1; Australia v New Zealand 3 - 3; Indonesia v New Zealand
1 - 0; Australia v Iraq 0 - 0; Iraq v Indonesia 3 - 2; Iraq v New Zealand
4 - 0; Australia v Indonesia 6 - 0

	P	W	D	L	F	A	Pts
Australia	6	3	3	0	15	6	9
Iraq	6	3	2	1	11	6	8
Indonesia	6	1	2	3	6	13	4
New Zealand	6	0	3	3	5	12	3

Sub-Group 2 (in Tehran)
North Korea v Iran 0 - 0; Syria v Kuwait 2 - 1; Iran v Kuwait 2 - 1; North
Korea v Syria 1 - 1; Iran v Syria 1 - 0; Kuwait v North Korea 0 - 0; North
Korea v Iran 1 - 2; Syria v Kuwait 2 - 0; Iran v Kuwait 2 - 0; North Korea v
Syria 3 - 0; Syria v Iran 1 - 0; Kuwait v North Korea 2 - 0

	P	W	D	L	F	A	Pts
Iran	6	4	1	1	7	3	9
Syria	6	3	1	2	6	7	7
North Korea	6	1	3	2	5	5	5
Kuwait	6	1	1	4	4	8	3

Final Round
Australia v Iran 3 - 0, 0 - 2; Australia v South Korea 0 - 0, 2 - 2
Play-off (in Hong Kong): Australia v South Korea 1 - 0
Australia qualified

Final Tournament WEST GERMANY
First round
GROUP 1
14.6.74 West Germany (1) 1, Chile (0) 0 WEST BERLIN
West Germany: Maier, Vogts, Schwarzenbeck, Beckenbauer, Breitner (1),
Hoeness, Cullmann, Overath (Holzbein), Grabowski, Muller, Heynckes
Chile: Vallejos, Garcia, Figueroa, Quintano, Arias, Valdes (Veliz), Rodriguez
(Lara), Reinoso, Caszely, Ahumada, Paez
Referee: Babacan (Turkey)

14.6.74 East Germany (0) 2, Australia (0) 0 HAMBURG
East Germany: Croy, Kische, Bransch, Weise, Watzlich, Sparwasser,
Irmscher, Pommerenke, Lowe (Hoffmann), Streich (1), Vogel
Australia: Reilly, Utjesenovic, Schafer, Wilson, Curran (o. g.), Richards,
Mackay, Rooney, Warren, Alston, Buljevic
Referee: N'Diaye (Senegal)

18.6.74 West Germany (2) 3, Australia (0) 0 HAMBURG
West Germany: Maier, Vogts, Schwarzenbeck, Beckenbauer, Breitner,
Hoeness, Cullmann (1) (Wimmer), Overath (1) , Grabowski, Muller (1) ,
Heynckes (Holzbein)
Australia: Reilly, Utjesenovic, Schafer, Wilson, Curran, Richards, Rooney,
Mackay, Campbell (Abonyi), Alston, Buljevic (Ollerton)
Referee: Kamel (Egypt)

18.6.74 Chile (0) 1, East Germany (0) 1 WEST BERLIN
Chile: Vallejos, Garcia, Figueroa, Quintano, Arias, Valdes (Yavar), Reinoso,
Paez, Socias (Farias), Ahumada (1), Veliz
East Germany: Croy, Kische, Bransch, Weise, Watzlich, Seguin (Kreische),
Irmscher, Sparwasser, Hoffmann (1), Streich, Vogel (Ducke)
Referee: Angonese (Italy)

22.6.74 Australia (0) 0, Chile (0) 0 WEST BERLIN
Australia: Reilly, Utjesenovic, Wilson, Schafer, Curran (Williams), Richards,
Rooney, Mackay, Abonyi, Alston (Ollerton), Buljevic
Chile: Vallejos, Garcia, Quintano, Figueroa, Arias, Paez, Caszely, Reinoso,
Valdes (Farias), Ahumada, Veliz (Yavar)
Referee: Namdar (Iran)

22.6.74 East Germany (0) 1, West Germany (0) 0 HAMBURG
East Germany: Croy, Kische, Weise, Bransch, Watzlich, Lauck, Irmscher
(Hamann), Kreische, Kurbjuweit, Sparwasser (1), Hoffmann
West Germany: Maier, Vogts, Schwarzenbeck (Hottges), Beckenbauer,
Breitner, Hoeness, Cullmann, Overath (Netzer), Grabowski, Muller, Flohe
Referee: Barreto (Uruguay)

	P	W	D	L	F	A	Pts
East Germany	3	2	1	0	4	1	5
West Germany	3	2	0	1	4	1	4
Chile	3	0	2	1	1	2	2
Australia	3	0	1	2	0	5	1

GROUP 2
13.6.74 Yugoslavia (0) 0, Brazil (0) 0 FRANKFURT
Yugoslavia: Maric, Buljan, Katalinski, Bogicevic, Hadziabdic, Muzinic, Oblak,
Acimovic, Petkovic, Surjak, Dzajic
Brazil: Leao, Nelinho, Mario Marinho, Pereira, Francesco Marinho, Piazza,
Rivelino, Paulo Cesar L, Valdomiro, Jairzinho, Leivinha
Referee: Scheurer (Switzerland)

14.6.74 Scotland (2) 2, Zaire (0) 0 DORTMUND
Scotland: Harvey, Jardine, McGrain, Bremner, Holton, Blackley, Dalglish
(Hutchison), Hay, Lorimer (1), Jordan (1), Law
Zaire: Kazadi, Mwepu, Mukombo, Buhanga, Lobilo, Kilasu, Myanga
(Kembo), Mana, Ndaye, Kidumu (Kibonge), Kakoko
Referee: Schulenberg (West Germany)

18.6.74 Yugoslavia (6) 9, Zaire (0) 0 GELSENKIRCHEN
Yugoslavia: Maric, Buljan, Katalinski (1), Bogicevic (1), Hadziabdic,
Acimovic, Oblak (1), Surjak (1), Petkovic (1), Bajevic (3), Dzajic (1)
Zaire: Kazadi (Tubilandu), Mwepu, Mukombo, Buhanga, Lobilo, Kilasu,
Ndaye, Mana, Kembo, Kidumu, Kakoko (Myanga)
Referee: Delgado (Colombia)

18.6.74 Scotland (0) 0, Brazil (0) 0 FRANKFURT
Scotland: Harvey, Jardine, McGrain, Buchan, Holton, Bremner, Dalglish,
Hay, Jordan, Lorimer, Morgan
Brazil: Leao, Nelinho, Pereira, Mario Marinho, Francesco Marinho, Piazza,
Rivelino, Paulo Cesar L, Jairzinho, Mirandinha, Leivinha (Paulo Cesar C)
Referee: Van Gemert (Netherlands)

22.6.74 Brazil (1) 3, Zaire (0) 0 GELSENKIRCHEN
Brazil: Leao, Nelinho, Pereira, Mario Marinho, Francesco Marinho, Piazza (Mirandhina), Rivelino (1), Paulo Cesar C, Jairzinho (1), Leivinha (Valdomiro (1)), Edu
Zaire: Kazadi, Mwepu, Mukombo, Buhanga, Lobilo, Kobonge, Tshinabu (Kembo), Mana, Ntumba, Kidumu (Kilasu), Myanga
Referee: Rainea (Rumania)

22.6.74 Yugoslavia (0) 1, Scotland (0) 1   FRANKFURT
Yugoslavia: Maric, Buljan, Katalinski, Bogicevic, Hadziabdic, Acimovic, Oblak, Surjak, Petkovic, Bajevic (Karasi (1)), Dzajic
Scotland: Harvey, Jardine, McGrain, Buchan, Holton, Bremner, Dalglish (Hutchison), Hay, Jordan (1), Lorimer, Morgan
Referee: Archundia (Mexico)

	P	W	D	L	F	A	Pts
Yugoslavia	3	1	2	0	10	1	4
Brazil	3	1	2	0	3	0	4
Scotland	3	1	2	0	3	1	4
Zaire	3	0	0	3	0	14	0

GROUP 3
15.6.74 Holland (1) 2, Uruguay (0) 0 HANOVER
Holland: Jongbloed, Suurbier, Rijsbergen, Haan, Krol, Jansen, Neeskens, Van Hanegem, Rep (2), Cruyff, Rensenbrink
Uruguay: Mazurkiewicz, Forlan, Masnik, Juaregui, Pavoni, Esparrago, Montero Castillo, Rocha, Cubilla (Milar), Morena, Mantegazza
Referee: Palotai (Hungary)

15.6.74 Sweden (0) 0, Bulgaria (0) 0 DUSSELDORF
Sweden: Hellstrom, Olsson, Karlsson, Bo Larsson, Andersson, Grahn, Kindvall (Magnusson), Tapper, Torstensson, Sandberg, Edstrom
Bulgaria: Goranov, Vassilev Z, Ivkov, Penev, Velitschkov, Kolev, Bonev, Nikodimov, Voinov (Michailov), Panov (Vassilev M), Denev
Referee: Nunez (Peru)

19.6.74 Holland (0) 0, Sweden (0) 0 DORTMUND
Holland: Jongbloed, Suurbier, Rijsbergen, Haan, Krol, Jansen, Neeskens, Van Hanegem (De Jong), Rep, Cruyff, Keizer
Sweden: Hellstrom, Olsson (Grip), Andersson, Karlsson, Nordqvist, Tapper (Persson), Grahn, Bo Larsson, Ejderstdt, Edstrom, Sandberg
Referee: Winsemann (Canada)

19.6.74 Bulgaria (1) 1, Uruguay (0) 1 HANOVER
Bulgaria: Goranov, Vassilev Z, Ivkov, Penev, Velitschkov, Kolev, Bonev (1), Nikodimov (Michailov), Voinov, Panov, Denev
Uruguay: Mazurkiewicz, Forlan, Garisto (Masnik), Jauregui, Pavoni (1), Esparrago, Mantegazza (Cardaccio), Rocha, Milar, Morena, Corbo
Referee: Taylor (England)

23.6.74 Holland (2) 4, Bulgaria (0) 1 DORTMUND
Holland: Jongbloed, Suurbier, Rijsbergen, Haan, Krol (o. g.), Jansen, Neeskens (2) (De Jong (1)), Van Hanegem (Israel), Rep (1), Cruyff, Rensenbrink
Bulgaria: Staikov, Vassilev Z, Ivkov, Penev, Velitschkov, Kolev, Bonev, Stoyanov (Michailov), Voinov, Panov (Borisov), Denev
Referee: Boskovic (Australia)

23.6.74 Sweden (0) 3, Uruguay (0) 0 DUSSELDORF
Sweden: Hellstrom, Andersson, Nordqvist, Karlsson, Grip, Grahn, Kindvall (Torstensson), Bo Larsson, Magnusson (Ahlstrom), Edstrom (2), Sandberg (1)
Uruguay: Mazurkiewicz, Forlan, Garisto (Masnik), Jauregui, Pavoni, Esparrago, Mantegazza, Rocha, Milar, Morena, Corbo (Cubilla)
Referee: Linemayr (Australia)

	P	W	D	L	F	A	Pts
Holland	3	2	1	0	6	1	5
Sweden	3	1	2	0	3	0	4
Bulgaria	3	0	2	1	2	5	2
Uruguay	3	0	1	2	1	6	1

GROUP 4
15.6.74 Italy (0) 3, Haiti (0) 1 MUNICH
Italy: Zoff, Spinosi, Morini, Burgnich, Facchetti, Mazzola, Capello, Rivera (1), Benetti, Chinaglia (Anastasi (1)), Riva
Haiti: Francillon, Bayonne, Nazaire, Jean-Joseph, Auguste, Francois, Vorbe, Desir, Antoine, Saint-Vil G (Barthelmy), Sanon (1)
Referee: Llobregat (Venezuela)

15.6.74 Poland (2) 3, Argentina (0) 2 STUTTGART
Poland: Tomaszewski, Szymanowski, Zmuda, Gorgon, Musial, Kasperczyk, Maszczyk, Deyna, Lato (2), Szarmach (1) (Domarski), Gadocha (Cmikiewicz)
Argentina: Carnevali, Wolff, Perfumo, Heredia (1), Sa, Bargas (Telch), Brindisi (Houseman), Babington (1), Balbuena, Ayala, Kempes
Referee: Thomas (Wales)

19.6.74 Poland (5) 7, Haiti (0) 0 MUNICH
Poland: Tomaszewski, Szymanowski, Zmuda, Gorgon (1), Musial (Gut), Kasperczyk, Maszczyk, Deyna (1), Lato (2), Szarmach (3), Gadocha
Haiti: Francillon, Bayonne, Nazaire, Vorbe, Auguste, Francois, Desir, Andre (Barthelmy), Sanon, Antoine, Saint-Vil R (Racine)
Referee: Suppiah (Singapore)

19.6.74 Argentina (1) 1, Italy (1) 1 STUTTGART
Argentina: Carnevali, Wolff (Glaria), Perfumo (o. g.), Heredia, Telch, Sa, Houseman (1), Babington, Ayala, Kempes, Yazalde (Chazarreta)
Italy: Zoff, Spinosi, Morini (Wilson), Burgnich, Facchetti, Mazzola, Capello, Rivera (Causio), Benetti, Riva, Anastasi
Referee: Kasakov (USSR)

23.6.74 Argentina (2) 4, Haiti (0) 1 MUNICH
Argentina: Carnevali, Wolff, Perfumo, Heredia, Sa, Telch, Houseman (1) (Brinidisi), Babington, Ayala (1), Kempes (Balbuena), Yazalde (2)
Haiti: Francillon, Ducoste, Bayonne, Nazaire (Leandre M), Louis, Vorbe, Desir, Saint-Vil G (Leandre F), Antoine, Racine, Sanon (1)
Referee: Sanchez-Ibanez (Spain)

23.6.74 Poland (2) 2, Italy (0) 1 STUTTGART
Poland: Tomaszewski, Szymanowski, Zmuda, Gorgon, Musial, Kasperczyk, Maszczyk, Deyna (1), Lato, Szarmach (1) (Cmikiewicz), Gadocha
Italy: Zoff, Spinosi, Morini, Burgnich (Wilson), Facchetti, Mazzola, Benetti, Capello (1), Causio, Chinaglia (Boninsegna), Anastasi
Referee: Weyland (West Germany)

	P	W	D	L	F	A	Pts
Poland	3	3	0	0	12	3	6
Argentina	3	1	1	1	7	5	3
Italy	3	1	1	1	5	4	3
Haiti	3	0	0	3	2	14	0

Second round
GROUP A
26.6.74 Brazil (0) 1, East Germany (0) 0 HANOVER
Brazil: Leao, Pereira, Ze Maria, Mario Marinho, Francesco Marinho, Rivelino (1), Paulo Cesar C, Paulo Cesar L, Valdomiro, Jairzinho, Dirceu
East Germany: Croy, Kische, Bransch, Weise, Watzlich, Lauck (Lowe), Hamann (Irmscher), Kurbjuweit, Streich, Sparwasser, Hoffmann
Referee: Thomas (Wales)

26.6.74 Holland (2) 4, Argentina (0) 0 GELSENKIRCHEN
Holland: Jongbloed, Suurbier (Israel), Rijsbergen, Haan, Krol (1), Jansen, Neeskens, Van Hanegem, Rep (1), Cruyff (2), Rensenbrink
Argentina: Carnevali, Wolff (Glaria), Perfumo, Heredia, Sa, Telch, Balbuena, Squeo, Yazalde, Ayala, Houseman (Kempes)
Referee: Davidson (Scotland)

30.6.74 Holland (1) 2, East Germany (0) 0 GELSENKIRCHEN
Holland: Jongbloed, Suurbier, Rijsbergen, Haan, Krol, Jansen, Neeskens (1), Van Hanegem, Rep, Cruyff, Rensenbrink (1)
East Germany: Croy, Kische, Weise, Bransch, Kurbjuweit, Lauck (Kreische), Schnuphase, Sparwasser, Pommerenke, Lowe (Ducke), Hoffmann
Referee: Scheurer (Switzerland)

30.6.74 Brazil (1) 2, Argentina (1) 1 HANOVER
Brazil: Leao, Pereira, Ze Maria, Mario Marinho, Francesco Marinho, Rivelino (1), Paulo Cesar C, Paulo Cesar L, Valdomiro, Jairzinho (1), Dirceu
Argentina: Carnevali, Glaria, Bargas, Heredia, Sa (Carrascosa), Brindisi (1), Squeo, Babington, Balbuena, Ayala, Kempes (Houseman)
Referee: Loraux (Belgium)

3.7.74 Holland (0) 2, Brazil (0) 0 DORTMUND
Holland: Jongbloed, Suurbier, Rijsbergen, Haan, Krol, Jansen, Neeskens (1) (Israel), Van Hanegem, Rep, Cruyff (1), Rensenbrink (De Jong)
Brazil: Leao, Pereira, Ze Maria, Mario Marinho, Francesco Marinho, Rivelino, Paulo Cesar C, Paulo Cesar L (Mirandhina), Valdomiro, Jairzinho, Dirceu
Referee: Tschenscher (West Germany)

3.7.84 East Germany (1) 1, Argentina (1) 1 GELSENKIRCHEN
East Germany: Croy, Kische, Weise, Bransch, Kurbjuweit, Sparwasser, Schnuphase, Pommerenke, Lowe (Vogel), Streich (1) (Ducke), Hoffmann
Argentina: Fillol, Wolff, Heredia, Bargas, Carrascosa, Telch, Brindisi, Babington, Houseman (1), Ayala, Kempes
Referee: Taylor (England)

	P	W	D	L	F	A	Pts
Holland	3	3	0	0	8	0	6
Brazil	3	2	0	1	3	3	4
East Germany	3	0	1	2	1	4	1
Argentina	3	0	1	2	2	7	1

GROUP B
26.6.74 West Germany (1) 2, Yugoslavia (0) 0 DUSSELDORF
West Germany: Maier, Vogts, Schwarzenbeck, Beckenbauer, Breitner, Wimmer (Hoeness), Overath, Bonhof, Holzenbein (Flohe), Muller (1), Herzog
Yugoslavia: Maric, Buljan, Katalinski, Muzinic, Hadziabdic, Oblak (Jerkovic), Acimovic, Surjak, Popivoda, Karasi, Dzajic (Petkovic)
Referee: Marques (Brazil)

26.6.74 Poland (1) 1, Sweden (0) 0 STUTTGART
Poland: Tomaszewski, Gut, Gorgon, Szymanowski, Zmuda, Kasperczyk, Deyna, Maszczyk, Lato (1), Szarmach (Kmiecik), Gadocha
Sweden: Hellstrom, Andersson (Augustsson), Grip, Karlsson, Nordqvist, Bo Larsson, Torstensson, Tapper (Ahlstrom), Edstrom, Grahn, Sandberg
Referee: Barreto (Uruguay)

30.6.74 West Germany (0) 4, Sweden (1) 2 DUSSELDORF
West Germany: Maier, Vogts, Schwarzenbeck, Beckenbauer, Breitner, Hoeness (1 pen), Bonhof (1), Overath (1), Holzenbein (Flohe), Muller, Herzog (Grabowski (1))
Sweden: Hellstrom, Olsson, Karlsson, Nordqvist, Augustsson, Tapper, Bo Larsson (Ejderstedt), Grahn, Torstensson, Edstrom (1), Sandberg (1)
Referee: Kasakov (USSR)

30.6.74 Poland (1) 2, Yugoslavia (1) 1 FRANKFURT
Poland: Tomaszewski, Szymanowski, Zmuda, Gorgon, Musial, Kasperczyk, Maszczyk, Deyna (1 pen) (Domarski), Lato (1), Szarmach (Cmikiewicz), Gadocha
Yugoslavia: Maric, Buljan, Katalinski, Bogicevic, Hadziabdic, Karasi (1), Oblak (Jerkovic), Acimovic, Petkovic (Petrovic), Bajevic, Surjak
Referee: Glockner (East Germany)

3.7.74 Sweden (1) 2, Yugoslavia (1) 1 DUSSELDORF
Sweden: Hellstrom, Olsson, Karlsson, Nordqvist, Augustsson, Tapper, Grahn, Persson, Torstensson (1), Edstrom (1), Sandberg
Yugoslavia: Maric, Buljan, Katalinski, Hadziabdic, Pavlovic (Peruzovic), Bogicevic, Acimovic, Jerkovic, Petrovic (Karasi), Surjak (1), Dzajic
Referee: Pestarino (Argentina)

3. 7. 74 West Germany (0) 1, Poland (0) 0 FRANKFURT
West Germany: Maier, Vogts, Schwarzenbeck, Beckenbauer, Breitner, Hoeness, Bonhof, Overath, Grabowski, Muller (1), Holzenbein
Poland: Tomaszewski, Szymanowski, Gorgon, Zmuda, Musial, Kasperczyk (Cmikiewicz), Deyna, Maszczyk (Kmiecik), Lato, Domarski, Gadocha
Referee: Linemayr (Austria)

	P	W	D	L	F	A	Pts
West Germany	3	3	0	0	7	2	6
Poland	3	2	0	1	3	2	4
Sweden	3	1	0	2	4	6	2
Yugoslavia	3	0	0	3	2	6	0

Match for third place
6.7.74 Poland (0) 1, Brazil (0) 0 MUNICH
Poland: Tomaszewski, Szymanowski, Zmuda, Gordon, Musial, Kasperczyk (Cmikiewicz), Maszczyk, Deyna, Lato (1), Szarmach (Kapka), Gadocha
Brazil: Leao, Ze Maria, Alfredo, Mario Marinho, Francesco Marinho, Rivelino, Paulo Cesar C, Ademir (Mirandhina), Valdomiro, Jairzinho, Dirceu
Referee: Angonese (Italy)

FINAL
7.7.74 West Germany (2) 2, Holland (1) 1 MUNICH
West Germany: Maier, Vogts, Schwarzenbeck, Beckenbauer, Breitner (1 pen), Hoeness, Bonhof, Overath, Grabowski, Muller (1), Holzenbein
Holland: Jongbloed, Suurbier, Rijsbergen (De Jong), Haan, Krol, Jansen, Neeskens (1 pen), Van Hanegem, Rep, Cruyff, Rensenbrink (Van der Kerkhof)
Referee: Taylor (England)

Argentina on the way to beating
Holland in the 1978 final on a
littered pitch in Buenos Aires.

ARGENTINA

1978

Argentina became the third host nation to win the competition in the last four tournaments, in a tense but flowing final in which the Dutch, though forcing extra time, again had to be content with runners-up medals. There was controversy before the match over the manner of Argentina's qualification for the final. They knew just how many goals were required against Peru to overtake Brazil on goal difference.

Gamesmanship also extended to the pre-match arrangements. Argentina kept the Dutch players waiting five minutes before they left their dressing-room. Then they complained about the plaster on the arm of Rene Van de Kerkhof; tactics designed to unsettle their opponents.

Although 102 goals were scored in the tournament, the average was only slightly better than the all-time low of 1974, with the gap widening between improved but uncompromising defences and impoverished attacks. Only two goals came from free-kicks and just one following a corner, though several memorable longer-range efforts succeeded from open play. There were three own goals, three players sent off and 58 cautioned.

Of the 14 penalty kicks awarded, only two failed, including another suspect incident involving Argentina, against Poland. Kazimierz Deyna, in his 100th international, was about to take his shot when the referee repositioned the ball, possibly disturbing his concentration. Scotland, the other spot-kick failures against Peru, had unwisely celebrated before the finals and clearly underestimated the South Americans. Two long-range efforts, one from a free-kick, by Teofilo Cubillas helped Peru to beat them 3-1.

The Scots were then held 1-1 by Iran but requiring a three-goal margin to deprive Holland of a place in the second stage, they gave their best performance by far,

Clive Thomas, the Welsh referee controversially blew for time seconds before Zico scored for Brazil against Sweden in Mar del Plata. The Brazilians were furious when he refused to allow the goal. (ASP)

A jubilant Mario Kempes (below) after opening the scoring in the final.

But Brazil, unbeaten in the three games, finished behind Austria to join Peru and Holland who had emerged from the other group. The Dutch, while still using the all-out attack and reinforced defence methods of their 'total football' era, badly missed Cruyff and lacked accuracy in front of goal.

In Group A of the second stage, West Germany and Italy played out a dull, negative scoreless draw before the Dutch produced their most successful win, 5-1 over Austria. A Paolo Rossi goal after 14 minutes gave Italy the points at the expense of the Austrians before West Germany and Holland replayed their 1974 final but shared four goals this time.

Erny Brandts scored for both sides in Holland's 2-1 win over Italy and Austria deprived the Germans of a chance of a medal by beating them 3-2, giving Italy the third-place tie behind Holland, who became finalists for the second series in a row.

In Group B, Argentina were well into their stride with Mario Kempes causing defences many anxious moments with his strong, long-striding runs and faultless finishing. He struck twice in the 16th and 71st minute in the opening match with Poland. Brazil also looked much better against Peru and deserved their three-goal victory and had the edge over Argentina in an absorbing if tension-ridden 0-0 draw with the hosts.

Though Poland kept their faint hopes alive by beating Peru 1-0, Brazil beat the Poles who had drawn level at 1-1 on half-time, scoring twice after the break in a 3-1 success. Four hours later the Argentines kicked-off against Peru knowing they needed a win of four goals to reach the final. They hit six against a totally demoralised Peruvian side, while rumours spread outside Argentina about the reasons for the collapse.

For Brazil it was a galling experience; unbeaten in six games and forced to play only in the game for third place, which they won, beating Italy 2-1 after being a goal down at half-time.

Argentina had strength, resolution and were quick in all departments. They also had outstanding individuals like their defence organiser Daniel Passarella, midfield genius Ossie Ardiles, who was at the hub of almost every attack, and Kempes, a rakish striker who deservedly won the player of the tournament award.

Against Holland they made the most of almost every opening, while the Dutch, well below their best, squandered the half-chances which came their way. Kempes' persistence gave them a 1-0 lead after 38 minutes and it seemed enough until substitute Dirk Nanninga equalised for Holland with eight minutes left. But in extra time Kempes' powers of penetration led to him scoring again after 105 minutes and making the opening for Daniel Bertoni to make it 3-1 eleven minutes later. Argentina, with racing inflation and military dictatorship, had something to celebrate.

winning 3-2. But there was more disgrace for Scotland as Willie Johnston was sent home after being found guilty of taking an illegal drug.

Argentina had started nervously themselves but finished second in their group to Italy, who had beaten them by a single goal in Buenos Aires. In Group 2 the traditional opener for the competition involving the holders resulted in a goalless draw between West Germany and Poland, who both went on to the second round, again based on two sections as in 1974.

In Group 3, Sweden and Brazil were drawing 1-1 when the South Americans were awarded a corner. Referee Clive Thomas allowed the kick to be taken although it was timed electronically at three seconds over the normal 90 minutes. Zico headed in at nine seconds on the clock but the goal was ruled out as Thomas insisted he had ended the match when the corner was taken.

Neither Italy nor West Germany managed a goal in this Group A match in Buenos Aires, but Antonio Cabrini appears to have cause for concern after being caught by Karl-Heinz Rummenigge (right).

Qualifying Tournament
106 entries

Europe (32): Austria, Belgium, Bulgaria, Cyprus, Czechoslovakia, Denmark, England, Finland, France, East Germany, West Germany, Greece, Holland, Hungary, Iceland, Republic of Ireland, Northern Ireland, Italy, Luxembourg, Malta, Norway, Poland, Portugal, Rumania, Scotland, Spain, Sweden, Switzerland, Turkey, USSR, Wales, Yugoslavia

Africa (26): Algeria, Cameroon, Central Africa, Congo, Egypt, Ethiopia, Ghana, Guinea, Ivory Coast, Kenya, Libya, Malawi, Mauritania, Morocco, Niger, Nigeria, Senegal, Sierra Leone, Sudan, Tanzania, Togo, Tunisia, Uganda, Upper Volta, Zaire, Zambia

Concacaf (17): Barbados, Canada, Costa Rica, Cuba, Dominican Republic, Guatemala, Guyana, Haiti, Honduras, Jamaica, Mexico, Netherlands Antilles, Panama, El Salvador, Surinam, Trinidad and Tobago, USA

South America (10): Argentina, Bolivia, Brazil, Chile, Colombia, Ecuador, Paraguay, Peru, Uruguay, Venezuela

Asia (18): Bahrain, Hong Kong, Indonesia, Iran, Iraq, Israel, Japan, North Korea, South Korea, Kuwait, Malaysia, Qatar, Saudi Arabia, Singapore, Sri Lanka, Syria, Thailand, United Arab Emirates

Oceania (3): Australia, New Zealand, Taiwan

Taiwan were transferred from the Asian zone into Oceania. In South America, the winners of the three groups were to play in a tournament in a neutral country. The first two teams were guaranteed final places but the third had to meet the winner of Group 9 in Europe. Sri Lanka became the first country to withdraw when its government refused to grant permission to pay the entrance fee.

Final places in Argentina were to be distributed as follows: Europe (9 + West Germany)*, South America (2 + Argentina)*, Concacaf (1), Africa (1), Asia/Oceania (1).

*Play-off between Hungary and Bolivia gave Europe a further final place

Europe
Group 1 (Poland, Portugal, Denmark, Cyprus)
Cyprus v Denmark 1 - 5; Portugal v Poland 0 - 2; Denmark v Cyprus 5 - 0; Poland v Cyprus 5 - 0; Cyprus v Portugal 1 - 2; Denmark v Poland 1 - 2; Cyprus v Poland 1 - 3; Poland v Denmark 4 - 1; Denmark v Portugal 2 - 4; Poland v Portugal 1 - 1; Portugal v Cyprus 4 - 0

	P	W	D	L	F	A	Pts
Poland	6	5	1	0	17	4	11
Portugal	6	4	1	1	12	6	9
Denmark	6	2	0	4	14	12	4
Cyprus	6	0	0	0	3	24	0

Poland qualified

Group 2 (Italy, England, Finland, Luxembourg)
Finland v England 1 - 4; Finland v Luxembourg 7 - 1; England v Finland 2 - 1; Luxembourg v Italy 1 - 4; Italy v England 2 - 0; England v Luxembourg 5 - 0; Luxembourg v Finland 0 - 1; Finland v Italy 0 - 3; Luxembourg v England 0 - 2; Italy v Finland 6 - 1; England v Italy 2 - 0; Italy v Luxembourg 3 - 0

	P	W	D	L	F	A	Pts
Italy	6	5	0	1	18	4	10
England	6	5	0	1	15	4	10
Finland	6	2	0	4	11	16	4
Luxembourg	6	0	0	6	2	22	0

Italy qualified

Group 3 (East Germany, Austria, Turkey, Malta)
Turkey v Malta 4 - 0; East Germany v Turkey 1 - 1; Malta v Austria 0 - 1; Malta v East Germany 0 - 1; Austria v Turkey 1 - 0; Austria v Malta 9 - 0; Austria v East Germany 1 - 1; East Germany v Austria 1 - 1; East Germany v Malta 9 - 0; Turkey v Austria 0 - 1; Turkey v East Germany 1 - 2; Malta v Turkey 0 - 3

	P	W	D	L	F	A	Pts
Austria	6	4	2	0	14	2	10
East Germany	6	3	3	0	15	4	9
Turkey	6	2	1	3	9	5	5
Malta	6	0	0	6	0	27	0

Austria qualified

Group 4 (Holland, Belgium, Northern Ireland, Iceland)
Iceland v Belgium 0 - 1; Iceland v Holland 0 - 1; Holland v Northern Ireland 2 - 2; Belgium v Northern Ireland 2 - 0; Belgium v Holland 0 - 2; Iceland v Northern Ireland 1 - 0; Holland v Iceland 4 - 1; Belgium v Iceland 4 - 0; Northern Ireland v Iceland 2 - 0; Northern Ireland v Holland 0 - 1; Holland v Belgium 1 - 0; Northern Ireland v Belgium 3 - 0

	P	W	D	L	F	A	Pts
Holland	6	5	1	0	11	3	11
Belgium	6	3	0	3	7	6	6
Northern Ireland	6	2	1	3	7	6	5
Iceland	6	1	0	5	2	12	2

Holland qualified

Group 5 (Bulgaria, France, Rep of Ireland)
Bulgaria v France 2 - 2; France v Rep of Ireland 2 - 0;
Rep of Ireland v France 1 - 0; Bulgaria v Rep of Ireland 2 - 1;
Rep of Ireland v Bulgaria 0 - 0; France v Bulgaria 3 - 1

	P	W	D	L	F	A	Pts
France	4	2	1	1	7	4	5
Bulgaria	4	1	2	1	5	6	4
Rep of Ireland	4	1	1	2	2	4	3

France qualified

Group 6 (Sweden, Switzerland, Norway)
Sweden v Norway 2 - 0; Norway v Switzerland 1 - 0;
Switzerland v Sweden 1 - 2; Sweden v Switzerland 2 - 1; Norway
v Sweden 2 - 1; Switzerland v Norway 1 - 0

	P	W	D	L	F	A	Pts
Sweden	4	3	0	1	7	4	6
Norway	4	2	0	2	3	4	4
Switzerland	4	1	0	3	3	5	2

Sweden qualified

Group 7 (Scotland, Czechoslovakia, Wales)
Czechoslovakia v Scotland 2 - 0; Scotland v Wales 1 - 0; Wales
v Czechoslovakia 3 - 0; Scotland v Czechoslovakia 3 - 1;
Wales v Scotland 0 - 2; Czechoslovakia v Wales 1 - 0

	P	W	D	L	F	A	Pts
Scotland	4	3	0	1	6	3	6
Czechoslovakia	4	2	0	2	4	6	4
Wales	4	1	0	3	3	4	2

Scotland qualified

Group 8 (Yugoslavia, Spain, Rumania)
Spain v Yugoslavia 1 - 0; Rumania v Spain 1 - 0; Yugoslavia v Rumania 0 - 2;
Spain v Rumania 2 - 0; Rumania v Yugoslavia 4 - 6; Yugoslavia v Spain 0 - 1

	P	W	D	L	F	A	Pts
Spain	4	3	0	1	4	1	6
Rumania	4	2	0	2	7	8	4
Yugoslavia	4	1	0	3	6	8	2

Spain qualified

Group 9 (USSR, Hungary, Greece)
Greece v Hungary 1 - 1; USSR v Greece 2 - 0; Hungary v USSR 2 - 1;
Greece v USSR 1 - 0; USSR v Hungary 2 - 0; Hungary v Greece 3 - 0

	P	W	D	L	F	A	Pts
Hungary	4	2	1	1	6	4	5
USSR	4	2	0	2	5	3	4
Greece	4	1	1	2	2	6	3

Play-off against third-placed team in South American play-off group:
Hungary v Bolivia 6 - 0, 3 - 2
Hungary qualified

South America
Group 1 (Brazil, Paraguay, Colombia)
Colombia v Brazil 0 - 0; Colombia v Paraguay 0 - 1; Paraguay v Colombia
1 - 1; Brazil v Colombia 6 - 0; Paraguay v Brazil 0 - 1; Brazil v Paraguay 1 - 1

	P	W	D	L	F	A	Pts
Brazil	4	2	2	0	8	1	6
Paraguay	4	1	2	1	3	3	4
Colombia	4	0	2	2	1	8	2

Group 2 (Uruguay, Venezuela, Bolivia)
Venezuela v Uruguay 1 - 1; Bolivia v Uruguay 1 - 0; Venezuela v Bolivia
1 - 3; Bolivia v Venezuela 2 - 0; Uruguay v Venezuela 2 - 0; Uruguay
v Bolivia 2 - 2

	P	W	D	L	F	A	Pts
Bolivia	4	3	1	0	8	3	7
Uruguay	4	1	2	1	5	4	4
Venezuela	4	0	1	3	2	8	1

Group 3 (Chile, Peru, Ecuador)
Ecuador v Peru 1 - 1; Ecuador v Chile 0 - 1; Chile v Peru 1 - 1; Peru
v Ecuador 4 - 0; Chile v Ecuador 3 - 0; Peru v Chile 2 - 0

	P	W	D	L	F	A	Pts
Peru	4	2	2	0	8	2	6
Chile	4	2	1	1	5	3	5
Ecuador	4	0	1	3	1	9	1

Play-off group (in Colombia)
Brazil v Peru 1 - 0; Brazil v Bolivia 8 - 0; Peru v Bolivia 5 - 0

	P	W	D	L	F	A	Pts
Brazil	2	2	0	0	9	0	4
Peru	2	1	0	1	5	1	2
Bolivia	2	0	0	2	0	13	0

Brazil and Peru qualified

Concacaf
Group 1 (North) (Canada, USA, Mexico)
Canada v USA 1 - 1; USA v Mexico 0 - 0; Canada v Mexico 1 - 0;
Mexico v USA 3 - 0; USA v Canada 2 - 0; Mexico v Canada 0 - 0

	P	W	D	L	F	A	Pts
Mexico	4	1	2	1	3	1	4
USA	4	1	2	1	3	4	4
Canada	4	1	2	1	2	3	4

Play-off for second place (in Haiti):
Canada v USA 3 - 0

Group 2 (Central) (Guatemala, El Salvador, Honduras, Costa Rica, Panama)
Honduras withdrew
Panama v Costa Rica 3 - 2; Panama v El Salvador 1 - 1; Costa Rica v Panama
3 - 0; El Salvador v Panama 4 - 1; Panama v Guatemala 2 - 4; Guatemala
v Panama 7 - 0; El Salvador v Costa Rica 1 - 1; Costa Rica v Guatemala
0 - 0; Guatemala v El Salvador 3 - 1; Guatemala v Costa Rica 1 - 1;
El Salvador v Guatemala 2 - 0; Costa Rica v El Salvador 1 - 1

	P	W	D	L	F	A	Pts
Guatemala	6	3	2	1	15	6	8
El Salvador	6	2	3	1	10	7	7
Costa Rica	6	1	4	1	8	6	6
Panama	6	1	1	4	7	21	3

Group 3 (Caribbean) (Netherlands Antilles, Barbados, Cuba, Guyana, Haiti, Jamaica, Surinam, Trinidad and Tobago, Dominican Republic)

Extra preliminary round
Dominican Republic v Haiti 0 - 3, 0 - 3

Preliminary round
Guyana v Surinam 2 - 0, 0 - 3; Netherlands Antilles v Haiti 1 - 2, 0 - 7;
Jamaica v Cuba 1 - 3, 0 - 2; Barbados v Trinidad and Tobago 2 - 1, 0 - 1;
Play-off: Trinidad and Tobago v Barbados 3 - 1

Final preliminary round
Surinam v Trinidad and Tobago 1 - 1, 2 - 2; Play-off: Surinam v Trinidad and
Tobago 3 - 2; Cuba v Haiti 1 - 1, 1 - 1. Play-off: Cuba v Haiti 0 - 2

Final Round
Guatemala v Surinam 3 - 2; El Salvador v Canada 2 - 1; Mexico v Haiti 4 - 1;
Canada v Surinam 2 - 1; Haiti v Guatemala 2 - 1; Mexico v El Salvador 3 - 1;
Mexico v Surinam 8 - 1; Canada v Guatemala 2 - 1; Haiti v El Salvador 1 - 0;
Mexico v Canada 3 - 1; Canada v Haiti 1 - 1; El Salvador v Surinam 3 - 2;
Mexico v Canada 3 - 1; Haiti v Surinam 1 - 0; Guatemala v El Salvador 2 - 2

	P	W	D	L	F	A	Pts
Mexico	5	5	0	0	20	5	10
Haiti	5	3	1	1	6	6	7
Canada	5	2	1	2	7	8	5
El Salvador	5	2	1	2	8	9	5
Guatemala	5	1	1	3	8	10	3
Surinam	5	0	0	5	6	17	0

Mexico qualified

Africa
Extra Preliminary Round
Sierra Leone v Niger 5 - 1, 1 - 2; Upper Volta v Mauritania 1 - 1, 2 - 0

1st Round
Algeria v Libya 1 - 0, 0 - 0; Morocco v Tunisia 1 - 1, 1 - 1 (Tunisia won 4 - 2
on penalties); Togo v Senegal 1 - 0, 1 - 1; Ghana v Guinea 2 - 1, 1 - 2;
Play-off: Guinea v Ghana 2 - 0; Zaire v Central Africa (withdrew); Sierra
Leone v Nigeria 0 - 0, 2 - 2; Congo v Cameroon 2 - 2, 2 - 1; Upper Volta
v Ivory Coast 1 - 1, 0 - 2; Egypt v Ethiopia 3 - 0, 2 - 1; Kenya v Sudan
(withdrew); Uganda v Tanzania (withdrew); Zambia v Malawi 4 - 0, 1 - 0

2nd Round
Zaire withdrew
Tunisia v Algeria 2 - 0, 1 - 1; Togo v Guinea 0 - 2, 1 - 2; Ivory Coast v Congo
3 - 2, 3 - 1; Kenya v Egypt 0 - 0, 0 - 1; Uganda v Zambia 1 - 0, 2 - 4

3rd Round

Guinea v Tunisia 1 - 0, 1 - 3; Ivory Coast v Nigeria 2 - 2, 0 - 4; Egypt v Zambia 2 - 0, 0 - 0

Final tournament

Tunisia v Nigeria 0 - 0; Nigeria v Egypt 4 - 0; Egypt v Nigeria 3 - 1; Nigeria v Tunisia 0 - 1; Egypt v Tunisia 3 - 2; Tunisia v Egypt 4 - 1

	P	W	D	L	F	A	Pts
Tunisia	4	2	1	1	7	4	5
Egypt	4	2	0	2	7	11	4
Nigeria	4	1	1	2	5	4	3

Tunisia qualified

Asia and Oceania

Oceania Group (Australia, New Zealand, Taiwan)

(In Australia)

Australia v Taiwan 3 - 0; Taiwan v Australia 1 - 2, New Zealand v Taiwan 6 - 0; Taiwan v New Zealand 0 - 6; Australia v New Zealand 3 - 1; New Zealand v Australia 1 - 1

	P	W	D	L	F	A	Pts
Australia	4	3	1	0	9	3	7
New Zealand	4	2	1	1	14	4	5
Taiwan	4	0	0	4	1	17	0

Asia Group 1 (Hong Kong, Indonesia, Malaysia, Thailand, Singapore)

(In Singapore)

Singapore v Thailand 2 - 0; Hong Kong v Indonesia 4 - 1; Malaysia v Thailand 6 - 4; Hong Kong v Singapore 2 - 2; Indonesia v Malaysia 0 - 0; Thailand v Hong Kong 1 - 2; Singapore v Malaysia 1 - 0; Thailand v Indonesia 3 - 2; Malaysia v Hong Kong 1 - 1; Indonesia v Singapore 4 - 0

	P	W	D	L	F	A	Pts
Hong Kong	4	2	2	0	9	5	6
Singapore	4	2	1	1	5	6	5
Malaysia	4	1	2	1	7	6	4
Indonesia	4	1	1	2	7	7	3
Thailand	4	1	0	3	8	12	2

Group Final: Singapore v Hong Kong 0 - 1

Asia Group 2 (Israel, Japan, South Korea, North Korea)

North Korea withdrew

Israel v South Korea 0 - 0; Israel v Japan 2 - 0; Japan v Israel 0 - 2; South Korea v Israel 3 - 1; Japan v South Korea 0 - 0; South Korea v Japan 1 - 0

	P	W	D	L	F	A	Pts
South Korea	4	2	2	0	4	1	6
Israel	4	2	1	1	5	3	5
Japan	4	0	1	3	0	5	1

Asia Group 3 (Iran, Saudi Arabia, Iraq, Syria)

Iraq withdrew

Saudi Arabia v Syria 2 - 0; Syria v Saudi Arabia 2 - 1; Saudi Arabia v Iran 0 - 3; Syria v Iran 0 - 1; Iran v Syria (withdrew), match awarded to Iran 2 - 0; Iran v Saudi Arabia 2 - 0

	P	W	D	L	F	A	Pts
Iran	4	4	0	0	8	0	8
Saudi Arabia	4	1	0	3	3	7	2
Syria	4	1	0	3	2	6	2

Asia Group 4 (Bahrain, Kuwait, Qatar, UAE)

(In Qatar)

UAE withdrew

Bahrain v Kuwait 0 - 2; Bahrain v Qatar 0 - 2; Qatar v Kuwait 0 - 2; Bahrain v Kuwait 1 - 2; Qatar v Bahrain 0 - 3; Qatar v Kuwait 1 - 4

	P	W	D	L	F	A	Pts
Kuwait	4	4	0	0	10	2	8
Qatar	4	1	0	3	3	9	2
Bahrain	4	1	0	3	4	6	2

Final round

Hong Kong v Iran 0 - 2; Hong Kong v South Korea 0 - 1; South Korea v Iran 0 - 0; Australia v Hong Kong 3 - 0; Australia v Iran 0 - 1; Australia v South Korea 2 - 1; Hong Kong v Kuwait 1 - 3; South Korea v Kuwait 1 - 0; Australia v Kuwait 1 - 2; South Korea v Australia 0 - 0; Iran v Kuwait 1 - 0; Hong Kong v Australia 2 - 5; Kuwait v South Korea 2 - 2; Iran v South Korea 2 - 2; Kuwait v Hong Kong 4 - 0; Iran v Hong Kong 3 - 0; Kuwait v Australia 1 - 0; Iran v Australia 1 - 0; Kuwait v Iran 1 - 2; South Korea v Hong Kong 5 - 2

	P	W	D	L	F	A	Pts
Iran	8	6	2	0	12	3	14
South Korea	8	3	4	1	12	8	10
Kuwait	8	4	1	3	13	8	9
Australia	8	3	1	4	11	8	7
Hong Kong	8	0	0	8	5	26	0

Iran qualified

Final Tournament ARGENTINA
First round
GROUP 1

2.6.78 Argentina (1) 2, Hungary (1) 1 BUENOS AIRES
Argentina: Fillol, Olguin, Galvan, Passarella, Tarantini, Ardiles, Gallego, Valencia (Alonso), Houseman (Bertoni (1)), Luque (1), Kempes
Hungary: Gujdar, Torok (Martos), Kereki, Kocsis, Toth J, Nyilasi, Pinter, Zombori, Csapo (1), Torocsik, Nagy
Refree: Garrido (Portugal)

2.6.78 Italy (1) 2, France (1) 1 MAR DEL PLATA
Italy: Zoff, Scirea, Gentile, Bellugi, Cabrini, Benetti, Causio, Tardelli, Antognoni (Zaccarelli (1)), Rossi (1), Bettega
France: Bertrand-Demanes, Tresor, Janvion, Rio, Bossis, Guillou, Michel, Platini, Dalger, Lacombe (1) (Berdoll), Six (Rouyer)
Referee: Rainea (Rumania)

6.7.78 Argentina (1) 2, France (0) 1 BUENOS AIRES
Argentina: Fillol, Olguin, Galvan, Passarella (1 pen), Tarantini, Ardiles, Gallego, Valencia (Alonso), Houseman, Luque (1), Kempes
France: Bertrand-Demanes (Baratelli), Tresor, Battiston, Lopez, Bossis, Bathenay, Michel, Platini (1), Rocheteau, Lacombe, Six
Referee: Dubach (Switzerland)

6.6.78 Italy (2) 3, Hungary (0) 1 MAR DEL PLATA
Italy: Zoff, Scirea, Gentile, Bellugi, Cabrini (Cuccureddu), Benetti (1), Causio, Tardelli, Antognoni, Rossi (1), Bettega (1) (Graziani)
Hungary: Meszaros, Kereki, Martos, Kocsis, Toth J, Csapo, Pinter, Zombori, Pusztai, Fazekas (Halasz), Nagy (Toth A (1 pen))
Referee: Barretto (Uruguay)

10.6.78 Italy (0) 1, Argentina (0) 0 BUENOS AIRES
Italy: Zoff, Scirea, Gentile, Bellugi (Cuccureddu), Cabrini, Benetti, Causio, Tardelli, Antognoni (Zaccarelli), Rossi, Bettega (1)
Argentina: Fillol, Olguin, Galvan, Passarella, Tarantini, Gallego, Ardiles, Valencia, Bertoni, Kempes, Ortiz (Houseman)
Referee: Klein (Israel)

10.6.78 France (3) 3, Hungary (1) 1 MAR DEL PLATA
France: Dropsy, Tresor, Janvion, Lopez (1), Bracci, Petit, Bathenay, Papi, Rocheteau (1), Berdoll (1), Rouyer
Hungary: Gujdar, Kereki, Balint, Martos, Toth J, Nyilasi, Pinter, Zombori (1), Pusztai, Torocsik, Nagy (Csapo)
Referee: Coelho (Brazil)

	P	W	D	L	F	A	Pts
Italy	3	3	0	0	6	2	6
Argentina	3	2	0	1	4	3	4
France	3	1	0	2	5	5	2
Hungary	3	0	0	3	3	8	0

GROUP 2

1.6.78 West Germany (0) 0, Poland (0) 0 BUENOS AIRES
West Germany: Maier, Kaltz, Vogts, Russmann, Zimmerman, Bonhof, Beer, Flohe, Muller H, Abramczik, Fischer
Poland: Tomaszewski, Gorgon, Maculewicz, Szymanowski, Zmuda, Masztaler (Kasperczak), Nawalka, Deyna, Lato, Lubanski (Boniek), Szarmach
Referee: Coerezza (Argentina)

2.6.78 Tunisia (0) 3, Mexico (1) 1 ROSARIO
Tunisia: Naili, Dhouieb (1), Jendoubi, Jebali, Kaabi (1), Ghommidh (1), Temine (Labidi), Agrebi, Akid, Tarak, Ben Aziza (Karoui)
Mexico: Reyes, Martinez Diaz, Vazquez Ayala (1 pen), Ramos, Tena, De la Torre, Cuellar, Mendizabal (Lugo Gomez), Isiordia, Rangel, Sanchez
Referee: Gordon (Scotland)

6.6.78 Poland (1) 1, Tunisia (0) 0 ROSARIO
Poland: Tomaszewski, Gordon, Szymanowski, Zmuda, Maculewicz, Nawalka, Deyna, Kasperczak, Lato (1), Lubanski (Boniek), Szarmach (Iwan)
Tunisia: Naili, Dhouieb, Jendoubi, Gasmi, Kaabi, Ghommidh, Temine, Agrebi, Akid, Tarak, Jebali
Referee: Martinez (Spain)

6.6.78 West Germany (4) 6, Mexico (0) 0 CORDOBA
West Germany: Maier, Kaltz, Vogts, Russmann, Dietz, Bonhof, Flohe (2), Muller H (1), Rummenigge (2), Fischer, Muller D (1)
Mexico: Reyes (Soto), Martinez Diaz, Tena, Ramos, Vazquez Ayala, Lopez Zarza (Lugo Gomez), Cuellar, De la Torre, Sanchez, Rangel, Mendizabal,
Referee: Bouzo (Syria)

10.6.78 West Germany (0) 0, Tunisia (0) 0 CORDOBA
West Germany: Maier, Kaltz, Vogts, Russmann, Dietz, Bonhof, Flohe, Rummenigge, Muller H, Fischer, Muller D
Tunisia: Naili, Jebali, Dhouieb, Jendoubi, Kaabi, Ghommidh, Gasmi, Tarak, Agrebi, Temine, Akid (Ben Aziza)
Referee: Orosco (Peru)

10.6.78 Poland (1) 3, Mexico (0) 1 ROSARIO
Poland: Tomaszewski, Gorgon, Szymanowski, Zmuda, Kasperczak, Deyna (1), Masztaler, Rudy (Maculewicz), Boniek (2), Lato, Iwan (Lubanski)
Mexico: Soto, Gomez C, Cisneros, De la Torre, Vazquez Ayala, Cuellar, Flores, Cardenas (Mendizabal), Ortega, Rangel (1), Sanchez
Referee: Namdar (Iran)

	P	W	D	L	F	A	Pts
Poland	3	2	1	0	4	1	5
West Germany	3	1	2	0	6	0	4
Tunisia	3	1	1	1	3	2	3
Mexico	3	0	0	3	2	12	0

GROUP 3
3.6.78 Austria (1) 2, Spain (1) 1 BUENOS AIRES
Austria: Koncilla, Pezzey, Sara, Breitenberger, Obermayer, Prohaska, Kreuz, Hickersberger (Weber), Jara, Schachner (1) (Pirkner), Krankl (1)
Spain: Miguel Angel, Marcelino, Pirri, Migueli, San Jose, De la Cruz, Asensi, Rexach (Quini), Cardenosa (Leal), Dani (1), Ruben Cano
Referee: Palotai (Hungary)

3.6.78 Sweden (1) 1, Brazil (1) 1 MAR DEL PLATA
Sweden: Hellstrom, Andersson R, Borg, Nordqvist, Erlandsson, Larsson L (Edstrom), Tapper, Linderoth, Bo Larsson, Sjoberg (1), Wendt
Brazil: Leao, Oscar, Toninho, Amaral, Edinho, Batista, Zico, Cerezo, Gil (Nelinho), Reinaldo (1), Rivelino
Referee: Thomas (Wales)

7.6.78 Austria (1) 1, Sweden (0) 0 BUENOS AIRES
Austria: Koncilia, Obermayer, Sara, Pezzey, Breitenberg, Prohaska, Hickersberger, Krieger (Weber), Jara, Krankl (1 pen), Kreuz
Sweden: Hellstrom, Andersson R, Borg, Nordqvist, Erlandsson, Larsson L, Tapper (Torstensson), Linderoth (Edstrom), Bo Larsson, Sjoberg, Wendt
Referee: Corver (Netherlands)

7.6.78 Brazil (0) 0, Spain (0) 0 MAR DEL PLATA
Brazil: Leao, Amaral, Nelinho (Gil), Oscar, Edinho, Cerezo, Batista, Zico (Mendonca), Dirceu, Toninho, Reinaldo
Spain: Miguel Angel, Olmo, Marcelino, Migueli (Biosca), Uria (Guzman), Leal, Asensi, Cardenosa, San Jose, Juanito, Santillana
Referee: Gonella (Italy)

11.6.78 Spain (0) 1, Sweden (0) 0 BUENOS AIRES
Spain: Miguel Angel, Olmo (Pirri), Marcelino, Biosca, San Jose, Uria, Leal, Asensi (1), Cardenosa, Juanito, Santillana
Sweden: Hellstrom, Andersson R, Borg, Nordqvist, Erlandsson, Larsson L, Bo Larsson, Nordin, Nilsson, Sjoberg (Linderoth), Edstrom (Wendt)
Referee: Biwersi (West Germany)

11.6.78 Brazil (1) 1, Austria (0) 0 MAR DEL PLATA
Brazil: Leao, Amaral, Toninho, Oscar, Rodrigues Neto, Batista, Cerezo (Chicao), Dirceu, Gil, Mendonca (Zico), Roberto (1)
Austria: Koncilia, Obermayer, Sara, Pezzey, Breitenberger, Prohaska, Hickersberger (Weber), Krieger (Happich), Jara, Krankl, Kreuz
Referee: Wurtz (France)

	P	W	D	L	F	A	Pts
Austria	3	2	0	1	3	2	4
Brazil	3	1	2	0	2	1	4
Spain	3	1	1	1	2	2	3
Sweden	3	0	1	2	1	3	1

GROUP 4
3.6.78 Holland (1) 3, Iran (0) 0 MENDOZA
Holland: Jongbled, Suurbier, Rijsbergen, Krol, Haan, Jansen, Neeskens, Van de Kerkhof W, Rep, Rensenbrink (3, 2 pens), Van de Kerkhof R (Nanninga)
Iran: Hejazi, Nazari, Abdullahi, Kazerani, Eskandarian, Parvin, Ghassempour, Sadeghi, Nayeb-Agha, Faraki (Rowshan), Jahani
Referee: Archundia (Mexico)

3.6.78 Peru (1) 3, Scotland (1) 1 CORDOBA
Peru: Quiroga, Chumpitaz, Duarte, Manzo, Diaz, Velasquez, Cueto (1) (Rojas), Cubillas (2), Munante, La Rosa (Sotil), Oblitas
Scotland: Rough, Kennedy, Burns, Rioch (Gemmill), Forsyth, Buchan, Dalglish, Hartford, Jordan, Masson (Macari), Johnston
Referee: Eriksson (Switzerland)

7.6.78 Scotland (1) 1, Iran (0) 1 CORDOBA
Scotland: Rough, Jardine, Donachie, Gemmill, Burns, Buchan (Forsyth), Dalglish (Harper), Hartford, Jordan, Macari, Robertson
Iran: Hejazi, Nazari, Abdullahi, Kazerani, Eskandarian (o. g.), Parvin, Ghassempour, Sadeghi, Danaifar (1) (Nayeb-Agha), Faraki (Rowshan), Jahani
Referee: N'Diaye (Senegal)

7.6.78 Holland (0) 0, Peru (0) 0 MENDOZA
Holland: Jongbled, Suurbier, Rijsbergen, Krol, Poortvliet, Neeskens (Nanninga), Van de Kerkhof W, Jansen, Haan, Van de Kerkhof R (Rep), Rensenbrink
Peru: Quiroga, Chumpitaz, Duarte, Manzo, Diaz, Velasquez, Cueto, Cubillas, Munante, La Rosa (Sotil), Oblitas
Referee: Prokop (East Germany)

11.6.78 Peru (3) 4, Iran (1) 1 CORDOBA
Peru: Quiroga, Chumpitaz, Duarte, Manzo (Leguia), Diaz, Velasquez (1), Cueto, Cubillas (3, 2 pens), Munante, La Rosa (Sotil), Oblitas
Iran: Hejazi, Nazari, Abdullahi, Kazerani, Allahvardi, Parvin, Ghassempour, Sadeghi, Danaifar, Faraki (Jahani), Rowshan (1) (Fariba)
Referee: Jarguz (Poland)

11.6.78 Scotland (1) 3, Holland (1) 2 MENDOZA
Scotland: Rough, Kennedy, Donachie, Rioch, Forsyth, Buchan, Dalglish (1), Hartford, Jordan, Gemmill (2, 1 pen), Souness
Holland: Jongbled, Suurbier, Rijsbergen (Wildschut), Krol, Poortvliet, Neeskens (Boskamp), Jansen, Van de Kerkhof W, Rep (1), Van de Kerkhof R, Rensenbrink (1 pen)
Referee: Linemayr (Austria)

	P	W	D	L	F	A	Pts
Peru	3	2	1	0	7	2	5
Holland	3	1	1	1	5	3	3
Scotland	3	1	1	1	5	6	3
Iran	3	0	1	2	2	8	1

Second round
GROUP A
14.6.78 West Germany (0) 0, Italy (0) 0 BUENOS AIRES
West Germany: Maier, Kaltz, Vogts, Russmann, Dietz, Bonhof, Flohe (Beer), Zimmermann (Konopa), Holzenbein, Rummenigge, Fischer
Italy: Zoff, Scirea, Gentile, Bellugi, Cabrini, Tardelli, Benetti, Antognoni (Zaccarelli), Causio, Rossi, Bettega
Referee: Maksimovic (Yugoslavia)

14.6.78 Holland (3) 5, Austria (0) 1 CORDOBA
Holland: Schrijvers, Wildschut, Brandts (1) (Van Kraay), Krol, Poortvliet, Jansen, Haan, Van de Kerkhof W (1), Rep (2), Van de Kerhof R (Schoenaker), Rensenbrink (1)
Austria: Koncilia, Obermayer (1), Sara, Pezzey, Breitenberger, Hickersberger, Prohaska, Jara, Krieger, Kreuz, Krankl
Referee: Gordon (Scotland)

18.6.78 Italy (1) 1, Austria (0) 0 BUENOS AIRES
Italy: Zoff, Scirea, Bellugi (Cuccureddu), Gentile, Cabrini, Benetti, Zaccarelli, Tardelli, Causio, Rossi (1), Bettega (Graziani)
Austria: Koncilia, Obermayer, Sara, Pezzey, Strasser, Hickersberger, Prohaska, Kreuz, Krieger, Schachner (Pirkner), Krankl
Referee: Rion (Belgium)

18.6.78 West Germany (1) 2, Holland (1) 2 Cordoba
West Germany: Maier, Kaltz, Vogts, Russmann, Dietz, Bonhof, Holzenbein, Beer, Abramczik (1), Muller D (1), Rummenigge
Holland: Schrijvers, Wildschut (Nanninga), Brandts, Krol, Poortvliet, Jansen, Haan (1), Van de Kerkhof W, Rep, Van de Kerkhof R (1), Rensenbrink
Referee: Barreto (Uruguay)

21.6.78 Holland (0) 2, Italy (1) 1 BUENOS AIRES
Holland: Schrijvers (Jongbloed), Brandts (o. g.), Krol, Poortvliet, Jansen, Haan (1), Neeskens, Van de Kerkhof W, Rep (van Kraay), Van de Kerkhof R, Rensenbrink
Italy: Zoff, Scirea, Gentile, Cuccureddu, Cabrini, Tardelli, Zaccarelli, Benetti (Graziani), Causio (Sala C), Rossi, Bettega
Referee: Martinez (Spain)

21.6.78 Austria (0) 3, West Germany (1) 2 CORDOBA
Austria: Koncilia, Obermayer, Sara, Pezzey, Strasser, Hickersberger, Prohaska, Kreuz, Krieger, Schachner (Oberacher), Krankl (2)
West Germany: Maier, Kaltz, Vogts (o. g.), Russmann, Dietz, Bonhof, Holzenbein (1), Beer (Muller H), Abramczik, Muller D (Fischer), Rummenigge (1)
Referee: Klein (Israel)

	P	W	D	L	F	A	Pts
Holland	3	2	1	0	9	4	5
Italy	3	1	1	1	2	2	3
West Germany	3	0	2	1	4	5	2
Austria	3	1	0	2	4	8	2

GROUP B
14.6.78 Argentina (1) 2, Poland (0) 0 ROSARIO
Argentina: Fillol, Olguin, Galvan, Passarella, Ardiles, Gallego, Valencia (Villa), Houseman (Ortiz), Bertoni, Kempes (2)
Poland: Tomaszewski, Kasperczak, Szymanowski, Zmuda, Maculewicz, Masztaler (Mazur), Deyna, Nawalka, Boniek, Lato, Szarmach
Referee: Eriksson (Sweden)

14.6.78 Brazil (2) 3, Peru (0) 0 MENDOZA
Brazil: Leao, Amaral, Toninho, Oscar, Rodrigues Neto, Batista, Cerezo (Chicao), Dirceu (2), Gil (Zico (1 pen)), Mendonca, Roberto
Peru: Quiroga, Chumpitaz, Diaz (Navarro), Manzo, Duarte, Velasquez, Cueto, Cubillas, La Rosa, Munante, Oblitas (Rojas P)
Referee: Rainea (Rumania)

18.6.78 Argentina (0) 0, Brazil (0) 0 ROSARIO
Argentina: Fillol, Olguin, Galvan, Passarella, Tarantini, Ardiles (Villa), Gallego, Ortiz (Alonso), Kempes, Bertoni, Luque
Brazil: Leao, Amaral, Toninho, Oscar, Rodrigues Neto (Edinho), Chicao, Batista, Dirceu, Mendonca (Zico), Gil, Roberto
Referee: Palotai (Hungary)

18.6.78 Poland (0) 1, Peru (0) 0 MENDOZA
Poland: Kukla, Gorgon, Szymanowski, Zmuda, Maculewicz, Masztaler (Kasperczak), Nawalka, Deyna, Lato, Boniek (Lubanski), Szarmach (1)
Peru: Quiroga, Chumpitaz, Duarte, Manzo, Navarro, Cueto, Quezada, Cubillas, La Rosa (Sotil), Munante (Rojas P), Oblitas
Referee: Partridge (England)

21.6.78 Brazil (1) 3, Poland (1) 1 MENDOZA
Brazil: Leao, Amaral, Toninho, Oscar, Nelinho (1), Cerezo (Rivelino), Batista, Dirceu, Zico (Mendonca), Gil, Roberto (2)
Poland: Kukla, Gorgon, Szymanowski, Zmuda, Maculewicz, Kasperczak (Lubanski), Nawalka, Deyna, Boniek, Lato (1), Szarmach
Referee: Silvagno (Chile)

21.6.78 Argentina (2) 6, Peru (0) 0 ROSARIO
Argentina: Fillol, Olguin, Galvan, Passarella, Tarantini (1), Larrosa, Gallego (Oviedo), Kempes (2), Bertoni (Houseman), Luque (2), Ortiz
Peru: Quiroga, Chumpitaz, Duarte, Manzo, Rojas R, Cueto, Velasquez (Gorriti), Cubillas, Quezada, Munante, Oblitas
Referee: Wurtz (France)

	P	W	D	L	F	A	Pts
Argentina	3	2	1	0	8	0	5
Brazil	3	2	1	0	6	1	5
Poland	3	1	0	2	2	5	2
Peru	3	0	0	3	0	10	0

Match for third place
24.6.78 Brazil (0) 2, Italy (1) 1 BUENOS AIRES
Brazil: Leao, Amaral, Nelinho (1), Oscar, Rodrigues Neto, Batista, Cerezo (Rivelino), Dirceu (1), Gil (Reinaldo), Roberto, Mendonca
Italy: Zoff, Scirea, Gentile, Cuccureddu, Maldera, Cabrini, Antognoni (Sala C), Sala P, Causio (1), Rossi, Bettega
Referee: Klein (Israel)

FINAL
25.6.78 Argentina (1) 3, Holland (0) 1 (aet, 1 - 1 at 90 mins) BUENOS AIRES
Argentina: Fillol, Olguin, Galvan, Passarella, Tarantini, Ardiles (Larrosa), Gallego, Kempes (2), Bertoni (1), Luque, Ortiz (Houseman)
Holland: Jongbloed, Poortvliet, Krol, Brandts, Jansen (Suurbier), Neeskens, Haan, Van de Kerkhof W, Van de Kerkhof R, Rep (Nanninga (1)), Rensenbrink
Referee: Gonella (Italy)

French defender Marius Tresor (8)
scores for France in the semi-final
with West Germany. But it was the
Germans who won on penalties
after extra time. (COLORSPORT)

SPAIN

1982

Italy's deserved success was a personal triumph for manager Enzo Bearzot, whose diligent endeavours to unfetter his international players from the defensive strictures of their domestic football proved successful. They were technically sound, professional and clinical in their finishing. Yet few would have given much for their prospects in the opening group phase. Even by their own standards they were abysmally negative.

Italy failed to win a match, drawing all three of these section games — as did modest Cameroon, who retired undefeated from the contest — yet progressed to the next stage by virtue of their superior goalscoring: two goals to Cameroon's one!

England could also rightly claim to have been forced out of the tournament by the vagaries of its system. They, too, remained unbeaten. However, just how much of the euphoria which surrounded their performance was borne of Bryan Robson scoring after 27 seconds of the first game is debatable. For the Scots, in a difficult group, defensive errors proved costly when they had revealed imagination and skill in combating teams of differing quality in Brazil and the rather overrated USSR.

Northern Ireland were one of the few teams to play above themselves. They reached a peak against their dismally disappointing Spanish hosts, beating them 1-0 despite having to play for the greater part of the second half with ten men following the dismissal of Mal Donaghy. Their defence did not waver or allow itself to be drawn into rash tackles that would inevitably have led to cries for a Spanish penalty. Such fears were understandable, for two of Spain's three previous goals had come from the spot.

The minnows — Honduras, Algeria, Kuwait and New Zealand in particular — certainly enlivened arguably the most unenterprising World Cup of all time, despite the increase in goalscoring. Forwards were scarce, most teams packed the midfield. But whereas some like Brazil and France used the midfield as a springboard to attack from all angles, too many relied on the mistakes of the opposition to goad them on to the offensive.

Unfortunately the Eastern Europeans were dreadfully dull and predictable, especially Czechoslovakia and Yugoslavia. Poland operated only fitfully, despite their third-place rating. But El Salvador managed to shore up their leaky defence after conceding 10 goals to the Hungarians.

For the South Americans, Chile and Peru failed to excite. The holders Argentina were physically dealt with by Italy in the first half, then beaten fairly and squarely after the interval. Diego Maradona, the Argentine with the multi-million pound reputation, was an expensive disappointment.

Conversely, the admirable Brazilians for whom Zico, Falcao, Socrates and Junior gave memorable performances, were finally let down by a goalkeeping weakness and the absence of a recognised spearhead. Unquestionably the outstanding team both for the quality of their play and for entertainment value, Brazil found themselves a goal down to Italy on three occasions, which was once too much for them.

French midfielder Patrick Battiston is stretchered off after being knocked unconscious by West German goalkeeper Harald Schumacher during the semi-final in Seville. (COLORSPORT)

The Italian goalscoring hero was Paolo Rossi, the prodigal son, returning from a two-year suspension following a bribery scandal. He struggled to find his form in the opening games, but became transformed in the second round to finish as the tournament's leading goalscorer with six goals.

Italy's victory over Brazil was the second-most rewarding encounter. The top game was the pulsating end-to-end semi-final between West Germany and France. The French had displayed enterprise and charm with Marius Tresor, Michel Platini, Jean Tigana and Alain Giresse shining. All square after extra time at 3-3, the emotionally and physically drained players were called upon to settle matters by penalty kicks. It was the first time that this unsatisfactory system had been used to determine a match in the World Cup finals.

The Germans emerged 5-4 winners from the shoot-out. Two goals down in the match itself at one stage, they salvaged part of their reputation against the French, who were only slightly inferior to Brazil in terms of attractiveness. However, there were less savoury aspects of German play. Humiliated by one of the outsiders, Algeria, they gave a miserly display on other occasions. They succumbed to the feigning of injury, which oddly

Paolo Rossi, the prodigal son of Italian football, scores the third of his hat-trick against Brazil. Italy won 3-2 to ensure a place in the semi-finals.
(POPPERFOTO)

Claudio Gentile (6) and his captain Dino Zoff (1) celebrate Italy's victory.

enough helped them reach the 1966 final, and a blatant foul on French substitute Patrick Battiston by goalkeeper Harald Schumacher at a crucial moment in the semi-final disrupted the French rhythm yet went unpunished. The standard of refereeing was no higher than that of the overall play.

Just as disturbing was the furore caused by the apparent arrangement between the Germans and Austria which prevented Algeria from progressing into the second round, West Germany winning 1-0.

The Germans could claim that Karl-Heinz Rummenigge, easily their most gifted player, was handicapped throughout by injury. Indeed, he seemed to be either coming on or going off late to preserve his fitness. Yet the Italians were hit more seriously in the final, having to start without Giancarlo Antognoni and losing Francesco Graziani in the early stages.

Italy's eventual success came as something of an anti-climax; they were far superior to the Germans and won as easily as 3-1 suggested. Dino Zoff, at 40, crowned a masterly tournament by collecting the trophy as Italy's skipper.

Qualifying Tournament

108 entries

Europe (33): Albania, Austria, Belgium, Bulgaria, Cyprus, Czechoslovakia, Denmark, England, Finland, France, East Germany, West Germany, Greece, Holland, Hungary, Iceland, Republic of Ireland, Northern Ireland, Italy, Luxembourg, Malta, Norway, Poland, Portugal, Rumania, Scotland, Spain, Sweden, Switzerland, Turkey, USSR, Wales, Yugoslavia

South America (10): Argentina, Bolivia, Brazil, Chile, Colombia, Ecuador, Paraguay, Peru, Uruguay, Venezuela

Africa (28): Algeria, Cameroon, Central Africa, Egypt, Ethiopia, Gambia, Ghana, Guinea, Kenya, Lesotho, Liberia, Libya, Madagascar, Malawi, Morocco, Mozambique, Niger, Nigeria, Senegal, Sierra Leone, Somalia, Sudan, Tanzania, Togo, Tunisia, Uganda, Zaire, Zambia

Asia (18): Bahrain, China, Hong Kong, Indonesia, Iran, Iraq, Israel, Japan, North Korea, South Korea, Kuwait, Macao, Malaysia, Qatar, Saudi Arabia, Singapore, Syria, Thailand

Concacaf (15): Canada, Costa Rica, Cuba, Grenada, Guatemala, Guyana, Haiti, Honduras, Mexico, Netherlands Antilles, Panama, El Salvador, Surinam, Trinidad and Tobago, USA

Oceania (4): Australia, Fiji, New Zealand, Taiwan

The People's Republic of China was re-admitted to FIFA in 1979. Israel was added to the European zone after the draw for the qualifying competition had left them isolated once more. The continuing political uncertainty in El Salvador caused Costa Rica to refuse to play there, but it cost them the points.

However the expansion from 16 to 24 finalists produced a record entry of 108 from a FIFA membership of 147 nations. Increased final places had an encouraging effect on third world participation.

Final places in Spain were to be distributed as follows: Europe (13 + Spain), South America (3 + Argentina), Africa (2), Concacaf (2), Asia/Oceania (2).

Europe

Group 1 (West Germany, Austria, Bulgaria, Finland, Albania)

Finland v Bulgaria 0 - 2; Albania v Finland 2 - 0; Finland v Austria 0 - 2; Bulgaria v Albania 2 - 1; Austria v Albania 5 - 0; Bulgaria v West Germany 1 - 3; Albania v Austria 0 - 1; Albania v West Germany 0 - 2; West Germany v Austria 2 - 0; Bulgaria v Finland 4 - 0; Finland v West Germany 0 - 4; Austria v Bulgaria 2 - 0; Austria v Finland 5 - 1; Finland v Albania 2 - 1; West Germany v Finland 7 - 1; Austria v West Germany 1 - 3; Albania v Bulgaria 0 - 2; Bulgaria v Austria 0 - 0; West Germany v Albania 8 - 0; West Germany v Bulgaria 4 - 0

	P	W	D	L	F	A	Pts
West Germany	8	8	0	0	33	3	15
Austria	8	5	1	2	16	6	11
Bulgaria	8	4	1	3	11	10	9
Albania	8	1	0	7	4	22	2
Finland	8	1	0	7	4	27	2

West Germany and Austria qualified

Group 2 (Holland, France, Belgium, Rep of Ireland, Cyprus)

Cyprus v Rep of Ireland 2 - 3; Rep of Ireland v Holland 2 - 1; Cyprus v France 0 - 7; Rep of Ireland v Belgium 1 - 1; France v Rep of Ireland 2 - 0; Belgium v Holland 1 - 0; Rep of Ireland v Cyprus 6 - 0; Cyprus v Belgium 0 - 2; Belgium v Cyprus 3 - 2; Holland v Cyprus 3 - 0; Holland v France 1 - 0; Belgium v Rep of Ireland 1 - 0; France v Belgium 3 - 2; Cyprus v Holland 0 - 1; Holland v Rep of Ireland 2 - 2; Belgium v France 2 - 0; Holland v Belgium 3 - 0; Rep of Ireland v France 3 - 2; France v Holland 2 - 0; France v Cyprus 4 - 0

	P	W	D	L	F	A	Pts
Belgium	8	5	1	2	12	9	11
France	8	5	0	3	20	8	10
Rep of Ireland	8	4	2	2	17	11	10
Holland	8	4	1	3	11	7	9
Cyprus	8	0	0	8	4	29	0

Belgium and France qualified

Group 3 (Czechoslovakia, USSR, Wales, Turkey, Iceland)

Iceland v Wales 0 - 4; Iceland v USSR 1 - 2; Turkey v Iceland 1 - 3; Wales v Turkey 4 - 0; USSR v Iceland 5 - 0; Wales v Czechoslovakia 1 - 0; Czechoslovakia v Turkey 2 - 0; Turkey v Wales 0 - 1; Turkey v Czechoslovakia 0 - 3; Czechoslovakia v Iceland 6 - 1; Wales v USSR 0 - 0; Iceland v Turkey 2 - 0; Czechoslovakia v Wales 2 - 0; Iceland v Czechoslovakia 1 - 1; USSR v Turkey 4 - 0; Turkey v USSR 0 - 3; Wales v Iceland 2 - 2; USSR v Czechoslovakia 2 - 0; USSR v Wales 3 - 0; Czechoslovakia v USSR 1 - 1

	P	W	D	L	F	A	Pts
USSR	8	6	2	0	20	2	14
Czechoslovakia	8	4	2	2	15	6	10
Wales	8	4	2	2	12	7	10
Iceland	8	2	2	4	10	21	6
Turkey	8	0	0	8	1	22	0

USSR and Czechoslovakia qualified

Group 4 (England, Norway, Rumania, Switzerland, Hungary)

England v Norway 4 - 0; Norway v Rumania 1 - 1; Rumania v England 2 - 1; Switzerland v Norway 1 - 2; England v Switzerland 2 - 1; Switzerland v Hungary 2 - 2; England v Rumania 0 - 0; Hungary v Rumania 1 - 0; Norway v Hungary 1 - 2; Switzerland v England 2 - 1; Rumania v Norway 1 - 0; Hungary v England 1 - 3; Norway v Switzerland 1 - 1; Norway v England 2 - 1; Rumania v Hungary 0 - 0; Rumania v Switzerland 1 - 2; Hungary v Switzerland 3 - 0; Hungary v Norway 4 - 1; Switzerland v Rumania 0 - 0; England v Hungary 1 - 0

	P	W	D	L	F	A	Pts
Hungary	8	4	2	2	13	8	10
England	8	4	1	3	13	8	9
Rumania	8	2	4	2	5	5	8
Switzerland	8	2	3	3	9	12	7
Norway	8	2	2	4	8	15	6

Hungary and England qualified

Group 5 (Italy, Yugoslavia, Greece, Denmark, Luxembourg)

Luxembourg v Yugoslavia 0 - 5; Yugoslavia v Denmark 2 - 1; Luxembourg v Italy 0 - 2; Denmark v Greece 0 - 1; Italy v Denmark 2 - 0; Italy v Yugoslavia 2 - 0; Denmark v Luxembourg 4 - 0; Greece v Italy 0 - 2; Greece v Luxembourg 2 - 0; Luxembourg v Greece 0 - 2; Yugoslavia v Greece 5 - 1; Luxembourg v Denmark 1 - 2; Denmark v Italy 3 - 1; Denmark v Yugoslavia 1 - 2; Greece v Denmark 2 - 3; Yugoslavia v Italy 1 - 1; Italy v Greece 1 - 1; Yugoslavia v Luxembourg 5 - 0; Greece v Yugoslavia 1 - 2; Italy v Luxembourg 1 - 0

	P	W	D	L	F	A	Pts
Yugoslavia	8	6	1	1	22	7	13
Italy	8	5	2	1	12	5	12
Denmark	8	4	0	4	14	11	8
Greece	8	3	1	4	10	13	7
Luxembourg	8	0	0	8	1	23	0

Yugoslavia and Italy qualified

Group 6 (Scotland, Sweden, Portugal, Northern Ireland, Israel)

Israel v Northern Ireland 0 - 0; Sweden v Israel 1 - 1; Sweden v Scotland 0 - 1; Northern Ireland v Sweden 3 - 0; Scotland v Portugal 0 - 0; Israel v Sweden 1 - 1; Portugal v Northern Ireland 1 - 0; Portugal v Israel 3 - 0; Israel v Scotland 0 - 1; Scotland v Northern Ireland 1 - 1; Scotland v Israel 3 - 1; Northern Ireland v Portugal 1 - 0; Sweden v Northern Ireland 1 - 0; Sweden v Portugal 3 - 0; Scotland v Sweden 2 - 0; Portugal v Sweden 1 - 2; Northern Ireland v Scotland 0 - 0; Israel v Portugal 4 - 1; Northern Ireland v Israel 1 - 0; Portugal v Scotland 2 - 1

	P	W	D	L	F	A	Pts
Scotland	8	4	3	1	9	4	11
Northern Ireland	8	3	3	2	6	3	9
Sweden	8	3	2	3	7	8	8
Portugal	8	3	1	4	8	11	7
Israel	8	1	3	4	6	10	5

Scotland and Northern Ireland qualified

Group 7 (Poland, East Germany, Malta)

Malta v Poland 0 - 2; Malta v East Germany 1 - 2; Poland v East Germany 1 - 0; East Germany v Poland 2 - 3; East Germany v Malta 5 - 1; Poland v Malta 6 - 0

	P	W	D	L	F	A	Pts
Poland	4	4	0	0	12	2	8
East Germany	4	2	0	2	9	6	4
Malta	4	0	0	4	2	15	0

Poland qualified

South America

Group 1 (Bolivia, Brazil, Venezuela)
Venezuela v Brazil 0 - 1; Bolivia v Venezuela 3 - 0; Bolivia v Brazil 1 - 2; Venezuela v Bolivia 1 - 0; Brazil v Bolivia 3 - 1; Brazil v Venezuela 5 - 0

	P	W	D	L	F	A	Pts
Brazil	4	4	0	0	11	2	8
Bolivia	4	1	0	3	5	6	2
Venezuela	4	1	0	3	1	9	2

Brazil qualified

Group 2 (Colombia, Peru, Uruguay)
Colombia v Peru 1 - 1; Uruguay v Colombia 3 - 2; Peru v Colombia 2 - 0; Uruguay v Peru 1 - 2; Peru v Uruguay 0 - 0; Colombia v Uruguay 1 - 1

	P	W	D	L	F	A	Pts
Peru	4	2	2	0	5	2	6
Uruguay	4	1	2	1	5	5	4
Colombia	4	0	2	2	4	7	2

Peru qualified

Group 3 (Chile, Ecuador, Paraguay)
Ecuador v Paraguay 1 - 0; Ecuador v Chile 0 - 0; Paraguay v Ecuador 3 - 1; Paraguay v Chile 0 - 1; Chile v Ecuador 2 - 0; Chile v Paraguay 3 - 0

	P	W	D	L	F	A	Pts
Chile	4	3	1	0	6	0	7
Ecuador	4	1	1	2	2	5	3
Paraguay	4	1	0	3	3	6	2

Chile qualified

Africa

1st Round (Zimbabwe, Sudan, Liberia, Togo byes)
Libya v Gambia 2 - 1, 0 - 0; Ethiopia v Zambia 0 - 0, 0 - 4; Sierra Leone v Algeria 2 - 2, 1 - 3; Senegal v Morocco 0 - 1, 0 - 0; Guinea v Lesotho 3 - 1, 1 - 1; Tunisia v Nigeria 2 - 0, 0 - 2 (Nigeria won 4 - 3 on penalties); Cameroon v Malawi 3 - 0, 1 - 1; Kenya v Tanzania 3 - 1, 0 - 5; Zaire v Mozambique 5 - 2, 2 - 1; Niger v Somalia 0 - 0, 1 - 1; Egypt v Ghana (withdrew); Madagascar v Uganda (withdrew)

2nd Round
Cameroon v Zimbabwe 2 - 0, 0 - 1; Sudan v Algeria 1 - 1, 0 - 2; Madagascar v Zaire 1 - 1, 2 - 3; Morocco v Zambia 2 - 0, 0 - 2 (Morocco won 5 - 4 on penalties); Nigeria v Tanzania 1 - 1, 2 - 0; Liberia v Guinea 0 - 0, 0 - 1; Niger v Togo 0 - 1, 2 - 1; Egypt v Libya (withdrew)

3rd Round
Guinea v Nigeria 1 - 1, 0 - 1; Zaire v Cameroon 1 - 0, 1 - 6; Morocco v Egypt 1 - 0, 0 - 0; Algeria v Niger 4 - 0, 0 - 1

4th Round
Nigeria v Algeria 0 - 2, 1 - 2; Morocco v Cameroon 0 - 2, 1 - 2
Algeria and Cameroon qualified

Asia/Oceania

Group 1 (Australia, Fiji, Indonesia, New Zealand, Taiwan)
New Zealand v Australia 3 - 3; Fiji v New Zealand 0 - 4; Taiwan v New Zealand 0 - 0; Indonesia v New Zealand 0 - 2; Australia v New Zealand 0 - 2; Australia v Indonesia 2 - 0; New Zealand v Indonesia 5 - 0; New Zealand v Taiwan 2 - 0; Fiji v Indonesia 0 - 0; Fiji v Taiwan 2 - 1; Australia v Taiwan 3 - 2; Indonesia v Taiwan 1 - 0; Taiwan v Indonesia 2 - 0; Fiji v Australia 1 - 4; Taiwan v Fiji 0 - 0; Indonesia v Fiji 3 - 3; Australia v Fiji 10 - 0; New Zealand v Fiji 13 - 0; Indonesia v Australia 1 - 0; Taiwan v Australia 0 - 0

	P	W	D	L	F	A	Pts
New Zealand	8	6	2	0	31	3	14
Australia	3	4	2	2	22	9	10
Indonesia	8	2	2	4	5	14	6
Taiwan	8	1	3	4	5	8	5
Fiji	8	1	3	4	6	35	5

Group 2 (Saudi Arabia, Bahrain, Iraq, Qatar, Syria)
(In Saudi Arabia)
Qatar v Iraq 0 - 1; Syria v Bahrain 0 - 1; Iraq v Saudi Arabia 0 - 1; Qatar v Bahrain 3 - 0; Syria v Saudi Arabia 0 - 2; Iraq v Bahrain 2 - 0; Qatar v Syria 2 - 1; Bahrain v Saudi Arabia 0 - 1; Iraq v Syria 2 - 1; Qatar v Saudi Arabia 0 - 1

	P	W	D	L	F	A	Pts
Saudi Arabia	4	4	0	0	5	0	8
Iraq	4	3	0	1	5	2	6
Qatar	4	2	0	2	5	3	4
Bahrain	4	1	0	3	1	6	2
Syria	4	0	0	4	2	7	0

Group 3 (South Korea, Iran (withdrew), Kuwait, Malaysia, Thailand)
(In Kuwait)
Malaysia v South Korea 1 - 2; Kuwait v Thailand 6 - 0; South Korea v Thailand 5 - 1; Kuwait v Malaysia 4 - 0; Malaysia v Thailand 2 - 2; Kuwait v South Korea 2 - 0

	P	W	D	L	F	A	Pts
Kuwait	3	3	0	0	12	0	6
South Korea	3	2	0	1	7	4	4
Malaysia	3	0	1	2	3	8	1
Thailand	3	0	1	2	3	13	1

Group 4 (China, North Korea, Hong Kong, Japan, Macao, Singapore)
(In Hong Kong)

Preliminary Round
Hong Kong v China 0 - 1; North Korea v Macao 3 - 0; Singapore v Japan 0 - 1

Sub-Group 4A
China v Macao 3 - 0; China v Japan 1 - 0; Japan v Macao 3 - 0

Sub-Group 4B
Hong Kong v Singapore 1 - 1; Singapore v North Korea 0 - 1; Hong Kong v North Korea 2 - 2

Semi-finals
North Korea v Japan 1 - 0; China v Hong Kong 0 - 0 (China won 5 - 4 on penalties)

Final
China v North Korea 4 - 2

Final round
China v New Zealand 0 - 0; New Zealand v China 1 - 0; New Zealand v Kuwait 1 - 2; China v Kuwait 3 - 0; Saudi Arabia v Kuwait 0 - 1; Saudi Arabia v China 2 - 4; China v Saudi Arabia 2 - 0; New Zealand v Saudi Arabia 2 - 2; Kuwait v China 1 - 0; Kuwait v Saudi Arabia 2 - 0; Kuwait v New Zealand 2 - 2; Saudi Arabia v New Zealand 0 - 5

	P	W	D	L	F	A	Pts
Kuwait	6	4	1	1	8	6	9
New Zealand	6	2	3	1	11	6	7
China	6	3	1	2	9	4	7
Saudi Arabia	6	0	1	5	4	16	1

Play-off: New Zealand v China 2 - 1 (in Singapore)
Kuwait and New Zealand qualified

Concacaf

Group 1 (Caribbean)
Preliminary Round
Guyana v Grenada 5 - 2, 3 - 2

Sub-Group 1A (Cuba, Surinam, Guyana)
Cuba v Surinam 3 - 0; Surinam v Cuba 0 - 0; Guyana v Surinam 0 - 1; Surinam v Guyana 4 - 0; Cuba v Guyana 1 - 0; Guyana v Cuba 0 - 3

	P	W	D	L	F	A	Pts
Cuba	4	3	1	0	7	0	7
Surinam	4	2	1	1	5	3	5
Guyana	4	0	0	4	0	9	0

Sub-Group 1B (Haiti, Trinidad and Tobago, Netherlands Antilles)
Haiti v Trinidad and Tobago 2 - 0; Trinidad and Tobago v Haiti 1 - 0; Haiti v Netherlands Antilles 1 - 0; Trinidad and Tobago v Netherlands Antilles 0 - 0; Netherlands Antilles v Trinidad and Tobago 0 - 0; Netherlands Antilles v Haiti 1 - 1

	P	W	D	L	F	A	Pts
Haiti	4	2	1	1	4	2	5
T'dad & Tobago	4	1	2	1	1	2	4
N'lands Antilles	4	0	3	1	1	2	3

Group 2 (North) (Mexico, Canada, USA)

Canada v Mexico 1 - 1; USA v Canada 0 - 0; Canada v USA 2 - 1; Mexico
v USA 5 - 1; Mexico v Canada 1 - 1; USA v Mexico 2 - 1

	P	W	D	L	F	A	Pts
Canada	4	1	3	0	4	3	5
Mexico	4	1	2	1	8	5	4
USA	4	1	1	2	4	8	3

Group 3 (Central) (Costa Rica, El Salvador, Guatemala, Honduras, Panama)

Panama v Guatemala 0 - 2; Panama v Honduras 0 - 2; Panama v Costa Rica
1 - 1; Panama v El Salvador 1 - 3; Costa Rica v Honduras 2 - 3; El Salvador
v Panama 4 - 1; Guatemala v Costa Rica 0 - 0; Honduras v Guatemala 0 - 0;
El Salvador v Costa Rica (awarded 2 - 0 to El Salvador when Costa Rica
refused to play there for security reasons); Costa Rica v Panama 2 - 0;
Guatemala v El Salvador 0 - 0; Guatemala v Panama 5 - 0; Honduras
v Costa Rica 1 - 1; El Salvador v Honduras 2 - 1; Costa Rica v Guatemala
0 - 3; Honduras v El Salvador 2 - 0; Guatemala v Honduras 0 - 1; Costa Rica
v El Salvador 0 - 0; Honduras v Panama 5 - 0; El Salvador v Guatemala 1 - 0

	P	W	D	L	F	A	Pts
Honduras	8	5	2	1	15	5	12
El Salvador	8	5	2	1	12	5	12
Guatemala	8	3	3	2	10	2	9
Costa Rica	8	1	4	3	6	10	6
Panama	8	0	1	7	3	24	1

Final round

(In Honduras)

Mexico v Cuba 4 - 0; Canada v El Salvador 1 - 0; Honduras v Haiti 4 - 0;
Haiti v Canada 1 - 1; Mexico v El Salvador 0 - 1; Honduras v Cuba 2 - 0;
El Salvador v Cuba 0 - 0; Mexico v Haiti 1 - 1; Honduras v Canada 2 - 1;
Haiti v Cuba 0 - 2; Mexico v Canada 1 - 1; Honduras v El Salvador 0 - 0;
Haiti v El Salvador 0 - 1; Cuba v Canada 2 - 2; Honduras v Mexico 0 - 0

	P	W	D	L	F	A	Pts
Honduras	5	3	2	0	8	1	8
El Salvador	5	2	2	1	2	1	6
Mexico	5	1	3	1	6	3	5
Canada	5	1	3	1	6	6	5
Cuba	5	1	2	2	4	8	4
Haiti	5	0	2	3	2	9	2

Honduras and El Salvador Qualified

Final Tournament SPAIN
GROUP 1

14.6.82 Italy (0) 0, Poland (0) 0 VIGO
Italy: Zoff, Gentile, Scirea, Collovati, Cabrini, Marini, Antognoni, Tardelli,
Conti, Rossi, Graziani
Poland: Mlynarczyk, Jalocha, Majewski, Zmuda, Janas, Buncol, Lato,
Boniek, Matysik, Iwan (Kusto), Smolarek
Referee: Vautrot (France)

15.6.82 Peru (0) 0, Cameroon (0) 0 LA CORUNA
Peru: Quiroga, Duarte, Salguero, Diaz, Olaechea, Uribe, Cueto, Velasquez,
Leguia (La Rosa), Cubillas (Barbadillo), Oblitas
Cameroon: N'Kono, M'Bom, Aoudou, Onana, Kaham, Abega, M'Bida,
Kunde, Milla (Tokoto), N'Djeya, N'Guea (Bakohen)
Referee: Wohrer (Austria)

18.6.82 Italy (1) 1, Peru (0) 1 VIGO
Italy: Zoff, Cabrini, Collovati, Gentile, Scirea, Antognoni, Marini, Tardelli,
Conti, Graziani, Rossi (Causio)
Peru: Quiroga, Duarte, Diaz (1), Salguero, Olaechea, Cueto, Velasquez (La
Rosa), Cubillas, Uribe, Oblitas, Barbadillo (Leguia)
Referee: Eschweiler (West Germany)

19.6.82 Poland (0) 0, Cameroon (0) 0 LA CORUNA
Poland: Mlynarczyk, Majewski, Janas, Zmuda, Jalocha, Lato, Buncol,
Boniek, Iwan (Szarmach), Palasz (Kusto), Smolarek
Cameroon: N'Kono, Kaham, Onana, N'Djeya, M'Bom, Aoudou, Abega,
Kunde, M'Bida, Milla, N'Guea (Tokoto)
Referee: Ponnet (Belgium)

22.6.82 Poland (0) 5, Peru (0) 1 LA CORUNA
Poland: Mlynarczyk, Majewski, Janas, Zmuda, Jalocha (Dziuba), Buncol
(1), Matysik, Kupcewiez, Lato (1), Boniek (1), Smolarek (1 (Ciolek [1])
Peru: Quiroga, Duarte, Diaz, Salguero, Olaechea, Cubillas (Uribe),
Velasquez, Cueto, Leguia, La Rosa (1), Oblitas (Barbadillo)
Referee: Rubio (Mexico)

23.6.82 Italy (0) 1, Cameroon (0) 1 VIGO
Italy: Zoff, Gentile, Collovati, Scirea, Cabrini, Oriali, Tardelli, Antognoni,
Conti, Rossi, Graziani (1)
Cameroon: N'Kono, Kaham, N'Djeya, Onana, M'Bom, Aoudou, Kunde,
M'Bida (1), Abega, Milla, Tokoto
Referee: Dotschev (Bulgaria)

	P	W	D	L	F	A	Pts
Poland	3	1	2	0	5	1	4
Italy	3	0	3	0	2	2	3
Cameroon	3	0	3	0	1	1	3
Peru	3	0	2	1	2	6	2

GROUP 2

16.6.82 Algeria (0) 2, West Germany (0) 1 GIJON
Algeria: Cerbah, Guendouz, Kourichi, Merzekane, Mansouri, Belloumi (1),
Dhaleb, Fergani, Madjer (1) (Larbes), Zidane (Bensaoula), Assad
West Germany: Schumacher, Kaltz, Stielike, Forster K H , Briegel, Breitner,
Magath (Fischer), Dremmler, Rummenigge (1), Hrubesch, Littbarski
Referee: Labo (Peru)

17.6.82 Austria (1) 1, Chile (0) 0 OVIEDO
Austria: Koncilia, Krauss, Obermayer, Pezzey, Degeorgi (Baumeister),
Hattenberger, Hintermaier, Weber (Jurtin), Prohaska, Krankl, Schachner
(1)
Chile: Osben, Garrido, Figueroa, Valenzuela, Bigorra, Bonvallet, Dubo,
Neira (Manuel Rojas), Moscoaso (Gamboa), Yanez, Caszely
Referee: Cardellino (Uruguay)

20.6.82 West Germany (1) 4, Chile (0) 1 GIJON
West Germany: Schumacher, Kaltz, Stielike, Forster K H , Briegel, Dremmler,
Breitner (Matthaus), Magath, Littbarski (Reinders [1]), Hrubesch,
Rummenigge (3)
Chile: Osben, Garrido, Figueroa, Valenzuela, Bigorra, Dubo, Bonvallet,
Soto (Letelier), Moscoso (1), Yanez, Gamboa (Neira)
Referee: Galler (Switzerland)

21.6.82 Algeria (0) 0, Austria (0) 2 OVIEDO
Algeria: Cerbah, Guendouz, Kourichi, Merzekane, Mansouri, Belloumi
(Bensaoula), Dhaleb (Tiemcani), Fergani, Madjer, Zidane, Assad
Austria: Koncilia, Krauss, Obermayer, Degeorgi, Pezzey, Hattenberger,
Hintermaier, Baumeister (Welzl), Prohaska (Weber), Krankl (1),
Schachner (1)
Referee: Boscovic (Austria)

24.6.82 Algeria (3) 3, Chile (0) 2 OVIEDO
Algeria: Cerbah, Guendouz, Marzekane, Guendouz, Larbes, Mansouri
(Dhaleb), Fergani, Assad (2), Bensaoula (1), Bourebbou (Yahi), Madjer
Chile: Osben, Galindo, Valenzuela, Figueroa, Bigorra, Bonvallet (Soto),
Dubo, Neira (1 pen), Yanez, Caszely (Letelier [1]), Moscoso
Referee: Mendez (Guatemala)

25.6.82 West Germany (1) 1, Austria (0) 0 GIJON
West Germany: Schumacher, Kaltz, Stielike, Forster K H , Briegel, Dremmler,
Breitner, Magath, Littbarski, Hrubesch (1) (Fischer), Rummenigge
(Matthaus)
Austria: Koncilia, Krauss, Pezzey, Obermayer, Degeorgi, Hattenberger,
Prohaska, Hintermaier, Weber, Schachner, Krankl
Referee: Valentine (Scotland)

	P	W	D	L	F	A	Pts
West Germany	3	2	0	1	6	3	4
Austria	3	2	0	1	3	1	4
Algeria	3	2	0	1	5	5	4
Chile	3	0	0	3	3	8	0

GROUP 3

13.6.82 Argentina (0) 0, Belgium (0) 1 BARCELONA
Argentina: Fillol, Olguin, Galvan, Passarella, Tarantini, Ardiles, Gallego, Maradona, Bertoni, Diaz (Valdano), Kempes
Belgium: Pfaff, Gerets, Millechamps L, de Schrijver, Baecke, Coeck, Vercauteren, Vandersmissen, Czerniatynski, Van den Bergh (1), Ceulemans
Referee: Christov (Czechoslovakia)

15.6.82 Hungary (3) 10, El Salvador (0) 1 ELCHE
Hungary: Meszaros, Martos, Balint, Toth (1), Garaba, Muller (Szentes [1]), Nyilasi (2), Sallai, Fazekas (2),Torocsik (Kiss [3]), Poloskei (1)
El Salvador: Mora, Castillo, Jovel, Rodriguez, Recinos, Rugamas (Zapata [1]), Ventura, Huezo, Hernandez F, Gonzalez, Rivas
Referee: Al-Doy (Bahrain)

18.6.82 Argentina (2) 4, Hungary (0) 1 ALICANTE
Argentina: Fillol, Olguin, Galvan, Passarella, Tarantini (Barbas), Ardiles (1), Gallego, Maradona (2), Bertoni (1), Valdano (Calderon), Kempes
Hungary: Meszaros, Martos (Fazekas),Balint, Toth, Varga, Garaba, Nyilasi, Sallai, Rab, Kiss (Szentes), Poloskei (1)
Referee: Lacarne (Algeria)

19.6.82 Belgium (1) 1, El Salvador (0) 0 ELCHE
Belgium: Pfaff, Gerets, Meeuws, Baecke, Millecamps L, Vandersmissen (Van der Elst), Coeck (1), Vercauteren, Ceulemans (Van Moer), Van den Bergh, Czerniatynski
El Salvador: Mora, Osorto (Diaz), Jovel, Rodriguez, Recinos, Fagoaga, Ventura, Huezo, Zapata, Gonzalez, Rivas
Referee: Moffat (Northern Ireland)

22.6.82 Belgium (0) 1, Hungary (1) 1 ELCHE
Belgium: Pfaff, Gerets (Plessers), Millecamps L, Meeuws, Baecke, Coeck, Vercauteren, Vandersmissen (Van Moer), Czerniatynski (1), Van den Bergh, Ceulemans
Hungary: Meszaros, Martos, Kerekes (Sallai), Garaba, Varga (1), Nyilasi, Muller, Fazekas, Torocsik, Kiss (Csongradi), Poloskei
Referee: White (England)

23.6.82 Argentina (1) 2, El Salvador (0) 0 ALICANTE
Argentina: Fillol, Olguin, Galvan, Passarella (1 pen), Tarantini, Ardiles, Gallego, Kempes, Bertoni (1) (Diaz), Maradona, Calderon (Santamaria)
El Salvador: Mora, Osorto (Arevalo), Jovel, Rodriguez, Rugamas, Fagoaga, Ventura (Alfaro), Huezo, Zapata, Gonzalez, Rivas
Referee: Barrancos (Bolivia)

	P	W	D	L	F	A	Pts
Belgium	3	2	1	0	3	1	5
Argentina	3	2	0	1	6	2	4
Hungary	3	1	1	1	12	6	3
El Salvador	3	0	0	3	1	13	0

GROUP 4

16.6.82 England (1) 3, France (1) 1 BILBAO
England: Shilton, Mills, Sansom (Neal), Thompson, Butcher, Robson (2), Coppell, Wilkins, Mariner (1), Francis, Rix
France: Ettori, Battiston, Bossis, Tresor, Lopez, Larios (Tigana), Girard, Giresse, Rocheteau (Six), Platini, Soler (1)
Referee: Garrido (Portugal)

17.6.82 Czechoslovakia (1) 1, Kuwait (0) 1 VALLADOLID
Czechoslovakia: Hruska, Barmos, Jurkemik, Fiala, Kukucka, Panenka (1 pen), Berger, Kriz (Bicovsky), Janecka (Petrzela), Nehoda, Vizek
Kuwait: Al Tarabulsi, Naeem Saed, Mayoof, Mahboub, Waleed Jasem, Al Buloushi, Saeed Al Houti, Karam (Fathi Kameel), Al Dakheel (1), Jasem Yacoub, Al Anbari
Referee: Dwomoha (Ghana)

20.6.82 England (0) 2, Czechoslovakia (0) 0 BILBAO
England: Shilton, Mills, Thompson, Butcher, Sansom, Coppell, Robson (Hoddle), Wilkins, Francis (1), Mariner (1), Rix
Czechoslovakia: Seman (Stromsik), Barmos, Fiala, Radimec, Vojacek, Jurkemik, Chaloupka, Vizek, Berger, Janecka (Masny), Nehodaf
Referee: Corver (Holland)

21.6.82 France (2) 4, Kuwait (0) 1 VALLADOLID
France: Ettori, Amoros, Tresor, Janvion, Bossis (1), Giresse, Platini (1) (Girard), Genghini (1), Soler, Lacombe, Six (1)
Kuwait: Al Tarabulsi, Naeem Saed, Mayoof, Mahboub, Waleed Jasem (Al Shemmari, Al Buloushi (1), Saed Al Houti, Karam (Fathi Kameel), Al Dakheel, Jasem Yacoub, Al Ambari
Referee: Stupar (USSR)

24.6.82 France (0) 1, Czechoslovakia (0) 1 VALLADOLID
France: Ettori, Amoros, Tresor, Janvion, Bossis, Giresse, Platini, Genghini, Soler (Girard), Lacombe (Couriol), Six (1)
Czechoslovakia: Stromsik, Barmos, Fiala, Stambacher, Vojacek, Jurkemik, Kriz (Masny), Bicovsky, Vizek, Janecka (Panenka [1 pen]), Nehoda
Referee: Casarin (Italy)

25.6.82 England (1) 1, Kuwait (0) 0 BILBAO
England: Shilton, Neal, Thompson, Foster, Mills, Coppell, Hoddle, Wilkins, Rix, Mariner, Francis (1)
Kuwait: Al Tarabulsi, Naeem Saed, Mahboub, Mayoof, Waleed Jasem (Al Shemmari), Saed Al Houti, Al Buloushi, Al Suwayed, Fathi Kameel, Al Dakheel, Al Anbari
Referee: Aristizabal (Colombia)

	P	W	D	L	F	A	Pts
England	3	3	0	0	6	1	6
France	3	1	1	1	6	5	3
Czechoslovakia	3	0	2	1	2	4	2
Kuwait	3	0	1	2	2	6	1

GROUP 5

16.6.82 Spain (0) 1, Honduras (1) 1 VALENCIA
Spain: Arconada, Gordillo, Camacho, Alonso, Alesanco, Tendillo (Saura), Joaquin (Sanchez), Satrustegui, Zamora, Lopez Ufarte (1 pen)
Honduras: Arzu, Gutierrez, Costly, Villegas, Bulnes, Zelaya (1), Gilberto, Maradiaga, Norales (Caballero), Betancourt, Figueroa
Referee: Ithurralde (Argentina)

17.6.82 Northern Ireland (0) 0, Yugoslavia (0) 0 ZARAGOZA
Northern Ireland: Jennings, Nicholl J, Nicholl C, McClelland, Donaghy, McIlroy, O'Neill M, McCreery, Armstrong, Hamilton, Whiteside
Yugoslavia: Pantelic, Gudelj, Zajec, Stojkovic, Petrovic, Sljivo, Zlatko Vujovic, Susic, Jovanovic, Hrstic, Surjak
Referee: Fredriksson (Sweden)

20.6.82 Spain (1) 2, Yugoslavia (1) 1 VALENCIA
Spain: Arconada, Camacho, Tendillo, Alesanco, Gordillo, Alonso, Sanchez (Saura [1]), Zamora, Juanito (1 pen), Satrustegui (Quini), Lopez Ufarte
Yugoslavia: Pantelic, Krmpotic, Zajec, Stojkovic, Jovanovic (Halilhodzic), Gudelj (1), Petrovic, Sljivo, Zlatko Vujovic (Sestic), Surjak, Susic
Referee: Lund-Sorensen (Denmark)

21.6.82 Honduras (0) 1, Northern Ireland (1) 1 ZARAGOZA
Honduras: Arzu, Gutierrez, Villegas, Cruz J L, Costly, Maradiaga, Gilberto, Zelaya, Norales (Laing [1]), Betancourt, Figueroa
Northern Ireland: Jennings, Nicholl J, Nicholl C, McClelland, Donaghy, O'Neill M (Healy), McCreery, McIlroy, Whiteside (Brotherston), Armstrong (1), Hamilton
Referee: Chan Tam Sun (Hong Kong)

24.6.82 Honduras (0) 0, Yugoslavia (0) 1 ZARAGOZA
Honduras: Arzu, Droumond, Villegas, Costly, Bulnes, Zelaya, Gilberto, Maradiaga, Cruz J (Laing), Betancourt, Figueroa
Yugoslavia: Pantelic, Krmpotic, Stojkovic, Zajec, Jovanovic (Halilhodzic), Sljivo, Gudelj, Surjak, Zlatko Vujovic (Sestic), Susic, Petrovic (1 pen)
Referee: Castro (Chile)

25.6.82 Northern Ireland (0) 1, Spain (0) 0 VALENCIA
Northern Ireland: Jennings, Nicholl J, Nicholl C, McClelland, Donaghy, O'Neill M, McCreery, McIlroy (Cassidy), Armstrong (1), Hamilton, Whiteside (Nelson)
Spain: Arconada, Camacho, Tendillo, Alesanco, Gordillo, Sanchez, Alonso, Saura, Juanito, Satrustegui (Quini), Lopez Ufarte (Gallego)
Referee: Ortiz (Paraguay)

	P	W	D	L	F	A	Pts
Northern Ireland	3	1	2	0	2	1	4
Spain	3	1	1	1	3	3	3
Yugoslavia	3	1	1	1	2	2	3
Honduras	3	0	2	1	2	3	2

GROUP 6

14.6.82 Brazil (0) 2, USSR (1) 1 SEVILLE
Brazil: Valdir Peres, Leandro, Oscar, Luizinho, Junior, Socrates (1), Serginho, Zico, Eder (1), Falcao, Dirceu (Paulo Isidoro)
USSR: Dasayev, Sulakvelidze, Chivadze, Baltacha, Demyanenko, Shengelia (Andreyev), Bessonov, Gavrilov (Susloparov), Blokhin, Bal (1), Daraselia
Referee: Lamo Castillo (Spain)

15.6.82 Scotland (3) 5, New Zealand (0) 2 MALAGA
Scotland: Rough, McGrain, Gray F, Hansen, Evans, Souness, Strachan (Narey), Dalglish (1), Wark (2), Brazil (Archibald [1]), Robertson (1)
New Zealand: Van Hattum, Elrick, Hill, Malcolmson (Cole), Almond (Herbert), Sumner (1), Mackay, Cresswell, Boath, Rufer W, Wooddin (1)
Referee: El Ghoul (Libya)

18.6.82 Brazil (1) 4, Scotland (1) 1 SEVILLE
Brazil: Valdir Peres, Leandro, Oscar (1), Luizinho, Junior, Cerezo, Falcao (1), Socrates, Serginho (Paulo Isidoro), Zico (1), Eder (1)
Scotland: Rough, Narey (1), Gray F, Souness, Hansen, Miller, Strachan (Dalglish), Hartford (McLeish), Archibald, Wark, Robertson
Referee: Siles (Costa Rica)

19.6.82 USSR (1) 3, New Zealand (0) 0 MALAGA
USSR: Dasayev, Sulakvelidze, Chivadze, Baltacha (1), Demyanenko, Shengelia, Bessonov, Bal, Daraselia (Oganesian), Gavrilov (1) (Rodionov), Blokhin (1)
New Zealand: Van Hattum, Dods, Herbert, Elrick, Boath, Cole, Sumner, Mackay, Cresswell, Rufer W, Wooddin
Referee: El Ghoul (Libya)

22.6.82 Scotland (1) 2, USSR (0) 2 MALAGA
Scotland: Rough, Narey, Gray F, Souness (1), Hansen, Miller, Strachan (McGrain), Archibald, Jordan (1) (Brazil), Wark, Robertson
USSR: Dasayev, Sulakvelidze, Chivadze (1), Baltacha, Demyanenko, Borovsky, Shengelia (1) (Andreyev), Bessonov, Gavrilov, Bal, Blokhin
Referee: Rainea (Rumania)

23.6.82 Brazil (2) 4, New Zealand (0) 0 SEVILLE
Brazil: Valdir Peres, Leandro, Oscar (Edinho), Luizinho, Junior, Cerezo, Socrates, Zico (2), Falcao (1), Serginho (1) (Paulo Isidoro), Eder
New Zealand: Van Hattum, Dods, Herbert, Elrick, Boath, Sumner, Mackay, Cresswell (Turner B), Almond, Rufer W (Cole), Wooddin
Referee: Matovinovic (Yugoslavia)

	P	W	D	L	F	A	Pts
Brazil	3	3	0	0	10	2	6
USSR	3	1	1	1	6	4	3
Scotland	3	1	1	1	8	8	3
New Zealand	3	0	0	3	2	12	0

Second round
GROUP A

28.6.82 Poland (2) 3, Belgium (0) 0 BARCELONA
Poland: Mlynarczyk, Dziuba, Zmuda, Janas, Majewski, Kupcewicz (Ciolek), Buncol, Matysik, Lato, Boniek (3), Smolarek
Belgium: Custers, Renquin, Millecamps L, Meeuws, Plessers (Baecke), Van Moer (Van der Elst), Coeck, Vercauteren, Czerniatynski, Van den Bergh, Ceulemans
Referee: Siles (Costa Rica)

1.7.82 Belgium (0) 0, USSR (0) 1 BARCELONA
Belgium: Munaron, Renquin, Millecamps L, Meeuws, de Schrijver (Millecamps M), Verheyen, Coeck, Vercauteren, Vandersmissen (Czerniatynski), Van den Bergh, Ceulemans
USSR: Dasayev, Borovsky, Chivadze, Baltacha, Demyanenko, Bal (Daraselia), Oganesian (1), Bessonov, Shengelia (Rodionov), Gavrilov, Blokhin
Referee: Vautrot (France)

4.7.82 Poland (0) 0, USSR (0) 0 BARCELONA
Poland: Mlynarczyk, Dziuba, Zmuda, Janas, Majewski, Kupcewicz (Ciolek), Buncol, Matysik, Lato, Boniek, Smolarek
USSR: Dasayev, Sulakvelidze, Chivadze, Baltacha, Demyanenko, Borovsky, Oganesian, Bessonov, Shengelia (Andreyev), Gavrilov (Daraselia), Blokhin
Referee: Valentine (Scotland)

	P	W	D	L	F	A	Pts
Poland	2	1	1	0	3	0	3
USSR	2	1	1	0	1	0	3
Belgium	2	0	0	2	0	4	0

GROUP B

29.6.82 West Germany (0) 0, England (0) 0 MADRID
West Germany: Schumacher, Kaltz, Forster K H, Stielike, Forster B, Muller (Fischer), Breitner, Dremmler, Briegel, Rummenigge, Reinders (Littbarski)
England: Shilton, Mills, Thompson, Butcher, Sansom, Coppell, Wilkins, Robson, Rix, Francis (Woodcock), Mariner
Referee: Coelho (Brazil)

2.7.82 Spain (0) 1, West Germany (0) 2 MADRID
Spain: Arconada, Camacho, Gordillo, Alonso, Tendillo, Alesanco, Juanito (Lopez Ufarte), Zamora (1), Urquiaga, Santillana, Quini (Sanchez)
West Germany: Schumacher, Kaltz, Forster K H, Stielike, Forster B, Breitner, Briegel, Dremmler, Littbarski (1), Fischer (1), Rummenigge (Reinders)
Referee: Casarin (Italy)

5.7.82 England (0) 0, Spain (0) 0 MADRID
England: Shilton, Mills, Thompson, Butcher, Sansom, Wilkins, Robson, Rix (Brooking), Francis, Mariner, Woodcock (Keegan)
Spain: Arconada, Camacho, Gordillo, Alonso, Tendillo (Macedo), Alesanco, Satrustegui, Zamora, Urquiaga, Saura (Uralde), Santillana
Referee: Ponnet (Belgium)

	P	W	D	L	F	A	Pts
West Germany	2	1	1	0	2	1	3
England	2	0	2	0	0	0	2
Spain	2	0	1	1	1	2	1

GROUP C

29.6.82 Italy (0) 2, Argentina (0) 1 BARCELONA
Italy: Zoff, Gentile, Collovati, Scirea, Cabrini (1), Oriali (Marini), Tardelli (1), Antognoni, Conti, Rossi (Altobelli), Graziani
Argentina: Fillol, Olguin, Passarella (1), Galvan, Tarantini, Ardiles, Gallego, Maradona, Bertoni, Diaz (Calderon), Kempes (Valencia)
Referee: Rainea (Rumania)

2.7.82 Brazil (1) 3, Argentina (0) 1 BARCELONA
Brazil: Valdir Peres, Leandro (Edevaldo), Oscar, Luizinho, Junior (1), Cerezo, Falcao, Socrates, Serginho (1), Zico (1) (Batista), Eder
Argentina: Fillol, Olguin, Barbas, Passarella, Tarantini, Ardiles, Galvan, Maradona, Bertoni (Santamaria), Calderon, Kempes (Diaz [1])
Referee: Rubio (Mexico)

5.7.82 Italy (2) 3, Brazil (1) 2 BARCELONA
Italy: Zoff, Collovati (Bergomi), Gentile, Scirea, Cabrini, Oriali, Antognoni, Tardelli (Marini), Conti, Graziani, Rossi (3)
Brazil: Valdir Peres, Leandro, Oscar, Luizinho, Junior, Cerezo, Falcao (1), Socrates (1), Zico, Serginho (Paulo Isidoro), Eder
Referee: Klein (Israel)

	P	W	D	L	F	A	Pts
Italy	2	2	0	0	5	3	4
Brazil	2	1	0	1	5	4	2
Argentina	2	0	0	2	2	5	0

GROUP D

28.6.82 France (1) 1, Austria (0) 0 MADRID
France: Ettori, Battiston, Janvion, Tresor, Bossis, Giresse, Genghini (1) (Girard), Tigana, Soler, Lacombe (Rocheteau), Six
Austria: Koncilia, Krauss, Obermayer, Pezzey, Degeorgi (Baumeister), Hattenberger, Hintermaier, Jara (Welzl), Schachner, Prohaska, Krankl
Referee: Palotai (Hungary)

1.7.82 Northern Ireland (1) 2, Austria (0) 2 MADRID
Northern Ireland: Platt, Nicholl J, Nicholl C, McClelland, Nelson, McCreery, O'Neill M, McIlroy, Armstrong, Hamilton (2), Whiteside (Brotherston)
Austria: Koncilia, Krauss, Obermayer, Pezzey (1), Schachner, Prohaska, Pichler, Hagmayr (Welzl), Baumeister, Pregesbauer (Hintermaier [1]), Jurtin
Referee: Prokop (East Germany)

84

4.7.82 Northern Ireland (0) 1, France (1) 4 MADRID
Northern Ireland: Jennings, Nicholl J, Nicholl C, McClelland, Donaghy, McIlroy, McCreery (O'Neill J), O'Neill M, Armstrong (1), Hamilton, Whiteside
France: Ettori, Amoros, Janvion, Tresor, Bossis, Giresse (2), Genghini, Tigana, Platini, Soler (Six), Rocheteau (2) (Couriol)
Referee: Jarguz (Poland)

	P	W	D	L	F	A	Pts
France	2	2	0	0	5	1	4
Austria	2	0	1	1	2	3	1
Northern Ireland	2	0	1	1	3	6	1

SEMI FINALS
8.7.82 Poland (0) 0, Italy (1) 2 BARCELONA
Poland: Mlynarczyk, Dziuba, Zmuda, Janas, Majewski, Kupcewicz, Buncol, Matysik, Lato, Ciolek (Palasz), Smolarek (Kusto)
Italy: Zoff, Bergomi, Collovati, Scirea, Cabrini, Oriali, Antognoni (Marini), Tardelli, Conti, Rossi (2), Graziani (Altobelli)
Referee: Cardellino (Uruguay)

8.7.82 West Germany (1) 3, France (1) 3 (aet, 1-1 at 90 mins, West Germany won 5 - 4 on penalties)   **SEVILLE**
West Germany: Schumacher, Kaltz, Forster K H, Stielike, Forster B, Briegel (Rummenigge [1]), Dremmler, Breitner, Littbarski (1), Fischer (1), Magath (Hrubesch)
France: Ettori, Amoros, Janvion, Tresor (1), Bossis, Genghini (Battiston) (Lopez), Platini (1 pen), Giresse (1), Rocheteau, Six, Tigana
Referee: Corver (Holland)

Match for third place
10.7.82 France (1) 2, Poland (2) 3 ALICANTE
France: Castaneda, Amoros, Mahut, Tresor, Janvion (Lopez), Tigana (Six), Girard (1), Larios, Couriol (1), Soler, Bellone
Poland: Mlynarczyk, Dziuba, Janas, Zmuda, Majewski (1), Matysik (Wojcicki), Kupcewicz (1), Buncol, Lato, Szarmach (1), Boniek
Referee: Garrido (Portugal)

FINAL
11.7.82 West Germany (0) 1, Italy (0) 3 MADRID
West Germany: Schumacher, Kaltz, Forster K H, Stielike, Forster B, Breitner (1), Dremmler (Hrubesch), Littbarski, Briegel, Fischer, Rummenigge (Muller)
Italy: Zoff, Bergomi, Cabrini, Collovati, Scirea, Gentile, Oriali, Tardelli (1), Conti, Graziani (Altobelli [1]) (Causio), Rossi (1)
Referee: Arnaldo Coelho (Brazil)

MEXICO
1986

To the English mind, the lasting memory of Mexico was of Diego Maradona. Alas, it was not as the genuinely outstanding individual of the tournament, but simply because he propelled the ball with his hand for Argentina's opening goal against England in the quarter-finals. Years afterwards, the infamy of this action was still being ridiculed in two separate advertisements on commercial television.

Commercial considerations had dominated the competition itself. To satisfy TV scheduling, matches were played in the hottest part of the day, with no time added on for stoppages. In one venue, Monterrey, in appalling conditions of heat and humidity, only nine goals were scored in the six group games played there.

Despite these restraints, the generally low goalscoring and the unsatisfactory matter of deciding games on penalty kicks, it was widely regarded as the best World Cup since the finals were previously held in Mexico 16 years earlier. Though France, Brazil, Denmark and the USSR produced floods of attacking fluency, they were eventually left flawed. Ultimately it was the Maradona-inspired aristry of Argentina which grappled with the doggedly determined West Germans.

Arguably the finest match was the quarter-final between France and Brazil; the best of the old and new worlds, but both linked with that inimitable Latin style of skill interwoven with improvisation. It was a travesty that it had to be decided on penalties.

Denmark took maximum points from their matches in Group E, including this 2 - 0 victory over West Germany. Danish striker Preben Elkjaer tussles for possession with Karl-Heinz Forster (white shirt).

(Above) Luis Brown (extreme right) heads Argentina into the lead in the 1986 World Cup final. Brown gallantly played out the final stages of the game despite suffering a dislocated shoulder.

Gary Lineker (10), about to complete a memorable hat-trick for England against Poland in Monterrey. A 3-0 win saw England through to the second round.

French skipper Platini in action against Canada. Having played some of the best football of the tournament, France again went out at the semi-final stage.

It had needed two weeks and 36 matches to eliminate just eight of the 24 finalists. England began disastrously, their 4-3-3 formation fortunately giving way, when injury and suspension hit Bryan Robson and Ray Wilkins respectively, to a 4-4-2 system which shot Gary Lineker to prominence with a hat-trick against Poland. Lineker snapped up two more goals against the ponderous Paraguayans and one against Argentina; these six goals made him the competition's leading marksman.

There was no doubting Argentina's superiority in the match against England. But that short-arm jab from Maradona let manager Bobby Robson off the hook by handing him the perfect excuse in defeat. Ironically, Maradona's second goal was arguably one of the finest ever seen in any match. Collecting the ball ten yards inside his own half on the right, he jinked his way past two opponents and accelerated before turning inside a third and rounding a fourth. His *coup de grace* was to dummy goalkeeper Peter Shilton before slipping the ball nonchalantly into the net. After that, Robson threw caution to the wind employing two wingers, but it was too little, too late.

France made light of the blistering heat and stamina-sapping altitude in Mexico City to dispose of the holders Italy with a display of flair and finesse which was reminiscent of their peak two years previously when they became European champions.

Though the USSR had given an early indication of the threat they posed, demoralising the Hungarians in a 6-0 win, their fast, attacking ideas foundered against the counter-punching Belgians. This 4-3 defeat echoed Italy's similar victory over the Germans in 1970.

Brazil, with question marks over their ageing stars like Socrates, Falcao and Junior plus the injured Zico, had a fortunate escape against Spain in their opening group game. Neither Australian referee Christopher Bambridge nor American linesman David Socha were positioned to notice that a drive by Michel which beat Carlos, the Brazilian goalkeeper, clearly bounced down off the crossbar over the line. Moreover there was a suspicion of offside when Socrates headed the only goal of the game.

The talented but indisciplined Uruguayans had had players sent off against Denmark and Scotland. Under the threat of expulsion from the competition they were subdued against Argentina, but restricted them to a 1-0 scoreline. As for the driving dynamics of the Danes, these faltered on defensive errors against the Spaniards who made them pay severely in a 5-1 success, while Brazil, who had been successfully rotating their veterans, lost out to France.

Meanwhile the Germans, underestimated as ever, had stumbled along to the final in characteristically unspectacular style. They were beaten 2-0 in the last group game by Denmark, almost held by Morocco and survived the penalty kick lottery against Mexico.

However their midfield held Michel Platini in a vice-like grip and the defence stifled everything else that the French could create in one semi-final, while a Maradona double accounted for Belgium in the other.

In the final, Argentina led 2-0 with 17 minutes remaining, only for the Germans to level the score with two goals in eight minutes. And for once it was Maradona in the role of goal maker who brought Argentina their second World Cup in eight years. He released a perfect pass to Jorge Burruchaga who ran half the length of the pitch before drawing Harald Schumacher and clinching victory in a spectacular climax to a memorable final. After 13 tournaments, FIFA had a competition more truly representative of its world-wide membership, if rather fewer great teams and referees. But without this sufficient guarantee of places its member nations would certainly fragment.

Qualifying Tournament

Record 119 entries*
Italy as champions and Mexico as hosts already qualified
Africa (29 entries): Algeria, Angola, Benin, Cameroon, Egypt, Ethiopia, Gambia, Ghana, Guinea, Ivory Coast, Kenya, Lesotho, Liberia, Libya, Madagascar, Malawi, Mauritius, Morocco, Niger, Nigeria, Senegal, Sierra Leone, Sudan, Tanzania, Togo, Tunisia, Uganda, Zambia, Zimbabwe
Asia (26): Bahrain, Bangladesh, Brunei, China, Hong Kong, India, Indonesia, Iran, Iraq, Israel, Japan, North Korea, South Korea, Kuwait, Macao, Malaysia, Nepal, Oman, Qatar, Saudi Arabia, Singapore, Syria, Thailand, UAE, North Yemen, South Yemen
Concacaf (18): Antigua, Barbados, Canada, Costa Rica, Grenada, Guatemala, Guyana, Haiti, Honduras, Jamaica, Mexico, Netherlands Antilles, Panama, Puerto Rico, El Salvador, Surinam, Trinidad and Tobago, USA
Europe (33): Albania, Austria, Belgium, Bulgaria, Cyprus, Czechoslovakia, Denmark, England, Finland, France, East Germany, West Germany, Greece, Holland, Hungary, Iceland, Northern Ireland, Rep of Ireland, Italy, Luxembourg, Malta, Norway, Poland, Portugal, Rumania, Scotland, Spain, Sweden, Switzerland, Turkey, USSR, Wales, Yugoslavia
Oceania (3): Australia, Taipei, New Zealand
South America (10): Argentina, Bolivia, Brazil, Chile, Colombia, Ecuador, Paraguay, Peru, Uruguay, Venezuela

Final places in Mexico were to be distributed as follows: Africa (2), Asia (2), Concacaf (1 + Mexico), Europe (13 + Italy)**, Oceania (0)**, South America (4).

*Subsequent additional entries for Lebanon in Asia and Israel added to Oceania, took the total to 121.

**Oceania's representative would be required to play the 13th placed team in Europe for a final place.

Europe
Group 1 (Poland, Belgium, Greece, Albania)
Belgium v Albania 3 - 1; Poland v Greece 3 - 1; Poland v Albania 2 - 2; Greece v Belgium 0 - 0; Albania v Belgium 2 - 0; Greece v Albania 2 - 0; Belgium v Greece 2 - 0; Belgium v Poland 2 - 0; Greece v Poland 1 - 4; Albania v Poland 0 - 1; Poland v Belgium 0 - 0; Albania v Greece 1 - 1

	P	W	D	L	F	A	Pts
Poland	6	3	2	1	10	6	8
Belgium	6	3	2	1	7	3	8
Greece	6	1	2	3	5	10	4
Albania	6	1	2	3	6	9	4

Poland qualified

Group 2 (West Germany, Czechoslovakia, Sweden, Portugal, Malta)
Sweden v Malta 4 - 0; Sweden v Portugal 0 - 1; Portugal v Czechoslovakia 2 - 1; West Germany v Sweden 2 - 0; Czechoslovakia v Malta 4 - 0; Portugal v Sweden 1 - 3; Malta v West Germany 2 - 3; Malta v Portugal 1 - 3; Portugal v West Germany 1 - 2; West Germany v Malta 6 - 0; Malta v Czechoslovakia 0 - 0; Czechoslovakia v West Germany 1 - 5; Sweden

v Czechoslovakia 2 - 0; Sweden v West Germany 2 - 2; Czechoslovakia v Portugal 1 - 0; Portugal v Malta 3 - 2; Czechoslovakia v Sweden 2 - 1; West Germany v Portugal 0 - 1; West Germany v Czechoslovakia 2 - 2; Malta v Sweden 1 - 2

	P	W	D	L	F	A	Pts
West Germany	8	5	2	1	22	9	12
Portugal	8	5	0	3	12	10	10
Sweden	8	4	1	3	14	9	9
Czechoslovakia	8	3	2	3	11	12	8
Malta	8	0	1	7	6	25	1

West Germany and Portugal qualified

Group 3 (England, Northern Ireland, Rumania, Turkey, Finland)
Finland v Northern Ireland 1 - 0; Northern Ireland v Rumania 3 - 2; England v Finland 5 - 0; Turkey v Finland 1 - 2; Northern Ireland v Finland 2 - 1; Turkey v England 0 - 8; Northern Ireland v England 0 - 1; Rumania v Turkey 3 - 0; Northern Ireland v Turkey 2 - 0; Rumania v England 0 - 0; Finland v England 1 - 1; Finland v Rumania 1 - 1; Rumania v Finland 2 - 0; Turkey v Northern Ireland 0 - 0; England v Rumania 1 - 1; England v Turkey 5 - 0; England v Northern Ireland 0 - 0; Turkey v Rumania 1 - 3

	P	W	D	L	F	A	Pts
England	8	4	4	0	21	2	12
Northern Ireland	8	4	2	2	8	5	10
Rumania	8	3	3	2	12	7	9
Finland	8	3	2	3	7	12	8
Turkey	8	0	1	7	2	24	1

England and Northern Ireland qualified

Group 4 (France, Yugoslavia, East Germany, Bulgaria, Luxembourg)
Yugoslavia v Bulgaria 0 - 0; Luxembourg v France 0 - 4; East Germany v Yugoslavia 2 - 3; Luxembourg v East Germany 0 - 5; France v Bulgaria 1 - 0; Bulgaria v Luxembourg 4 - 0; France v East Germany 2 - 0; Yugoslavia v Luxembourg 1 - 0; Yugoslavia v France 0 - 0; Bulgaria v East Germany 1 - 0; Luxembourg v Yugoslavia 0 - 1; Bulgaria v France 2 - 0; East Germany v Luxembourg 3 - 1; Bulgaria v Yugoslavia 2 - 1; East Germany v France 2 - 0; Luxembourg v Bulgaria 1 - 3; Yugoslavia v East Germany 1 - 2; France v Luxembourg 6 - 0; France v Yugoslavia 2 - 0; East Germany v Bulgaria 2 - 1

	P	W	D	L	F	A	Pts
France	8	5	1	2	15	4	11
Bulgaria	8	5	1	2	13	5	11
East Germany	8	5	0	3	16	9	10
Yugoslavia	8	3	2	3	7	8	8
Luxembourg	8	0	0	8	2	27	0

France and Bulgaria qualified

Group 5 (Austria, Hungary, Holland, Cyprus)
Cyprus v Austria 1 - 2; Hungary v Austria 3 - 1; Holland v Hungary 1 - 2; Austria v Holland 1 - 0; Cyprus v Hungary 1 - 2; Cyprus v Holland 0 - 1; Holland v Cyprus 7 - 1; Hungary v Cyprus 2 - 0; Austria v Hungary 0 - 3; Holland v Austria 1 - 1; Austria v Cyprus 4 - 0; Hungary v Holland 0 - 1

	P	W	D	L	F	A	Pts
Hungary	6	5	0	1	12	4	10
Holland	6	3	1	2	11	5	7
Austria	6	3	1	2	9	8	7
Cyprus	6	0	0	6	3	18	0

Hungary qualified
Play-off between the runners-up of Groups 1 and 5
Belgium v Holland 1 - 0, 1 - 2
Belgium qualified

Group 6 (USSR, Denmark, Rep of Ireland, Switzerland, Norway)

Rep of Ireland v USSR 1 - 0; Norway v Switzerland 0 - 1; Denmark v Norway 1 - 0; Norway v USSR 1 - 1; Switzerland v Denmark 1 - 0; Norway v Rep of Ireland 1 - 0; Denmark v Rep of Ireland 3 - 0; Switzerland v USSR 2 - 2; Rep of Ireland v Norway 0 - 0; USSR v Switzerland 4 - 0; Rep of Ireland v Switzerland 3 - 0; Denmark v USSR 4 - 2; Switzerland v Rep of Ireland 0 - 0; Denmark v Switzerland 0 - 0; Norway v Denmark 1 - 5; USSR v Rep of Ireland 2 - 0; USSR v Norway 1 - 0; Switzerland v Norway 1 - 1; Rep of Ireland v Denmark 1 - 4

	P	W	D	L	F	A	Pts
Denmark	8	5	1	2	17	6	11
USSR	8	4	2	2	13	8	10
Switzerland	8	2	4	2	5	10	8
Rep of Ireland	8	2	2	4	5	10	6
Norway	8	1	3	4	4	10	5

Denmark and USSR qualified.

Group 7 (Spain, Scotland, Wales, Iceland)

Iceland v Wales 1 - 0; Spain v Wales 3 - 0; Scotland v Iceland 3 - 0; Scotland v Spain 3 - 1; Wales v Iceland 2 - 1; Spain v Scotland 1 - 0; Scotland v Wales 2 - 0; Wales v Spain 3 - 0; Iceland v Scotland 0 - 1; Iceland v Spain 1 - 2; Wales v Scotland 1 - 1; Spain v Iceland 2 - 1

	P	W	D	L	F	A	Pts
Spain	6	4	0	2	9	8	8
Scotland	6	3	1	2	8	4	7
Wales	6	3	1	2	7	6	7
Iceland	6	1	0	5	4	10	2

Spain qualified

Runner-up played winner of Oceania group
Scotland v Australia 2 - 0, 0 - 0
Scotland qualified

Oceania

1st Round

Israel v Taipei 6 - 0; Taipei v Israel 0 - 5; New Zealand v Australia 0 - 0; New Zealand v Taipei 5 - 1; Israel v Australia 1 - 2; Taipei v New Zaaland 0 - 5; Australia v Israel 1 - 1; Australia v Tapei 7 - 0; New Zealand v Israel 3 - 1; Taipei v Australia 0 - 8; Australia v New Zealand 2 - 0; Israel v New Zealand 3 - 0

	P	W	D	L	F	A	Pts
Australia	6	4	2	0	20	2	10
Israel	6	3	1	2	17	6	7
New Zealand	6	3	1	2	13	7	7
Taipei	6	0	0	6	1	36	0

Australia qualified for play-off: see above

South America

Group 1 (Argentina, Peru, Colombia, Venezuela)

Colombia v Peru 1 - 0; Venezuela v Argentina 2 - 3; Colombia v Argentina 1 - 3; Venezuela v Peru 0 - 1; Peru v Colombia 0 - 0; Argentina v Venezuela 3 - 0; Peru v Venezuela 4 - 1; Argentina v Colombia 1 - 0; Venezuela v Colombia 2 - 2; Peru v Argentina 1 - 0; Colombia v Venezuela 2 - 0; Argentina v Peru 2 - 2

	P	W	D	L	F	A	Pts
Argentina	6	4	1	1	12	6	9
Peru	6	3	2	1	8	4	8
Colombia	6	2	2	2	6	6	6
Venezuela	6	0	1	5	5	15	1

Argentina qualified

Group 2 (Chile, Ecuador, Uruguay)

Ecuador v Chile 1 - 1; Uruguay v Ecuador 2 - 1; Chile v Ecuador 6 - 2; Chile v Uruguay 2 - 0; Ecuador v Uruguay 0 - 2; Uruguay v Chile 2 - 1

	P	W	D	L	F	A	Pts
Uruguay	4	3	0	1	6	4	6
Chile	4	2	1	1	10	5	5
Ecuador	4	0	1	3	4	11	1

Uruguay qualified

Group 3 (Brazil, Paraguay, Bolivia)

Bolivia v Paraguay 1 - 1; Bolivia v Brazil 0 - 2; Paraguay v Bolivia 3 - 0; Paraguay v Brazil 0 - 2; Brazil v Paraguay 1 - 1; Brazil - Bolivia 1 - 1

	P	W	D	L	F	A	Pts
Brazil	4	2	2	0	6	2	6
Paraguay	4	1	2	1	5	4	4
Bolivia	4	0	2	2	2	7	2

Brazil qualified

Play-off between the runners-up of Groups 1 and 2
Chile v Peru 4 - 2, 1 - 0

Play-off between the runners-up of Group 3 and third-placed team in Group 1
Paraguay v Colombia 3 - 0, 1 - 2

Final qualifier from above matches
Paraguay v Chile 3 - 0, 2 - 2
Paraguay qualified

Africa

1st Round

Egypt v Zimbabwe 1 - 0, 1 - 1; Kenya v Ethiopia 2 - 1, 3 - 3; Mauritius v Malawi 0 - 1, 0 - 4; Zambia v Uganda 3 - 0, 0 - 1; Madagascar v Lesotho (withdrew); Tanzania v Sudan 1 - 1, 0 - 0; Sierra Leone v Morocco 0 - 1, 0 - 4; Libya v Niger (withdrew); Benin v Tunisia 0 - 2, 0 - 4; Ivory Coast v Gambia 4 - 0, 2 - 3; Nigeria v Liberia 3 - 0, 1 - 0; Angola v Senegal 1 - 0, 0 - 1 (Angola won 4 - 3 on penalties); Guinea v Togo (withdrew)

2nd Round

Zambia v Cameroon 4 - 1, 1 - 1; Morocco v Malawi 2 - 0, 0 - 0; Angola v Algeria 0, 2 - 3; Kenya v Nigeria 0 - 3, 1 - 3; Egypt v Madagascar 1 - 0, 0 - 1 (Egypt won 4 - 2 on penalties); Guinea v Tunisia 1 - 0, 0 - 2; Sudan v Libya 0 - 0, 0 - 4; Ivory Coast v Ghana 0 - 0, 0 - 2

3rd Round

Algeria v Zambia 2 - 0, 1 - 0; Ghana v Libya 0 - 0, 0 - 2; Nigeria v Tunisia 1 - 0, 0 - 2; Egypt v Morocco 0 - 0, 0 - 2

4th Round

Tunisia v Algeria 1 - 4, 0 - 3; Morocco v Libya 3 - 0, 0 - 1
Algeria and Morocco qualified

Concacaf

1st Round

Group 1 (El Salvador, Puerto Rico, Canada, Jamaica (expelled), Netherlands Antilles, USA)
El Salvador v Puerto Rico 5 - 0, 3 - 0; Netherlands Antilles v USA 0 - 0, 0 - 4; Canada (walked over)

Group 2 (Barbados (withdrew), Costa Rica (walked over), Panama, Honduras, Guatemala (walked over))
Panama v Honduras 0 - 3, 0 - 1

Group 3 (Trinidad and Tobago, Grenada (withdrew), Antigua, Haiti, Surinam, Guyana)
Antigua v Haiti 0 - 4, 2 - 1; Surinam v Guyana 1 - 0, 1 - 1; Trinidad and Tobago (walked over)

2nd Round

Group 1 (El Salvador, Honduras, Surinam)
Surinam v El Salvador 0 - 3; El Salvador v Surinam 3 - 0; Surinam v Honduras 1 - 1; Honduras v Surinam 2 - 1; El Salvador v Honduras 1 - 2; Honduras v El Salvador 0 - 0

	P	W	D	L	F	A	Pts
Honduras	4	2	2	0	5	3	6
El Salvador	4	2	1	1	7	2	5
Surinam	4	0	1	3	2	9	1

Group 2 (Canada, Haiti, Guatemala)
Canada v Haiti 2 - 0; Canada v Guatemala 2 - 1; Haiti v Guatemala 0 - 1; Guatemala v Canada 1 - 1; Haiti v Canada 0 - 2; Guatemala v Haiti 4 - 0

	P	W	D	L	F	A	Pts
Canada	4	3	1	0	7	2	7
Guatemala	4	2	1	1	7	3	5
Haiti	4	0	0	4	0	9	0

Group 3 (USA, Costa Rica, Trinidad and Tobago)
Trinidad and Tobago v Costa Rica 0 - 3; Costa Rica v Tinidad and Tobago 1 - 1; Trinidad and Tobago v USA 1 - 2; USA v Trinidad and Tobago 1 - 0; Costa Rica v USA 1 - 1; USA v Costa Rica 0 - 1

	P	W	D	L	F	A	Pts
Costa Rica	4	2	2	0	6	2	6
USA	4	2	1	1	4	3	5
T'dad & Tobago	4	0	1	3	2	7	1

3rd Round

Costa Rica v Honduras 2 - 2; Canada v Costa Rica 1 - 1; Honduras v Canada 0 - 1; Costa Rica v Canada 0 - 0; Honduras v Costa Rica 3 - 1; Canada v Honduras 2 - 1

	P	W	D	L	F	A	Pts
Canada	4	2	2	0	4	2	6
Honduras	4	1	1	2	6	6	3
Costa Rica	4	0	3	1	4	6	3

Canada qualified

Asia

1st Round

Group 1

Sub-Group 1A (Saudi Arabia, UAE, Oman (withdrew))
Saudi Arabia v UAE 0 - 0, 0 - 1

Sub - Group 1B (Iraq, Lebanon, Qatar, Jordan)
Jordan v Qatar 1 - 0; Lebanon v Iraq 0 - 6; Qatar v Lebanon 7 - 0 (Lebanon subsequently withdrew, record expunged); Jordan v Iraq 2 - 3; Qatar v Iraq 3 - 0; Qatar v Jordan 2 - 0; Iraq v Jordan 2 - 0; Iraq v Qatar 2 - 1

	P	W	D	L	F	A	Pts
Iraq	4	3	0	1	7	6	6
Qatar	4	2	0	2	6	3	4
Jordan	4	1	0	3	3	7	2

Group 2

Sub-Group 2A (Kuwait, North Yemen, Syria)
Syria v Kuwait I - 0; North Yemen v Syria 0 - 1; Kuwait v North Yemen 5 - 0; Kuwait v Syria 0 - 0; Syria v North Yemen 3 - 0; North Yemen v Kuwait 1 - 3

	P	W	D	L	F	A	Pts
Syria	4	3	1	0	5	0	7
Kuwait	4	2	1	1	8	2	5
North Yemen	4	0	0	4	1	12	0

Sub-Group 2B (Bahrain, South Yemen, Iran excluded)
South Yemen v Bahrain 1 - 4; Bahrain v South Yemen 3 - 3

Group 3

Sub-Group 3A (Malaysia, Nepal, South Korea)
Nepal v South Korea 0 - 2; Malaysia v South Korea 1 - 0; Nepal v Malaysia 0 - 0; Malaysia v Nepal 5 - 0; South Korea v Nepal 4 - 0; South Korea v Malaysia 2 - 0

	P	W	D	L	F	A	Pts
South Korea	4	3	0	1	8	1	6
Malaysia	4	2	1	1	6	2	5
Nepal	4	0	1	3	0	11	1

Sub-Group 3B (Thailand, India, Bangladesh, Indonesia)
Indonesia v Thailand 1 - 0; Indonesia v Bangladesh 2 - 0; Indonesia v India 2 - 1; Thailand v Bangladesh 3 - 0; Thailand v India 0 - 0; Thailand v Indonesia 0 - 1; Bangladesh v India 1 - 2; Bangladesh v Indonesia 2 - 1; Bangladesh v Thailand 1 - 0; India v Indonesia 1 - 1; India v Thailand 1 - 1; India v Bangladesh 2 - 0

	P	W	D	L	F	A	Pts
Indonesia	6	4	1	1	8	4	9
India	6	2	3	1	7	6	7
Thailand	6	1	2	3	4	4	4
Bangladesh	6	2	0	4	5	10	4

Group 4

Sub-Group 4A (China, Hong Kong, Macao, Brunei)
Macao v Brunei 2 - 0; Hong Kong v China 0 - 0; Macao v China 0 - 4; Hong Kong v Brunei 8 - 0; China v Brunei 8 - 0; Brunei v China 0 - 4; Brunei v Hong Kong 1 - 5; Brunei v Macao 1 - 2; Macao v Hong Kong 0 - 2; Hong Kong v Macao 6 - 0; China v Macao 6 - 0; China v Hong Kong 1 - 2

	P	W	D	L	F	A	Pts
Hong Kong	6	5	1	0	19	2	11
China	6	4	1	1	23	2	9
Macao	6	2	0	4	4	15	4
Brunei	6	0	0	6	2	29	0

Sub-Group 4B (Japan, North Korea, Singapore)
Singapore v North Korea 1 - 1; Singapore v Japan 1 - 3; Japan v North Korea 1 - 0; North Korea v Japan 0 - 0; Japan v Singapore 5 - 0; North Korea v Singapore 2 - 0

	P	W	D	L	F	A	Pts
Japan	4	3	1	0	9	1	7
North Korea	4	1	2	1	3	2	4
Singapore	4	0	1	3	2	11	1

2nd Round

UAE v Iraq 2 - 3, 2 - 1; Bahrain v Syria 1 - 1, 0 - 1; South Korea v Indonesia 2 - 0, 4 - 1; Japan v Hong Kong 3 - 0, 2 - 1

3rd Round

Syria v Iraq 0 - 0; Iraq v Syria 3 - 1
Japan v South Korea 1 - 2; South Korea v Japan 1 - 0
Iraq and South Korea qualified

Final Tournament MEXICO
First round
GROUP A

31.5.86 Bulgaria (0) 1, Italy (1) 1 MEXICO CITY
Bulgaria: Mikhailov, Arabov, Zdravkov, Dimitrov, Markov A, Sirakov (1), Iskrenov (Kostadinov), Sadkov, Mladenov, Gospodinov (Jeliaskov), Getov
Italy: Galli, Bergomi, Cabrini, De Napoli, Vierchowod, Scirea, Conti (Vialli), Di Gennaro, Galderisi, Bagni, Altobelli (1)
Referee: Fredriksson (Sweden)

2.6.86 Argentina (2) 3, South Korea (0) 1 MEXICO CITY
Argentina: Pumpido, Clausen, Brown, Ruggeri (1), Garre, Giusti, Batista (Olarticoechea), Burruchaga, Pasculli (Tapia), Maradona, Valdano (2)
South Korea: Oh Yun-Kyo, Park Kyung-Hoon, Jung Yong-Hwan, Cho Min-Kook, Kim Yong-See (Byun Byung-Joo), Huh Jung-Moo, Kim Pyung- Suk (Cho Kwang-Rae), Park Chang-Sun (1), Choi Soon-Ho, Kim Joo- Sung, Cha Bum-Kun
Referee: Sanchez Arminio (Spain)

5.6.86 Italy (1) 1, Argentina (1) 1 PUEBLA
Italy: Galli, Bergomi, Cabrini, De Napoli (Baresi), Vierchowod, Scirea, Conti (Vialli), De Gennaro, Galderisi, Bagni, Altobelli (1 pen)
Argentina: Pumpido, Cuciuffo, Brown, Ruggeri, Garre, Giusti, Batista (Olarticoechea), Burruchaga, Borghi (Enrique), Maradona (1), Valdano
Referee: Keizer (Holland)

2.6.86 South Korea (0) 1, Bulgaria (1) 1 MEXICO CITY
South Korea: Oh Yun-Kyo, Park Kyung-Hoon, Jung Yong-Hwan, Cho Young-Jeung, Cho Kwang-Rae (Choe Min-Kook), Huh Jung-Moo, Park Chang-Sun, No Soo-Jin (Kim Jong-Boo [1]), Byun Byung-Joo, Kim Joo-Sung, Cha Bum-Kun
Bulgaria: Mikhailov, Arabov, Zdravkov, Dimitrov, Petrov, Sirakov, Iskrenov, Sadkov, Mladenov, Gospodinov (Jeliaskov), Getov (1) (Kostadinov)
Referee: Al-Shanar (Saudi Arabia)

10.6.86 Argentina (1) 2, Bulgaria (0) 0 MEXICO CITY
Argentina: Pumpido, Cuciuffo, Brown, Ruggeri, Garre, Giusti, Batista (Enrique), Burruchaga, Borghi (Olarticoechea), Maradona, Valdano (1)
Bulgaria: Mikhailov, Sirakov, Markov A., Dimitrov, Jordanov, Markov P., Petrov, Jeliaskov, Mladenov (Velitchkov), Sadkov, Getov
Referee: Ulloa (Costa Rica)

10.6.86 South Korea (0) 2, Italy (1) 3 PUEBLA
South Korea: On Yun-Kyo, Park Kyung-Hoon, Jung Yong-Hwan, Cho Young-Jeung, Cho Kwang-Rae (o. g.), Huh Jung-Moo, Park Chang-Sun, Byun Byung-Joo (Kim Jong-Boo), Choi Soon-Ho (1), Kim Joo-Sung (Chung Jong-Soo), Cha Bum-Kun
Italy: Galli, Collovati, Cabrini, De Napoli, Vierchowod, Scirea, Conti, Di Gennaro, Galderisi (Vialli), Bagni (Baresi), Altobelli (2)
Referee: Socha (USA)

	P	W	D	L	F	A	Pts
Argentina	3	2	1	0	6	2	5
Italy	3	1	2	0	5	4	4
Bulgaria	3	0	2	1	2	4	2
South Korea	3	0	1	2	4	7	1

GROUP B

3.6.86 Belgium (1) 1, Mexico (2) 2 MEXICO CITY
Belgium: Pfaff, Gerets, Van der Elst F, Broos, De Wolf, Scifo, Vandereyncken, Vercauteren, Desmet (Claesen), Vandenbergh (1) (Demol), Ceulemans
Mexico: Larios, Trejo, Quirarte (1), Felix Cruz, Servin, Munoz, Aguirre, Negrete, Boy (Espana), Sanchez (1), Flores (Javier Cruz)
Referee: Esposito (Argentina)

4.6.86 Paraguay (1) 1, Iraq (0) 0 TOLUCA
Paraguay: Fernandez, Torales, Zabula, Schettina, Delgado, Nunez, Ferreira, Romero (1), Cabanas, Canete, Mendoza (Guasch)
Iraq: Hammoudi, Allawi, Shaker N, Shaker B, Hussein, Mohammed (Hameed), Radi, Saeed, Gorgis (Quassen), Hashem, Uraibi
Referee: Picon (Mauritius)

7.6.86 Mexico (1) 1, Paraguay (0) 1 MEXICO CITY
Mexico: Larios, Trejo, Quirarte, Felix Cruz, Servin, Munoz, Aguirre, Negrete, Boy (Espana), Sanchez, Flores (1) (Javier Cruz)
Paraguay: Fernandez, Torales (Hicks), Zabala, Schettina, Delgado, Nunez, Ferreira, Romero (1), Cabanas, Canete, Mendoza (Guasch)
Referee: Courtney (England)

8.6.86 Iraq (0) 1, Belgium (2) 2 TOLUCA
Iraq: Hammoudi, Allawi, Shaker N, Shaker B, Hussein, Mohammed, Radi (1), Saddam (Hameed), Gorgis, Hashem, Uraibi
Belgium: Pfaff, Gerets, Van der Elst F, Demol (Grun), De Wolf, Scifo (1) (Clysters), Vandereyncken, Vercauteren, Desmet, Claesen (1 pen), Ceulemans
Referee: Diaz (Colombia)

11.6.86 Paraguay (0) 2, Belgium (1) 2 TOLUCA
Paraguay: Fernandez, Torales, Zabala, Delgado, Guasch, Nunez, Ferreira, Romero, Cabanas (2), Canete, Mendoza (Hicks)
Belgium: Pfaff, Grun (Van der Elst L), Broos, Renquin, Vervoort, Scifo, Demol, Ceulemans, Vercauteren (1), Veyt (1), Claesen
Referee: Dochev (Bulgaria)

11.6.86 Iraq (0) 0, Mexico (0) 1 MEXICO CITY
Iraq: Jasim, Majeed, Allawi, Nadhum, Hussein, Ghanem, Hashem, Radi, Abid (Shaker N), Minshed, Kassim (Hameed)
Mexico: Larios, Amador (Dominguez), Quirarte (1), Felix Cruz, Servin, De los Cobos (Javier Cruz), Aguirre, Negrete, Boy, Espana, Flores
Referee: Petrovic (Yugoslavia)

	P	W	D	L	F	A	Pts
Mexico	3	2	1	0	4	2	5
Paraguay	3	1	2	0	4	3	4
Belgium	3	1	1	1	5	5	3
Iraq	3	0	0	3	1	4	0

GROUP C

1.6.86 Canada (0) 0, France (0) 1 LEON
Canada: Dolan, Lenarduzzi, Wilson, Bridge, Samuel, Ragan, Valentine, Norman, James (Segota), Sweeney (Lowery), Vrablic
France: Bats, Amoros, Tusseau, Battiston, Bossis, Fernandez, Giresse, Tigana, Papin (1), Platini, Rocheteau (Stopyra)
Referee: Silva Arce (Chile)

2.6.86 USSR (3) 6, Hungary (0) 0 IRAPUATO
USSR: Dasayev, Larionov, Bessonov, Kuznetsov, Demyanenko, Yaremchuk (2), Yakovenko (1) (Yevtushenko), Rats, Belanov (1 pen) (Rodionov [1]), Zavarov, Aleinikov (1)
Hungary: Disztl P, Sallai, Roth (Burcsa), Garaba, Kardos, Kiprich, Nagy, Detari, Peter (Dajka), Esterhazy, Bognar
Referee: Agnolin (Italy)

5.6.86 France (0) 1, USSR (0) 1 LEON
France: Bats, Amoros, Ayache, Battiston, Bossis, Fernandez (1), Giresse (Vercruysse), Tigana, Papin (Bellone), Platini, Stopyra
USSR: Dasayev, Larionov, Bessonov, Kuznetsov, Demyanenko, Yaremchuk, Yakovenko, Rats (1), Belanov, Zavarov (Blokhin), Aleinikov
Referee: Arrpi Filho (Brazil)

6.6.86 Hungary (1) 2, Canada (0) 0 IRAPUATO
Hungary: Szendrei, Sallai, Varga, Garaba, Kardos, Kiprich, Nagy (Dajka), Detari (1), Burcsa (Roth), Esterhazy (1), Bognar
Canada: Lettieri, Lenarduzzi, Wilson (Sweeney), Bridge, Samuel, Ragan, Valentine, Norman, James (Segota), Gray, Vrablic
Referee: Al-Sharis (Syria)

9.6.86 Hungary (0) 0, France (1) 3 LEON
Hungary: Disztl P, Sallai, Roth, Varga, Kardos, Garaba, Hannich (Nagy), Detari, Dajka, Esterhazy, Kovacs (Bognar)
France: Bats, Ayache, Amoros, Battiston, Bossis, Fernandez, Giresse, Tigana (1), Papin (Rocheteau [1]), Platini, Stopyra (1) (Ferreri)
Referee: Silva (Portugal)

9.6.86 USSR (0) 2, Canada (0) 0 IRAPUATO
USSR: Chanov, Morozov, Bubnov, Kuznetsov, Bal, Litovchenko, Yevtushenko, Aleinikov, Rodionov, Protasov (Belanov), Blokhin (1) (Zavarov [1])
Canada: Lettieri, Lenarduzzi, Wilson, Bridge, Samuel, Ragan, Valentine, Norman, James (Segota), Gray (Pakos), Mitchell
Referee: Traore (Mali)

	P	W	D	L	F	A	Pts
USSR	3	2	1	0	9	1	5
France	3	2	1	0	5	1	5
Hungary	3	1	0	2	2	9	2
Canada	3	0	0	3	0	5	0

GROUP D

1.6.86 Spain (0) 0, Brazil (0) 1 GUADALAJARA
Spain: Zubizarreta, Tomas, Camacho, Maceda, Giocoechea, Julio Alberto, Michel, Victor, Butragueno, Francisco (Senor), Julio Salinas
Brazil: Carlos, Branco, Edson, Edhino, Julio Cesar, Junior (Falcao), Alemao, Casagrande (Muller), Careca, Socrates (1), Elzo
Referee: Bambridge (Australia)

3.6.86 Algeria (0) 1, Northern Ireland (1) 1 GUADALAJARA
Algeria: Larbi, Medjadi, Mansouri, Kourichi, Guendouz, Kaci Said, Assad, Benmabrouk, Zidane (1) (Belloumi), Maroc, Madjer (Harkouk)
Northern Ireland: Jennings, Nicholl, Donaghy, O'Neill, McDonald, Worthington, Penney (Stewart), McIlroy, McCreery, Hamilton, Whiteside (1) (Clarke)
Referee: Butenko (USSR)

7.6.86 Northern Ireland (0) 1, Spain (2) 2 GUADALAJARA
Northern Ireland: Jennings, Nicholl, Donaghy, O'Neill, McDonald, Worthington (Hamilton), Penney (Stewart), McIlroy, McCreery, Clarke (1), Whiteside
Spain: Zubizarreta, Tomas, Camacho, Gallego, Giocoechea, Gordillo (Caldere), Michel, Victor, Butragueno (1), Francisco, Julio Salinas (1) (Senor)
Referee: Brummener (Austria)

6.6.86 Brazil (0) 1, Algeria (0) 0 GUADALAJARA
Brazil: Carlos, Edson (Falcao), Branco, Edinho, Julio Cesar, Junior, Alemao, Casagrande (Muller), Careca (1), Socrates, Elzo
Algeria: Drid, Medjadi, Mamsouri, Megharia, Guendouz, Kaci Said, Assad (Bensaoula), Benmabrouk, Menad, Belloumi (Zidane), Madjer
Referee: Molina (Guatemala)

12.6.85 Algeria (0) 0, Spain (1) 3 MONTERREY
Algeria: Drid (Larbi), Megharia, Mansouri, Kourichi, Guendouz, Kaci Said, Madjer, Maroc, Harkouk, Belloumi, Zidane (Menad)
Spain: Zubizarreta, Tomas, Camacho, Gallego, Goicoechea, Caldere (2), Michel (Senor), Victor, Butragueno (Eloy [1]), Francisco, Julio Salinas
Referee: Takada (Japan)

12.6.86 Northern Ireland (0) 0, Brazil (2) 3 GUADALAJARA
Northern Ireland: Jennings, Nicholl, Donaghy, O'Neill, McDonald, McCreery, McIlroy, Stewart, Clarke, Whiteside (Hamilton), Campbell (Armstrong)
Brazil: Carlos, Josimar (1), Julio Cesar, Edinho, Branco, Elzo, Alemao, Junior, Socrates (Zico), Muller (Casagrande), Careca (2)
Referee: Kirschen (East Germany)

	P	W	D	L	F	A	Pts
Brazil	3	3	0	0	5	0	6
Spain	3	2	0	1	5	2	4
Northern Ireland	3	0	1	2	2	6	1
Algeria	3	0	1	2	1	5	1

GROUP E

4.6.86 Uruguay (1) 1, West Germany (0) 1 QUERETARO
Uruguay: Alvez, Gutierrez, Acevedo, Diogo, Bossio, Batista, Alzamendi (1) (Ramos), Barrios (Saralegui), Da Silva, Francescoli, Santin
West Germany: Schumacher, Briegel, Berthold, Forster, Augenthaler, Eder, Matthaus (Rummenigge), Magath, Brehme (Littbarski), Voller, Allofs (1)
Referee: Christov (Czechoslovakia)

4.6.86 Scotland (0) 0, Denmark (0) 1 NEZA
Scotland: Leighton, Gough, Malpas, Souness, McLeish, Miller, Strachan (Bannon), Aitken, Nicol, Nicholas, Sturrock (McAvennie)
Denmark: Rasmussen, Busk, Olsen M, Nielsen, Lerby, Olsen J (Molby), Berggreen, Elkjaer (1), Laudrup, Bertelsen, Arnesen (Sivebaek)
Referee: Nemeth (Hungary)

8.6.86 Denmark (2) 6, Uruguay (1) 1 NEZA
Denmark: Rasmussen, Busk, Olsen M, Nielsen, Lerby (1), Andersen, Berggreen, Elkjaer (3), Laudrup (1) (Olsen J [1]), Bertelsen (Molby), Arnesen
Uruguay: Alvez, Gutierrez, Acevedo, Diogo, Bossio, Batista, Alzamendi (Ramos), Saralegui, Da Silva, Francescoli (1), Santin (Salazar)
Referee: Marquez (Mexico)

8.6.89 West Germany (1) 2, Scotland (1) 1 QUERETARO
West Germany: Schumacher, Briegel (Jakobs), Berthold, Forster, Augenthaler, Eder, Matthaus, Magath, Littbarski (Rummenigge), Voller (1), Allofs (1)
Scotland: Leighton, Gough, Malpas, Souness, Narey, Miller, Strachan (1), Aitken, Nicol (McAvennie), Archibald, Bannon (Cooper)
Referee: Igna (Romania)

13.6.86 Scotland (0) 0, Uruguay (0) 0 NEZA
Scotland: Leighton, Gough, Albiston, Aitken, Narey, Miller, Strachan, McStay, Sharp, Nicol (Cooper), Sturrock (Nicholas)
Uruguay: Alvez, Diogo, Acevedo, Gutierrez, Pereyra, Batista, Ramos (Saralegui), Barrios, Cabrera, Francescoli (Alzamendi), Santin
Referee: Quiniou (France)

13.6.86 Denmark (1) 2, West Germany (0) 0 QUERETARO
Denmark: Hogh, Sivebaek, Busk, Olsen M, Andersen, Arnesen, Lerby, Molby, Laudrup, Olsen J (1 pen) (Simonsen), Elkjaer (Eriksen [1])
West Germany: Schumacher, Berthold, Jakobs, Forster (Rummenigge), Herget, Eder, Brehme, Matthaus, Voller, Rolff (Littbarski), Allofs
Referee: Ponnet (Belgium)

	P	W	D	L	F	A	Pts
Denmark	3	3	0	0	9	1	6
West Germany	3	1	1	1	3	4	3
Uruguay	3	0	2	1	2	7	2
Scotland	3	0	1	2	1	3	1

GROUP F

2.6.86 Morocco (0) 0, Poland (0) 0 MONTERREY
Morocco: Zaki, Labd, Lemriss, El-Biyaz, Bouyahiaoui, Mustapha El-Haddaoui (Souleimani), Dolmy, Bouderbala, Krimau, Timoumi (Khairi), Merry
Poland: Milynarczyk, Ostrowski, Wojcicki, Majewski, Matysik, Kubicki, Komornicki (Przybys), Buncol, Smolarek, Dziekanowski (Urban), Boniek
Referee: Martinez Bazan (Uruguay)

3.6.86 Portugal (0) 1, England (0) 0 MONTERREY
Portugal: Bento, Alvaro, Frederico, Oliveira, Inacio, Diamantino (Jose Antonio), Andre, Carlos Manuel (1), Pacheco, Sousa, Gomes (Futre)
England: Shilton, Stevens, Sansom, Hoddle, Fenwick, Butcher, Robson (Hodge), Wilkins, Hateley, Lineker, Waddle (Beardsley)
Referee: Roth (West Germany)

6.6.86 England (0) 0, Morocco (0) 0 MONTERREY
England: Shilton, Stevens, Sansom, Hoddle, Fenwick, Butcher, Robson (Hodge), Wilkins, Hateley (Stevens G A), Lineker, Waddle
Morocco: Zaki, Labd, Lemriss (Heina), El-Biyaz, Bouyahiaoui, Khairi, Dolmy, Bouderbala, Krimau, Timoumi, Merry (Souleimani)
Referee: Gonzalez (Paraguay)

7.6.86 Poland (0) 1, Portugal (0) 0 MONTERREY
Poland: Mlynarczyk, Ostrowski, Wojcicki, Majewski, Matysik, Urban, Komornicki (Karas), Pawlak, Smolarek (1) (Zgutczynski), Dziekanowski, Boniek
Portugal: Damas, Alvaro, Frederico, Oliveira, Inacio, Diamantino, Andre (Magalhaes), Carlos Manuel, Pacheco, Sousa, Gomes (Futre)
Referee: Ali ben Nasser (Tunisia)

11.6.86 England (3) 3, Poland (0) 0 MONTERREY
England: Shilton, Stevens, Sansom, Hoddle, Fenwick, Butcher, Steven, Reid, Lineker (3) (Dixon), Beardsley (Waddle), Hodge
Poland: Milynarczyk, Ostrowski, Wojcicki, Matysik (Buncol), Urban, Majewski, Smolarek, Komonicki (Karas), Pawlak, Dziekanowski, Boniek
Referee: Daina (Switzerland)

11.6.86 Portugal (0) 1, Morocco (2) 3 GUADALAJARA
Portugal: Damas, Alvaro (Aguas), Frederico, Oliveira, Inacio, Magalhaes, Carlos Manuel, Pacheco, Sousa (Diamantino [1]), Gomes, Futre
Morocco: Zaki, Labd, Lemriss, El-Biyaz, Bouyahiaoui, Dolmy, Mustapha El-Haddaoui (Souleimani), Bouderbala, Krimau (1), Timouni, Khairi (2)
Referee: Snoddy (Northern Ireland)

	P	W	D	L	F	A	Pts
Morocco	3	1	2	0	3	1	4
England	3	1	1	1	3	1	3
Poland	3	1	1	1	1	3	3
Portugal	3	1	0	2	2	4	2

Second round

15.6.86 Mexico (1) 2, Bulgaria (0) 0 MEXICO CITY
Mexico: Larios, Amador, Quirarte, Felix Cruz, Servin (1), Espana, Aguirre, Munoz, Boy (De los Cobos), Sanchez, Negrete (1)
Bulgaria: Mikhailov, Arabov, Zdravkov, Dimitrov, Petrov, Jordanov, Sadkov, Kostadinov, Getov (Sirakov), Gospodinov, Paschev (Iskrenov)
Referee: Arppi Filho (Brazil)

15.6.86 USSR (1) 3, Belgium (0) 4 (aet, 2 - 2 at 90 mins) LEON
USSR: Dasayev, Bessonov, Bal, Kuznetsov, Demyanenko, Yaremchuk, Yakovenko (Yevtushenko), Aleinikov, Rats, Belanov (3, 1 pen), Zavarov (Rodionov)
Belgium: Pfaff, Gerets, Grun (Clijsters), Vervoort, Demol (1), Renquin, Scifo (1), Vercauteren, Claesen (1), Veyt, Ceulemans (1)
Referee: Frederiksson (Sweden)

16.6.86 Brazil (1) 4, Poland (0) 0 GUADALAJARA
Brazil: Carlos, Josimar (1), Branco, Edinho (1), Julio Cesar, Alemao, Muller (Silas), Socrates (1 pen) (Zico), Careca (1 pen), Junior, Elzo
Poland: Mlynarczyk, Ostrowski, Majewski, Wojcicki, Przybs (Furtok), Urban (Zmuda), Karas, Tarasiewicz, Dziekanowski, Boniek, Smolarek
Referee: Roth (West Germany)

16.6.86 Argentina (1) 1, Uruguay (0) 0 PUEBLA
Argentina: Pumpido, Cuciuffo, Brown, Garre, Giusti, Ruggeri, Batista (Olarticoechea), Burruchaga, Pasculli (1), Maradona, Valdano
Uruguay: Alvez, Rivero, Bossio, Gutierrez, Acevedo (Paz), Pereyra, Ramos, Cabrera (Da Silva), Francescoli, Barrios, Santin
Referee: Agnolin (Italy)

17.6.86 France (1) 2, Italy (0) 0 MEXICO CITY
France: Bats, Ayache, Amoros, Battiston, Bossis, Fernandez (Tusseau), Giresse, Tigana, Rocheteau, Platini (1) (Ferreri), Stopyra (1)
Italy: Galli, Bergomi, Cabrini, De Napoli, Vierchowod, Scirea, Conti, Bagni, Galderisi (Vialli), Baresi (Di Gennaro), Altobelli
Referee: Esposito (Argentina)

17.6.86 Morocco (0) 0, West Germany (0) 1 MONTERREY
Morocco: Zaki, Labd, Lemriss, Bouyahiaoui, Dolmy, Mustapha El-Haddaoui, Bouderbala, Krimau, Timoumi, Hcina, Khairi
West Germany: Schumacher, Berthold, Briegel, Jakobs, Forster, Eder, Matthaus (1), Rummenigge, Voller (Littbarski), Magath, Allofs
Referee: Petrovic (Yugoslavia)

18.6.86 England (1) 3, Paraguay (0) 0 MEXICO CITY
England: Shilton, Stevens, Sansom, Hoddle, Martin, Butcher, Steven, Reid (Stevens G A), Lineker (2), Beardsley (1) (Hateley), Hodge
Paraguay: Fernandez, Torales (Guasch), Zabala, Schettina, Delgado, Nunez, Ferreira, Romero, Cabanas, Canets, Mendoza
Referee: Al-Sharif (Syria)

18.6.86 Denmark (1) 1, Spain (1) 5 QUERETARO
Denmark: Hogh, Andersen (Eriksen), Olsen M, Busk, Nielsen, Lerby, Olsen J (1 pen) (Molby), Bertelsen, Laudrup, Berggreen, Elkjaer
Spain: Zubizarreta, Tomas, Camacho, Gallego, Giocoechea (1 pen) Julio Alberto,Victor, Michel (Francisco), Butragueno (4, 1 pen), Caldere, Julio Salinas (Eloy)
Referee: Keizer (Holland)

QUARTER FINALS
21.6.86 Brazil (1) 1, France (1) 1 (aet, 1 - 1 at 90 mins, France won 4 - 3 on penalties)   **GUADALAJARA**
Brazil: Carlos, Josimar, Branco, Edinho, Julio Cesar, Elzo, Muller (Zico), Alemao, Careca (1), Socrates, Junior (Silas)
France: Bats, Amoros, Tusseau, Battiston, Bossis, Fernandez, Giresse (Ferreri), Tigana, Rocheteau (Bellone), Platini (1), Stopyra
Referee: Igna (Romania)

21.6.86 West Germany (0) 0, Mexico (0) 0 (aet, West Germany won 4 - 1 on penalties)   **MONTERREY**
West Germany: Schumacher, Berthold, Briegel, Jakobs, Forster, Eder (Littbarski), Matthaus, Brehme, Rummenigge (Hoeness), Magath, Allofs
Mexico: Larios, Amador (Javier Cruz), Felix Cruz, Quirarte, Servin, Munoz, Aguirre, Espana, Boy (De los Cobos), Negrete, Sanchez
Referee: Diaz (Colombia)

22.6.86 Argentina (0) 2, England (0) 1 MEXICO CITY
Argentina: Pumpido, Ruggeri, Cuciuffo, Olarticoechea, Brown, Giusti, Batista, Burruchaga (Tapia), Enrique, Maradona (2), Valdano
England: Shilton, Stevens, Sansom, Hoddle, Butcher, Fenwick, Steven (Barnes), Reid (Waddle), Lineker (1), Beardsley, Hodge
Referee: Ali ben Nasser (Tunisia)

22.6.86 Spain (0) 1, Belgium (1) 1 (aet, 1 - 1 at 90 mins, Belgium won 5 - 4 on penalties)   **PUEBLA**
Spain: Zubizarreta, Chendo, Camacho, Gallego, Tomas (Senor [1]), Michel, Victor, Caldere, Butragueno, Julio Alberto, Julio Salinas (Eloy)
Belgium: Pfaff, Gerets, Renquin, Demol, Vervoort, Grun, Scifo, Veyt (Broos), Claesen, Ceulemans (1), Vercauteren (Van der Elst L)
Referee: Kirschen (East Germany)

SEMI FINALS
25.6.86 Argentina (0) 2, Belgium (0) 0 MEXICO CITY
Argentina: Pumpido, Cuciuffo, Olarticoechea, Giusti, Batista, Burruchaga (Bochini), Enrique, Maradona (2), Valdano
Belgium: Pfaff, Gerets, Renquin (Desmet), Demol, Vervoort, Veyt, Grun, Scifo, Claesen, Ceulemans, Vercauteren
Referee: Marquez (Mexico)

25.6.86 France (0) 0, West Germany (1) 2 GUADALAJARA
France: Bats, Amoros, Ayache, Battiston, Bossis, Fernandez, Giresse (Vercruysse), Tigana, Bellone (Xuereb), Platini, Stopyra
West Germany: Schumacher, Brehme (1), Briegel, Jakobs, Forster, Eder, Matthaus, Rolff, Rummenigge (Voller [1]), Magath, Allofs
Referee: Agnolin (Italy)

Match for third place
28.6.86 Belgium (1) 2, France (2) 4 PUEBLA
Belgium: Pfaff, Gerets, Vervoort, Demol, Renquin (Van der Elst F), Grun, Scifo (Van der Elst L), Mommens, Claesen (1), Ceulemans (1), Veyt
France: Rust, Bibard, Amoros (1 pen), Le Roux (Bossis), Battiston, Vercruysse, Genghini (1), Tigana (Tusseau), Papin (1), Ferreri (1), Bellone
Referee: Courtney (England)

FINAL
29.6.86 Argentina (1) 3, West Germany (0) 2 MEXICO CITY
Argentina: Pumpido, Cuciuffo, Olarticoechea, Ruggeri, Brown (1), Giusti, Burruchaga (1) (Trobbiani), Batista, Valdano (1), Maradona, Enrique
West Germany: Schumacher, Berthold, Briegel, Jakobs, Forster, Eder, Brehme, Matthaus, Allofs (Voller [1]), Magath (Hoeness), Rummenigge (1)
Referee: Arppi Filho (Brazil)

ITALY

1990

In a reversal of the result of the final in Mexico four years earlier, West Germany gained revenge over Argentina in a totally unsatisfactory match which was an affront to the game and an appalling advertisement for the world championship. It epitomised much of what had been an undistinguished tournament.

Argentina finished the game with nine men and the Germans won with a disputed penalty five minutes from time. Pedro Monzon became the first player to be sent off in a World Cup final and was later followed by team-mate Gustavo Dezotti. West Germany equalled Brazil's and Italy's record of three World Cup wins and Franz Beckenbauer, who had captained their 1974 side, became the first manager to win the trophy having led the team to victory as a player in a previous tournament.

With four players suspended, Argentina concentrated on defence in the final. They had reached this stage in fortuitous circumstances while piling up a disgraceful total of red and yellow cards. They rarely showed any ambition to attack the opposition's goal, often resorting to attacking the opposing player. At the end of the tournament they had amassed 22 yellow and three red cards in an overall tally of 164 bookings and 16 dismissals, a record total as match officials threw cautions to the wind. FIFA's insistence on clamping down on infringements of the law put incredible pressure on the referees, who were struggling to understand the offside law in many instances and were falling foul of the idea that they had to decide whether a tackle was legitimate or not by the antics of the victim. Again a wide interpretation of the laws meant a wholly unsatisfactory outcome.

In the first half of the final the physically formidable Germans attacked relentlessly without sufficient guile. Rudi Voller missed three reasonable scoring opportunities

while Argentina's only reply came from a poorly directed free kick from Diego Maradona, who had gone through the entire tournament with a bored and bemused countenance. He had made one telling contribution in the second round when he contrived a defence-splitting pass which sealed Brazil's fate, but apart from being the most fouled player, he contributed little and was surrounded by a set of quite ordinary colleagues.

At the start of the second half, Monzon replaced Oscar Ruggeri in the Argentine defence but played only 20 minutes before he brought down Jurgen Klinsmann and was shown the red card. Worse followed, as Voller was tripped by Robert Sensini and the impressive Andreas Brehme converted low to the right of the Argentine goalkeeper Goycochea with five minutes remaining. Two minutes from the final whistle Dezotti wrestled Kohler for the ball and was sent off. Maradona joined Sensini among the yellow cards for protesting amidst a group of furious Argentines.

The game for third place was this time one of the more enjoyable of the entire month-long extravaganza. Instead of adopting the approach of beaten semi-finalists with little heart for the fray, both Italy and England put on a creditable performance. The Italians won 2-1 in a closely fought affair which confirmed England as worthy winners of the fair play award. They had only five players booked throughout the tournament and committed just 106 fouls. At the end of the game Peter Shilton announced his retirement from international football after collecting 125 caps. He had been unable to bow out in style; he was at fault with Italy's first goal, dallying in front of goal and allowing himself to be dispossessed. He had also been caught off his line in the semi-final with West Germany when a free-kick took a high deflection off the wall.

The hosts Italy were always going to struggle for goals.

Marco Tardelli (above), scorer of Italy's second goal in the 1982 final, celebrates his country's third World Cup triumph. (ALLSPORT)

Overpage England (in red shirts) defend in depth against West Germany at Wembley in the 1966 World Cup final. George Cohen and Martin Peters (foreground) turn; Gordon Banks sits it out. (SYNDICATION INTERNATIONAL)

Alf Ramsey (Inset, left) with his right-hand man Harold Shepherdson. Ramsey led England to victory in the 1966 World Cup and was again in charge for the 1970 finals. (ALLSPORT)

England pushed Brazil in 1970 on several occasions. Felix diverted one shot from Geoff Hurst (above) and in another incident (right) had to receive attention after Francis Lee collided with him. (SYNDICATION INTERNATIONAL)

Sepp Maier was a commanding figure in goal for West Germany in three World Cups, including their success in 1974. (ALLSPORT)

Two Polish defenders who did much to prevent England reaching the 1974 World Cup finals were Jerzy Gorgon (6) and Wladyslaw Zmuda. It was Zmuda who went on to equal Uwe Seeler's record of appearances in World Cup finals matches. (SYNDICATION INTERNATIONAL)

(Above) Bjorn Nordqvist (blue shirt, centre) in action for Sweden against Brazil in 1978. This centre-back made 115 appearances for his country. (COLORSPORT)

Daniel Passarella (far left, holding trophy) was an inspirational captain for Argentina as centre-back in the 1978 World Cup. (COLORSPORT)
Mario Kempes (left) was the leading scorer in the 1978 World Cup finals with six goals and epitomised the fresh, attacking flavour of the Argentine success. (COLORSPORT)

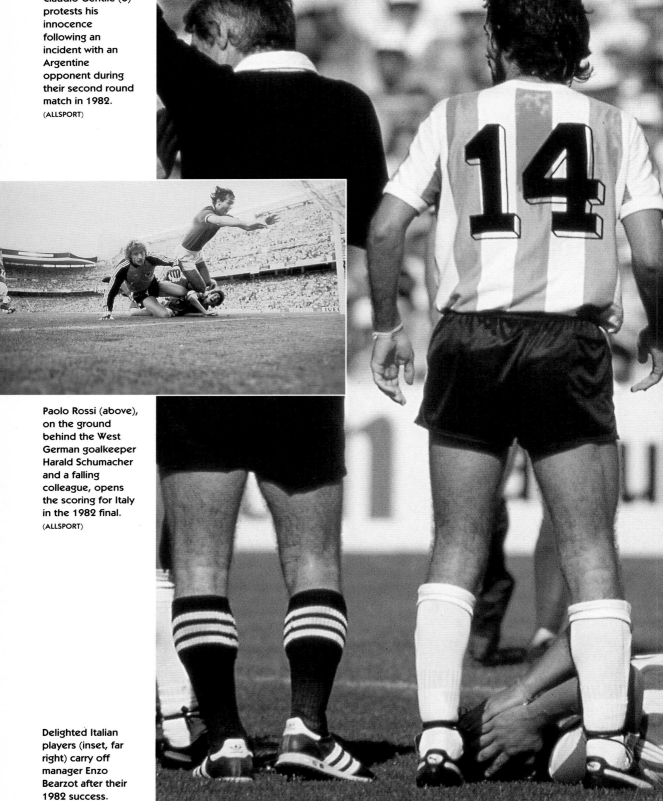

(Main picture) Italy's Claudio Gentile (6) protests his innocence following an incident with an Argentine opponent during their second round match in 1982.
(ALLSPORT)

Paolo Rossi (above), on the ground behind the West German goalkeeper Harald Schumacher and a falling colleague, opens the scoring for Italy in the 1982 final.
(ALLSPORT)

Delighted Italian players (inset, far right) carry off manager Enzo Bearzot after their 1982 success.
(ALLSPORT)

Michel Platini (left) directing the French operations against West Germany in the semi-final of 1986. Alas for him, they came to nothing as the Germans won 2-0. (ALLSPORT)

Platini (inset) celebrates his equaliser in the classic quarter-final with Brazil in Guadalajara. (ALLSPORT)

England's Gary Lineker 'sent flying' (right) by Romero of Paraguay. Lineker scored twice in this match as England won 3-0. (ALLSPORT)

Argentina's supporters are keen to show the flag. (ALLSPORT)
(Inset, top) Brazilian fans are more traditional. (ALLSPORT)
(Inset, centre) Mexican fans appear frightful. (ALLSPORT)
(Inset, below) A mini-Mexican is far more appealing. (ALLSPORT)

(Above) West German defender Dietmar Jakobs clears from Argentina's Jorge Valdano. (ALLSPORT)

Previous page Diego Maradona tries a swallow dive against West Germany in the 1986 final, but the referee does not apparently swallow it. (ALLSPORT)

The 'hand of God' (Inset) helps Diego Maradona to score Argentina's first goal against England in the 1986 series. (ALLSPORT)

England celebrate as a goal by David Platt (kneeling) in the last minute of extra time wins the second round match against Belgium.

The unmistakeable expression of Salvatore 'Toto' Schillaci, top scorer in the 1990 finals.

Although they had discovered a marksman in the Sicilian, Salvatore Schillaci, a chunky, ebullient little man, they could not provide him with the support up front which he obviously needed. He finished top scorer in the competition with six goals. Yet for all the Italians technical accomplishments on the ball, they lacked the necessary drive in the last third of the field. Individually there was much to admire in Giannini, Donadoni, Baresi and even the £7.7 million Roberto Baggio, who had some inspired moments. But the penalty shoot-out with Argentina was to provide a cruel exit. Schillaci was the player caught most offside during Italia '90.

So ironically, the tournament which began with Argentina being humiliated in losing to the Cameroon, who finished the match with nine men, ended with the South Americans themselves losing two men and the match to a theatrical West Germany, for whom Lothar Matthaus proved a midfield dynamo.

There was little doubt that the 1990 finals revealed a levelling of standards. Of the lesser nations only South Korea and the United Arab Emirates failed to make an impression. The Cameroon, unbeaten in their only previous appearance in the World Cup finals eight years earlier, were a revelation. With better discipline they might have reached the final itself. Their combined play and individual flair was a joy to behold and they went some way towards assuming the mantle of Brazil.

Egypt excelled in defence with Hany Ramzi outstanding at the heart of their rearguard and the USA recovered from a naive display in their opening game when they were thrashed 5-1 by the Czechs to improve noticeably in their remaining group matches though they still lost 1-0 to Italy and 2-1 to Austria. Indeed against the Italians they might well have scored on the counter attack on at least two occasions. Costa Rica, given little chance by the critics or themselves, began by beating Scotland 1-0 and at times mirrored the best passing movements of

Brazil. But they had a vulnerability in defence which was exposed in the second round when the aerial threat posed by Czechoslovakia resulted in Tomas Skuhravy scoring a rare headed hat-trick in a 4-1 win.

Arguably the two most disappointing teams were Sweden and Austria. The Austrians had clearly played their best football in the warm up games before the finals and well though the Swedes played at times in their group, they had nothing to show for their endeavours. Again the Soviet Union were exasperating. After a lethargic opening in which they were well beaten 2-0 by a lively Rumanian team, they were unlucky to lose by the same margin to Argentina, having a player sent off rather harshly it seemed, and being denied a penalty when Diego Maradona showed he had added a further dimension to his handling prowess at the other end of the field. The Argentines were clearly determined to show that it was not only their stocky captain who could use his hands to good effect. Alas, others lacked his subtle approach and Claudio Caniggia was booked for leaping up basketball fashion in midfield, the resultant yellow card costing him a place in the final.

Of the more fancied sides, Holland were arguably the most disappointing. Their big four of Marco Van Basten, Ruud Gullit, Ronald Koeman and Frank Rijkaard all had problems. Van Basten scarcely did anything right and appeared uninterested for long periods. Gullit was a shadow of his former buccaneering self but having had a year out with injury he at least had an excuse. Koeman did not have the same reason for a low-key performance and Rijkaard disgraced himself in the second round game with West Germany when he was sent off for spitting twice at the West German Rudi Voller, whom he apparently goaded into also being dismissed with him.

Brazil might have progressed further than the second round had they played with the conviction in attack that the previous wearers of the yellow shirts had done. They were beaten by a late goal against Argentina after controlling almost the entire game. Uruguay, having cleaned up their act from four years earlier, were a curious mixture; their defensive organisation was almost faultless but they were let down by players like Enzo Francescoli and Ruben Sosa who had been expected to shine during the finals. Sosa missed a penalty against Spain after Villaroya handled under the crossbar, the misdemeanour passing unpunished by the referee, who had previously booked the Spaniard for another handling offence.

The Scots were dreadful against Costa Rica despite missing chances close in, but lifted themselves against the Swedes and were denied a place in the second round when they conceded a late scrambled goal to the Brazilians. As for the Republic of Ireland, they reached the second round by giving every ounce of energy they possessed and came through the first of the penalty shoot-out lotteries against Rumania. They were narrowly beaten by Italy in the quarter-final. Yet their opening fixture with England might well have been a poor First Division game in the Football League and received widespread criticism.

However England did better against the uninspired, dispirited Dutch who obviously had trouble in the camp; the players had apparently wanted Johan Cruyff to take over as coach after they had succeeded in having Thijs Libregts removed, and were unhappy with Leo Beenhakker's appointment. This game ended goalless and for periods against the Egyptians, England were nonplussed. They were outplayed for long periods against Belgium, who twice hit a post, before David Platt snatched a memorable late winner in extra time; and they had to dig deep into their determination to come back against the Cameroon to win 3-2 with two penalties from Gary Lineker, after trailing 2-1.

Ironically England's good fortune evaporated after their most convincing performance in the semi-final with West Germany. This was also decided on penalties; the quartet of German efforts were despatched with teutonic efficiency leaving Stuart Pearce and Chris Waddle to fail in their attempts. But England had had many plusses. Des Walker and Mark Wright excelled in defence as did Lineker in attack. Paul Gascoigne was accuracy itself with dead ball kicks, many of which he himself earned through his tireless running with the ball.

The tournament failed to reveal many new outstanding individuals. Indeed one of the most effective to emerge was 38-year-old Roger Milla of the Cameroon, brought out of semi-retirement on the island of Reunion, which said little for others ten years his junior. Yugoslavia's Dragan Stojkovic was often influential in a team which threatened to do better but never quite achieved it, while several teams suffered from having one outstanding player through whom almost everything had to flow. Belgium, who had a purple patch in one of the better contests with Uruguay, had above-average players but invariably looked to the scurrying expertise of Enzo Scifo. Michel was in a similar position for Spain, who proved to be as inconsistent as ever, and Gheorghe Hagi often ventured individual sorties for Rumania which came to nothing, when the team as a unit had been more effective in the first game against the Soviet Union without him. To a lesser extent Colombia relied on Carlos Valderrama, but he was overshadowed by the eccentricities of goalkeeper Rene Higuita, who was finally caught out attempting some sleight of foot outside his penalty area against the Cameroon in extra time. The incident just about summed up the entire tournament, which despite ultimately producing worthy champions in West Germany, will be remembered most for its errors and omissions.

Andreas Brehme (3) scores from the penalty spot to win the World Cup for West Germany.

Qualifying Tournament

112 entries*

Argentina as champions and Italy as hosts already qualified

AFRICA (24): Algeria, Angola, Burkina Faso, Cameroon, Egypt, Gabon, Ghana, Guinea, Ivory Coast, Kenya, Lesotho, Liberia, Libya, Malawi, Morocco, Nigeria, Rwanda, Sudan, Togo, Tunisia, Uganda, Zaire, Zambia, Zimbabwe

CONCACAF(15): Antigua, Canada, Costa Rica, Cuba, Guatemala, Guyana, Honduras, Jamaica, Mexico, Netherlands Antilles, Panama, Puerto Rico, El Salvador, Trinidad and Tobago, USA

EUROPE(33): Albania, Austria, Belgium, Bulgaria, Cyprus, Czechoslovakia, Denmark, England, Finland, France, East Germany, West Germany, Greece, Holland, Hungary, Iceland, Northern Ireland, Rep of Ireland, Italy, Luxembourg, Malta, Norway, Poland, Portugal, Rumania, Scotland, Spain, Sweden, Switzerland, Turkey, USSR, Wales, Yugoslavia

OCEANIA (4 + 1): Australia, Fiji, New Zealand, Taipei + Israel

SOUTH AMERICA(10): Argentina, Bolivia, Brazil, Chile, Colombia, Ecuador, Paraguay, Peru, Uruguay, Venezuela

ASIA (25): Bahrain, Bangladesh, China, Hong Kong, India, Indonesia, Iran, Iraq, Japan, Jordan, North Korea, South Korea, Kuwait, Malaysia, Nepal, Oman, Pakistan, Qatar, Saudi Arabia, Singapore, Syria, Thailand, UAE, North Yemen, South Yemen

*India subsequently withdrew.

Final places in Italy were to be distributed as follows: Africa (2), Asia (2), Concacaf (2), Europe (13 + Italy), Oceania (0)**, South America (3;+ Argentina)**

**Oceania's representative would be required to play the winner of Group 2 in South America for a final place.

Europe

Group 1 (Denmark, Bulgaria, Rumania, Greece)

Greece v Denmark 1 - 1; Bulgaria v Rumania 1 - 3; Rumania v Greece 3 - 0; Denmark v Bulgaria 1 - 1; Greece v Rumania 0 - 0; Bulgaria v Denmark 0 - 2; Rumania v Bulgaria 1 - 0; Denmark v Greece 7 - 1; Bulgaria v Greece 4 - 0; Denmark v Rumania 3 - 0; Greece v Rumania 1 - 0; Rumania v Denmark 3 - 1

	P	W	D	L	F	A	Pts
Rumania	6	4	1	1	10	5	9
Denmark	6	3	2	1	15	6	8
Greece	6	1	2	3	3	15	4
Bulgaria	6	1	1	4	6	8	3

Rumania qualified

Group 2 (England, Poland, Sweden, Albania)

England v Sweden 0 - 0; Poland v Albania 1 - 0; Albania v Sweden 1 - 2; Albania v England 0 - 2; England v Albania 5 - 0; Sweden v Poland 2 - 1; England v Poland 3 - 0; Sweden v England 0 - 0; Sweden v Albania 3 - 1; Poland v England 0 - 0; Poland v Sweden 0 - 2; Albania v Poland 1 - 2

	P	W	D	L	F	A	Pts
Sweden	6	4	2	0	9	3	10
England	6	3	3	0	10	0	9
Poland	6	2	1	3	4	8	5
Albania	6	0	0	6	3	15	0

Sweden and England qualified

Group 3 (USSR, East Germany, Austria, Iceland, Turkey)

Iceland v USSR 1 - 1; Turkey v Iceland 1 -1 ; USSR v Austria 2 - 0; East Germany v Iceland 2 - 0; Austria v Turkey 3 - 2; Turkey v East Germany 3 - 1; East Germany v Turkey 0 - 2; USSR v East Germany 3 - 0; Turkey v USSR 0 - 1; East Germany v Austria 1 - 1; USSR v Iceland 1 - 1; Iceland v Austria 0 - 0; Austria v Iceland 2 - 1; Austria v USSR 0 - 0; Iceland v East Germany 0 - 3; Iceland v Turkey 2 - 1; East Germany v USSR 2 - 1; Turkey v Austria 3 -0; USSR v Turkey 2 - 0; Austria v East Germany 3 - 0

	P	W	D	L	F	A	Pts
USSR	8	4	3	1	11	4	11
Austria	8	3	3	2	9	9	9
Turkey	8	3	1	4	12	10	7
East Germany	8	3	1	4	9	13	7
Iceland	8	1	4	3	6	11	6

USSR and Austria qualified

Group 4 (West Germany, Holland, Wales, Finland)

Finland v West Germany 0 - 4; Holland v Wales 1 - 0; Wales v Finland
2 - 2; West Germany v Holland 0 - 0; Holland v West Germany 1 - 1; Wales
v West Germany 0 - 0; Finland v Holland 0 - 1; Finland v Wales
1 - 0; West Germany v Finland 6 - 1; Wales v Holland 1 - 2; West Germany
v Wales 2 - 1; Holland v Finland 3 - 0

	P	W	D	L	F	A	Pts
Holland	6	4	2	0	8	2	10
West Germany	6	3	3	0	13	3	9
Finland	6	1	1	4	4	16	3
Wales	6	0	2	4	4	8	2

Holland and West Germany qualified

Group 5 (France, Scotland, Yugoslavia, Norway, Cyprus)

Norway v Scotland 1 - 2; France v Norway 1 - 0; Scotland v Yugoslavia
1 - 1; Cyprus v France 1 - 1; Cyprus v Norway 0 - 3; Yugoslavia v France
3 - 2; Yugoslavia v Cyprus 4 - 0; Scotland v Cyprus 2 - 3; Scotland
v France 2 - 0; Scotland v Cyprus 2 - 1; France v Yugoslavia 0 - 0; Norway
v Cyprus 3 - 0; Norway v Yugoslavia 1 - 2; Norway v France 1 - 1;
Yugoslavia v Scotland 3 - 1; Yugoslavia v Norway 1 - 0; France v Scotland 3 -
0; Cyprus v Yugoslavia 1 - 2; Scotland v Norway 1 - 1; France v Cyprus 2 - 0

	P	W	D	L	F	A	Pts
Yugoslavia	8	6	2	0	16	6	14
Scotland	8	4	2	2	12	12	10
France	8	3	3	2	10	7	9
Norway	8	2	2	4	10	9	6
Cyprus	8	0	1	7	6	20	1

Yugoslavia and Scotland qualified

Group 6 (Spain, Hungary, Northern Ireland, Rep of Ireland, Malta)

Northern Ireland v Malta 3 - 0; Northern Ireland v Rep of Ireland 0 - 0;
Hungary v Northern Ireland 1 - 0; Spain v Rep of Ireland 2 - 0; Malta
v Hungary 2 - 2; Spain v Northern Ireland 4 - 0; Malta v Spain 0 - 2;
Northern Ireland v Spain 0 - 2; Hungary v Rep of Ireland 0 - 0; Spain
v Malta 4 - 0; Hungary v Malta 1 -1 ; Malta v Northern Ireland 0 - 2; Rep of
Ireland v Spain 0 - 2; Rep of Ireland v Malta 2 - 0; Rep of
Ireland v Hungary 2 - 0; Northern Ireland v Hungary 1 - 2; Hungary v Spain 2 - 2;
Rep of Ireland v Northern Ireland 3 - 0; Spain v Hungary 4 - 0; Malta
v Rep of Ireland 0 - 2

	P	W	D	L	F	A	Pts
Spain	8	6	1	1	20	3	13
Rep of Ireland	8	5	2	1	10	2	12
Hungary	8	2	4	2	8	12	8
Northern Ireland	8	2	1	5	6	12	5
Malta	8	0	2	6	3	18	2

Spain and Rep of Ireland qualified

Group 7 (Belgium, Portugal, Czechoslovakia, Switzerland, Luxembourg)

Luxembourg v Switzerland 1 - 4; Luxembourg v Czechoslovakia 0 - 2;
Belgium v Switzerland 1 - 0; Czechoslovakia v Belgium 0 - 0; Portugal
v Luxembourg 1 - 0; Portugal v Belgium 1 - 1; Portugal v Switzerland 3 - 1;
Belgium v Czechoslovakia 2 - 1; Czechoslovakia v Luxembourg 4 - 0;
Luxembourg v Belgium 0 - 5; Switzerland v Czechoslovakia 0 - 1; Belgium
v Portugal 3 - 0; Switzerland v Portugal 1 - 2; Czechoslovakia v Portugal
2 - 1; Luxembourg v Portugal 0 - 3; Switzerland v Belgium 2 - 2;
Czechoslovakia v Switzerland 3 - 0; Belgium v Luxembourg 1 - 1; Portugal
v Czechoslovakia 0 - 0; Switzerland v Luxembourg 2 - 1

	P	W	D	L	F	A	Pts
Belgium	8	4	4	0	15	5	12
Czechoslovakia	8	5	2	1	13	3	12
Portugal	8	4	2	2	11	8	10
Switzerland	8	2	1	5	10	14	5
Luxembourg	8	0	1	7	3	22	1

Belgium and Czechoslovakia qualified

Africa

1st Round
Group 1

Angola v Sudan 0 - 0, 2 - 1; Zimbabwe v Lesotho (withdrew); Zambia
v Rwanda (withdrew); Uganda v Malawi 1 - 0, 1 - 3

Group 2

Libya v Burkina Faso 3 - 0, 0 - 2; Ghana v Liberia 0 - 0, 0 - 2; Tunisia
v Guinea 5 - 0, 0 - 3; Gabon v Togo (withdrew)

2nd Round
Group A (Algeria, Ivory Coast, Zimbabwe, Libya)

Algeria v Zimbabwe 3 - 0; Ivory Coast v Libya 1 - 0; Libya v Algeria (Libya
refused to play claiming state of war against the USA; match awarded
2 - 0 to Algeria); Zimbabwe v Ivory Coast 0 - 0;(Libya withdrew at this
point and their record was expunged); Ivory Coast v Algeria 0 - 0;
Zimbabwe v Algeria 1 - 2; Ivory Coast v Zimbabwe 5 - 0; Algeria v Ivory
Coast 1 - 0

	P	W	D	L	F	A	Pts
Algeria	4	3	1	0	6	1	7
Ivory Coast	4	1	2	1	5	1	4
Zimbabwe	4	0	1	3	1	10	1

Group B (Egypt, Kenya, Malawi, Liberia)

Egypt v Liberia 2 - 0; Kenya v Malawi 1 - 1; Malawi v Egypt 1 - 1;Liberia
v Kenya 0 - 0; Kenya v Egypt 0 - 0; Liberia v Malawi 1 - 0; Malawi v Kenya
1 - 0; Liberia v Egypt 1 - 0; Egypt v Malawi 1 - 0; Kenya v Liberia 1 - 0;
Egypt v Kenya 2 - 0; Malawi v Liberia 0 - 0

	P	W	D	L	F	A	Pts
Egypt	6	3	2	1	6	2	8
Liberia	6	2	2	2	2	3	6
Malawi	6	1	3	2	3	4	5
Kenya	6	1	3	2	2	4	5

Group C (Cameroon, Nigeria, Gabon, Angola)

Nigeria v Gabon 1 - 0; Cameroon v Angola 1 - 1; Gabon v Cameroon
1 - 3; Angola v Nigeria 2 - 2; Nigeria v Cameroon 2 - 0; Angola v Gabon
2 - 0; Angola v Cameroon 1 - 2; Gabon v Nigeria 2 - 1; Nigeria v Angola
1 - 0; Cameroon v Gabon 2 - 1; Cameroon v Nigeria 1 - 0; Gabon v Angola
1 - 0

	P	W	D	L	F	A	Pts
Cameroon	6	4	1	1	9	6	9
Nigeria	6	3	1	2	7	5	7
Angola	6	1	2	3	6	7	4
Gabon	6	2	0	4	5	9	4

Group D (Morocco, Zaire, Tunisia, Zambia)

Morocco v Zambia 1 - 0; Zaire v Tunisia 3 - 1; Tunisia v Morocco 2 - 1;
Zambia v Zaire 4 - 2; Zaire v Morocco 0 - 0; Zambia v Tunisia 1 - 0; Zambia
v Morocco 2 - 1; Tunisia v Zaire 1 - 0; Morocco v Tunisia 0 - 0; Zaire
v Zambia 1 - 0; Tunisia v Zambia 1 - 0; Morocco v Zaire 1 - 1

	P	W	D	L	F	A	Pts
Tunisia	6	3	1	2	5	5	7
Zambia	6	3	0	3	7	6	6
Zaire	6	2	2	2	7	7	6
Morocco	6	1	3	2	4	5	5

3rd Round

Algeria v Egypt 0 - 0,0 - 1; Cameroon v Tunisia 2 - 0, 1 - 0

Egypt and Cameroon qualified

Asia

1st Round
Group 1 (Iraq, Qatar, Jordan, Oman)

Qatar v Jordan 1 - 1; Oman v Iraq 1 - 1; Oman v Qatar 0 - 0; Jordan v Iraq
0 - 1; Jordan v Oman 2 - 0; Qatar v Iraq 1 - 0; Jordan v Qatar 1 - 1; Iraq
v Oman 3 - 1; Qatar v Oman 3 - 0; Iraq v Jordan 4 - 0; Oman v Jordan
0 - 2; Iraq v Qatar 2 - 2

	P	W	D	L	F	A	Pts
Qatar	6	3	3	0	8	3	9
Iraq	6	3	2	1	11	5	8
Jordan	6	2	1	3	5	7	5
Oman	6	0	2	4	2	11	2

Group 2 (Saudi Arabia, Syria, North Yemen, Bahrain (withdrew))

North Yemen v Syria 0 - 1; Saudi Arabia v Syria 5 - 4; North Yemen v Saudi
Arabia 0 - 1; Syria v North Yemen 2 - 0; Syria v Saudi Arabia 0 - 0; Saudi
Arabia v North Yemen 1 - 0

	P	W	D	L	F	A	Pts
Saudi Arabia	4	3	1	0	7	4	7
Syria	4	2	1	1	7	5	5
North Yemen	4	0	0	4	0	5	0

Group 3 (Kuwait, UAE, Pakistan, South Yemen (withdrew))
Pakistan v Kuwait 0 - 1; Kuwait v UAE 3 - 2; UAE v Pakistan 5 - 0; Kuwait
v Pakistan 2 - 0; UAE v Kuwait 1 - 0; Pakistan v UAE 1 - 4

	P	W	D	L	F	A	Pts
UAE	4	3	0	1	12	4	6
Kuwait	4	3	0	1	6	3	6
Pakistan	4	0	0	4	1	12	0

Group 4 (South Korea, Singapore, Malaysia, Nepal, India (withdrew))
All matches played in Singapore
Malaysia v Nepal 2 - 0; Singapore v South Korea 0 - 3; Malaysia v
Singapore 1 - 0; Nepal v South Korea 0 - 9; Singapore v Nepal 3 - 0; South
Korea v Malaysia 3 - 0 (all matches played in South Korea); Singapore
v Malaysia 2 - 2; South Korea v Nepal 4 - 0; Malaysia v South Korea 0 - 3;
Nepal v Singapore 0 - 7; Singapore v South Korea 0 - 3; Malaysia v Nepal
3 - 0

	P	W	D	L	F	A	Pts
South Korea	6	6	0	0	25	0	2
Malaysia	6	3	1	2	8	8	7
Singapore	6	2	1	3	12	9	5
Nepal	6	0	0	6	0	28	0

Group 5 (China, Iran, Thailand, Bangladesh)
Thailand v Bangladesh 1 - 0; China v Bangladesh 2 - 0; Thailand v Iran 0 - 3;
Bangladesh v Iran 1 - 2; Thailand v China 0 - 3; Bangladesh v China 0 - 2;
Bangladesh v Thailand 3 - 1; Iran v Bangladesh 1 - 0; Iran v Thailand 3 - 0;
China v Iran 2 - 0; Iran v China 3 - 2; China v Thailand 2 - 0

	P	W	D	L	F	A	Pts
China	6	5	0	1	13	3	10
Iran	6	5	0	1	12	5	10
Bangladesh	6	1	0	5	4	9	2
Thailand	6	1	0	5	2	14	2

Group 6 (North Korea, Japan, Indonesia, Hong Kong)
Indonesia v North Korea 0 - 0; Hong Kong v Japan 0 - 0; Hong Kong v
North Korea 1 - 2; Indonesia v Japan 0 - 0; Hong Kong v Indonesia 1 - 1;
Japan v North Korea 2 - 1; Japan v Indonesia 5 - 0; Japan v Hong Kong 0 -
0; Indonesia v Hong Kong 3 - 2; North Korea v Japan 2 - 0; North Korea
v Hong Kong 4 - 1; North Korea v Indonesia 2 - 1

	P	W	D	L	F	A	Pts
North Korea	6	4	1	1	11	5	9
Japan	6	2	3	1	7	3	7
Indonesia	6	1	3	2	5	10	5
Hong Kong	6	0	3	3	5	10	3

2nd Round (in Singapore)
UAE v North Korea 0 - 0; China v Saudi Arabia 2 - 1; South Korea v Qatar
0 - 0; Qatar v Saudi Arabia 1 - 1; South Korea v North Korea 1 - 0; China
v UAE 1 - 2; China v South Korea 0 - 1; North Korea v Qatar 0 - 0; Saudi
Arabia v UAE 0 - 0; UAE v Qatar 1 - 1; North Korea v China 0 - 1; Saudi
Arabia v South Korea 0 - 2; UAE v South Korea 1 - 1; Saudi Arabia v North
Korea 2 - 0; Qatar v China 2 - 1

	P	W	D	L	F	A	Pts
South Korea	5	3	2	0	5	1	8
UAE	5	1	4	0	4	3	6
Qatar	5	1	3	1	4	5	5
China	5	2	0	3	5	6	4
Saudi Arabia	5	1	2	2	4	5	4
North Korea	5	1	1	3	2	4	3

South Korea and UAE qualified

Concacaf
1st Round
Guyana v Trinidad and Tobago 0 - 4, 0 - 1; Cuba v Guatemala 0 - 1, 1 - 1;
Jamaica v Puerto Rico 1 - 0, 2 - 1; Antigua v Netherlands Antilles 0 - 1,
1 - 0 (Netherlands Antilles won 3 - 1 on penalties); Costa Rica v Panama
1 - 1, 2 - 0

2nd Round
Netherlands Antilles v El Salvador 0 - 1, 0 - 5; Jamaica v USA 0 - 0, 1 - 5;
Trinidad and Tobago v Honduras 0 - 0, 1 - 1; Costa Rica v Mexico
(disqualified); Guatemala v Canada 1 0, 2 - 3

3rd Round
Guatemala v Costa Rica 1 - 0; Costa Rica v Guatemala 2 - 1; Costa Rica
v USA 1 - 0; USA v Costa Rica 1 - 0; USA v Trinidad and Tobago 1 - 0;
Trinidad and Tobago v Costa Rica 1 - 1; Costa Rica v Trinidad and Tobago
1 - 0; USA v Guatemala 2 - 1; El Salvador v Costa Rica 2 - 4 (match
abandoned after 84 mins; score allowed to stand), Costa Rica
v El Salvador 1 - 0; Trinidad and Tobago v El Salvador 2 - 0; El Salvador
v Trinidad and Tobago 0 - 0; Guatemala v Trinidad and Tobago 0 - 1;
Trinidad and Tobago v Guatemala 2 - 1; El Salvador v USA (in Honduras)
0 - 1; Guatemala v USA 0 - 0; USA v El Salvador 1 - 0; Trinidad and Tobago
v USA 0 - 1; Guatemala v El Salvador and El Salvador v Guatemala not
played due to deterioration of the political situation in El Salvador, FIFA
annulled the fixtures

	P	W	D	L	F	A	Pts
Costa Rica	8	5	1	2	10	6	11
USA	8	4	3	1	6	3	11
T'dad/Tobago	8	3	3	2	7	5	9
Guatemala	6	1	1	4	4	7	3
El Salvador	6	0	2	4	2	8	2

Costa Rica and USA qualified

South America
Group 1 (Uruguay, Peru, Bolivia)
Bolivia v Peru 2 - 1; Peru v Uruguay 0 - 2; Bolivia v Uruguay 2 - 1;
Peru v Bolivia 1 - 2; Uruguay v Bolivia 2 - 0; Uruguay v Peru 2 - 0

	P	W	D	L	F	A	Pts
Uruguay	4	3	0	1	7	2	6
Bolivia	4	3	0	1	6	5	6
Peru	4	0	0	4	2	8	0

Uruguay qualified

Group 2 (Paraguay, Colombia, Ecuador)
Colombia v Ecuador 2 - 0; Paraguay v Colombia 2 - 1; Ecuador v Colombia
0 - 0; Paraguay v Ecuador 2 - 1; Colombia v Paraguay 2 - 1; Ecuador
v Paraguay 3 - 1

	P	W	D	L	F	A	Pts
Colombia	4	2	1	1	5	3	5
Paraguay	4	2	0	2	6	7	4
Ecuador	4	1	1	2	4	5	3

Colombia qualified for play-off with Oceania winner

Group 3 (Brazil, Chile, Venezuela)
Venezuela v Brazil 0 - 4; Venezuela v Chile 1 - 3; Chile v Brazil 1 - 1; Brazil v
Venezuela 6 - 0; Chile v Venezuela 5 - 0; Brazil v Chile 1 - 0 (abandoned
59th minute; match awarded 2 - 0 to Brazil)

	P	W	D	L	F	A	Pts
Brazil	4	3	1	0	13	1	7
Chile	4	2	1	1	9	4	5
Venezuela	4	0	0	4	1	18	0

Brazil qualified

Oceania
1st round
Group 1
Taipei v New Zealand 0 - 4, 1-4

Group 2
Fiji v Australia 1 - 0, 1 - 5

2nd round
Israel v New Zealand 1 - 0; Australia v New Zealand 4 - 1; Israel
v Australia 1 - 1; New Zealand v Australia 2 - 0; New Zealand v Israel 2 - 2;
Australia v Israel 1 - 1

	P	W	D	L	F	A	Pts
Israel	4	1	3	0	5	4	5
Australia	4	1	2	1	6	5	4
New Zealand	4	1	1	2	5	7	3

Play-off: Colombia v Israel 1 - 0, 0 - 0
Colombia qualified

Final Tournament ITALY
First Round
GROUP A

9.6.90 Italy (0) 1, Austria (0) 0 ROME
Italy: Zenga, Maldini, Ferri, Baresi, Bergomi, De Napoli, Ancelotti (De Agostini), Donadoni, Giannini, Carnevale (Schillaci (1)), Vialli
Austria: Lindenberger, Russ, Streiter, Pecl, Aigner, Artner (Zsak), Herzog, Schottel, Linzmaier (Hortnagl), Ogris, Polster
Referee: Wright (Brazil)

10.6.90 Czechoslovakia (2) 5, USA (0) 1 FLORENCE
Czechoslovakia: Stejskal, Hasek (1), Kocian, Kadlec, Straka, Moravcik (Weiss), Chovanec, Kubik, Bilek (1 pen), Knoflicek (Luhovy (1)), Skuhravy (2)
USA: Meola, Armstrong, Stollmeyer (Balboa), Windischmann, Trittschuh, Caligiuri (1), Ramos, Harkes, Wynalda, Vermes, Murray (Sullivan)
Referee: Rothlisberger (Switzerland)

14.6.90 Italy (1) 1, USA (0) 0 ROME
Italy: Zenga, Bergomi, Ferri, Baresi, Maldini, De Napoli, Berti, Giannini (1), Donadoni, Carnevale (Schillaci), Vialli
USA: Meola, Armstrong, Windischmann, Doyle, Banks (Stollmeyer), Ramos, Balboa, Caligiuri, Harkes, Vermes, Murray (Sullivan)
Referee: Codesal (Mexico)

15.6.90 Austria (0) 0, Czechoslovakia (0) 1 FLORENCE
Austria: Lindenberger, Russ (Ogris), Aigner, Pecl, Pfeffer, Hortnagl, Zsak, Schottel (Streiter), Herzog, Rodax, Polster
Czechoslovakia: Stejskal, Hasek, Kadlec, Kocian, Nemecek, Moravcik, Chovanec (Bielik), Kubik, Bilek (1 pen), Skuhravy, Knoflicek (Weiss)
Referee: Smith (Scotland)

19.6.90 Italy (1) 2, Czechoslovakia (0) 0 ROME
Italy: Zenga, Bergomi, Ferri, Baresi, Maldini, Donadoni (De Agostini), De Napoli (Vierchowod), Giannini, Berti, Baggio (1), Schillaci (1)
Czechoslovakia: Stejskal, Hasek, Kadlec, Kinier, Nemecek (Bielik), Moravcik, Chovanec, Weiss (Griga), Bilek, Skuhravy, Knoflicek
Referee: Quiniou (France)

19.6.90 Austria (0) 2, USA (0) 1 FLORENCE
Austria: Lindenberger, Streiter, Aigner, Pecl, Pfeffer, Artner, Zsak, Herzog, Rodax (1) (Glatzmeyer), Polster (Reisinger), Ogris (1)
USA: Meola, Doyle, Windischmann, Banks (Wynalda), Armstrong, Caligiuri (Bliss), Harkes, Ramos, Balboa, Murray (1), Vermes
Referee: Sharif Jamal (Egypt)

	P	W	D	L	F	A	Pts
Italy	3	3	0	0	4	0	6
Czechoslovakia	3	2	0	1	6	3	4
Austria	3	1	0	2	2	3	2
United States	3	0	0	3	2	8	0

GROUP B

8.6.90 Argentina (0) 0, Cameroon (0) 1 MILAN
Argentina: Pumpido, Ruggeri (Caniggia), Fabbri, Simon, Lorenzo, Batista, Sensini (Calderon), Balbo, Basualdo, Burruchaga, Maradona
Cameroon: Nkono, Tataw, Ebwelle, Massing, Ndip, Kunde, Mbouh, Kana-Biyik, Mfede (Libih), Makanaky (Milla), Omam-Biyik (1)
Referee: Vautrot (France)

9.6.90 USSR (0) 0, Rumania (1) 2 BARI
USSR: Dasayev, Kuznetsov, Khidiatulin, Gorlukovich, Rats, Aleinikov, Bessonov, Litovchenko (Yaremchuk), Zavarov, Protasov, Dobrovolski (Borodyuk)
Rumania: Lung, Rednic, Andone, Popescu, Klein, Rotariu, Timofte, Sabau, Lupescu, Lacatus (2, 1 pen) (Dumitrescu), Raducioiu (Balint)
Referee: Cardellino (Uruguay)

13.6.90 Argentina (1) 2, USSR (0) 0 NAPLES
Argentina: Pumpido (Goycochea), Monzon (Lorenzo), Serrizuela, Simon, Olarticoechea, Batista, Basualdo, Burruchaga (1), Troglio (1), Maradona, Caniggia
USSR: Uvarov, Bessonov, Kuznetsov, Khidiatulin, Gorlukovich, Zygmantovich, Aleinikov, Shalimov, Zavarov (Liuti), Dobrovolski, Protasov (Litovchenko)
Referee: Fredriksson (Sweden)

14.6.90 Cameroon (0) 2, Rumania (0) 1 BARI
Cameroon: Nkono, Tataw, Onana, Ndip, Ebwelle, Kunde (Pagal), Mbouh, Mfede, Maboang (Milla (2)), Makanaky, Omam-Biyik
Rumania: Lung, Rednic, Andone, Popescu, Klein, Rotariu, Sabau, Timofte, Hagi (Dumitrescu), Raducioiu (Balint (1)), Lacatus
Referee: Valente (Portugal)

18.6.90 Argentina (0) 1, Rumania (0) 1 NAPLES
Argentina: Goycochea, Simon, Serrizuela, Monzon (1), Troglio (Giusti), Batista, Burruchaga (Dezotti), Basualdo, Olarticoechea, Maradona, Caniggia
Rumania: Lung, Rednic, Andone, Popescu, Klein, Rotariu, Sabau (Mateut), Lupescu, Hagi, Lacatus, Balint (1) (Lupu)
Referee: Valente (Portugal)

18.6.90 USSR (2) 4, Cameroon (0) 0 BARI
USSR: Uvarov, Khidiatulin, Kuznetsov, Demianenko, Gorlukovich, Aleinikov, Litovchenko (Yaremchuk), Zygmantovich (1), Shalimov (Zavarov (1)), Protasov (1), Dobrovolski (1)
Cameroon: Nkono, Onana, Ebwelle, Kunde (Milla), Tataw, Ndip, Kana-Biyik, Mbouh, Mfede, Makanaky (Pagal), Omam-Biyik
Referee: Wright (Brazil)

	P	W	D	L	F	A	Pts
Cameroon	3	2	0	1	3	5	4
Rumania	3	1	1	1	4	3	3
Argentina	3	1	1	1	3	2	3
USSR	3	1	0	2	4	4	2

GROUP C

10.6.90 Brazil (1) 2, Sweden (0) 1 TURIN
Brazil: Taffarel, Mauro Galvao, Mozer, Ricardo Gomes, Jorginho, Branco, Dunga, Alemao, Valdo (Silas), Muller, Careca (2)
Sweden: Ravelli, Nilsson R, Larsson P, Ljung (Stromberg), Limpar, Thern, Schwarz, Ingesson, Nilsson J, Brolin (1), Magnusson (Pettersson)
Referee: Lanese (Italy)

11.6.90 Costa Rica (0) 1, Scotland (0) 0 GENOA
Costa Rica: Conejo, Chavarria, Flores, Marchena, Montero, Chavez, Gonzalez, Gomez, Ramirez, Jara (Medford), Cayasso (1)
Scotland: Leighton, Gough (McKimmie), McPherson, McLeish, Malpas, McStay, Aitken, McCall, Bett (McCoist), Johnston, McInally
Referee: Loustau (Argentina)

16.6.90 Brazil (1) 1, Costa Rica (0) 0 TURIN
Brazil: Taffarel, Mauro Galvao, Jorginho, Mozer, Ricardo Gomes, Branco, Dunga, Alemao, Valdo (Silas), Careca (Bebeto), Muller (1)
Costa Rica: Conejo, Flores, Chavarria, Marchena, Gonzalez, Montero, Chavez, Gomez, Ramirez, Jara (Myers), Cayasso (Guimaraes)
Referee: Jouini (Tunisia)

16.6.90 Scotland (1) 2, Sweden (0) 1 GENOA
Scotland: Leighton, McPherson, Levein, McLeish, Malpas, Aitken, MacLeod, McCall (1), Fleck (McCoist), Durie (McStay), Johnston (1 pen)
Sweden: Ravelli, Nilsson R, Larsson P (Stromberg (1)), Hysen, Schwarz, Ingesson, Thern, Limpar, Nilsson J, Brolin, Pettersson (Ekstrom)
Referee: Maciel (Paraguay)

20.6.90 Brazil (0) 1, Scotland (0) 0 TURIN
Brazil: Taffarel, Jorginho, Mauro Galvao, Ricardo Rocha, Ricardo Gomes, Branco, Alemao, Dunga, Valdo, Careca, Romario (Muller (1))
Scotland: Leighton, McKimmie, McPherson, Aitken, McLeish, Malpas, McCall, McStay, MacLeod (Gillespie), Johnston, McCoist (Fleck)
Referee: Kohl (Austria)

20.6.90 Costa Rica (0) 2, Sweden (1) 1 GENOA
Costa Rica: Conejo, Marchena, Flores (1), Gonzalez, Montero, Chavarria, Gomez (Medford (1)), Chaves, Cayasso, Ramirez, Jara
Sweden: Ravelli, Nilsson R, Larsson P, Hysen, Schwarz, Pettersson, Stromberg (Engqvist), Ingesson, Nilsson J, Ekstrom (1), Brolin (Gren)
Referee: Petrovic (Yugoslavia)

	P	W	D	L	F	A	Pts
Brazil	3	3	0	0	4	1	6
Costa Rica	3	2	0	1	3	2	4
Scotland	3	1	0	2	2	3	2
Sweden	3	0	0	3	3	6	0

GROUP D

9.6.90 Colombia (0) 2, UAE (0) 0 BOLOGNA
Colombia: Higuita, Escobar, Gildardo Gomez, Herrera, Perea, Gabriel Gomez, Valderrama (1), Redin (1), Alvarez, Rincon, Iguaran (Estrada)
UAE: Faraj, Mubarak K G, Abdulrahman I, Abdulrahman E (Sultan), Mohamed Y, Juma'a, Abdullah Moh, Abbas, Mubarak N, Mubarak K (Bilal), Talyani
Referee: Courtney (England)

10.6.90 Yugoslavia (0) 1, West Germany (2) 4 MILAN
Yugoslavia: Ivkovic, Vulic, Hadzibegic, Jozic (1), Spasic, Katanec, Baljic, Susic (Brnovic), Savicevic (Prosinecki), Stojkovic, Vujovic
West Germany: Illgner, Reuter, Berthold, Augenthaler, Brehme, Buchwald, Matthaus (2), Bein (Moller), Hassler (Littbarski), Klinsmann (1), Voller (1)
Referee: Mikkelsen (Denmark)

14.6.90 Yugoslavia (0) 1, Colombia (0) 0 BOLOGNA
Yugoslavia: Ivkovic, Stanojkovic, Spasic, Hadzibegic, Jozic (1), Brnovic, Susic, Katanec (Jarni), Stojkovic, Sabanadzovic, Vujovic (Pancev)
Colombia: Higuita, Herrera, Perea, Gildardo Gomez, Escobar, Gabriel Gomez, Alvarez, Valderrama, Redin (Estrada), Rincon (Hernandez), Iguaran
Referee: Agnolin (Italy)

15.6.90 West Germany (2) 5, UAE (0) 1 MILAN
West Germany: Illgner, Reuter, Buchwald, Augenthaler, Brehme, Berthold (Littbarski), Matthaus (1), Hassler, Bein (1), Klinsmann (1) (Riedle), Voller (2)
UAE: Faraj, Abdulrahman E, Mubarak K G, Mohamed Y, Abdulrahman I, (Al Haddad), Addullah Moh, Juma'a, Mubarak N, Mubarak K (1) (Hussain), Abbas, Talyani
Referee: Spirin (USSR)

19.6.90 West Germany (0) 1, Colombia (0) 1 MILAN
West Germany: Illgner, Reuter, Buchwald, Augenthaler, Pflugler, Berthold, Matthaus, Hassler (Thon), Bein (Littbarski (1)), Klinsmann, Voller
Colombia: Higuita, Herrera, Escobar, Perea, Gildardo Gomez, Gabriel Gomez, Alvarez, Estrada, Fajardo, Valderrama, Rincon (1)
Referee: Snoddy (N. Ireland)

19.6.90 Yugoslavia (2) 4, UAE (1) 1 BOLOGNA
Yugoslavia: Ivkovic, Stanojkovic, Spasic, Hadzibegic, Jozic, Brnovic, Susic (1), Stojkovic, Sabanadzovic (Prosinecki), Pancev (2), Vujovic (Vulic)
UAE: Faraj, Mubarak K G, Abdulrahman I, Abdulrahman E, Al Haddad, Juma'a (1), (Mubarak F K), Abdullah Moh, Abbas, Mubarak N (Sultan), Mubarak I, Talyani
Referee: Takada (Japan)

	P	W	D	L	F	A	Pts
West Germany	3	2	1	0	10	3	5
Yugoslavia	3	2	0	1	6	5	4
Colombia	3	1	1	1	3	2	1
UAE	3	0	0	3	2	11	0

GROUP E

12.6.90 Belgium (0) 2, South Korea (0) 0 VERONA
Belgium: Preud'homme, Gerets, Clijsters, Demol, Dewolf (1), Emmers, Van der Elst, Scifo, Versavel, De Gryse (1), Van der Linden (Ceulemans)
South Korea: Choi In-Young, Choi Kang-Hee, Chung Yong-Hwan, Hong Myung-Bo, Park Kyung-Joon, Gu Sang-Bum, Lee Young-Jin (Cho Min-Kook), Noh Soo-Jin (Lee Tae-Hoo), Choi Soon-Ho, Hwang Seon-Hong, Kim Joo-Sung
Referee: Mauro (USA)

13.6.90 Spain (0) 0, Uruguay (0) 0 UDINE
Spain: Zubizarreta, Chendo, Sanchis, Andrinua, Jimenez, Martin Vazquez, Roberto, Villaroya (Gorriz), Michel, Manolo (Paz), Butragueno
Uruguay: Alvez, Herrera, Gutierrez, De Leon, Dominguez, Ruben Pereira (Correa), Perdomo, Paz, Alzamendi (Aguilera), Francescoli, Sosa
Referee: Kohl (Austria)

17.6.90 Spain (1) 3, South Korea (1) 1 UDINE
Spain: Zubizarreta, Chendo, Andrinua, Sanchis, Gorriz, Michel (3), Villaroya, Roberto (Bakero), Martin Vazquez, Butragueno (Fernando), Julio Salinas
South Korea: Choi In-Young, Park Kyung-Joon (Chung Jong-Soo), Choi Kang-Hee, Hong Myung-Bo, Yoon Deuk-Yeo, Hwang Kwan-Bo (1), Chung Hae-Won (Noh Soo-Jin), Kim Joo-Sung, Gu Sang-Bum, Byun Byung-Joo, Choi Soon-Ho
Referee: Guerrero (Ecuador)

17.6.90 Belgium (2) 3, Uruguay (0) 1 VERONA
Belgium: Preud'homme, Gerets, Grun, Clijsters (1) (Emmers), Demol, Dewolf, Versavel (Vervoort), Van der Elst, Scifo (1), De Gryse, Ceulemans (1)
Uruguay: Alvez, Herrera, Gutierrez, De Leon, Dominguez, Ostolaza (Bengoechea)), Perdomo, Paz, Alzamendi (Aguilera), Francescoli, Sosa
Referee: Kirschen (East Germany)

21.6.90 Spain (2) 2, Belgium (1) 1 VERONA
Spain: Zubizarreta, Chendo, Sanchis, Andrinua, Villaroya, Gorriz (1), Michel (1 pen), Roberto, Martin Vazquez, Butragueno (Alcorta), Julio Salinas (Pardeza)
Belgium: Preud'homme, Staelens (Van der Linden), Albert, Demol, Dewolf, Van der Elst, Emmers (Plovie), Vervoort (1), Scifo, De Gryse, Ceulemans
Referee: Loustau (Argentina)

21.6.90 Uruguay (0) 1, South Korea (0) 0 UDINE
Uruguay: Alvez, Gutierrez, De Leon, Herrera, Dominguez, Perdomo, Ostolaza (Aguilera), Francescoli, Paz, Martinez, Sosa (Fonseca (1))
South Korea: Choi In-Young, Park Kyung-Joon, Choi Kang-Hee, Chung Jong-Soo, Hong Myung-Bo, Yoon Deuk-Yeo, Hwang Kwan-Bo (Chung Hae-Won), Lee Heung-Sil, Kim Joo-Sung (Hwang Seon-Hong), Byun Byung-Joo, Choi Soon-Ho
Referee: Lanese (Italy)

	P	W	D	L	F	A	Pts
Spain	3	2	1	0	5	2	5
Belgium	3	2	0	1	6	3	4
Uruguay	3	1	1	1	2	3	3
South Korea	3	0	0	3	1	6	0

GROUP F

11.6.90 England (1) 1, Rep of Ireland (0) 1 CAGLIARI
England: Shilton, Stevens, Walker, Butcher, Pearce, Robson, Beardsley (McMahon), Gascoigne, Waddle, Barnes, Lineker (1) (Bull)
Rep of Ireland: Bonner, Morris, McCarthy, Moran, Staunton, McGrath, Houghton, Sheedy (1), Aldridge (McLoughlin), Townsend, Cascarino
Referee: Schmidhuber (West Germany)

12.6.90 Egypt (0) 1, Holland (0) 1 PALERMO
Egypt: Shoubeir, Hassan I, Yaken, Ramzi H, Yassine, Youssef, Ramzi A (Abdel Rahmane), Hassan H, Abdelhamid (Tolba), Abdelghani (1 pen), Abdou
Holland: Van Breukelen, Van Aerle, Rutjes, Koeman R, Van Tiggelen, Vanenburg (Kieft (1)), Wouters, Rijkaard, Koeman E (Witschge), Van Basten, Gullit
Referee: Aladren (Spain)

16.9.90 England (0) 0, Holland (0) 0 CAGLIARI
England: Shilton, Parker, Walker, Wright, Butcher, Pearce, Robson (Platt), Waddle (Bull), Gascoigne, Barnes, Lineker
Holland: Van Breukelen, Van Aerle, Rijkaard, Koeman R, Van Tiggelen, Wouters, Gullit, Witschge, Van't Schip (Kieft), Gillhaus, Van Basten
Referee: Petrovic (Yugoslavia)

17.6.90 Egypt (0) 0, Rep of Ireland (0) 0 PALERMO
Egypt: Shoubeir, Hassan I, Yaken, Ramzi H, Yassine, Abdelghani, Orabi, Tolba (Abou Seid), Youssef, Abdou (Abdelhamid), Hassan H
Rep of Ireland: Bonner, Morris, McCarthy, Moran, Staunton, McGrath, Houghton, Townsend, Sheedy, Aldridge (McLoughlin), Cascarino (Quinn)
Referee: Van Langehove (Belgium)

21.6.90 England (0) 1, Egypt (0) 0 CAGLIARI
England: Shilton, Parker, Wright (1), Walker, Pearce, Waddle (Platt), McMahon, Gascoigne, Barnes, Lineker, Bull (Beardsley)
Egypt: Shoubeir, Hassan I, Yaken, Ramzi H, Yassine, Youssef, Abdelghani, Abdou (Soliman), Ramzi A, Abdelhamid (Abdel Rahmane), Hassan H
Referee: Rothlisberger (Switzerland)

21.6.90 Rep of Ireland (0) 1, Holland (1) 1 PALERMO
Rep of Ireland: Bonner, Morris, McCarthy, Moran, Staunton, McGrath, Houghton, Townsend, Sheedy (Whelan), Aldridge (Cascarino), Quinn (1)
Holland: Van Breukelen, Van Aerle, Rijkaard, Koeman R, Van Tiggelen, Wouters, Witschge (Fraser), Van Basten, Gullit (1), Gillhaus, Kieft (Van Loen)
Referee: Vautrot (France)

	P	W	D	L	F	A	Pts
England	3	1	2	0	2	1	4
Rep of Ireland	3	0	3	0	2	2	3
Holland	3	0	3	0	2	2	3
Egypt	3	0	2	1	1	2	2

Second round

23.6.90 Cameroon (0) 2, Colombia (0) 1 (aet, 0-0 at 90 mins) NAPLES
Cameroon: Nkono, Tataw, Ndip, Onana, Ebwelle, Kana-Biyik, Mbouh, Maboang, Mfede (Milla (2)), Omam-Biyik, Makanaky (Djonkep)
Colombia: Higuita, Herrera, Perea, Escobar, Gildardo Gomez, Alvarez, Gabriel Gomez (Redin (1)), Rincon, Fajardo (Iguaran), Valderrama, Estrada
Referee: Lanese (Italy)

23.6.90 Czechoslovakia (1) 4, Costa Rica (0) 1 BARI
Czechoslovakia: Stejskal, Hasek, Kadlec, Kocian, Straka, Moravcik, Chovanec, Kubik (1), Bilek, Skuhravy (3), Knoflicek
Costa Rica: Barrantes, Chavarria (Guimaraes), Marchena, Flores, Montero, Chavez, Ramirez, Gonzalez (1), Obando (Medford), Cayasso, Jara
Referee: Kirschen (East Germany)

24.6.90 Argentina (0) 1, Brazil (0) 0 TURIN
Argentina: Goycochea, Basualdo, Monzon, Simon, Ruggeri, Olarticoechea, Giusti, Burruchaga, Maradona, Troglio (Calderon), Caniggia (1)
Brazil: Taffarel, Jorginho, Ricardo Rocha, Ricardo Gomes, Mauro Galvao (Renato), Branco, Alemao (Silas), Dunga, Valdo, Careca, Muller
Referee: Quiniou (France)

24.6.90 West Germany (0) 2, Holland (0) 1 MILAN
West Germany: Illgner, Reuter, Kohler, Augenthaler, Brehme (1), Buchwald, Berthold, Matthaus, Littbarski, Voller, Klinsmann (1) (Riedle)
Holland: Van Breukelen, Van Aerle (Kieft), Koeman R (1 pen), Van Tiggelen, Wouters, Rijkaard, Witschge (Gillhaus), Winter, Gullit, Van Basten, Van't Schip
Referee: Loustau (Argentina)

25.6.90 Rep of Ireland (0) 0, Rumania (0) 0
(aet, Rep of Ireland won 5-4 on penalties) GENOA
Rep of Ireland: Bonner, Morris, McCarthy, Moran, Staunton (O'Leary), McGrath, Townsend, Houghton, Sheedy, Aldridge (Cascarino), Quinn
Rumania: Lung, Rednic, Andone, Popescu, Klein, Rotariu, Lupescu, Sabau (Timofte), Hagi, Raducioiu (Lupu), Balint
Referee: Wright (Brazil)

25.6 90 Italy (0) 2, Uruguay (0) 0 ROME
Italy: Zenga, Bergomi, Ferri, Baresi, Maldini, De Agostini, De Napoli, Berti (Serena (1)) Giannini, Schillaci (1), Baggio (Vierchowod)
Uruguay: Alvez, Saldana, Gutierrez, De Leon, Dominguez, Ostolaza (Alzamendi), Perdomo, Francescoli, Ruben Pereira, Aguilera (Sosa), Fonseca
Referee: Courtney (England)

26.6.90 Spain (0) 1, Yugoslavia (0) 2 (aet, 1-1 at 90 mins) VERONA
Spain: Zubizarreta, Chendo, Gorriz, Andrinua (Jimenez), Sanchis, Villaroya, Martin Vazquez, Roberto, Michel, Butragueno (Rafa Paz), Julio Salinas (1)
Yugoslavia: Ivkovic, Sabanadzovic, Spasic, Brnovic, Katanec (Vulic), Hadzibegic, Jozic, Susic, Stojkovic, Pancev (Savicevic (2)), Vujovic
Referee: Schmidhuber (West Germany)

26.6.90 England (0) 1, Belgium (0) 0 (aet) BOLOGNA
England: Shilton, Parker, Butcher, Wright, Walker, Pearce, Waddle, Gascoigne, McMahon (Platt (1)), Barnes (Bull), Lineker
Belgium: Preud'homme, Gerets, Grun, Demol, Clijsters, Dewolf, Van der Elst, Scifo, Versavel (Vervoort), Ceulemans, De Gryse (Claesen)
Referee: Middelsen (Denmark)

QUARTER FINALS

30.6.90 Argentina (0) 0, Yugoslavia (0) 0
(aet, Argentina won 3-2 on penalties) FLORENCE
Argentina: Goycochea, Simon, Ruggeri, Serrizuela, Basualdo, Olarticoechea (Troglio), Giusti, Burruchaga, Calderon (Dezotti), Caniggia, Maradona
Yugoslavia: Ivkovic, Hadzibegic, Spasic, Brnovic, Vulic, Sabanadzovic, Jozic, Susic (Savicevic), Prosinecki, Stojkovic, Vujovic
Referee: Rothlisberger (West Germany)

30.6.90 Rep of Ireland (0) 0, Italy (1) 1 ROME
Rep of Ireland: Bonner, Morris, McCarthy, Moran, Staunton, McGrath, Houghton, Townsend, Sheedy, Quinn (Cascarino), Aldridge (Sheridan)
Italy: Zenga, Bergomi, Ferri, Baresi, Maldini, De Agostini, Donadoni, De Napoli, Giannini (Ancelotti), Baggio (Serena), Schillaci (1)
Referee: Valente (Portugal)

1.7.90 Czechoslovakia (0) 0, West Germany (1) 1 MILAN
Czechoslovakia: Stejskal, Hasek, Straka, Kocian, Kadlec, Moravcik, Chovanec, Bilek (Nemecek), Kubik (Griga), Skuhravy, Knoflicek
West Germany: Illgner, Berthold, Kohler, Augenthaler, Brehme, Buchwald, Matthaus (1 pen), Bein (Moller), Littbarski, Riedle, Klinsmann
Referee: Kohl (Austria)

1.7.90 Cameroon (0) 2, England (1) 3 (aet, 2-2 at 90 mins) NAPLES
Cameroon: Nkono, Tataw, Massing, Kunde (1 pen), Ebwelle, Maboang (Milla), Libih, Pagal, Makanaky, Mfede (Ekeke (1)), Omam-Biyik
England: Shilton, Parker, Butcher (Steven), Wright, Walker, Pearce, Waddle, Platt (1), Gascoigne, Barnes (Beardsley), Lineker (2 pens)
Referee: Codesal (Mexico)

SEMI FINALS

3.7.90 Argentina (0) 1, Italy (1) 1
(aet, 1-1 at 90 mins, Argentina won 4-3 on penalties) NAPLES
Argentina: Goycochea, Simon, Ruggeri, Serrizuela, Giusti, Calderon (Troglio), Burruchaga, Basualdo (Batista), Olarticoechea, Caniggia (1), Maradona
Italy: Zenga, Bergomi, Baresi, Ferri, De Napoli, De Agostini, Donadoni, Maldini, Giannini (Baggio), Schillaci (1), Vialli (Serena)
Referee: Vautrot (France)

4.7.90 West Germany (0) 1, England (0) 1
(aet, 1-1 at 90 mins, West Germany won 4-3 on penalties) TURIN
West Germany: Illgner, Berthold, Augenthaler, Buchwald, Kohler, Hassler (Reuter), Matthaus, Thon, Brehme (1), Klinsmann, Voller (Riedle)
England: Shilton, Parker, Butcher (Steven), Wright, Walker, Pearce, Platt, Gascoigne, Waddle, Beardsley, Lineker (1)
Referee: Wright (Brazil)

Match for third place

7.7.9 Italy (0) 2, England (0) 1 BARI
Italy: Zenga, Bergomi, Baresi, Ferrara, Maldini, Vierchowod, De Agostini (Berti), Ancelotti, Giannini (Ferri), Baggio (1), Schillaci (1 pen)
England: Shilton, Stevens, Wright (Waddle), Parker, Walker, Dorigo, Steven, Platt, McMahon (Webb), Beardsley, Lineker
Referee: Quiniou (France)

FINAL

8.7.90 West Germany (0) 1, Argentina (0) 0 ROME
West Germany: Illgner, Berthold (Reuter), Kohler, Augenthaler, Buchwald, Brehme (1 pen), Littbarski, Hassler, Matthaus, Voller, Klinsmann
Argentina: Goycochea, Lorenzo, Serrizuela, Sensini, Ruggeri (Monzon), Simon, Basualdo, Burruchaga (Calderon), Maradona, Troglio, Dezotti
Referee: Codesal (Mexico)

21 WORLD CUP ALL-TIME GREATS

The great Pele in action for Brazil in the 1970 World Cup final against Italy.

GORDON BANKS

ENGLAND

If goalkeeper Gordon Banks is remembered for one isolated incident in his career, it must be the one-handed save he made from Pele in the 1970 World Cup. The Brazilian's downward header into the corner of the goal was a text-book example of correctness. Yet Banks prevented the ball from entering the net.

Jairzinho had scampered around the England defence and crossed to the far post where Pele powered the ball into the ground only to see Banks' reflexes function perfectly in response. He flung himself low to his right, outstretched fingers managing to divert the ball upwards and over the bar.

England eventually lost the game 1-0 but Banks kept the opposition out in the next game against Czechoslovakia, an Allan Clarke penalty dividing the teams. But illness deprived him of a place in the side against West Germany and fate decreed that Banks would not play in another World Cup match.

Born in Sheffield on 30 December 1937, he played his early football in the locality. After making a name for himself with Sheffield Schools he played for Millspaugh Steelworks and then graduated to Rawmarsh Welfare.

His first chance with a Football League club came when he signed for Chesterfield in October 1955. Banks was nearly 18 and National Service was soon upon him. Posted to Germany for part of his period in uniform, he had to wait for his chance in League football. In fact by the time Leicester City succeeded in obtaining his signature, he had made only 23 League appearances.In 1956 he had appeared in the FA Youth Cup final.

That transfer was in May 1959 and he soon settled down at Filbert Street to become the club's regular choice. Two Under-23 caps against Wales and Scotland followed as a prelude to his full international debut for England against the Scots at Wembley in April 1963.

It was not the happiest of baptisms as Scotland won 2-1, but Banks had shown enough promise to be given further opportunities. Despite his height and large frame his agility was exceptional. A commanding figure in goal, he was a courageous keeper with that split-second sense of timing which distinguishes the exceptional from the accepted. Safe handling and fine positional sense added to his qualities.

In the next few years, Banks established himself for club and country. His understudy with Leicester was a teenager called Peter Shilton who was given his senior debut in 1965-66. Banks was preparing to defend the England goal in the World Cup.

He remained unbeaten in England's opening group games against Uruguay, Mexico and France and then the quarter-final with Argentina. It was only from the penalty spot against Portugal that Eusebio succeeded in putting the ball past him for the first time. By the time England had collected the World Cup after beating West Germany 4-2 at Wembley, Banks' reputation was world-wide.

At Leicester, Banks had been on the losing side in two FA Cup finals in 1961 and 1963 plus the two-legged League Cup finals in 1964 and 1965; he had taken his number of League appearances for Leicester to 293 when the club decided to look to the future. Banks, their first choice goalkeeper, was 29, his stand-in Shilton 12 years younger. So when Stoke City approached them for Banks, they agreed to transfer him for £52,000. At the time it was not even a record fee for a goalkeeper.

Thus in April 1967, with 37 international appearances for England, he moved to his third 'unfashionable' club. He had already overtaken Ron Springett as his country's most capped goalkeeper, set a record of caps for a Leicester player and now he proceeded to reach a similar milestone at Stoke.

Gordon Banks hugs Nobby Stiles following the 2-1 win by England over Portugal in 1966. Banks conceded his first goal in the competition on that evening.
(HULTON)

But little did he realise when he played against Scotland at Hampden Park in May 1972, that this was to be his last international cap. He was still only 34 years old. Banks was not beaten by the Scots; Alan Ball gave England a 1-0 win.

He had achieved recognition for his services to the game in 1970 with the announcement of an OBE. In 1972 he had collected a winner's medal with Stoke in the League Cup after a thrilling semi-final struggle with West Ham United. During the second leg, Banks memorably saved a blistering penalty from his old World Cup colleague Geoff Hurst. He became Player of the Year.

At the start of 1972-73, Banks had one or two injury problems. But he played at Liverpool on 21 October in a 2-1 defeat for Stoke and the following day reported for treatment at the Victoria Ground. On the way from the ground he was involved in a car accident and suffered serious damage to his right eye.

After several attempts at a come-back, including one with Morton in the Scottish League which was denied him by insurance companies, Banks went to the USA where he had two seasons with Fort Lauderdale in 1977 and 1978 before resuming a coaching role which he had taken up with England's intermediate and youth teams in the aftermath of his departure from Stoke. At his height he had been as safe as 'the Banks of England'.

FRANZ BECKENBAUER

WEST GERMANY

Few experts would argue against giving Franz Beckenbauer the title of the most complete footballer produced by West Germany. He had twelve years at the top in the international arena, made 103 appearances for his country and led his team to World Cup success as captain in 1974 and as manager in 1990.

As a schoolboy he played for 1906 Munchen, then at 13 he joined Bayern Munich. It was 1958 and he graduated through the club's junior ranks. Schools and youth matches provided an honours background which was to be handsomely enhanced in later years at higher level.

Born in Munich on 11 September 1945, he was 18 when he made his debut in Bayern's first team. In those days he was a left-winger, but soon found himself playing more in a midfield role. The Bayern coaches realised that his was no ordinary talent.

From his earliest games, it was evident that he had a maturity about his play far above his years. There was much more. He had speed, control and vision. Beckenbauer was also inclined to be an introvert and from this stemmed the beginnings of the accusations of a certain arrogance. The legend of 'Kaiser Franz' was born.

But a wider audience for his attributes was not yet visible. Bayern Munich were not members of the Bundesliga when it was formed in 1963-64. The top club in the city was 1860 Munich.

However, two seasons later Bayern found themselves promoted into the new German super-league, challenging their established rivals. That season 1860 Munich won the Bundesliga, but Bayern and Beckenbauer finished third.

Beckenbauer had by this time added a couple of appearances for West Germany's 'B' team but his prowess was such that in his club's initial season in the highest grade, he found himself selected to play for the full national team.

Appropriately it was in a World Cup qualifying match, against Sweden in Stockholm and the Germans won 2-1. In his fourth international he was on the losing side at Wembley in a 1-0 defeat inflicted by England. Five months later he returned, to face even greater disappointment in the World Cup Final.

Interestingly enough, these two games were the only ones in which the Germans lost during Beckenbauer's first 14 appearances. In fact there might have been a happier ending for him in that World Cup Final had it not been for the role handed to him by manager Helmut Schoen.

The Germans rightly considered Bobby Charlton to be the danger. But instead of detailing a more defensive player to shadow the Manchester United maestro, Schoen put the responsibility on Beckenbauer. Moreover, despite Charlton's comparatively quiet afternoon, the two cancelled each other out.

It was two years before Beckenbauer had the chance to restore pride lost in these defeats by England. In June 1968 in Hanover he did so with a vengeance, scoring the only goal of the match. Even more satisfaction was to come his way two years later.

On the way to the 1970 World Cup in Mexico, West Germany had a useful run of success which stretched to ten games without defeat. Morocco, Bulgaria and Peru were also accounted for in the finals themselves before a quarter-final with England.

Beckenbauer was to be switched to playing as a sweeper where his capacity for reading the game found a fresh dimension. Against England he needed all his skill to extricate West Germany from the position in which they found themselves. Two goals down and looking well beaten, the Germans discovered hidden reserves of stamina and concentration, inspired by Beckenbauer's presence.

In fact it was his low, penetrating drive which reduced the deficit to 2-1 and led to the Germans coming back to win the game 3-2. It was only Beckenbauer's second goal since his effort against England in Hanover two years before.

But if that was a high point in his career, the next was the lowest. The semi-final with Italy also went into extra

1972 to 1977 he was to become permanent skipper.

In 1972 West Germany won the European Championship impressively under Beckenbauer's command. At the end of the year he was elected European Footballer of the Year, an honour he was to receive again in 1976. For three successive years he helped Bayern to European Cup honours.

With a technique rarely matched anywhere, he appeared almost casual but always in charge of the

Helmut Schoen, the West German team manager and his captain Franz Beckenbauer. This partnership followed a similar association between Sepp Herberger and Fritz Walter and even earlier between Otto Nerz and Fritz Szepan.

time before West Germany lost 4-3. For Beckenbauer, it was a tragedy. He was seriously injured and forced to play with a dislocated shoulder, his arm being strapped across his chest. Schoen had already used both substitutes.

Yet his career developed further at club and country level. Bayern were to start their domination of domestic and European football and the national team about to reach its peak. Beckenbauer was himself appointed captain for the first time against Turkey in April 1971. From

situation. His distribution was faultless and he could take the ball past opponents with either speed or a neat swerve. More importantly he could change pace and direction at will.

In 1974 he led West Germany to a World Cup victory and continued his career outside Germany in 1977 with New York Cosmos, returning to finish his playing career at Hamburg. In 1984, he became West Germany's team manager, taking them to the runners-up spot in the 1986 World Cup, before bowing out as a winner again in 1990.

BOBBY CHARLTON

ENGLAND

Bobby Charlton was the epitome of the spirit that helped to revive Manchester United after the Munich air disaster in 1958 and the conscientious will-to-succeed that led England to its World Cup triumph eight years later. Of more practical importance, when he had the ball the crowd expected something positive to happen and were rarely disappointed.

Charlton established three records for his club and another for his country which might well stand for all time. He played in more games, scored more goals and was United's most capped player as well as being the highest goalscorer in his country's history.

But there was far more to Charlton than mere records. At his peak there was no more explosive forward anywhere in the country, combining that rare commodity for an Englishman, flair,with his powerful shooting ability.

Born into the famous footballing family of Ashington known as the Milburn club, he was the nephew of Jackie Milburn and the younger brother of Jack Charlton. He signed for Manchester United in 1953 straight from school and in doing so thwarted the aims of 17 other clubs who were chasing this schoolboy starlet.

He played with the other Matt Busby Babes in three FA Youth Cup winning teams from 1954 to 1956 inclusive and was given his first opportunity in the League side on 6 October 1956 as deputy for the injured Tommy Taylor, ironically against Charlton Athletic, scoring twice on this impressive debut. That season United won the championship and he scored ten goals in only 14 appearances.

The following season he had won a regular place in the side when the heart of the club was ripped out by the air crash in West Germany. Charlton miraculously escaped injury, being flung to safety, strapped to his seat with his shoes torn off. Despite the mental torment which must

have resulted from this traumatic experience, he was quickly back in action.

Charlton assumed a responsibility which matured and enhanced him as a player and he became the focal point of the United reconstruction. Moreover he made his debut for England in the aftermath of the same tragedy, scoring in a 4-0 win over Scotland. Two more goals in the next success 2-1 against Portugal brought him his third appearance in Yugoslavia. But a 5-0 defeat cost him his place in the World Cup team in Sweden, his inside-right berth going to Bobby Robson.

In hindsight his omission proved to be a costly error. After that he was rarely absent on international duty, taking his total of appearances to 106 and a record 49 goals. Without doubt his finest moments came in the 1966 World Cup.

Yet England began the series looking anything but potential champions. They gave a lack-lustre performance against Uruguay and in subsequent matches needed the spark provided by Charlton's pace and blistering shots to ignite them. He scored two unforgettable goals against Portugal in the semi-final which set up the final accolade at West Germany's expense. Deservedly he had already been elected as Footballer of the Year and added the European crown later in the year.

In 1968 Charlton was on hand for another Wembley moment, when he scored twice in Manchester United's 4-1 win over Benfica in the European Cup final, one of his goals being a rare header.

But there had been disappointments during his career. His first FA Cup Final appearance against Aston Villa in 1957 ended in defeat as did the following year's effort against Bolton Wanderers when United's courageous post-Munich team lost 2-0. Charlton had a shot which rebounded off a post in the latter game, when Bolton were still only one goal ahead.

In the 1962 World Cup, Charlton, now settled at outside-left, was one of England's outstanding players in an ordinary squad. His acceleration and unexpected shooting from long range made him the most dangerous of opponents. His sweeping crossfield passes could also change the point of attack in impressively accurate fashion.

Subsequently he moved to inside-left and later wore the No.9 shirt as a deep-lying centre-forward, from which position he plotted the 1966 World Cup successes.

Born 11 October 1937, he was 32 at the time of the 1970 World Cup in Mexico. His last game for England was in the 3-2 defeat sustained against West Germany. Perhaps his greatest compliment has come since then, as his country has never been able to replace him with a player of similar calibre.

Charlton captained Manchester United from 1968 to 1973. He had won two League championsip medals in 1965 and 1967, an FA Cup winners medal in 1963, six Under-23 caps, an OBE in 1969 and the CBE in 1974.

In April 1973 he left Old Trafford and became player-manager of Preston North End. But like many an outstanding player before and since, his flirtation with the managerial side was not a success and he resigned over a disagreement with the board. He did have a short spell as Wigan Athletic's caretaker-manager while on that club's board but later became a director of Manchester United and organised a school for youngsters learning soccer skills.

His total number of League appearences for Manchester United came to 606 with 199 goals. In all senior club games he appeared 754 times and scored 247 goals.

The Charlton brothers Jack and Bobby (right) were stalwarts in England's World Cup triumph in 1966. (HULTON)

JOHAN CRUYFF

HOLLAND

Probably the outstanding European player in the 1970s and certainly the most gifted Dutchman of the same era, Johan Cruyff's name was synonymous with the 'total football' which brought fame to Holland during this exciting period in the country's history.

Born in a poor quarter of Amsterdam on 25 April 1947, he had close connections with Ajax. In fact his mother worked at the ground as a cleaner. He joined them when he was still at school as a ten-year-old. By the age of 17 he was making his first team debut and in that 1964-65 season scored four goals.

The following season he was a regular choice and his 16 League goals contributed to Ajax winning the championsnip. In 1966-67 they achieved the League and Cup double and Cruyff led the Dutch League goalscorers with 33 goals. A third title win in succession underlined Ajax's supremacy at home but in 1968-69 they made strenuous efforts to extend their dominance to the European Cup.

Ajax reached the final — Cruyff contributing five goals on the way — where they met AC Milan. Unfortunately they were exposed by the tactically wise Italian side, whose counter-attacking produced an emphatic 4-1 win.

Cruyff had been given the Dutch Footballer of the Year awards in 1968 and 1969. Moreover he had already been blooded into the national team, although his early experiences had been shattering to his morale. After his debut against Hungary in 1966 at the age of 19, he played his second game against Czechoslovakia. During the game he was involved in a stormy argument with the East German referee Rudi Glockner and was sent off for apparently striking the official.

Film of the event make it clear that it had been a gesture rather than a blow, but the Dutch Federation still suspended him from the national team for a year, later commuting the sentence to six months, though it was ten months before he was restored to the side against, ironically, East Germany.

Slightly built, this lanky forward had razor-sharp reactions, excellent control, speed, acceleration and the ability to change direction instantly. His problem was a demonstrative temperament which certainly cost him dearly in his younger days.

Ajax had another determined try for the European Cup in 1970-71, but made an inauspicious start in Albania where they were held to a 2-2 draw by 17 Nentori. They did better in the return leg winning 2-0 and took a 3-0 lead over Basle in the first leg of the second round. In Switzerland they won again, 2-1.

In the quarter-finals they were drawn against Celtic and Cruyff put them ahead at home with his first goal in the competition that season. Ajax went on to win 3-0 and though they lost 1-0 away, they emerged 3-1 on aggregate and faced Atletico Madrid in the semi-final. Again they were beaten by a single goal in Spain but retrieved the deficit 3-0 in Amsterdam.

The European Cup final was played at Wembley and Panathinaikos, the Greek team, found Ajax far too clever for them. The Dutch side won 2-0, without convincing sceptics that they were a team of all the talents. But their coach Rinus Michels had knocked them into shape and surprisingly decided to move on to Barcelona.

Michels was succeeded by the Rumanian Stefan Kovacs who allowed the players far more relaxation in the playing system he adapted from Michels' more disciplined strategy. The change added comprehensively to Ajax's potential and they crowned their performances with a stunning 2-0 final win over Internazionale, Cruyff scoring both goals. Ajax again retained the trophy in 1973, beating Juventus 1-0 in the final in Belgrade.

Johan Cruyff in full flight for Holland on the way to the 1974 final in West Germany.

Then, following protracted negotiations, Cruyff was transferred to Barcelona where he joined his former boss Michels. The fee was £922,300 with some £400,000 going to Cruyff, who thus became one of the best-paid professional sportsmen in the world at the time.

Later that year he was voted European Footballer of the Year for the second time, having first received the award in 1971. Although his goalscoring output was not phenomenal he had taken his total of League goals to 187 by the time he moved to Spain. In 1971-72 he had been top scorer in the Dutch League with 25 goals. However the danger he posed to defenders was enough to create havoc and his final pass was invariably of pin-point accuracy, leaving colleagues with inviting openings. Overall he was to score 215 goals in Dutch League games, 47 League goals for Barcelona and 25 in the North American Soccer League.

Holland qualified for the World Cup finals in 1974 and improved as the tournament progressed in West Germany, revealing the all-out attack and defence in depth epitomised by Ajax. When in possesion, the entire complement of outfield players supported the ball carrier and made the best use of space. When the opposition had the ball, everybody fell back to cover. But they were frustrated in the final by a shrewd German team. Two years on, Holland finished third in the European Championship and Cruyff helped them to reach the 1978 World Cup finals, but decided to retire before the games in Argentina. He had scored 33 goals in 48 internationals.

Subsequently he came out of retirement, playing for Los Angeles, Washington, Feyenoord, Ajax again and the Spanish club Levante. Then as coach he won the Cup Winners' Cup with Ajax in 1987 and Barcelona in 1989.

KENNY DALGLISH

SCOTLAND

The game is littered with examples of clubs having to pay for the failure to recognise talent in a player. It happened to Liverpool with Kenny Dalglish, 11 years before they paid a then record fee for British clubs of £440,000 for his services.

Born in Glasgow on 4 March 1951, he played for Glasgow Schools, represented his country at that level and then joined Drumchapel Amateurs. His next club was Glasgow United and shortly after linking up with Celtic, he went on a two-week trial with Liverpool.

While at Anfield, he played in their 'B' team on 20 August 1966 wearing the No. 8 shirt in a match lost 1-0 to Southport. Afterwards he returned to Celtic who farmed him out to Cumbernauld to help develop his skills. Back at Parkhead, he made a couple of appearances in Celtic's League side in 1969-70 and three in the following term. But from 1971-72 he became an automatic choice.

With Youth and Under-23 representative honours already gained, he won his first full cap for Scotland as substitute against Belgium on 10 November 1971. He was given a full outing in the next match with Holland, but did not appear again until the following year when he again came on, during the match with Denmark.

This time he kept his place and was not out of the squad up to the 1974 World Cup finals in West Germany, playing either a complete game or being used as a substitute in every match. The Scots began their quest against Zaire but only managed to score twice without reply against their naive opponents.

Yugoslavia went on to score nine goals against Zaire, and even though Scotland drew 0-0 with Brazil, their 1-1 draw with Yugoslavia in the last game left the Brazilians needing to score at least three against the Africans. They achieved just that. Thus the Scots were eliminated on goal difference, with all three leading teams on the same number of points. Being undefeated was little consolation.

However Dalglish remained a vital part of the team. In fact he made 33 consecutive appearances before missing a match with Wales in 1976. He returned to complete 43 in a row up to 1981.

Meanwhile at Celtic he had won four championship medals, another four in the Scottish Cup and one in the League Cup. He had scored 112 goals in 204 League games, 34 in 60 Scottish League Cup matches and 11 in 28 Scottish Cup ties. In European games he had scored a further nine goals.

Then in August 1977 Liverpool signed him as a replacement for Kevin Keegan. In his first season on Merseyside he played at Wembley three times in the Charity Shield, League Cup and European Cup finals and was not once on the losing side.

This compact forward with keen-edged awareness in the penalty area, fine reflexes and the close control to make space and finish in clinical style, continued his consistency at Anfield. The changeover from Scottish to English League appeared not to have been a real problem for Dalglish. He made 177 consecutive League and Cup appearances before missing a League Cup game against Bradford City on 27 August 1980.

Honours fell to Liverpool with almost predictable regularity. The 1983-84 season was of special personal significance to him. In the European Cup he overtook Denis Law's total of 14 goals to become the highest-scoring British player in this competition. On 26 November 1983 he scored his 100th League goal for Liverpool, becoming only the third player to achieve a century of goals at this level on both sides of the border. He also equalled the record number of goals scored by a Scottish international.

114

No other Scottish player has made more appearances for his country than Kenny Dalglish. He made 102 in a distinguished career.

On the international front, Dalglish had added handsomely to his total of full appearances. In the 1978 World Cup finals there was understandable sorrow over Scotland's poor showing in the early games in Argentina. But when already certain of having to make the return trip without glory of any kind, they beat Holland 3-2, Dalglish opening the scoring for the Scots.

Even at the age of 31 in 1982, he was again a member of the squad in Spain and was on the mark in the opening game with New Zealand. Once more the Scots faded, but not so the career of Dalglish.

Liverpool swept practically everything before them, winning five League championships, four League Cups and three European Cup trophies. Dalglish was rarely absent. In five out of nine seasons he did not miss a game. Then in May 1985 in the wake of the Heysel disaster, he accepted an invitation to become player-manager of Liverpool.

Since then the winning formula perfected on the field and off it has not altered. Dalglish has gradually withdrawn from the playing side having won 102 record caps for Scotland, equalled Law's 30 goals for his country and scored 118 goals in 354 League matches for Liverpool. Dalglish did not figure in the Scottish squad for the 1986 World Cup in Mexico. But he did reappear the his country's colours the following season.

DIDI

BRAZIL

The illustrious career of Waldir Pereira, otherwise known simply as Didi, might never have happened. At the age of 14 he suffered a ferocious kick on his right knee during an amateur game. An abscess developed and medical advice was moving towards amputation of the limb.

Fortunately for him, this extreme measure was avoided by skilful treatment and nursing. But he had to spend six months in a wheelchair and the result was that he slightly dragged his right leg.

Once pronounced fit, Didi was determined to make up for the years he had lost and it said much for his perseverance and courage that by the age of 18 he was able to join a local club Americano of Campos. After a spell with Lencoense of Sao Paulo, he moved to Madureira in 1949.

Born in Campos on 8 October 1928, Didi reached his 21st birthday as a leading inside-forward in the Rio League. His progress had been such that the top clubs in the area were vying for his services. Fluminense were the successful club, obtaining his signature in 1950.

Having made the grade and mindful of his experiences as a partial cripple in his youth, Didi spent hours and hours practising on his own. It was while he was with Fluminense that he fashioned his famous dead-ball kick which curved, then faded. In Brazil it was known as the *folha seca* (dry leaf).

In order to perfect this ability, he would take every opportunity to use the ball and did not neglect other requirements. In fact he sharpened up his ordinary shooting skills and distribution over short and long distances.

This voluntary training and willingness to improve his game made him one of the most promising players in Rio. The same year he joined Fluminense, the city was preparing for the World Cup finals. The Maracana Stadium was heading towards completion and a match was arranged to commemorate its opening.

Didi was selected in a team of Rio young professionals and had the honour of scoring the first ever goal in that famous venue. The Brazilian national team had an inside-forward trio of Zizinho, Ademiri and Jair that was considered untouchable at the time, but by 1951 Didi's prompting of the Fluminense attack had resulted in the team taking the Rio League title.

Brazil's manager, Zeze Moreira, decided to give him a chance in the 1952 Pan-American championships in Chile. In April he made his debut in a 2-0 win over Mexico and was rarely absent from subsequent line-ups.

By 1954 and the World Cup in Switzerland, Didi was a permanent fixture, masterminding the Brazilian offensive play. Frayed tempers on the field caused the side to lose concentration against Hungary and hopes of a second World Cup final appearance vanished.

Two years later he was transferred to Botafogo, who oddly enough did not encourage him to practise on his own. In no time, his famous swerving free-kicks became less and less a part of his game. Luckily for club and country, he managed to recapture his knack in time to score probably the most important goal in his career.

It came in the World Cup qualifying game against Peru which enabled Brazil to go to Sweden. Didi's performance in the final tournament was outstanding. While the teenaged Pele attracted most of the attention, it was Didi who linked defence and attack with a marvellous control of the midfield which seemed to have been manipulated by off-the-field planning.

In October 1959 Real Madrid bought him in a £30,000 transfer deal. Didi was 31 and at the peak of his game. A commanding figure, tall and upright, he possessed a presence on the field that was difficult to ignore. The

prospect of him playing in a forward line which listed Kopa, Didi, Di Stefano, Puskas and Gento seemed too good to be true.

He arrived at Chamartin, Real's home ground, with the media freely talking about him as the 'world's greatest player'. Alfredo di Stefano already considered himself to be the top forward at Real Madrid and was determined that Didi would receive no assistance in dislodging him from his exalted position.

It went further. Didi was made to feel totally unwanted. He did not even manage to play in any of Real's European Cup ties on their way to winning a fifth successive trophy. For a while Didi was loaned to Valencia before he requested his contract to be terminated. In 1960 he returned to Botafogo.

Mercifully for club and country, his experience in Spain had not affected his inherent qualities as a player. Botafogo won the Rio League in 1961 and 1962. In the World Cup, despite having slowed a trifle, Didi was the most consistent Brazilian as they collected a second winner's title.

Shortly afterwards he accepted an invitation to become Sporting Cristal's player-coach in Peru. They finished second. For Brazil he had played in 72 internationals and scored 21 goals. Now he had another career as coach. In 1970 he was in charge of the Peruvian national team in the World Cup. Next to Brazil they were the most enterprising and entertaining on view.

GIACINTO FACCHETTI

ITALY

The second most honoured player in Italian history, Giacinto Facchetti appeared on 94 occasions for the national team and captained them 70 times. Although he began his career as a full-back he ended it as a sweeper.

However his early development was as slow as a footballer as it was quick as an athlete. At school he clocked 8.8 seconds for the 80 metres and 10.6 for the 80 metres hurdles. He was Italian junior champion at the time.

But as to his prowess on the field of play, he was tall, inclined to be ungainly, but quick. Unfortunately he had limited control of the ball . Originally a centre-forward he moved back to play in the defence.

Born 18 July 1942 in Treviglio, he eventually joined his local club CS Trevigliese. Helenio Herrera, often referred to as the high priest of *catenaccio* (blanket defence), was coach of Internazionale and had an idea that Facchetti 's rough edges could be smoothed out.

In 1960 he signed this tall, well-built teenager and proceeded to knock him into the kind of shape necessary to be a top-flight player. Herrera used Facchetti at left-back, despite the player 's tendency to favour his right foot. This did not prevent him from becoming an excellent overlapping defender. In fact the problem was to dissuade him from continually attacking.

In 1960-61 he made three League appearances, scoring in one of the games, and the following season added a further 15 outings. By the age of 20 he had become a regular choice. In 1962-63 Inter won the Italian championship and Facchetti was awarded his first cap for his country against Turkey in a European Nations Cup game in Istanbul. It was an inexperienced team, but the Italians managed to win 1-0 and went on to improve.

Facchetti scored four League goals for Inter that season and in the years that followed, invariably contributed a useful share of goalscoring. In 1965-66 he reached double figures, an excellent total for any defender, but astonishing by Italian standards. Facchetti added championship medals in 1965, 1966 and 1971 and European Cup success also came his way.

In 1964 he achieved a winner 's medal when Inter beat Real Madrid 3-1 in the Champions Cup final. A year later he won a second, having scored against Liverpool in the semi-final. His marksmanship was of even more value in the semi-final with CSKA Sofia in 1966-67 when he scored in two 1-1 draws against the Bulgarian Army team.

Internationally, he remained a regular choice but there was disappointment for him personally and the team in general over their miserable performance in the 1966 World Cup. But a few months later he became captain of Italy, this honour being given to the most capped player in the team.

Facchetti led the team out for the first time in Milan in a friendly with the USSR on 1 November 1966 in his 25th international. Italy won 1-0. Though settled at left-back, Inter tried to utilise his attacking gifts in a different way.

He was tried on the left-wing in a game with relegation-threatened Sampdoria. Inter won 5-0, Facchetti scored one goal and had another disallowed. But he had a nightmare game in the following match with Bologna, missing an easy chance. Finding little room in which to work, he was totally frustrated. That was the end of Facchetti as a forward, but back in his usual position of left-back he was irresistible. He could shorten or lengthen his stride and had a subtle change of pace which frequently wrong-footed opponents. He was most effective when moving into the middle of the field.

In 1968 he led Italy to victory in the European Championships, and though the 1970 World Cup left the team as beaten finalists, Facchetti and his side were

Giacinto Facchetti was an outstanding outfield player for both club and country, captaining the national side on numerous occasions.
(POPPERFOTO)

critically appraised. In October 1971 he won his 60th cap against Sweden in a European Championship game, to become Italy's most capped player. The previous holder had been Umberto Caligaris, also a left-back.

That 1971-72 season saw another milestone passed when he overtook the record total of goals scored by a full-back in Italian League football. The previous holder Sergio Cervato had contributed most of his from free-kicks and penalties, while Facchetti had scored chiefly from open play.

However he was dropped from the national team after losing the quarter-final of the European Championship to Belgium 2-1 in 1972, only to return for his 65th cap against Turkey in a World Cup game the following February. Facchetti played in the 1974 World Cup finals but was switched to sweeper in the next friendly with Yugoslavia in the following September.

He went on to play 94 times, his last appearance being against England at Wembley in 1977. Unassuming off the field, forceful on it, Facchetti held a justifiable reputation as a sportsman in 476 League games which yielded 59 goals for Internazionale. He became their most capped player and still holds the club record for League appearances.

JUST FONTAINE

FRANCE

Just Fontaine suffered two serious injuries at the height of his career which led to his premature retirement from the game. Yet in the 1958 World Cup he had scored a record 13 goals in the competition and overall registered 30 for France in only 21 matches.

His international debut was bizarre to say the least. It was on 17 December 1953 in a World Cup qualifying match against Luxembourg in Paris. The French fielded their Under-23 team and have never considered the game to be a full international! France won 8-0 and Fontaine scored a hat-trick.

He was subsequently included in the list of 40 players originally named for the 1954 World Cup but did not make the squad for the final stages in Switzerland.

Born in Marrakesh, Morocco on 18 August 1933 he developed as a goalscoring inside-forward with USM Casablanca before moving to France, where he turned professional with OGC Nice. He made an impressive start, scoring 17 League goals as Nice finished eighth in the championship. His team reached the French Cup final, beating Marseille 2-1. Though the side slipped to ninth in the League during 1954-55, Fontaine increased his scoring rate to 20 goals. Yet strangely enough, the following season was one of considerable disappointment for Fontaine even though Nice won the championship. He was in and out of the side, had one or two injury problems and contributed just six goals to the proceedings.

As a result of his indifferent displays that season, Nice decided to accept an offer of £12,000 from Reims and Fontaine could not have made a better move. In 1956-57 he scored 30 goals and was recalled to the full international side. He had played for the French Army and also at B level, but now found himself playing against Hungary in October 1956. It was Ferenc Puskas' last game

for the Hungarians who won 2-1.

That defeat delayed further progress for Fontaine on the international scene, and it was another year before he was chosen again for the return encounter with Hungary in Budapest. Again France lost, and again Fontaine was axed. But if there had been problems in this area, at domestic level he was blossoming. In 1957-58 he was the leading scorer in the championship with 34 goals. Reims achieved the League and Cup double, Fontaine scoring once in the 3-1 victory over Nimes.

In March 1958 he was given another opportunity to show his paces in the French team in a friendly with Spain at the Parc des Princes in Paris. This time Fontaine scored in a 2-2 draw and kept his place for the match with Switzerland which ended in a goalless draw.

With France having qualified for the 1958 World Cup finals in Sweden, his next game was in Norrkoping against Paraguay in the opening match of the series. By now, Fontaine was reaching his peak. Gone was the indecision of three years previously. He was quick, confident, had superb control and could score goals with his head and either foot.

He was included at inside-right against Paraguay, with Raymond Kopa named as centre-forward. But Fontaine had always been the spearhead whatever his nominal position and with Kopa lying deep and providing the clear-cut openings with penetrating and imaginative passes, the famous pairing known as 'le tandem terrible' was born.

Fontaine scored a hat-trick against Paraguay in a 7-3 win and followed it with both goals in the 3-2 defeat sustained against Yugoslavia and then one in the 2-1 win over Scotland. He also hit two goals in the 4-0 win over Northern Ireland and one in the 5-2 defeat by Brazil. In this match France were handicapped by an injury to

Robert Jonquet, who was a virtual passenger.

Still, France made up for this reverse in the match for third place and Fontaine joined the select band of World Cup players who have scored four goals in a match, in the 6-3 win over West Germany.

In 1958-59, Fontaine scored 24 goals but Reims had to settle for second place to Real Madrid in the European Cup, losing 2-0 with Kopa now playing for the Spanish club. And although Reims won their second domestic championship the following season, Fontaine's season ended in February when he sustained a double fracture of his left leg at Sochaux. At the time he was leading scorer with 28 goals and remained as such.

It was a tragedy for Fontaine, whose international career had been continuing to develop. He had scored two hat-tricks in succession against Austria and Spain followed by a couple of goals against Chile.

Then after a painful time recovering and returning to fitness, he made his comeback for France in a World Cup qualifying match against Bulgaria in December 1960. Unfortunately the New Year brought another leg fracture and this effectively ended his playing career at 28.

Fontaine became a sports writer, was awarded a coaching diploma, had two matches in charge of the French national team and later coached Paris St Germain back to the First Division.

In eight years with Nice and Reims he had scored 163 League goals, ten in the European Cup for Reims and formed a unique partnership with Kopa in the national team in a brief but memorable period.

French players carry four-goal Just Fontaine from the field after the 6-3 win over West Germany in the match for third place.

NANDOR HIDEGKUTI

HUNGARY

Although Nandor Hidegkuti became synonymous with the Magic Magyars of the early 1950s, his own career was well advanced at the time and he reached his peak when he was past 30 years of age. Yet if any one player was responsible for Hungary's success during this period, he certainly earned the recognition.

The Second World War interrupted his development as a footballer. Born 3 March 1922, it was not until international football was restarted in 1945 that Hidegkuti found himself pitched into the team in unusual circumstances.

At the time, he was with the Second Division team Herminamezo. The national team manager Tibor Gallovich had a problem to solve when his first choice inside-right, Ferenc Szusza, cried off with illness. Few people outside his own club knew of Hidegkuti's ability and he was not a popular replacement. But he silenced his critics by scoring twice in Hungary's 7-2 win over Rumania.

This promising debut did not ensure Hidegkuti of a place. He was chosen only fitfully during the next seven years, making a mere handful of appearances in various forward positions. His real chance came in the 1952 Olympics in Helsinki. The Hungarian side was already taking shape in a most exciting way.

After the gold medal success in Finland he replaced his club colleague Peter Palotas at centre-forward in a full international with Switzerland. Here he was used in a deep-lying role where he was able to prompt the attack, composed of two fast-raiding wingers and two strikers. His exceptional control, ability to unravel weaknesses in the opposition and exploit them with accurate passes was allied to a keen intellect for the game.

Although Ferenc Puskas and Sandor Kocsis, the two strikers, earned most of the goalscoring accolades during Hungary's purple period, Hidegkuti managed to record at

least one goal every two games. His finest scoring moment arrived at Wembley in the autumn of 1953.

England had not lost on their own soil to a continental team. They had scraped a 4-4 draw with FIFA in a commemorative game, thanks to a last-minute penalty, but defeat did not seem to have crossed the minds of the insular English.

The events of the opening seconds disturbed this blinkered vision. Receiving the ball on the edge of the penalty-area, Hidegkuti veered one way, swerved past his marker Harry Johnston and then beat Gil Merrick in the England goal with a rising right-foot shot from 15 yards.

Though England levelled the scores, Hidegkuti restored Hungary's lead in the 21st minute and completed his hat-trick and his team's scoring in the 53rd minute of their 6-3 victory. Johnston, his unfortunate shadow, was put through a gruelling afternoon. At first Hidegkuti kept well upfield to lure Johnston into thinking he was to operate as an orthodox centre-forward.

Then he dropped back into his accustomed withdrawn position and Johnston followed, leaving a gaping hole in the middle of the England defence which Puskas and Kocsis exploited to the full. As the game wore on, Billy Wright and Jimmy Dickinson both tried to mark the elusive Hidegkuti, with no more success than Johnston had achieved.

The Hungarians had revolutionised forward play, and this ultimately led to defences adopting an extra man to cope with the twin-striking strategy. But that counter measure was some years ahead and Hungary were able to sweep almost everything before them.

Between June 1950 and November 1955 they won 43 of 51 matches, scored in every game with a goal record of 220 for and 58 against and lost just once. Unfortunately for them it was the 1954 World Cup final against West

Germany. Hidegkuti was influential in the fine start made by the team, but control of the game was wrested from them by the determination of the Germans.

Apart from his speed, distribution and shooting ability, Hidegkuti was masterly in the air, specialising in diving headers. In the 1954 World Cup semi-final with Uruguay, he delivered one of his special aerial goals.

In domestic football, Hidegkuti joined Magyar Testgyakorlok Kore shortly after the war. Better known as MTK they subsequently changed their name to Textiles, Bastya, Voros Lobogo and then back to MTK. They won three championships and one cup trophy.

His association with MTK came by a twist of fate. Originally prepared to sign for Ferencvaros, he overheard local supporters grumbling about the proposed arrival of this unknown newcomer, and Hidegkuti walked away.

In 1958 he was again on World Cup duty in Sweden, but was 36 and no longer the dynamic force of old. He became a respected coach, guiding teams both at home, and in Italy and Poland. Always a fit man, he

Nandor Hidegkuti (back row, third from left) touched the heights late in his career but made an impact when he did so in the 1950s as a deep-lying centre-forward.
(TOPHAM)

star for his country in veteran internationals.

Hidegkuti scored 39 goals in 68 internationals but was responsible for creating twice as many for his colleagues and was unquestionably the switch which turned on the ignition for Hungary's driving force in an era of free, unfettered attacking football. He was instrumental in heaping further humiliation on England in 1954 when Hungary won 7-1 in Budapest.

RUDI KROL

HOLLAND

The 'total football' tag which was justifiably attached to Ajax and the Dutch national team in the early 1970s, tended to ignore the defensive qualities required as a basis for its attacking flair. But the presence of Rudi Krol at the back was equally as important to the overall success.

Born in Amsterdam on 24 March 1949 he was an outstanding youngster when only nine years old. At 13 he joined Ruud-Wit (Red and White) and found himself making his first team debut at the still tender age of 16. Selection for an Amsterdam youth representative side at 17 brought offers from three local clubs: Ajax, DWS Amsterdam and Blauw-Wit (Blue and White).

He made his mind up and chose Ajax, being given his first outing in a friendly when he was 20. The following season 1969-70 saw him make his first appearance in a League game against Groningen. From then onwards his career took off.

After only ten games he was selected to play for the full national team against England in November 1969 as left-back. Gradually he settled down and appeared to be on the threshold of a European Cup final place in 1971 when he broke his leg in the Dutch Cup semi-final against NEC Nijmegen and missed the Wembley occasion against Panathinaikos.

Actually Krol did accompany the squad, but had to be content with hobbling around the greyhound track on crutches. A year later it was a different story for him, as Ajax achieved their second successive victory in a European final. This time their victims were Internazionale. In 1973 Ajax completed a hat-trick as Juventus became the second Italian side to lose to the Dutchmen.

Krol's prospects at international level also looked promising as the nucleus of the crack Ajax team was providing the backbone of Holland's squad for the 1974 World Cup. In the qualifying competition, he was an ever present and duly took his place in the final stages in West Germany. Although Holland got as far as facing the host nation in the final, the outcome was disappointing and a similar tale had to be told four years later in Argentina, where the Dutch again succumbed to the locals at the final stage.

By this period, Krol had become the sweeper. His uncanny ability to stop opposing attacks and launch his own team onto the offensive, by either a sweeping pass or individual sortie, almost in one movement, put him head and shoulders above his contemporaries. This could be taken literally since his height and weight made him a commanding figure anyway.

On 26 April 1980 he appeared in his 450th game for Ajax against Den Haag. He was coming to the end of his contract with the Amsterdam club and his career was apparently at the crossroads.

His service for Holland had also seen him reach a milestone the previous year. On 22 May 1979 he led the team against Argentina in the 75th anniversary match for FIFA. It was his 65th game for his country and in appearing, Krol had overtaken the previous holder Puck Van Heel.

Krol had long since assumed the captaincy of the Netherlands but it came as a surprise when he decided to accept a three-year contract with the North American Soccer League club Vancouver Whitecaps. The American scene was in decline. Pele had retired from New York Cosmos, and Franz Beckenbauer was about to return to West Germany from the same club.

Yet it was merely academic. Krol had scarcely settled down in Canada when Napoli moved in to sign him. In his first season the team finished third. Krol made an easy adjustment to the different tempo of Italian football. The *catenaccio* system was ideal for a player of his class.

No goals between Holland and Sweden in 1974 but friendship exists between Ruud Krol (left) and Ralf Edstrom, the Swedish striker.

He found that the style of counter-attacking was one admirably suited to his talents. Meanwhile the Dutch national team continued to call upon him. Off the field the various business interests into which he had invested continued to broaden his general view of life outside football.

At one stage in Holland he owned a couple of snack bars, personally modelled clothes and dabbled in interior design. As captain of Ajax and the Netherlands he was a much sought-after product. But in Italy he had to concentrate totally on his game and this presented no problems for him.

In 1980-81 Napoli finished third. Their defence was more than competent, marshalled as it was by Krol, but their attack lacked penetration. Incredibly the following season in which they were placed fourth, their goal record of 31-21 was identical with that of 1980-81.

However in the next two seasons Napoli slumped.

After 107 appearances for the team, Krol left Italy to play in the French Second Division for Cannes. During his stint with Napoli, there had been a blow to Dutch prestige when Holland failed to qualify for the 1982 World Cup finals in Spain.

For such a gifted player who had studied the game throughout his active career, the temptation to become a coach was overwhelming. With the experience of 83 international games behind him he decided to take on the exacting role of instructor. His appointment with Mechelen, the leading Belgian club in 1989, marked another highspot in Krol's life.

Alas it was to be a short-lived feeling of euphoria, for Krol had had little experience of controlling the affairs of a leading club. Mid-way through his first season, he was relieved of his duties. Mechelen as a team had not been unsuccessful, but Krol had quickly learned the harsh realities of life as a coach.

GARY LINEKER

ENGLAND

In the 1990 World Cup finals in Italy, Gary Lineker enhanced his reputation as a top-class marksman by scoring four times, including two penalties. It took his overall goals tally in World Cup finals to 10, and meant that in 58 games for England he had scored 35 goals.

Born in Leicester on 30 November 1960 and raised locally, he became an apprentice with City and developed as a striker, despite the fact that he stood only 5ft 6in at the time. He made his debut in 1978-79 and scored once in seven outings. But it took him three seasons before he could command a regular place.

In 1981-82 he scored 17 goals in 39 League games, finishing as Leicester's leading scorer. In the next three seasons he was top each time with 26, 22 and 24 goals respectively.

It was a difficult period for Leicester. They had lost their First Division status by the time Lineker was given his initial chance in League football. They had been promoted and relegated again before he established himself.

However, he was able to take his full part in Leicester returning to Division One at the end of the 1982-83 season, and in the full glare of First Division publicity the following term, he showed enough promise to find himself selected for international honours. His first taste at top level came as substitute for England against Scotland in May 1984.

But he had to wait until the following year and nine more matches before being given a further outing. This time he began in the No.10 shirt and scored one of England's goals in a 2-1 win. Yet again he was not retained. He was used as substitute in three of the next four matches, but was not chosen to start a game until West Germany provided the opposition. That was in Mexico City in June 1985.

England won 3-0 and although Lineker did not figure among the scorers, he kept his position for five more matches. In those ten games he had scored six goals, but still critics pointed to the fact that three had been achieved against Turkey and two more against the USA.

Domestically, other moves were afoot. Everton had been sufficiently impressed with him to contact Leicester where he had rejected a new contract. A tribunal set the fee at £800,000 even though City wanted £1 million.

Lineker was yet to be given a complete vote of confidence in the run-up to the World Cup finals in Mexico. Thus he went into the tournament with something to prove not only for England but to himself and his critics. Yet the hallmarks of a goalscorer above the average were already evident in his play. In his first season for Everton he had scored 30 goals.

He had shown directness and speed, allied to an ability to dart into scoring positions in the penalty area. An accuracy in finishing had also made him a marked man, but he had finished with a highly respectable total of League goals in the First Division.

In the opening two matches against Portugal and Morocco, the England attack failed miserably and there were no goals. Lineker was paired with Mark Hateley for these games. But changes were forced upon Bobby Robson for the game with Poland which included a switch of tactics from 4-3-3 to 4-4-2. This, allied to the fact that he was now partnered by Peter Beardsley, changed Lineker's fortunes in dramatic style.

He responded with a hat-trick against Poland and almost overnight became a sensation. Two more goals came from the in-form Lineker against Paraguay and one in the controversial quarter-final with Argentina. By the end of the World Cup he was being hailed as a world-class striker.

The 1986 World Cup transformed Gary Lineker from a more than useful club player into an international class striker.

Barcelona stepped in to sign him in a £2.75 million transfer and Lineker made the transition to Spanish League football in a surprisingly smooth way. Though the Catalan club finished second behind of Real Madrid in the Spanish championship, Lineker's marksmanship won full acclaim from the Barcelona faithful. If there was any lingering doubt over his ability, it was dispelled when England played Spain on their own territory.

He scored four times as England won 4-2. It had been a splendid year for him. He had entered the World Cup as both the Football Writers Association and Professional Footballers Association choice as player of the year. At the end of the period he came second in the European poll, largely as a result of the impression his goalscoring had made in the Mexico World Cup.

The arrival of Johan Cruyff as coach at Barcelona in the wake of Terry Venables' departure, was the beginning of the end of Lineker's association with the Spanish club. Cruyff insisted on playing him wide on the right, and it was no surprise when, after Lineker had helped Barcelona to beat Sampdoria in the Cup Winners Cup in 1989, he joined Tottenham Hotspur for a fee of £1.25 million.

Lineker had been understandably lethargic during the 1988 European Championships due to a bout of jaundice but 24 league goals for Tottenham in 1989-90, and his performances in Italy, showed he was back to his best.

DIEGO MARADONA

ARGENTINA

Many cynics have said that Diego Maradona won the 1986 World Cup for Argentina single-handed. His contribution to the overall team effort was indeed substantial, and he might well have tipped the scales of victory towards half a dozen teams engaged in the tournament, had he changed sides accordingly.

Born in Buenos Aires on 30 October 1960 into a poor family, he revealed exceptional ability at an early age. His debut in senior circles came with Argentinos Juniors when he was still ten days short of his 16th birthday. Maradona's team lost 1-0 to Talleres Cordoba on that occasion, but it was not long before he was on the winning side more often than not.

In his first half-season with the club he scored twice in 11 matches but in the following term increased his output to 19 in 49 matches. In February of that same year, 1977, he was selected to play for the national team against Hungary in a 4-1 win. He had already become something of a boy wonder, being compared with Brazil's Pele at the same age.

He had made such progress that the Argentina team manager Luis Cesar Menotti was worried about his future. He felt the pressures on the youngster would increase, especially as the country was getting prepared to host the 1978 World Cup. At the time it seemed that Maradona would be a certainty. But Menotti left him out, hoping that he could develop towards the 1982 series at a steadier pace.

It was a brave move on the part of Menotti, and one which could have backfired on him had Argentina failed to win the World Cup; the fans would never have forgiven him for omitting Maradona in those circumstances.

However it was a shattering blow to the young player's ego when he was omitted. Yet he continued to show outstanding form for Argentinos Juniors and by 1980 had scored 116 goals in 166 League games. Then Boca Juniors signed him and he added 28 goals for them in 40 matches.

By the time he had settled down with his new club, the 1982 World Cup finals were due to be played in Spain. Maradona had become a marked man and it was obvious that he would be given special attention during the tournament. Unfortunately for him, Maradona's temperament was not of the same maturity as his football and he was sent off against Brazil for retaliation.

After the finals, Maradona remained in Spain having been transferred to Barcelona for a then world record fee of £4,235,000. But it was not a happy time for him. He suffered a bout of hepatitis, which kept him out of action for three months, and then a severe ankle injury, the result of many blatant fouls committed on him.

In two seasons with the Catalan club he appeared in only 36 League games and scored 22 goals. But with friendlies and cup games added on he reached an overall total of 74 matches with 45 goals, though he was used in a number of games when he was not fully fit.

In the summer of 1984, he was the subject of the most costly transfer in the history of the game. The fee has been scaled up and down in the years since the move, but Napoli had to pay £6.9 million for his services at the moment they secured his signature. It was a calculated gamble and one which also brought huge receipts to the club, who sold 40,000 season tickets at £150 each within hours of the capture.

There was little respite for Maradona in Italian football. Alas, Napoli could do no better than finish eighth in his first season. Maradona's contribution was 14 goals in 30 games. But there was no denying his ability.

An attacking player of exceptional quality, as well as supreme confidence, he often attempted and many times succeeded in beating player after player with speed and alacrity. His chief fault was wanting to keep possession. Another vital part of his make-up was the accuracy of his free-kicks.

Napoli did a little better in 1985-86, winning more games to finish third. Maradona scored 11 goals but had problems with knee ligament damage, the result of a bizarre incident in a World Cup qualifying game with Venezuela in 1985. As the players were leaving the field surrounded by spectators, Maradona received a kick on the knee.

There was some doubt as to whether he would be fit enough to play in Mexico, but it was unthinkable that Argentina would even contemplate leaving him out. They included him and kept their fingers crossed. In the opening game with South Korea, he contributed to all three Argentine goals and took his share of knocks from the effervescent Asians. In the next he gave his Italian friends the runaround, pouncing on a half-chance to score in a 1-1 draw.

He inspired victory over Bulgaria and was the difference between winning and being held by Uruguay. Then came his amazing double over England and two more goals at the expense of Belgium. In the final he was again the player to catch the eye. He returned to Italy and helped Napoli to the League and Cup double. By the end of the 1989-90 season he had helped the club win the UEFA Cup and then the league once again, but in the 1990 World Cup, suffering with an injury and jeered outside Naples, he was a pale shadow of his former self.

The 1986 World Cup finals were a personal triumph for Diego Maradona. He gave a hint of what was to come in Argentina's opening match (right) against South Korea.

BOBBY MOORE

ENGLAND

Few players can have looked back on such a distinguished international career as Bobby Moore's. It lasted eleven and a half years, during which he was absent from the England team on just 12 occasions, and those due to injury or the need to give other players a chance.

Born in Barking on 12 April 1941, his early football was played with Barking and Leyton Schools then Woodford Youth Club. He joined West Ham United in June 1958 and was soon given his first League outing in the September of that year against Manchester United at Upton Park. That same season he was capped by England at youth level and played in the Hammers' FA Youth Cup final side.

He played 18 times for the England youth team and graduated to the Under-23's. He was awarded his first full cap in a pre-World Cup friendly against Peru in 1962, wearing the No. 4 shirt. In the finals in Chile, Moore was one of only two real successes in the side.

He was never absent on more than two occasions in succession and he reached his zenith when he captained England superbly in the 1966 World Cup. As one of the twin centre-backs his role was not restricted to the tight-marking of an opponent. His impeccable positioning enabled him to give the extra cover and depth required.

Moore's other outstanding capabilities were centred on his expert reading of the game, vision and constructive prowess in quickly turning defence into attack with precision and accuracy. These characteristics and his strong physique more than compensated for a slight lack of pace and suspect heading ability. Again, to offset this his tackling was well judged and measured and he was rarely caught off balance; in Moore, England truly had a world class player.

At club level, Moore helped West Ham to their 1964 FA

Cup and 1965 European Cup Winners' Cup successes. He played in a record 544 League games for them before ending his career at Fulham where he added a further 124 before retiring. In all, he made 1,000 senior appearances for club and country.

Although there were much publicised differences between him and Ron Greenwood, the West Ham manager, and to a lesser extent with Sir Alf Ramsey who led England, his conduct on the field and off it was usually free of indiscretion.

However his greatest test came in Colombia before the 1970 World Cup when he was involved in the notorious affair of the 'stolen' bracelet. This was not the most suitable preliminary exercise to a tough campaign in Mexico, but Moore survived it.

He remained as calm and self-controlled in the days which followed the incident as he was cool and disciplined on the field. In Mexico he probably played better than he had four years earlier; that performance had led to the award of an OBE in January 1967.

Moore's other slip off the field was on a Friday night at Blackpool before West Ham's cup tie in January 1971. The late, late show received considerable publicity. The following day Blackpool beat West Ham 4-0. Then Moore was dropped. He missed the next two games and was required to sit on the bench for a third before making his only league appearance in a No. 12 shirt as a completion of his penance.

The following season he was called upon to deputise in goal for the injured Bobby Ferguson in a League Cup semi-final with Stoke when the goalkeeper was concussed. Moore pulled off a penalty save but was beaten by the rebound shot.

He captained England on numerous occasions. His first match leading his country was in 1963 against

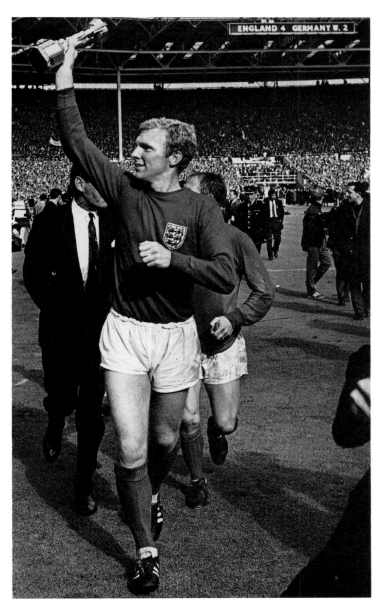

Bobby Moore trots round Wembley with the World Cup in 1966 after leading England to success.

Czechoslovakia in the absence of Jimmy Armfield. It was only his second time in the No.6 shirt he made famous. At the time he was 22.

Moore became the permanent skipper the following year, succeeding Armfield in a match with Uruguay. His last appearance was against Italy in 1973 when England had still not quite recovered from the shock of failing to qualify for the World Cup.

The following spring, Moore was transferred to Fulham for £20,000. In 1975 he made one last appearance at Wembley in the FA Cup Final. Ironically it was for Fulham against his old club West Ham. But it was to receive a runners-up medal. Then when he left Fulham he had a brief association with Seattle Sounders in the USA.

His first appointment as manager was in charge of the non-league club Oxford City. After a spell in Hong Kong, he satisfied his ambition of taking charge of a Football League club when he accepted the managership of Southend United. After two years with them he remained on their board of directors. Subsequently he had interests in journalism and publishing outlets.

Although his final appearance at Wembley had ended in defeat, the hallowed turf at the home of English football had provided Moore with arguably his three finest moments: the 1964 FA Cup win, the 1965 European Cup Winners' success and the 1966 World Cup triumph. In 1964 he had been the recipient of the Footballer of the Year award.

In 1966 when he captained England to World Cup glory, he was also voted the outstanding player in the entire tournament; there could have been few dissenters from this honour justly awarded.

GERD MULLER

WEST GERMANY

In West Germany he became known as 'Der Bomber', but the best description of Gerd Muller as a marksman could be summed up by the phrase 'pouncing poacher'. Few players of international class can have been so lethal inside the penalty area. Only 5ft 8in, this chunky, thick-thighed centre-forward had a low centre of gravity, fine balance and an agile sense of anticipation.

His record merely serves to underline his expertise as a goalscorer. Between 1966 and 1974 he scored 68 goals in 62 appearances for West Germany. In all competitive games he scored 628 times, and in a short extension of his career in the USA, he added 38 goals for Fort Lauderdale.

Born 11 November 1945 in the Bavarian village of Zinsen, he grew up to discover that there was no proper football pitch in his area. He had to travel seven miles by bus to have a trial with TSV Nordlingen. Muller's father died and the youngster had to leave school at 15 whereupon he became an apprentice weaver.

But Nordlingen had been impressed and signed him. Muller had made a scoring debut in what was his first game on a marked-out pitch, despite wearing borrowed boots. In fact he scored two goals. Still, he had a problem: he was overweight and earned the nickname of 'Dicker' (fatty).

Even so, in two seasons for Nordlingen he scored 46 goals. His scoring ability was duly noted by several clubs although the man who took most interest in him was Wilhelm Neudecker, President of Bayern Munich. Neudecker persuaded his coach Tchik Cajkovski, the former Yugoslavian international, to sign him. But Cajkovski regarded Muller as 'a bear among racehorses'!

Muller's debut for Bayern's reserves was a painful one; he broke his arm. In those days, Bayern was still a club in the Regional League of Southern Germany and eventually Muller made his senior bow against Freiburger and scored twice in an 11-2 win. His 35 goals that season helped Bayern win promotion to the Bundesliga.

In 1965-66 he hit 15 goals in 33 games and also deputised in goal for the injured Sepp Maier against Hamburg. By this time, Muller had had reduced his weight by more than 20 lb and his reactions sharpened. In 1966-67 he was joint top scorer in the League with 28 goals.

There were German Cup victories in 1966 and 1967 and the European Cup Winners' Cup trophy in the latter year, in which Muller scored eight goals, including four against Standard Liege in the semi-finals.

More domestic honours followed. In 1968-69 Bayern achieved their first Bundesliga title and Muller was confirmed as their ace marksman with 30 goals. Moreover he had also established himself in the national side.

His first appearance was the match after West Germany had lost the 1966 World Cup final to England at Wembley. It was on 12 October. His colleagues that day included Maier, Grabowski and Netzer. West Germany won 2 - 0 but Muller did not score. In fact he was left out until the game with Albania in the following April, when he scored four times in a 6 - 0 win.

Despite this haul, he was far from a regular choice until 1969. In the 1969-70 domestic season he scored 38 League goals as well as nine in World Cup qualifying games which helped West Germany reach the finals in Mexico. There he finished as leading scorer in the tournament with 10 goals. Recognition of his performances at club and country level followed when he was voted European Footballer of the Year.

After winning the Cup in 1971, Bayern won three Bundesliga titles in a row and each season Muller was West Germany's leading League scorer with 40, 36 and then joint top with 30 goals from 1972 to 1974.

In 1974 West Germany reached the World Cup final itself and though the team was past its peak, it achieved a notable victory. Muller's winning goal in the final against Holland was a half-chance from his only opening in the match. He retired from international football after this game, but continued to take the honours at Bayern.

That same year, Bayern had won the first of three successive European Cup Finals. He was joint top scorer for the last time in the Bundesliga with 24 goals in 1978. The following season he wanted to retire completely, but went to the North American Soccer League instead.

His tally of goals in the Bundesliga had been 365 goals in 427 games. Muller's 350th effort had arrived against Werder Bremen on 21 January 1978. He also reached his 600th competitive goal in the same season. Between 1969-70 and 1976-77 he scored 36 goals for Bayern in the European Cup. His aggregate of 14 goals in World Cup finals came from 10 in 1970, four in 1974.

In 1972 he led the West German attack in the European Championships, scoring two goals in the 3 - 0 win over the USSR in the final. It was Germany's most accomplished performance, and Muller with his uncanny positioning and accuracy was its ideal spearhead.

Gerd Muller (right, dark shirt) heads West Germany's third and final goal in the 3-0 win over Australia in the 1974 World Cup. Aussie goalkeeper Jack Reilly is well beaten. (POPPERFOTO)

PELE

BRAZIL

It says much for Pele, arguably the most accomplished footballer of all time, that two of his most audacious attempts at scoring, both of which failed to produce a goal, are remembered as fondly as the many that proved successful. Both were in the 1970 World Cup; a lob from his own half against Czechoslovakia and a brilliant dummy he sold the Uruguayan goalkeeper.

Among those unforgettably recorded was his first goal in the 1958 World Cup finals against Wales when he controlled the ball on his thigh, hooked it over his head, pivoted and drove the ball in. Then there was the occasion for Santos against Fluminense in the Maracana Stadium in Rio when from his own penalty area he dribbled past seven opponents before scoring.

Born 23 October 1940 in Tre Coracoes in the state of Minas Gerais, he came from a footballing family. His father, Joao Ramos do Nascimento, known as Dondinho, was a professional. Moreover, the nickname of Pele for someone born Edson Arantes do Nascimento has never been properly explained. To this day, the family always refer to Pele as Dico.

Pele's footballing career began when the family moved to Bauru in Sao Paulo. His first games were for a team called Ameriquinha, organised by his school friends. But it was when he joined Baquinha — little BAC, the junior team run by Bauru Athletic Club — that his fortunes changed.

Pele was 13 years old. Bauru had appointed Waldemar de Brito as coach. A member of Brazil's 1934 World Cup team, Waldemar was a friend of Pele's father. He proved of exceptional influence in Pele's formative years.

Waldemar was strict but fair and a thorough coach. He taught his young players everything he knew. But without Pele's inherent ability there would have been no outstanding talent to develop. Waldemar never attempted to curb the youngster's natural gifts, rather concentrating on his weaknesses.

He kept in close contact with Dondinho and the family, to such an extent that when Bangu tried to persuade Pele to sign for them Waldemar persuaded the family to wait, and suggested that Santos would prove a better grounding for Pele.

Thus at 15, Pele moved on, graduating from youth team to senior status. He was still 16 when he played his first game for the first team, a friendly against AIK Stockholm. Santos won with a late penalty but in Pele's next game against Corinthians of Santo Andre he scored his first goal in a 7-1 win on 7 September 1956.

While still not 17, he was chosen to play in Brazil's Roca Cup squad for the two games with Argentina. In his first on 7 July 1957 he made his debut as substitute midway through the second half and scored within 10 minutes. Brazil lost 2-1, but in the return game Pele was on from the start and scored again in a 2-0 success which clinched the trophy for Brazil.

That season with Santos he was the leading scorer in the Sao Paulo League with 36 goals. The following year he hit a record 53. But his prospects for the World Cup team looked bleak. He was almost left behind because of a knee injury.

In fact he did not play until Brazil's third game, against the USSR. He hit a post in the 2-0 win and scored the only goal of the next game with Wales. In the semi-final against France he produced a hat-trick, and two more goals followed in the final with Sweden.

The next two World Cup tournaments ended in personal despair for Pele. In 1962 he began well enough, scoring in the 2-0 success over Mexico, but was injured in the goalless draw with Czechoslovakia and took no further part in the tournament, which Brazil won. Four

Pele (10) receives the outstretched arms of Rivelino (11) and Tostao (9) having scored the opening goal of the 1970 World Cup final against Italy.
(POPPERFOTO)

years later in England, he was severely mauled by Bulgarian and Portuguese defenders and had to be assisted from the pitch in the latter encounter.

But in 1970 everything went according to plan. At 29, Pele had achieved just about everything possible in the game. His best scoring year had been 1959 when he reached 126 goals in all matches. In 1969 he reached his 1000th goal in his 909th game. Pele even completed his national service in the Army, serving in the 6th Coast Guard.

Frequently the victim of unscrupulous defenders, Pele, rarely retaliated though he was sent off early in his career when he did so. In later years he invariably humiliated his opponents with feints and footwork achieving his own kind of retribution with consummate ease.

In Mexico in 1970 he revealed his full range of artistry. His wide peripheral vision, made acute by Waldemar's insistence that players should glance around before receiving the ball, kept him vital seconds ahead in reading the game. His control was peerless and the final in particular showed his unselfishness as he memorably laid on a goal for his captain, Carlos Alberto.

His 111th and last international was against Austria in July 1971, his last game for Santos in October 1974. He retired, only to reappear for New York Cosmos and almost single-handedly popularised the game in the USA. He played his last match in New Jersey on 1 October 1977, before a crowd of 75,646. During the game he appeared for both sides — New York and Santos. It was his 1,363rd match and he scored his 1,281st goal. Later he added two more goals in special appearances. For Brazil alone he had scored 97.

Pele has remained in the public eye at home and abroad. He remains an excellent ambassador for the game, though he has been critical of Brazilian football. His popularity is such that he has considered entering politics. He continues to make public appearances on World Cup occasions and was on hand for the 1990 World Cup draw in December 1989.

MICHEL PLATINI

FRANCE

Michel Platini was the midfield inspiration of the French team which won the European Championship with an irresistible display of incisive, attacking play in the 1984 tournament. It was a memorable year for him. He became European Footballer of the Year for the second time and helped Juventus to the Italian championship in which he finished as leading goalscorer.

Platini also played in the 1978, 1982 and 1986 World Cup competitions, stamping his own authority on the fluidly attractive style for which the French became renowned.

Born in Joeuf on 21 June 1955 his early football was played with Nancy, where his father Aldo was one of the coaches. In seven seasons there he scored 98 goals in 175 League appearances. He also made his first steps in international football as a member of the French team in the 1976 Olympics in Montreal, after his full debut against Czechoslovakia in March of the same year. In this game he scored in a 2-2 draw.

In 1978 he scored the goal in the French Cup final which took the trophy to Nancy at the expense of Nice and went on to play in the World Cup finals in Argentina. The French took the lead in under a minute in the opening match with Italy, but while they promised much, results were ultimately disappointing.

But for Platini there was a move to St Etienne which was to produce a championship in 1981 in which he contributed 21 invaluable goals, and two cup final appearances on the losing side. In 107 League games he scored 58 goals for St Etienne.

In the 1982 World Cup, France's hopes were finally dashed after an exhausting 3-3 draw with West Germany and the subsequent penalty shoot-out which ended 5-4 in the Germans' favour. After the tournament, Platini moved to Italy, Juventus having paid £1.2 million for him.

Although Juventus had to be content with the runners-up position in the Italian First Division, Platini enjoyed an excellent initial season finishing as the League's leading goalscorer on 16 goals. In 1983-84 both club and player did better than that, Juventus winning the title and Platini again top scoring with 20 goals.

In 1984 France had the advantage of hosting the final tournament in the European Championship. Platini scored the only goal of the game with Denmark, three of the five against Belgium including a penalty and all three at the expense of Yugoslavia, who were beaten 3-2. He then hit the winner in the thrilling 3-2 win in extra time against Portugal, and to complete a remarkable tournament, scored the first goal in the final, which saw Spain defeated 2-0.

He had scored more goals for France than any other player in the country's history and overtook Just Fontaine's previous record of 31 goals. At 29, Platini was at his most assertive. Truly a mercurial midfield master, he initiated and completed attacks with skilled understanding and control.

His dead-ball expertise was honed by hours of practice, swerving the ball round wooden dummies. Free-kicks and penalties swelled his tally of goals. But it was his mobile contribution which made him such a dangerous opponent, able to elude the closest of markers. Platini would patiently hover for just one lapse to steal into a space and produce an opening either for a colleague or for himself.

Juventus won the 1985 European Cup, Platini converting a penalty against Liverpool in the awful aftermath of the Heysel Stadium disaster. The previous year he had won a Cup Winners' Cup medal in the 2-1 victory over Porto. In 1985-86 Juventus won another championship, Platini scoring 12 goals. The season before that he had been leading scorer with 18 goals. His last campaign for Juventus was in 1986-87.

In the 1986 World Cup in Mexico, Platini was a closely watched player. Although he equalised for France in the absorbing clash with Brazil, the match had to be decided on penalties and Platini missed from the spot. It was not the first set-back in his career, but as a player it was one of his last.

In his first season with Juventus, Platini had to settle for a runners-up medal in the European Cup, the Italian champions losing to Hamburg. But his experiences at club and international level had included nine consecutive seasons in one or other of the three European competitions. He had scored 27 goals in these three tournaments.

For Juventus in League games alone, he scored 68 goals in 147 matches. For France, whom he captained in the European Championship, Platini appeared on 72 occasions and added 41 goals to his record.

His ability to direct the ball with precision either for other players or for himself had made him unique in his era, where specialists had increasingly become uncommon and individual accomplishment rarer. At the age of 32 he decided to retire.

However he was not kept out of the spotlight for long. Having dabbled in television as a football commentator, he was asked to take over the French national team and had to wrestle with the problem faced by all outstanding players when required to manage others: transferring their own natural ability to those less gifted.

Michel Platini in aerial action for France against Hungary in the 1986 World Cup in Mexico.

DJALMA SANTOS

BRAZIL

Djalma Santos, or Dejalma dos Santos to give him his full name, was something of a late developer. This was due in part to his father who caught him playing truant from school and banned him from playing football until his studies were satisfactorily completed.

Unfortunately for the young Santos, this meant a two-year lapse in his career and it was not until 1948, when he was 19, that he was able to join a senior club in Brazil. Born in Sao Paulo on 27 February 1929, it was to Portuguesa that he departed with parental approval at last.

He had made his impression as a central defender of the old school, with an attacking flair which in more modern systems would see him called a sweeper in front of the back four. But Portuguesa switched him quickly to a more obvious midfield role.

Santos had 11 years with his first senior club and achieved his initial international honours with them in 1952. The event was the Pan-American Games in Santiago, Chile. Brazil's first game was against Peru. Santos made his debut in it and had the satisfaction of helping to keep the Brazilian defence intact in a goalless draw.

In the other two matches in which his team were involved, Santos assisted them to a 5-0 win over Panama and a 4-2 success against Uruguay which gave Brazil the gold medal in the tournament. Beginning to settle into the national team set-up, he next looked towards the 1954 World Cup.

Brazil's qualifying group included Chile and Paraguay and Santos was on duty in all four games which produced a quartet of wins. In Switzerland for the finals, Brazil were among the favourites outside Europe along with the holders Uruguay.

In the quarter-finals Brazil found their opponents to be the hot favourites from Europe, Hungary. But the game was a disgrace; Brazil lost 4-2 in the 'Battle of Berne' and though Santos had the satisfaction of scoring from the penalty-spot, the entire squad was under something of a cloud.

He made only one appearance in 1955 but in the same year collected his second Rio-Sao Paulo Cup winners medal with Portuguesa. The first had been achieved three years earlier. In fact, his impact on the domestic scene had been such that Bauer, the Brazilian wing-half in the 1950 World Cup and captain in 1954, was switched to the left side of midfield to accommodate Santos before the latter became the regular choice right-back.

However in 1956 Santos appeared in 19 matches for Brazil. By now he had developed a style which made him one of the most respected defenders in the country. His partnership with left-back Nilton Santos was progressing well.

Nilton Santos was unrelated and white. The two were perfecting the overlapping full-back strategy, which was to become a feature of Brazilian teams in the years ahead. But during 1956, Djalma Santos came across a problem when he played against England at Wembley.

Brazil were destroyed. Although the final score was 4-2 in England's favour, they missed two penalties and several other clear-cut scoring opportunities. The recalled Stanley Matthews, at 41, created havoc in the Brazilian defence.

Djalma Santos survived this experience and doubtless became a wiser defender for it. He was adept at never allowing himself to be committed by an opponent. He preferred to position himself rather than move in quickly. Santos would wait until the right moment to dispossess the opposing player.

In spite of his cautious though admirably effective defensive qualities, his attacking features were just the opposite. Whenever in possession himself, he would revert to his sharp, attacking style on the flank.

For the 1958 World Cup, Brazil were fortunate that their qualifying group consisted of just one other opponent, Peru. Santos played in both games, a 1-1 draw in Lima and a 1-0 win in Rio. But Brazilian team manager Vicente Feola was still toying with his team selection.

De Sordi was selected at right-back instead of Santos who did not figure in a match until the final itself. Santos' opponent was the elusive Swedish winger Nacka

fans in Sao Paulo, finished with a 2-0 win for Brazil. Before the end of the game he was replaced by Carlos Alberto who was to go on and captain his country in their 1970 World Cup triumph. For Djalma Santos, 1968 saw him move on to Atletico Parana.

One of his most memorable appearances was being selected for the Rest of the World against England at Wembley in 1963, to mark the Football Association's Centenary. He was the only Brazilian chosen for the occasion.

Djalma Santos the Brazilian right-back, pictured with Zito the captain and Pele after the 1962 World Cup.
(HULTON DEUTSCH)

Skoglund. The Brazilian defender's wait and see tactics proved immensely successful and confounded Sweden's hopes of turning the Brazilians on the wings.

In 1959, he changed clubs, signing for Palmeiras. In the years ahead he achieved three Sao Paulo championship medals with them as well as another Rio-Sao Paulo honour. Internationally, he was still a firm selection and helped Brazil to their second successive World Cup win in 1962. In the final he provided the cross from which Brazil scored their third goal.

He was again in favour for the 1966 World Cup in England but the 3-1 defeat by Hungary was his last international until given a final outing two years later to mark his retirement. The match chosen as a farewell was against Uruguay. Djalma Santos was in his familiar position at right-back and the game, played in front of his local

JUAN ALBERTO SCHIAFFINO

URUGUAY

Years after Uruguay's 1950 World Cup victory over Brazil, Juan Schiaffino referred to the triumph as 'a miracle'. The comment, though understandably modest, detracted from his own vital performance and that of the team as a whole.

However, this rather unassuming character preferred to let his actions speak for him, and his career in Uruguay and Italy was of sufficient substance to vindicate this attitude.

Born in Montevideo on 28 July 1925 of Italian parentage,he developed a keen interest in the game and showed considerable ability even at an early age. Unfortunately since he was of slight build and inclined towards playing centre-forward, his prospects of high attainment seemed remote.

But in 1943 at the age of 18 he joined Penarol, ostensibly to play in their lower ranks. Despite his physical problems, he revealed such promise that a first team chance was awaiting him. This opportunity came in 1944. By the following year he had become a regular choice, now switched to inside-left where his all-round talents were finding even more success.

Juan — nicknamed Pepe — had an older brother at Penarol called Raul who was two years his senior. With Walter Gomez at inside-right they formed a formidable attacking trio. Pepe had already displayed his prowess as a goalscorer with an uncanny knack of being in the right place at the precise moment that scoring opportunities presented themselves. Now he produced a full range of skills.

With a vision and intelligence which stood out, his elegant stature was allied to finely-tuned distribution, speed, control and finishing accuracy. An international appearance was not far off, but arrived in unusual circumstances.

A strike of professional players in Uruguay coincided with the 1949 South American Championships. Rather than withdraw their entry, Uruguay decided to send a team of its best amateur players. Juan Schiaffino was one of them.

This makeshift side finished fourth. The winners were Brazil who beat Uruguay 5-1. But the young Uruguayans learned a valuable lesson that day. A year later they were able to put it to practical use during the World Cup.

The finals held in Brazil were marred by late withdrawals. Uruguay's group shrunk to just two competitors and they had a field day against the weak Bolivians. Schiaffino scored four goals in an 8-0 win.

This solitary game put Uruguay into the final pool of four. Twice they came back from being a goal down to Sweden to win 3-2, and despite taking an early lead against Spain, found themselves behind again before forcing a 2-2 draw. The last match against Brazil seemed a formality for the hosts who needed only a draw to win the World Cup.

The Brazilians penned Uruguay into their own half for most of the first half and when they went ahead two minutes after the break, the contest looked as good as over. But the goal simply served to inspire Uruguay who had conceded territory but not spirit to their opponents.

Chasing every loose ball, not allowing Brazil to settle when in possession and throwing more players forward, they seized the initiative for themselves. Schiaffino, who had worked tirelessly throughout, stunned the vast crowd in the Maracana Stadium with a drive which rippled the Brazilian rigging. Sixty-six minutes had elapsed but Brazil still only required a draw.

Then Schiaffino conjured up a move which ended with Alcide Ghiggia cracking the winner with 11 minutes remaining. Once in the lead, there was no way the combative Uruguayans were going to surrender.

Back at home in Montevideo, Schiaffino and company received a tremendous reception. Then it was back to playing successfully with Penarol until the 1954 World Cup. Uruguay reached the semi-final where they met Hungary, Europe's outstanding representatives.

The match was memorable, played in driving rain. Uruguay, two goals down, fought back to force extra time and it was only when Schiaffino was slowed by injury that Hungary gained supremacy. But Schiaffino's reputation had soared. At 29, he was at the peak of his career and had made 22 appearances for Uruguay.

AC Milan broke the world transfer fee by paying £72,000 for him. At San Siro he masterminded Milan's championship successes in 1955, 1957 and 1959. The slender frame withstood everything the rigours of the Italian game could pitch against it, and in Milan's 1955 success he scored 15 goals. As a tactician he was instrumental in providing the launching pad for the team's attacking strength.

In 1958 AC Milan reached the European Cup Final. Schiaffino scored a typical goal but it was not enough to prevent Real Madrid winning 3-2. Italy had already capped him, and appropriately one of four caps was in a World Cup qualifying game for the 1958 competition. In 1962 he retired after two years in the service of Roma.

Back home in Montevideo he scouted for Penarol, managed them for a six-month spell, even took charge of the national side for two games. But business interests kept him out of full-time football, though he continued coaching youngsters.

Juan Alberto Schiaffino burst onto the World Cup scene in 1950 with four goals in the opening game with Bolivia and masterminded the Uruguayan offensive in two World Cups. (HULTON DEUTSCH)

FRITZ WALTER

WEST GERMANY

Had the Second Word War not interrupted his career, Fritz Walter would probably have become the first German to make 100 appearances for his country. Between 1942 and 1950 the Germans did not play any internationals.

In fact, having played in Germany's last fixture against the satellite state of Slovakia in November 1942, Walter missed the next game with Switzerland in November 1950 and did not resume until the following April in the return game with the Swiss.

Born in Kaiserslautern on 31 October 1920 he made a sensational start to his international career in July 1940 against Rumania in Frankfurt, scoring a hat-trick in a 9-3 win. He was still only 19 years old.

By the time it had become impossible to continue international fixtures, Walter had made 24 appearances and scored 19 goals including another hat-trick against Rumania. He usually played at inside-left, but also led the attack on occasions.

Despite his relative youth, he had shown an instinct for leadership and tactics, combining midfield foraging with an eye for goalscoring opportunities. Walter joined a paratroop regiment in the war and as a result of this experience, refused to fly to matches in later years.

When hostilities ceased, Walter returned to his only club, Kaiserslautern, and was instrumental in rebuilding the team as football struggled to regain its pre-war place in the ruins that were post-war Germany. The championship did not restart until 1948 and was still organised on a regional basis.

But Kaiserslautern reached the final before losing 2-1 to Nuremberg. In 1949 they were placed third and two years later won the championship for the first time in the club's history, beating Preussen Munster 2-1. They repeated this success in 1953 with a 4-1 win over Stuttgart. Walter was often used at inside-right, the vital link between scheming and scoring, with his younger brother Ottmar at centre-forward.

West Germany's national team was still prevented from competing in international football, but was allowed back into FIFA in 1950, though not in time to take part in the World Cup that year.

In the draw for the qualifying competition in the 1954 series, West Germany's group opponents were modest Saarland and Norway. Not surprisingly they dropped only one point, in the away match with the Norwegians. Fritz Walter was the lynch-pin of the team. Moreover he had a fine understanding with his manager Sepp Herberger.

This relationship had started in a small way during the three years in which Walter had been launched into the international arena before the war closed in. So impressed had Herberger been that he now made Walter captain.

Walter led the Germans for the first time in April 1951. Herberger treated him with more consideration than any father would care for his own son. The manager knew how vital was the well being of Walter to his plans for West Germany.

Herberger was conscious of Walter's sensitivity, his proneness to nervous strain. But all the manager's careful planning seemed to have been scuppered by the events at the end of the West German championship. Kaiserslautern, with five of the World Cup squad on duty for them, were slaughtered 5-1 by Hanover who did not have a single player going to Switzerland.

Morale was at rock bottom. With three weeks to go before the opening game with Turkey, Herberger decided to put his captain in the same room as the extrovert winger Helmut Rahn in a bid to get him to relax. Fortunately, all the tension seemed to disappear when the Turks were beaten 4-1.

Fritz Walter, holding the World Cup, is congratulated by Ferenc Puskas after the 1954 final in Berne. (POPPERFOTO)

The next match was against the favourites to win the World Cup, Hungary. Herberger knew that the peculiar arrangement of fixtures in the group could give him a unique opportunity to fool the Hungarians. He deliberately fielded a weakened side under Walter's captaincy, knowing that defeat would put them into a play-off situation with Turkey.

Hungary duly obliged with a crushing 8-3 win, but Herberger's gamble paid off as the Turks were trounced 7-2 in the play-off. Yugoslavia and Austria then fell victim to the Germans in the run up to the final in Berne against Hungary.

In the semi-final against Austria, Walter was inspirational, prompting his fast-raiding wingers and supporting the spearhead of the attack which ripped through the opposing defence. West Germany won 6-1, with Walter scoring twice from the penalty spot.

Although his presence was essential to Germany's success, Walter was economical in his dwellings on the ball, preferring to bring others into the game to such an extent that his contribution often appeared minimal.

But in the final, with Hungary two goals ahead in the opening minutes, he needed all his powers of skill and determination to turn the game, which he did in outstanding fashion. At the end he collected the cup after the 3-2 win.

Four years later Walter was again on duty in the finals in Sweden. But for his crippling injury sustained against the Swedes, the Germans might have reached the final. He retired from the international scene with 61 appearances and 33 goals to his credit. However, he continued to play for Kaiserslautern until he was 40 and Herberger even wanted him to play in the 1962 World Cup.

ZICO

BRAZIL

Artur Antunes Coimbra, known as Zico, experienced varying degrees of disappointment in three World Cup competitions. In his last World Cup game for Brazil, he even had the misfortune to miss a crucial penalty minutes after coming on as substitute. Yet this unluckiest of players always remained a world class performer.

A quick, unselfish midfield-attacker with fine control, precision passing and tireless application, he was last in the line of those known as the 'White Pele'. As a boy in his native Rio de Janeiro he had played with a ball made of rags on the beaches and was later to enjoy the riches associated with a top-flight career.

Born on 3 March 1953 into a footballing family — his three brothers were professionals and his father formerly a goalkeeper — he joined Flamengo as a frail 15-year-old. The club immediately put him on a body-building course and a year later the elderly Paraguayan coach of the club Fleitas Solich, gave him a chance in the first team. He managed to score twice in 15 games but often seemed out of his depth.

Clearly he needed more time to develop, and was sent back to play in the youth team where he had scored his first goal on 18 March 1970 against Sao Cristobal. It worked wonders for his confidence and he proceeded to score 20 goals in 22 games.

His next appearance in the senior side was the beginning of a permanent place and he also appeared in the Brazilian Olympic side. He was given his bow in the full national team and made it a memorable occasion by scoring the winner against Uruguay in 1975.

After the inadequacy of the Brazilian attack was exposed in the 1974 World Cup finals, there was a need to discover a versatile player who could operate behind the front line but function both as a maker and taker of scoring chances. Zico looked to be the answer.

Brazil appointed Claudio Coutinho as coach. Unfortunately for Zico he wanted him to adopt a different role from the one he was used to playing with Flamengo. This was one problem. Another was the niggling injury which Zico carried into the finals themselves.

The opening match in Argentina was against Sweden. Brazil did not succeed in getting to grips with the opposition. The score was 1-1 when in the dying seconds, Brazil took a corner. Zico headed in from almost under the bar, only to find that referee Clive Thomas had already blown his whistle for full time. In the next game with Spain, Zico was taken off seven minutes before the end in a goalless draw and with the pressure on the team in the last game with Austria he was on the substitutes bench. His contribution to the 1-0 win was a seven minute appearance towards the end.

Brazil had managed to qualify for the second stage but morale generally was not too high. The next fixture was against Peru and Zico was again on the bench. Dirceu cracked in two swerving shots to give the Brazilians a 2-0 lead. Then they were awarded a penalty in the second half. Zico came on to take it and scored. In the following goalless draw with Argentina, he was restricted to 22 minutes as substitute once more.

But for the vital game with Poland, Zico was restored to the team. He lasted just seven minutes before being taken off with injury. Brazil won 3-1 but Argentina needed just to wait for the result and then hit as many goals as required against Peru. Brazil secured third place but Zico was out of action.

However in 1979, Zico regained all his lost confidence, and restored to fitness he scored 89 goals; 65 of them in the League for Flamengo, 16 in friendlies, seven for Brazil and one for the Rest of Europe. The same year he set up a

Zico scored 66 goals in 88 internationals for Brazil. At club level he hit more than 500 senior goals for Flamengo.

new scoring record in the Rio 'Carioca' League with his 245th goal for Flamengo.

A dead ball expert, he was able to add to his haul of goals with free-kicks and penalties. In 1981 he became South American Footballer of the Year for the second time, his first award having been in 1977.

In 1982, Brazil went to Spain hoping for better fortune in the World Cup. They had to claw their way back into the game with USSR, scoring twice in the last quarter of an hour to win 2-1. Zico scored one of the goals by which Brazil beat Scotland 4-1 and two in the 4-0 win over New Zealand.

After giving his team the lead over Argentina he was injured in the 83rd minute of Brazil's 3-1 win but recovered in time to play against Italy, only to discover the frail nature of his team's defence. However he was voted South American Player of the Year again.

In 1983 after 630 goals, three Brazilian championships, six Rio State titles and South American and World Cup Championship honours he went to Italy where Udinese paid £2.5 million for his services. In his first season he topped their scoring list with 19 goals, but after an injury-hit second season he returned in June 1985 to his former club Flamengo.

He had a knee operation and returned to the national side with three goals against Yugoslavia but at 33 and still not fully fit, was doubtful for the World Cup. In the opening group games he played just 22 minutes, as substitute against Northern Ireland, but at half-pace scarcely put a foot wrong. He made a similar late but effective appearance against Poland. Then came his penalty miss against France, though to his credit he appeared unaffected by the failure and was one of Brazil's scorers in the shoot-out.

DINO ZOFF

ITALY

Like a vintage wine, Dino Zoff improved with age. He was 40 when he captained Italy to their 1982 World Cup success and although he had one or two disappointments in his career, consistency was a key factor in his longevity as an international goalkeeper.

Born at Mariano del Friuli in the north-east province of Gorizia on 28 February 1942, he developed with Udinese but had a severe baptism in the first team, conceding five goals in a 5-2 defeat away to Fiorentina when he was 19. It was not a happy period for the club. Zoff made four League appearances in that 1961-62 season, at the conclusion of which Udinese found themselves relegated.

In 1962-63 he was the regular choice and before the beginning of the following season, he moved on to Mantova who were in the First Division at the time. That season he played the first of three intermediate internationals for Italy.

However there was another set-back at the end of 1964-65 when Mantova were relegated. But they bounced back after just one term in Division Two and it was not until 1967 that Zoff switched clubs again. His destination was Napoli and in April 1968 he found himself capped for Italy at full level on his home ground in a European Championship game against Bulgaria, before an ecstatic crowd of 90,000.

His second international was in the semi-final of the same competition against USSR. Zoff remained unbeaten after extra time, with the Italians rather fortunately going through on the toss of a coin!

In the final in Rome, he was beaten for the first time in a 1-1 draw which also went to the extra period. But in the replay he kept the opposition out as Italy took the trophy in a 2-0 success. Before his debut in national colours, the Italians' first choice goalkeeper had been Enrico Albertosi. Now both players were tried on an alternate basis in the run up to the World Cup in Mexico. But after Zoff's tenth appearance in a 2-2 draw with Spain in Madrid, a match notable for the double own goal by Italy's Sandro Salvadore, Albertosi was made first choice.

Zoff's next outing was as second-half substitute against Switzerland in Berne in which he was not beaten in a 1-1 draw. Shortly afterwards he edged out Albertosi, and in 1972 was transferred to Juventus. The following year he finished runner-up in the European Footballer of the Year award.

It was the beginning of the goalkeeper's most rewarding period at club and country level. He was rarely absent from either the Juventus team or the national side. The club won five championships and two cups.

After conceding a goal to Yugoslavia 17 minutes from the end of a 3-1 win in September 1972 he was unbeaten in 12 entire matches. In the 13th, against Haiti in the 1974 World Cup, he finally conceded a goal a minute after half-time. His 1,143 minutes without letting the opposition score against him created a world record. It included two matches against England.

Noted for his agility, courage and anticipation, his reflexes were honed intensely by the defensive methods used in Italian football. In fact it often appeared far easier for him to deal with shots in international games where he often had more time to see the ball. However his prowess in the Italian League was such that he also established a record of 903 minutes without letting in a goal.

Zoff won his 64th cap in the opening World Cup game in Argentina in 1978. Having beaten the host nation to finish top of their group, the Italians went on to reach the semi-final and met Holland. In the second half, with Italy leading by an own goal, Zoff was twice beaten by

searing, long-range drives. He looked every part of his 36 years. His career seemed to be in the balance.

But it was not in jeopardy. He continued to be called upon by Italy even though other players were tried out for the day when Zoff would retire. The 1982 World Cup arrived with him poised to make his 100th appearance for Italy, and he marked the occasion with a clean sheet against Poland in a goalless draw.

Despite the Italians giving three low-key performances in the opening group matches, Zoff had kept his best for the second round tie with Brazil. He succeeded in keeping the Italians ahead when Brazil pressed desperately in the closing stages, trying to save the game. But Zoff remained cool, commanding and belied his age as he pulled out every morsel of know-how derived from 20 years in top class football.

In the World Cup final itself, Zoff again looked supreme. He collected the trophy after his 106th game for Italy, and went on to complete 112 appearances. His last international was against Sweden in May 1983 in a European Championship qualifying match in which he was beaten twice.

His 570 First Division matches included 332 consecutive appearances and with his two seasons in the Second Division added on, he had made a total of 644 League appearances. Upon retiring he took charge of the Italian Olympic team in 1988 and then assumed control of his favourite Juventus team.

Dino Zoff moves smartly to cut off the ball before it reaches Ray Wilkins. England beat Italy 2-0 at Wembley, but the Italians and Zoff qualified for the 1978 finals at the expense of the home side.
(HULTON)

THE 1990 FINALISTS'
WORLD CUP PEDIGREE

Assessing a country's prospects for any World Cup tournament is never simply a question of looking at the current strengths and weaknesses of the team. Almost as much significance is attached to the record of the nation in past World Cups.

FIFA, for one, now base the Group seedings for the final tournament strictly according to this criterion, preferring to award seeded places on the basis of recent World Cup performances. In 1982 they even decided to make seeds of all past winners who had qualified, despite the fact that one of them, England, had not even qualified for the previous two finals.

European Championship wins, as Holland discovered when the 1990 draw was made, count for very little. Denmark, strongly fancied to do well in 1986 but making their first ever appearance in the finals, found themselves bracketed for seeding purposes with vastly inferior sides such as Iraq and Canada, a fate which mercifully did not befall the Republic of Ireland in 1990. The Danes had the last laugh, though, as they took maximum points from their group!

It is true, nonetheless, that some countries have proved unexpectedly resilient in maintaining their World Cup track records. Brazil have never failed to qualify for the finals and since 1934, have only once failed to progress beyond the opening stages. Uruguay, the first winners of the trophy in 1930, did not lose a World Cup match until the semi-final in 1954. More recently, West Germany have maintained a remarkably consistent level of achievement in the World Cup finals, no matter how unfancied they may have been at the outset.

Since the introduction of greater representation in the finals for Africa, Asia and Central America, these nations

Brazil's first World Cup triumph was in 1958. Back row, left to right: Feola (trainer), Djaima Santos, Zito, Bellini, Nilton Santos, Orlando, Gylmar. Front: Garrincha, Didi, Pele, Vava, Zagalo.
(POPPERFOTO)

have been able to develop a World Cup pedigree of their own, Algeria, Cameroon and South Korea being notable examples, while each tournament now invariably sees some countries making their first appearances in the finals, Costa Rica, the United Arab Emirates and the Republic of Ireland doing so in 1990.

Each national side now has every incentive to establish, maintain or add to its country's World Cup history. This section looks at the achievements so far of every qualifier for Italy 1990.

AUSTRIA

Austria have had a chequered history as far as the World Cup is concerned. They performed well below expectations in 1990, failing to reach the second round, and third place in 1954 remains their best achievement.

In 1934 wins over France and Hungary took them through to the the semi-finals, where they lost 1-0 to the hosts, Italy. Germany accounted for them 3-2 in the match for third place. They qualified in 1938 but the annexation by Germany deprived them of a final place.

After withdrawing in 1950, they reached Switzerland in 1954. A 1-0 win over Scotland was followed by beating Czechoslovakia 5-0. In the quarter-finals with the Swiss, they won a free-scoring affair 7-5 only to be crushed 6-1 by the Germans in the semi-finals. However they beat Uruguay 3-1 for third place.

In 1958 they began by losing 3-0 to Brazil, were then beaten 2-0 by the USSR and a 2-2 draw with England was not enough to save them. They did not enter in 1962 and failed to qualify four years later. It was a similar story of failure in 1970 and 1974, but they qualified for Argentina in 1978.

Indeed the Austrians started well, beating Spain 2-1, and then had a single goal win over Sweden before losing 1-0 to Brazil. But in the second round they crashed 5-1 to Holland and lost 1-0 to Italy. Their 3-2 win over West Germany was merely a consolation for past reverses at their neighbours' hands.

They reached Spain in 1982 ironically in company with West Germany. A 1-0 success over Chile was followed by a 2-0 win over Algeria which allowed them the luxury of losing 1-0 to the Germans again in a controversial match. But in the second round they were edged out 1-0 by France held 2-2 by Northern Ireland and were eliminated. In 1986 they did not qualify.

Manfred Linzmaier indulges in some neat hurdling during the decisive 1990 World Cup qualifying match against East Germany. Austria won 3-0.

AUSTRIA

Formed: *1904*
Joined FIFA: *1905*
Honours: *3rd 1954; 4th 1934*
Clubs: *1992*
Players: *253,576*
Division I clubs: *12*
Season: *August-December; February-June*
Colours: *White shirts, black shorts, black stockings*
Manager: *Josef Hickersberger*
Highest World Cup win: *9-0 v Malta, 1978 qualifying*

WORLD CUP RECORD

1930	*Did not enter*
1934	*4th*
1938	*Withdrew after qualifying*
1950	*Withdrew*
1954	*3rd*
1958	*First Round*
1962	*Did not enter*
1966	*Did not qualify*
1970	*Did not qualify*
1974	*Did not qualify*
1978	*Second Round*
1982	*Second Round*
1986	*Did not qualify*
1990	*First Round*

CZECHOSLOVAKIA

Having twice finished as runners-up in the World Cup, Czechoslovakia can justifiably claim to be among the best of the Eastern European countries in the tournament, along with Hungary, twice beaten finalists themselves.

In 1934 they beat Rumania 2-1 in the first round, Switzerland. 3-2 in the quarter-finals and Germany 3-1 in Rome in the semi-finals. They forced Italy to extra time in the final before losing 2-1. In 1938 Czechoslovakia needed the extra period before they could defeat Holland 3-0 and again had to play over 90 minutes against Brazil in the quarter-finals. The sides were still 1-1 at the end but it was Brazil who won the replay 2-1.

They did not enter in 1950 but reached the finals in 1954 only to lose 2-0 to Uruguay and 5-0 to Austria. They did manage to survive slightly longer in 1958 after a slow start in which they lost 1-0 to Northern Ireland. The West Germans were held 2-2 and then Argentina were well beaten 6-1. But the Czechs lost the play-off with the Irish 2-1, again after extra time.

It was not a convincing opening in 1962; they beat Spain 1-0, held Brazil to a goalless draw but lost 3-1 to Mexico. In the quarter-finals they accounted for Hungary 1-0 and Yugoslavia were beaten 3-1 in the semi-finals. Still despite taking the lead in the final with the Brazilians, they were beaten 3-1 in Santiago.

They did not qualify in 1966 and lost all three games in 1970: 4-1 to Brazil, 2-1 to Rumania, as well as 1-0 to England. There was no qualification in either 1974 or 1978, but the Czechs reached Spain in 1982. However they were held 1-1 by Kuwait, lost 2-0 to England and a 1-1 draw with France was not enough to save them. Four years later they did not qualify for Mexico but regained some credibility by reaching the quarter-finals in 1990.

Josef Masopust opens the scoring for Czechoslovakia in the 1962 final.
(CZECHOSLOVAKIAN FA)

CZECHOSLOVAKIA

Formed: *1901*
Joined FIFA: *1906*
Honours: *Runners-up 1934, 1962*
Clubs: *5972*
Players: *374,421*
Division I clubs: *16*
Season: *August-November; February-June*
Colours: *Red shirts, white shorts, blue stockings*
Manager: *Josef Venglos*
Highest World Cup win: *7-1 v Rep of Ireland 1962 Qualifying*

WORLD CUP RECORD

1930	*Did not enter*
1934	*Runners-up*
1938	*Second round*
1950	*Did not enter*
1954	*First Round*
1958	*First Round*
1962	*Runners-up*
1966	*Did not qualify*
1970	*First Round*
1974	*Did not qualify*
1978	*Did not qualify*
1982	*First Round*
1986	*Did not qualify*
1990	*Quarter-finals*

ITALY

Italy equalled Brazil's record of three World Cup wins in 1982, having won their first two in 1934 and 1938, and had high hopes of a record-breaking fourth win in 1990 before losing on penalties to Argentina in the semi-finals.

In 1934 they beat the USA 7-1, Spain 1-0 after a 1-1 draw and Austria 1-0 to reach the final in which they defeated Czechoslovakia 2-1 after extra time. Four years on and Norway forced them to extra time before the Italians won 2-1 and then it was France, beaten 3-1, Brazil 2-1 and finally Hungary 4-2.

However in 1950 they had just two games: a 3-2 defeat against Sweden and a 2-0 win over Paraguay. More disappointment came in 1954 after losing 2-1 to Switzerland and beating Belgium 4-1; they lost a play-off 4-1 to the Swiss. After failing to qualify in 1958 they reached Chile to hold West Germany 0-0, lose 2-0 to the hosts and beat Switzerland 3-0 only to be knocked out. Worse, in 1966 after revenge against Chile by 2-0, they lost 1-0 to the USSR and humiliatingly 1-0 to North Korea.

There was better fortune in 1970. Sweden were beaten 1-0, Uruguay and Israel held 0-0. Mexico were defeated 4-1 and West Germany 4-3 after extra time before.the Italians finally lost 4-1 to Brazil. In 1974 Haiti were beaten 3-1, Argentina held 1-1 before they lost 2-1 to Poland.

In 1978 the tournament began with victories over France, Hungary and Argentina. West Germany were held 0-0 and Austria beaten 1-0, before the Italians lost 2-1 to Holland and 2-1 to Brazil in the game for third place.

More successfully in 1982 Italy won their third trophy. Beginning slowly with three draws, 0-0 with Poland, 1-1 with Peru and 1-1 with Cameroon, they survived to beat Argentina 2-1, Brazil 3-2, Poland 2-0 and West Germany 3-1 in the final. In 1986 there were further 1-1 draws with Bulgaria and Argentina before a 3-2 win over South Korea. Elimination came in the second round, 2-0 against France.

Not all Italians were behind manager Enzo Bearzot (left) when he selected Paolo Rossi for the 1982 World Cup squad. But his choice was vindicated when Rossi helped Italy to win the Cup for the third time.

ITALY		WORLD CUP RECORD	
Formed: *1898*		**1930**	*Did not enter*
Joined FIFA: *1905*		**1934**	*Winners*
Honours: *Winners 1934, 1938, 1982;*		**1938**	*Winners*
runners-up 1970; 3rd 1990; 4th 1978		**1950**	*First Round*
Clubs: *19,191*		**1954**	*First Round*
Players: *1,612,404*		**1958**	*Did not qualify*
Division I clubs: *18*		**1962**	*First Round*
Season: *September-June*		**1966**	*First Round*
Colours: *Blue shirts, white shorts,*		**1970**	*Runners-up*
blue stockings, white trim		**1974**	*First Round*
Manager: *Azeglio Vicini*		**1978**	*4th*
Highest World Cup win: *7-1 v USA 1934*		**1982**	*Winners*
		1986	*Second Round*
		1990	*3rd*

USA

The United States of America can claim to be one of a comparatively small number of countries to have entered every World Cup competition. Their most rewarding tournament came in 1930 and their best performance achieved in one game in 1950.

In 1930 they began impressively with 3-0 wins over Belgium and Paraguay to reach the semi-finals where they were beaten 6-1 by Argentina, but only after suffering several injuries. Four years later they made the long journey to Italy before playing a qualifying game with Mexico, winning 4-2 only to find themselves subsequently crushed 7-1 by the host nation. In 1938 they did enter but withdrew before playing.

They were required to play in a tournament in Mexico before qualifying in 1950. But they lost 3-1 to Spain in the opening match in the final series and were expected to finish well beaten against England. Instead they won 1-0 in arguably the most sensational result ever achieved in the World Cup. However they came down to earth in the next match, losing 5-2 to Chile.

Not having the benefit of any home matches in 1954 robbed them of any real chance of qualifying but they could not use this as an excuse four years later. There was similar disappointment in 1962 and 1966, though in the latter competition they were slightly handicapped by

having to play both games with Honduras away and they did manage to hold Mexico to a 2-2 draw in Los Angeles.

They failed again in 1974 but in 1978 prospects slightly improved, as a better performance was ended only by defeat in a play-off against Canada. The US made little progress in 1982 or 1986 but finally reached the finals again in 1990 thanks to a dramatic win away to Trinidad and Tobago. In Italy, they were by no means disgraced.

Brian Bliss, one of the American squad which enabled his country to qualify for the finals for only the fourth time in their history in 1990.

USA	WORLD CUP RECORD	
Formed: *1913*	**1930**	*Semi-finals*
Joined FIFA: *1913*	**1934**	*First Round*
Honours: *Nil*	**1938**	*Withdrew*
Clubs: *6500*	**1950**	*First Round*
Players: *1,700,000*	**1954**	*Did not qualify*
Division I clubs: *No national league,*	**1958**	*Did not qualify*
ASL 10; WSL 9	**1962**	*Did not qualify*
Season: *April-September*	**1966**	*Did not qualify*
Colours: *White shirts, blue shorts, red*	**1970**	*Did not qualify*
stockings	**1974**	*Did not qualify*
Manager: *Bob Gansler*	**1978**	*Did not qualify*
Highest World Cup win: *6-2 v Bermuda,*	**1982**	*Did not qualify*
1970 qualifying	**1986**	*Did not qualify*
	1990	*First Round*

CAMEROON

Cameroon were unquestionably the sensation of the 1990 World Cup, defeating Argentina, Rumania and Colombia to reach the quarter-finals, where they were unlucky to lose 3-2 to England.

In 1966 they entered the competition for the first time but were among the mass exodus of African nations before a qualifying game was played. Four years later they were knocked out in the first match against Nigeria, but in 1974 forced a play-off with Zaire after being given a bye through a withdrawal in the first round. But Zaire won this game 2-0.

In 1978 Cameroon lost to the Congo but there was a transformation in their fortunes in 1982. In the first round, they beat Malawi 3-0 at home and then drew the return game 1-1 to progress into the next stage. Again they won on their own soil, beating Zimbabwe 2-0 and edged through into the third round despite losing the return match 1-0. But it looked bleak for them when Zaire won the first game by a single goal. However Cameroon swept through after winning 6-1 at home. This put them into the final round and they needed to beat Morocco for a place in the finals in Spain. They began well by winning 2-0 in Kenitra and eased through in Yaounde during their home clash with a 2-1 success.

Cameroon's group in Spain included Poland, Italy and

Peru. In the opening game with the Peruvians in La Coruna they drew 0-0 and repeated the scoreline against Poland. They entered the last group game with Italy knowing that a win would put them into the second stage, but a draw would be of no use since the Italians had at least scored one goal. The outcome was a 1-1 draw. Cameroon were eliminated unbeaten and Italy went on to win the Cup.

Ebwere Bertin in action for the Cameroon in their final qualifying game against Tunisia in Tunis which clinched a place in Italy for the Africans.

CAMEROON	WORLD CUP RECORD	
Formed: *1960*	**1930**	*Not eligible*
Joined FIFA: *1962*	**1934**	*Not eligible*
Honours: *Nil*	**1938**	*Not eligible*
Clubs: *380*	**1950**	*Not eligible*
Players: *18,578*	**1954**	*Not eligible*
Division I clubs: *16*	**1958**	*Not eligible*
Season: *October-August*	**1962**	*Not eligible*
Colours: *Green shirts, red shorts, yellow*	**1966**	*Withdrew*
stockings	**1970**	*Did not qualify*
Manager: *Valery Nepomniaschi*	**1974**	*Did not qualify*
Highest World Cup win: *6-1 v Zaire 1982*	**1978**	*Did not qualify*
qualifying	**1982**	*First Round*
	1986	*Did not qualify*
	1990	*Quarter-finals*

ARGENTINA

Having finished as runners-up in the initial tournament in 1930, Argentina had to wait until the 1970s before their first success but they have now appeared in three of the last four finals, losing to West Germany in 1990.

In 1930 they beat France 1-0, Mexico 6-3 and Chile 3-1 to reach the semi-finals where they defeated the USA 6-1. But they went down 4-2 to neighbouring Uruguay in the final. They did not enter in 1934, withdrew in 1938 and 1950 and did not enter in 1954. They qualified in 1958 only to find erratic form in Sweden, losing 3-1 to West Germany but beating Northern Ireland by the same score before crashing out 6-1 to Czechoslovakia.

In 1962 they edged out Bulgaria 1-0 but were beaten 3-1 by England and were held to a goalless draw by Hungary. However they began promisingly enough in 1966 with a 2-1 win over Spain, a goalless draw with West Germany and a 2-0 success over Switzerland. But it fell apart in the controversial quarter-final where they again lost to England by a single goal.

They did not qualify in 1970 but in 1974 reached the second round. After losing 3-2 to Poland, drawing 1-1 with Italy and beating Haiti 4-1, Holland beat them 4-0 as did Brazil by 2-1. The 1-1 draw with East Germany was of no assistance.

With home advantage in 1978 they made the most of it.

There were 2-1 wins over Hungary and France before a 1-0 defeat against Italy. In the second round they beat Poland 2-0, held Brazil to a 0-0 draw and took six goals off Peru without reply. In the final they beat Holland 3-1.

In 1982 a 1-0 defeat by Belgium was retrieved with a 4-1 win over Hungary and a 2-0 win over El Salvador. But then came a 2-1 defeat by Italy and a 3-1 reverse against Brazil. Yet in 1986 South Korea were despatched 3-1, Italy held 1-1 and Bulgaria beaten 2-0. Then Uruguay were beaten 1-0, England 2-1 and Belgium 2-0. In the final West Germany became their victims in a 3-2 success.

ARGENTINA	WORLD CUP RECORD	
Formed: *1893*	1930	*Runners-up*
Joined FIFA: *1912*	1934	*Did not enter*
Honours: *Winners 1978, 1986; runners-up*	1938	*Withdrew*
1930, 1990	1950	*Withdrew*
Clubs: *3350*	1954	*Did not enter*
Players: *307,000*	1958	*Did not enter*
Division I clubs: *20*	1962	*Did not enter*
Colours: *Blue and white shirts, black shorts,*	1966	*Quarter-finals*
white stockings	1970	*Did not qualify*
Manager: *Carlos Bilardo*	1974	*Second Round*
Highest World Cup win: *6-0 v Peru 1978*	1978	*Winners*
	1982	*Second Round*
	1986	*Winners*
	1990	*Runners-up*

Argentina fell at the quarter-final stage in 1966 after captain Antonio Rattin was sent off. England beat the ten-man South Americans 1-0. (POPPERFOTO)

USSR

The USSR emerged from its post-war isolation to participate in the World Cup for the first time in the 1958 series. But fourth place in 1966 represents the Soviets' best performance and they never threatened to improve on that in 1990, as they failed to reach the second round.

However in 1958 they qualified at the first attempt in a group which included Poland and Finland. In Helsinki they beat the Finns 10-0 and dropped only two points, losing 2-1 to the Poles. In Sweden they began by drawing 2-2 with England, Austria were beaten 2-0 before the Soviets lost to the Brazilians by the same score. In the play-off for second place in the group, they beat England 1-0.

They lost 2-0 to Sweden in the quarter-finals and having qualified again in 1962 they began with another 2-0 victory over Yugoslavia. They were held 4-4 in an error-ridden game with Colombia before edging out Uruguay 2-1. But again the host nation knocked them out; Chile winning 2-1.

In 1966 they beat North Korea 3-0, the Italians by a single goal and gained revenge over Chile with a 2-1 win. The quarter-finals saw them defeat Hungary 2-1 at Roker Park, but West Germany beat them in the semi-finals and in the match for third place at Wembley, they lost 2-1 to Portugal.

In Mexico they opened the series with a goalless draw against the host nation, then defeated Belgium 4-1 and El Salvador 2-0 only to lose 1-0 to Uruguay in extra time in the quarter-finals.

After two failures the 1982 finals were reached. They recovered from a 2-1 defeat by Brazil to beat New Zealand 3-0 and then drew 2-2 with Scotland. In the second round they beat Belgium 1-0 but were held scoreless by Poland and eliminated. Four years later they were off to a fine start taking six goals off Hungary without reply. The Soviets then held France 1-1 and beat Canada 2-0. But in the second round they lost 4-3 to Belgium after extra time in Leon.

The Soviet Union were involved in a classic second round match in the 1986 finals in Mexico, eventually losing 4-3 to Belgium. Dasayev makes the catch, watched by Belgium's Nico Claesen (dark shirt), scorer of the winning goal.

USSR

Formed: *1912*
Joined FIFA: *1946*
Honours: *4th 1966*
Clubs: *50,198*
Players: *4,800,300*
Division I clubs: *16*
Season: *April-November*
Colours: *Red shirts, white shorts, red stockings*
Manager: *Valery Lobanovski*
Highest World Cup win: *10-0 v Finland, 1958 qualifying*

WORLD CUP RECORD

1930	*Not eligible*
1934	*Not eligible*
1938	*Not eligible*
1950	*Did not enter*
1954	*Did not enter*
1958	*Quarter-finals*
1962	*Quarter-finals*
1966	*4th*
1970	*Quarter-finals*
1974	*Did not qualify*
1978	*Did not qualify*
1982	*Second Round*
1986	*Second Round*
1990	*First Round*

RUMANIA

One of the four European countries to enter the first tournament in 1930, they participated in all three of the pre-war series but have not carried on the tradition. 1990 saw only their second post-war appearance in the finals.

Rumania did make a useful start in Uruguay beating Peru 3-1 but then lost 4-0 to the hosts and eventual winners. But in 1934 they almost found themselves the first team to be disqualified from the World Cup. In the qualifying competition Switzerland complained that Rumania had fielded an ineligible player but the Rumanians were reinstated on appeal. Alas it proved a short-lived reprieve as Rumania lost by 2-1 to the eventual runners-up Czechoslovakia in the first round.

In 1938 the withdrawal of Egypt gave Rumania a free pass to the finals in France where they were surprised by Cuba who held them to a 3-3 draw. More shocks came in the replay when Cuba beat them 2-1. They did not enter in 1950 and failed to qualify in 1954 and 1958. In 1962 they withdrew and in 1966 again found themselves out of the finals despite winning all their home qualifying games. This was particularly disappointing for them.

At last in 1970 Rumania succeeded in emerging from the qualifying tournament to win a place in Mexico. But they found themselves in a strong group which included Brazil, England and Czechoslovakia who had been their initial opponents in 1934. Luck was against them.

England provided the first hurdle and Rumania lost 1-0. But revenge was obtained against the Czechs in a 2-1 win before Rumania faced the might of Brazil. Almost certain of reaching the knock-out stage, the Brazilians rested a couple of key players. Even so after a slow start, Rumania were not disgraced in their 3-2 defeat.

RUMANIA	WORLD CUP RECORD	
Formed: *1908*	**1930**	*First Round*
Joined FIFA: *1930*	**1934**	*First Round*
Honours: *Nil*	**1938**	*First Round*
Clubs: *5453*	**1950**	*Did not enter*
Players: *179,987*	**1954**	*Did not qualify*
Division I clubs: *18*	**1958**	*Did not qualify*
Season: *August-November; March-July*	**1962**	*Withdrew*
Colours: *Yellow shirts, blue shorts,*	**1966**	*Did not qualify*
red stockings	**1970**	*First Round*
Manager: *Emerich Jenei*	**1974**	*Did not qualify*
Highest World Cup win: *9-0 v Finland,*	**1978**	*Did not qualify*
1974 qualifying	**1982**	*Did not qualify*
	1986	*Did not qualify*
	1990	*Second Round*

Marius Lacatus scored twice in Rumania's opening game of the 1990 finals, but suspension caused him to miss the crucial second round match against Ireland. Rumania were eliminated on penalties.

COSTA RICA

Costa Rica's association with the World Cup dates back to pre-war times but success had invariably eluded them until their first qualification for the 1990 series.

In 1938 they entered but withdrew along with most other countries in the vicinity before playing a match. In fact they did not attempt another tournament until 1958 when they finished top of their sub-group above Guatemala and Curacao to reach the second stage. Here they lost 2-0 to Mexico and drew 1-1 at home.

In 1962 they were required to play-off with Honduras and a 1-0 win put them again into the second stage, where they made a fine start by beating Mexico 1-0 at home. This was followed by a 6-0 win over the Netherlands Antilles. But Costa Rica lost both away fixtures.

The 1966 series again saw them safely through the initial group games above Trinidad and Surinam, but Mexico again proved the stumbling block in the next round, though Costa Rica beat Jamaica 7-0 in one of the matches.

However in 1970 they failed at the first stage and were similarly affected in 1974. Again in 1978 and 1982 their results were most disappointing and left them trailing in the opening phase of each series. However there was a marked improvement in the qualifying games for the 1986 World Cup.

When they reached the finals four years later, few expected them to score a goal, let alone win two matches and progress to the second phase. Having defeated Scotland 1-0 in their opening game they grew in confidence and after losing to Brazil by a single goal they beat Sweden 2-1 to finish second in their group. Facing Czechoslovakia in the next round, they looked the likelier winners at one stage, but eventually lost 4-1.

After years of trying to reach the finals, Costa Rica finally succeeded in the 1990 series. Here they put the pressure on the outnumbered United States player in a qualifying game.

COSTA RICA	WORLD CUP RECORD	
Formed: *1921*	**1930**	*Did not enter*
Joined FIFA: *1927*	**1934**	*Did not enter*
Honours: *Nil*	**1938**	*Withdrew*
Clubs: *431*	**1950**	*Did not enter*
Players: *12,429*	**1954**	*Did not enter*
Division I clubs: *10*	**1958**	*Did not qualify*
Season: *March-October*	**1962**	*Did not qualify*
Colours: *Red shirts, blue shorts, white stockings*	**1966**	*Did not qualify*
Manager: *Bora Milutinovic*	**1970**	*Did not qualify*
Highest World Cup win: *7-0 v Jamaica, 1966 qualifying*	**1974**	*Did not qualify*
	1978	*Did not qualify*
	1982	*Did not qualify*
	1986	*Did not qualify*
	1990	*Second Round*

BRAZIL

Brazil were the first country to win the World Cup three times and are the only one to have appeared in all the final competitions. They won the Jules Rimet Trophy outright in 1970 but have not reached the final since then, always falling short when looking like potential winners.

In 1930 they won one game and lost another; four years later they went out in the first round but improved in 1938. They edged out Poland 6-5 after extra time and beat Czechoslovakia 2-1 after a 1-1 draw, but then lost 2-1 to Italy in the semi-finals. Still they secured third place by beating Sweden 4-2.

In 1950 a 4-0 win over Mexico, a 2-2 draw with Switzerland and a 2-0 victory against Yugoslavia put them into the final pool where, after crushing Sweden 7-1 and Spain 6-1 they had to settle for runners-up spot, losing 2-1 to Uruguay.

Brazil were eliminated by Hungary in the quarter-finals in the 1954 series but impressed everyone in 1958. They beat Austria 3-0, drew 0-0 with England and beat the USSR 2-0, Wales 1-0 and France 5-2. In the final they also accounted for Sweden 5-2.

Retaining the cup in 1962 their victims were Mexico 2-0, Czechoslovakia held 0-0, Spain 2-1, England 3-1, Chile 4-2 and the Czechs finally overcome 3-1. But they were knocked out in the first stage in 1966.

Yet it was vintage Brazil in 1970. Czechoslovakia were beaten again this time 4-1, England 1-0, Rumania 3-2, Peru 4-2, Uruguay 3-1 and ultimately Italy 4-1. Even fourth place was disappointing in 1974. Brazil were third in 1978, thwarted by the vagaries of the schedule as much as anything else.

In 1982 defensive errors proved costly against Italy in the second stage and tragically they made a glorious exit after the lottery of a penalty shoot-out four years later, following a memorable game with France.

BRAZIL

Formed: *1914*
Joined FIFA: *1923*
Honours: *Winners 1958, 1962, 1970; runners-up 1950; 3rd 1938, 1978; 4th 1974*
Clubs: *12,890*
Players: *552,000*
Division I clubs: *National Championship: 22 clubs*
Season: *January-December*
Colours: *Yellow shirts, blue shorts, white stockings, green trim*
Manager: *Sebastiao Lazaroni*
Highest World Cup win: *7-1 v Sweden 1950*

WORLD CUP RECORD

1930	*First Round*
1934	*First Round*
1938	*3rd*
1950	*Runners-up*
1954	*Quarter-finals*
1958	*Winners*
1962	*Winners*
1966	*First Round*
1970	*Winners*
1974	*4th*
1978	*3rd*
1982	*Second Round*
1986	*Quarter-finals*
1990	*Second Round*

Brazil's captain in the 1970 World Cup was Carlos Alberto, the right-back; he managed to get himself on the score sheet in the final with the last goal of the game.
(SYNDICATION INTERNATIONAL)

SCOTLAND

Scotland have had a strange relationship with the World Cup, but one which has improved slowly. They have successfully played through five qualifying competitions, something unusual in the history of the tournament, after apparent lack of interest in it at one time.

In 1950 they were guaranteed a place in the finals on finishing second to England in the British Championship, but declined to take up the offer. Four years later they were again runners-up in the four nations tournament but this time went to Switzerland.

Unlucky to lose 1-0 to Austria, they crumpled completely against Uruguay and were beaten 7-0. However they fared much better when the qualifying necessity was taken away from the British Championship and became part of the overall draw. In fact they reached Sweden in 1958 only to return with one point; a draw with Yugoslavia at 1-1 followed by 3-2 and 2-1 defeats against Paraguay and France respectively.

They just failed to qualify in 1962 but were out of contention in 1966 and again in 1970. The Scots made sure in 1974 only to retire undefeated after beating Zaire 2-0 and drawing 0-0 with Brazil and 1-1 with Yugoslavia. But 1978 was a tragically disappointing experience. A 3-1 defeat by Peru was followed by an ignominious 1-1 draw with Iran and the 3-2 revitalisation at the expense of

Holland was too late to save them. Then in 1982 they found themselves in a formidable group with Brazil, the USSR and New Zealand as their opponents.

They were able to start well enough with a 5-2 win over the Kiwis but crashed 4-1 to Brazil after scoring first and ended with a gallant 2-2 draw against the Soviet Union. Again in 1986 the draw had them paired with Denmark, West Germany and Uruguay. Narrow 1-0 and 2-1 defeats respectively against the Danes and Germans left them with the physical Uruguayans, but they were held in scoreless draw by ten men. It was another disappointing performance for the Scots, who have invariably promised more than they have delivered. Even when expectations were low in 1990 they managed to sink below them, losing to Costa Rica and suffering another early exit.

Scotland made an inglorious exit from the 1986 finals, held 0-0 by the 10 men of Uruguay. Here Roy Aitken's path is blocked by Cabrera (white shirt).

SCOTLAND

Formed: *1873*
Joined FIFA: *1910-1920; 1924-1928; 1946*
Honours: *Nil*
Clubs: *5700*
Players: *137,000*
Division I clubs: *10 (Premier)*
Season: *July-May*
Colours: *Dark blue shirts, white shorts, red stockings*
Manager: *Andy Roxburgh*
Highest World Cup win: *8-0 v Cyprus 1970 qualifying*

WORLD CUP RECORD

1930	*Not eligible*
1934	*Not eligible*
1938	*Not eligible*
1950	*Withdrew after qualifying*
1954	*First Round*
1958	*First Round*
1962	*Did not qualify*
1966	*Did not qualify*
1970	*Did not qualify*
1974	*First Round*
1978	*First Round*
1982	*First Round*
1986	*First Round*
1990	*First Round*

SWEDEN

Sweden's best performance came in 1958 when they finished runners-up to Brazil in the tournament held on their own territory. Apart from the initial competition, they have entered every series.

In 1934 they beat Argentina 3-2 before losing to Germany 2-1 and were given a first round bye in 1938 when Austria pulled out. They then took eight goals off Cuba without reply but were beaten 5-1 by Hungary in the semi-finals and 4-2 by Brazil in the match for third place. A 3-2 win over Italy and a 2-2 draw with Paraguay in 1950 put them in the final group where they were trounced 7-1 by Brazil, edged out 3-2 by Uruguay but ensured of third place by beating Spain 3-1.

Sweden did not qualify again until staging their own tournament in 1958. They beat Mexico 3-0, Hungary 2-1 and drew 0-0 with Wales. In the quarter-finals they overcame the Soviet Union 2-0 and West Germany 3-1 in the semi-finals. Against any other team but Brazil in the final, they might have caused an upset, but a 5-2 defeat was no disgrace.

They did not qualify again until 1970 where they were eliminated on goal difference after losing 1-0 to Italy and drawing 1-1 with Israel, because their 1-0 win over Uruguay was not enough. There was a better outcome in 1974, when after goalless draws with Bulgaria and Holland they again beat Uruguay 3-0 to reach the next stage. But they lost 1-0 to Poland and 4-2 to West Germany giving them merely the consolation of a 2-1 win over Yugoslavia.

Sweden managed a 1-1 draw with Brazil at the beginning of the 1978 final tournament but then lost by a single goal to both Austria and Spain. They did not qualify in either 1982 or 1986, and in 1990 must have wished they hadn't, as they lost all three matches in Italy.

SWEDEN	WORLD CUP RECORD	
Formed: *1904*	**1930**	*Did not enter*
Joined FIFA: *1904*	**1934**	*Second Round*
Honours: *Runners-up 1958; 3rd 1950;*	**1938**	*4th*
4th 1938	**1950**	*3rd*
Clubs: *3400*	**1954**	*Did not qualify*
Players: *437,000*	**1958**	*Runners-up*
Division I clubs: *12*	**1962**	*Did not qualify*
Season: *April-October*	**1966**	*Did not qualify*
Colours: *Yellow shirts, blue shorts, yellow*	**1970**	*First Round*
and blue stockings	**1974**	*Second Round*
Manager: *Olle Nordin*	**1978**	*First Round*
Highest World Cup win: *8-0 v Cuba 1938*	**1982**	*Did not qualify*
	1986	*Did not qualify*
	1990	*First Round*

Sweden's most successful World Cup was as hosts in 1958. Right-back Orvar Bergmark heads clear during a 2-1 win over Hungary

161

WEST GERMANY

Only Brazil has a better record in terms of matches won in the World Cup than West Germany but the Germans are catching up fast, and since they did not enter in 1930 and were not allowed back into FIFA until after the 1950 tournament, their record is even more impressive.

In 1934 they accounted for Belgium 5-2 and Sweden 2-1 before losing 3-1 to the eventual beaten finalists Czechoslovakia. They took third place beating Austria 3-2. Ironically the overrunning of Austria by Germany gave the Germans several Austrian players in the 1938 campaign in which they were surprisingly beaten 4-2 by Switzerland in a replay after a 1-1 draw.

In 1954, shrewd manipulation of the oddities of the system allowed them to qualify for the quarter-finals. They defeated Yugoslavia 2-0 and then trounced Austria 6-1 in the semi-finals to face the favourites Hungary in the final. Against all the odds they won 3-2.

They were far more cautious in 1958 but still reached the semi-finals where they lost 3-1 to Sweden and were well beaten 6-3 by France in the match for third place. But the quarter-final was their downfall in 1962 when Yugoslavia beat them by a single goal.

In 1966 a 2-1 semi-final win over the Soviet Union put them into the final against England which ended in their controversial 4-2 defeat in extra time. Although they took

revenge on England in the 1970 quarter-finals they had to settle for third after the exhausting 4-3 defeat by Italy.

Home advantage helped in 1974 and their disciplined performance in the final against Holland produced a worthy 2-1 win, but they lost in 1978 at the second stage, ironically beaten 3-2 by Austria. Since then they have not failed to reach the final. They lost disappointingly 3-1 to Italy in 1982 and 3-2 to Argentina in 1986 after clawing their way back into the match. But in 1990 they gained revenge by beating the South Americans 1-0.

WEST GERMANY	WORLD CUP RECORD	
Formed: *1900*	1930	*Did not enter*
Joined FIFA: *1904-1945; 1950*	1934	*3rd*
Honours: *Winners 1954, 1974, 1990;*	1938	*First Round*
runners-up 1966, 1982, 1986; 3rd 1934, 1970;	1950	*Not eligible*
4th 1958	1954	*Winners*
Clubs: *21,510*	1958	*4th*
Players: *4,765,146*	1962	*Quarter-finals*
Division I clubs: *18*	1966	*Runners-up*
Season: *August-June*	1970	*3rd*
Colours: *White shirts, black shorts, white*	1974	*Winners*
stockings	1978	*Second Round*
Manager: *Franz Beckenbauer*	1982	*Runners-up*
Highest World Cup win: *12-0 v Cyprus 1970*	1986	*Runners-up*
qualifying	1990	*Winners*

The victorious West German team of 1954. Left to right: Fritz Walter, Turek, Eckel, Rahn, Ottmar Walter, Liebrich, Posipal, Schafer, Kohlmeyer, Mai. Coal-scuttle helmeted soldiers are in attendance. (JR)

COLOMBIA

Colombia's practical link with the World Cup dates back to the latter part of the post-war period. They had entered in 1938 but withdrew without playing a match. They did not enter in 1950 or 1954 and failed to reach the finals in 1958. However the Colombians made their bow in 1962 without causing too much concern to their opponents apart from the Soviet Union.

The first fixture was against fellow South Americans from Uruguay who beat them 2-1 in Arica. Then came the 4-4 draw with the Soviet Union and a 5-0 defeat by Yugoslavia. Finishing bottom of their qualifying group in 1966 and third out of four in 1970 was a disappointment in both instances. But there was an improvement in 1974 when they were only deprived of a place in the finals above Uruguay on goal difference.

In 1978 Colombia again finished bottom of their three-team qualifying group and four years later only succeeded in drawing their home matches 1-1 with Peru and Uruguay while losing both games away. In 1986 they were eliminated in a play-off with Paraguay, but four years later they finished top of their qualifying group and faced Israel in a play-off for a place in the finals. A 1-0 win in Bogota proved decisive.

They started the 1990 tournament with a 2-0 win against the United Arab Emirates, which meant that they needed just one more point to progress. But they lost 1-0 to Yugoslavia and looked to be going out when West Germany led 1-0 against them in the final minute. But a dramatic equaliser in injury time saw them reach the second round, only to lose 2-1 to Cameroon. They showed glimpses of Latin style and flair but were unable to impose themselves on the opposition.

COLOMBIA	WORLD CUP RECORD	
Formed: *1925*	**1930**	*Not eligible*
Joined FIFA: *1931*	**1934**	*Did not enter*
Honours: *Nil*	**1938**	*Withdrew*
Clubs: *3805*	**1950**	*Did not enter*
Players: *209,580*	**1954**	*Did not enter*
Division I clubs: *15*	**1958**	*Did not qualify*
Season: *February-December*	**1962**	*First Round*
Colours: *Red shirts, blue shorts, tricolour*	**1966**	*Did not qualify*
stockings	**1970**	*Did not qualify*
Manager: *Francisco Maturana*	**1974**	*Did not qualify*
Highest World Cup win: *2-0 v United Arab*	**1978**	*Did not qualify*
Emirates 1990	**1982**	*Did not qualify*
	1986	*Did not qualify*
	1990	*Second Round*

Carlos Valderrama played his club football in France for Montpellier before the 1990 finals. He was luckier than many of his Colombian colleagues, whose league fixtures were abandoned because of terrorist attacks organised by drug barons.

UNITED ARAB EMIRATES

Of the 24 finalists in the 1990 World Cup, the United Arab Emirates had the least experience in the competition, and their inexperience showed as they lost all three matches, including a 5-1 defeat against the eventual winners West Germany.

In 1978 they withdrew before playing in their group games and did not enter in 1982. But they made a useful start to their campaign in the following tournament, aided by the withdrawal of Oman which left their sub-group with just Saudi Arabia as their opponents.

The draw forced them to play their initial match in Riyadh and they did well to return from the match with a goalless draw. A week later at home in Dubai, the United Arab Emirates took a first half lead over the Saudis and retained it until the final whistle.

The UAE had to wait five months before they were required to play in the next stage and they were paired with Iraq. This time they had the advantage of a home first leg and though they were drawing 1-1 at half-time, it was Iraq who won 3-2.

A week later the team went to Taif for the return encounter and prospects looked good at half-time when the UAE led by a single goal. Mindful that they needed to achieve at least three goals in order to cancel Iraq's away goals advantage, they continued on the offensive but at

the final whistle were 2-1 ahead; not enough for victory.

Interestingly, the late Don Revie quit as England's national team manager in 1977 and took up a position with the UAE. The move certainly gave the country a higher profile in international football. But managerial comings and goings overshadowed their build-up to the 1990 finals. Brazilian Mario Zagalo was axed as manager and replaced by the Polish coach Bernard Blaut and then Blaut was replaced by Carlos Alberto.

United Arab Emirates players appear to be enjoying this warming up exercise during a training spell. They had to say goodbye to coach Mario Zagalo after he had taken them to the finals for the first time in their comparatively short footballing history.

UNITED ARAB EMIRATES

Formed: *1971*
Joined FIFA: *1972*
Honours: *Nil*
Clubs: *23*
Players: *690*
Division I clubs: *11*
Season: *October-May*
Colours: *All white*
Manager: *Carlos Alberto*
Highest World Cup win: *5-0 v Pakistan 1990 qualifying*

WORLD CUP RECORD

1930	*Not eligible*
1934	*Not eligible*
1938	*Not eligible*
1950	*Not eligible*
1954	*Not eligible*
1958	*Not eligible*
1962	*Not eligible*
1966	*Not eligible*
1970	*Not eligible*
1974	*Did not enter*
1978	*Withdrew*
1982	*Did not enter*
1986	*Did not qualify*
1990	*First Round*

YUGOSLAVIA

Although Yugoslavia have never won the World Cup they can be proud of their record of having entered for every tournament held so far. They have twice reached the semi-finals, in 1930 and 1962, an achievement they were prevented from matching in 1990 only by elimination on penalties against Argentina.

In 1930 they were one of only four European teams to embark on the then gruelling journey by sea to Uruguay. After beating Brazil 2-1 and Bolivia 4-0 they scored first against the Uruguayans but were well beaten 6-1.

Twenty years later they made an impressive start in Brazil, beating Switzerland 3-0 and Mexico 4-1 before losing 2-0 to the hosts in a closely-fought encounter. In 1954 they beat France 1-0 and then had another excellent match with the Brazilians which ended 1-1 after extra time. But in the quarter-finals, poor finishing let them down badly against West Germany. Moreover they conceded an own goal and one suspiciously close to offside in a 2-0 defeat. In 1958, Yugoslavia again reached the quarter-final only to lose again to the Germans.

Happily in 1962 they avoided a hat-trick of defeats against West Germany, once more at the quarter-final stage. This time Yugoslavia gained revenge winning 1-0. But in the semi-final, Czechoslovakia outwitted them tactically to win 3-1 and Chile beat them with the only goal of the game in the third place meeting.

In 1974 Yugoslavia were unbeaten in their opening three games which included a 9-0 win over Zaire, but lost all three second round matches. They did not qualify again until 1982 but managed to win only one match against Honduras 1-0.

Yugoslavia were unbeaten in the 1974 finals until they came across West Germany in the second round (above). Muller (13) was on target as the Germans won 2-0.

YUGOSLAVIA

Formed: *1919*
Joined FIFA: *1919*
Honours: *4th 1962*
Clubs: *7455*
Players: *270,229*
Division I clubs: *18*
Season: *August-November; March-June*
Colours: *Blue shirts, white shorts, red stockings*
Manager: *Ivica Osim*
Highest World Cup win: *9-0 v Zaire 1974*

WORLD CUP RECORD

1930	*Semi-finals*
1934	*Did not qualify*
1938	*Quarter-finals*
1950	*First Round*
1954	*Quarter-finals*
1958	*Quarter-finals*
1962	*4th*
1966	*Did not qualify*
1970	*Did not qualify*
1974	*Second Round*
1978	*Did not qualify*
1982	*First Round*
1986	*Did not qualify*
1990	*Quarter-finals*

BELGIUM

Belgium were one of the four original European entries in 1930 and have since qualified for the finals seven times. Fourth place in 1986 remains their best performance, though they were possibly more impressive in 1990.

In 1930 they lost 3-0 to the United States and 1-0 to Paraguay, but after qualifying in 1934 lost 5-2 in the first round to Germany. There was similar first round disappointment in 1938 when France beat them 3-1, but they withdrew in 1950.

They succeeded in 1954 and began their programme by drawing 4-4 with England, but were well beaten 4-1 by the Italians. They failed to qualify in 1958 and 1962 but at least forced a play-off with Bulgaria in the 1966 version, before losing 2-1 in Florence.

However they played in Mexico in 1970 and started by beating El Salvador 3-0. The Belgians then lost 4-1 to the USSR and 1-0 to the host nation. Neighbours Holland edged them out of a place in 1974 and repeated the exercise in 1978. But the Belgians were able to turn the tables on the Dutch in the run-up to the 1982 finals. A 3-0 defeat in Holland did not prevent them qualifying along with France, thanks to an earlier 1-0 win over the Dutch.

El Salvador were again in Belgium's group, but it was Argentina who fell victims to the Belgians 1-0 in the opening match. A similar win was recorded over El Salvador and then came a 1-1 draw with Hungary. But they lost 3-0 to Poland and 1-0 to the USSR in the second stage.

Belgium qualified again in 1986 and it was back to Mexico where they started by losing 2-1 to the hosts once more. A 2-1 win over Iraq was followed by a 2-2 draw with Paraguay. However in the second round they surpassed themselves beating the USSR 4-3 after extra time and Spain 5-4 on penalties after a 1-1 draw in the quarter-finals. Argentina took revenge in the semi-final winning 2-0 and Belgium lost third place to France 4-2.

Wilfred Van Moer had over a decade as a midfield player with Belgium, dictating the course of many World Cup games during his era; he was still good enough in 1982 to be included in the Belgian squad for the finals.
(BELGIAN FA)

BELGIUM

Formed: *1895*
Joined FIFA: *1904*
Honours: *4th 1986*
Clubs: *3362*
Players: *289,770*
Division I clubs: *18*
Season: *July-June*
Colours: *Red shirts with tri-coloured trim, red shorts, red stockings with trim*
Manager: *Guy Thys*
Highest World Cup win: *8-3 v Iceland, 1953 qualifying*

WORLD CUP RECORD

1930	*First Round*
1934	*First Round*
1938	*First Round*
1950	*Withdrew*
1954	*First Round*
1958	*Did not qualify*
1962	*Did not qualify*
1966	*Did not qualify*
1970	*First Round*
1974	*Did not qualify*
1978	*Did not qualify*
1982	*Second Round*
1986	*4th*
1990	*Second Round*

SPAIN

Spain have never quite managed to live up to their reputation in the World Cup since finishing fourth in 1950 and they were disappointing again in the 1990 finals.

They began their World Cup challenge well enough in 1934, beating Brazil 3-1 but then lost 1-0 to the eventual winners Italy after a bruising 1-1 draw after extra time. In 1938 the civil war robbed them of any participation but in 1950 they showed something of their potential. They defeated the USA 3-1, Chile 2-0 and even England 1-0 to reach the last four. But after a 2-2 draw with Uruguay they were well beaten 6-1 by Brazil and 3-1 by Sweden.

In 1954 and 1958 they failed to qualify only to find themselves in a difficult group in Chile for the 1962 finals. They lost the opening game 1-0 to Czechoslovakia but managed to beat Mexico 1-0. However a narrow 2-1 reverse against Brazil eliminated them.

In 1966 the draw again did them no favours. Argentina beat them 2-1 before the Spaniards reversed the scoreline against Switzerland, but another 2-1 defeat by West Germany ended their interest. Again there were two competitions in which they missed out before qualifying again for the 1978 finals in Argentina. Yet they were beaten 2-1 by Austria in the first match and though they held Brazil to a goalless draw and defeated Sweden 1-0

they were still eliminated.

Staging the finals in 1982 seemed to provide Spain with the right platform to display their ability. But they just scraped into the second stage where they lost 2-1 to West Germany and were held 0-0 by England. However 1986 was much better. They were unfortunate to lose 1-0 to Brazil but impressively beat Denmark 5-1 before losing on penalty kicks to Belgium after a 1-1 draw.

Emilio Butragueno (right), nicknamed 'The Vulture', swooped down on Denmark four times in a 5-1 win for Spain in 1986.

SPAIN

Formed: *1913*
Joined FIFA: *1904*
Honours: *4th 1950*
Clubs: *30,920*
Players: *343,657*
Division I clubs: *20*
Season: *September-June*
Colours: *Red shirts, dark blue shorts, black stockings, yellow trim*
Manager: *Luis Suarez*
Highest World Cup win: *9-0 v Portugal, 1934 qualifying*

WORLD CUP RECORD

1930	*Did not enter*
1934	*Second Round*
1938	*Could not enter*
1950	*4th*
1954	*Did not qualify*
1958	*Did not qualify*
1962	*First Round*
1966	*First Round*
1970	*Did not qualify*
1974	*Did not qualify*
1978	*First Round*
1982	*Second Round*
1986	*Quarter-finals*
1990	*Second Round*

URUGUAY

Uruguay won the inaugural competition in 1930 in impressive style and pulled off a splendid surprise win 20 years later. Since then their performances have become more disappointing and 1990 proved no exception.

Before the 1930 final they conceded only one goal in the semi-final in a 6-1 win over Yugoslavia. Previously they had beaten Peru 1-0 and Rumania 4-0. In the final they defeated neighbours Argentina 4-2. However, so annoyed were the Uruguayans over the lack of interest shown by European teams in their tournament that they did not enter either the 1934 or 1938 series. Thus it was not until 1950 that they competed again.

They were aided by withdrawals in the qualifying section and farcically in the finals, too, which left them with just one opponent, Bolivia who were despatched 8-0. Then in the final group they were held 2-2, by Spain and just edged out Sweden 3-2. They had to beat Brazil to win the tournament and did so courageously, 2-1.

In 1954 they beat Czechoslovakia 2-0 and Scotland 7-0 before overcoming England 4-2 in the quarter-finals. Then in a memorable semi-final they lost 4-2 to Hungary after extra time to suffer their first World Cup defeat. The 3-1 reverse against Austria in the match for third place was an anti-climactic reaction.

After failing to qualify in 1958 they disappointed in 1962 and when refereeing decisions went against them in 1966, disintegrated in a 4-0 defeat by West Germany.

The 1970 vintage was slightly better and with a reliable marksman they might have taken third place, but the 1974 squad was poor. After two abortive attempts to qualify they reached the 1986 finals as one of the favourites. Alas their talented team degenerated into indiscipline and were almost expelled from the competition.

Uruguay did everything but score in the match for third place with West Germany in 1970, but the Germans won 1-0.

URUGUAY	WORLD CUP RECORD	
Formed: *1900*	1930	*Winners*
Joined FIFA: *1923*	1934	*Did not enter*
Honours: *Winners 1930, 1950; 4th 1954, 1970*	1938	*Did not enter*
Clubs: *1102*	1950	*Winners*
Players: *155,000*	1954	*4th*
Division I clubs: *13*	1958	*Did not qualify*
Season: *March-December*	1962	*First Round*
Colours: *Light blue shirts, black shorts, black stockings*	1966	*Quarter-finals*
Manager: *Oscar Washington Tabarez*	1970	*4th*
Highest World Cup win: *8-0 v Bolivia 1950*	1974	*First Round*
	1978	*Did not qualify*
	1982	*Did not qualify*
	1986	*Second Round*
	1990	*Second Round*

SOUTH KOREA

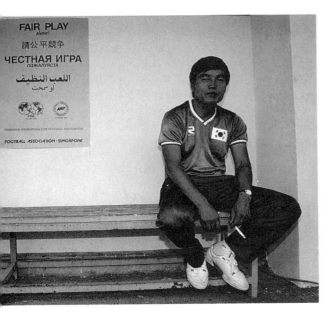

South Korea have shown some consistency in qualifying for recent finals, but progressing past the first round has proved beyond them.

Their initial achievement in reaching the 1954 tournament in Switzerland proved to be a chastening experience. Having overcome Japan to qualify, they were torn apart by the Hungarians in Zurich losing 9-0 and even lost 7-0 to Turkey.

They did not enter in 1958 but in 1962 again overcame Japan winning 2-1 in Seoul and 2-0 in Tokyo which meant they had to play Yugoslavia for a final place. In Belgrade they were beaten 5-1 and also lost at home 3-1.

They pulled out in 1966 and despite staging their sub-group in Seoul in 1970, failed to make any progress. But in 1974 they emerged from their initial matches to beat Israel 1-0 in the sub-group final and forced Australia to a play-off in the zone final before losing 1-0 in Hong Kong.

In 1978 they again negotiated the opening phase to finish second to Iran in the final round but were beaten 2-0 by Kuwait in a four-team group in 1982, though this was their only defeat in the tournament staged in Kuwait.

At last 1986 brought just reward. They beat Nepal 2-0 away and 4-0 at home, and after losing 1-0 in Malaysia, won the return game 2-0 to move on to the second round where they defeated Indonesia 2-0 and 4-1. In the final stage they beat Japan 2-1 in Tokyo and 1-0 in Seoul.

In Mexico their misfortune was to start the competition by playing Argentina. This 3-1 defeat was followed by holding Bulgaria to a 1-1 draw and they surprised Italy in the last group match before being edged out 3-2.

SOUTH KOREA

Formed: *1928*
Joined FIFA: *1948*
Honours: *Nil*
Clubs: *476*
Players: *2047*
Division I clubs: *5*
Season: *March-November*
Colours: *All red*
Manager: *Lee Hoe-Taik*
Highest World Cup win: *9-0 v Nepal 1990 qualifying*

WORLD CUP RECORD

1930	*Not eligible*
1934	*Not eligible*
1938	*Not eligible*
1950	*Did not enter*
1954	*First Round*
1958	*Did not enter*
1962	*Did not qualify*
1966	*Withdrew*
1970	*Did not qualify*
1974	*Did not qualify*
1978	*Did not qualify*
1982	*Did not qualify*
1986	*First Round*
1990	*First Round*

A coach's life can be a lonely one; certainly this appears to be the case for Lee Hoe-Taik, South Korea's man in the hot seat as he takes time out to think tactics.

EGYPT

Egypt have qualified for the finals just twice but were not disgraced on either occasion.

In 1934, they were required to play a qualifying match against neighbouring Palestine and in the home game in Cairo had a comfortable 7-1 win which virtually assured them of a final place. In the return in Jerusalem they completed an impressive double with a 4-1 success.

In Naples they were drawn to play Hungary in the first round. Far from being overawed by the occasion, they gave the Hungarians a hard game. At the interval Egypt trailed 2-1 but stayed in contention until the end when they finished as 4-2 losers.

Egypt entered in 1938 but withdrew before meeting Rumania. They did not compete in 1950, resuming in 1954 when they were required to play Italy in the qualifying stages. They were narrowly beaten 2-1 by the Italians in Cairo but lost the return game in Milan 5-1.

In the 1958 series they found their original qualifying opponents Cyprus unwilling to play and had a bye into the second round. But Egypt themselves then withdrew when paired with Sudan and when the same two countries were drawn together in 1962, they both pulled out!

In 1966, they were among the mass withdrawals of African states, did not enter four years later and were eliminated in the first preliminary round in 1974.

In 1978 they were just edged out by Tunisia and failed against Morocco in 1982 and 1986. But they reached the finals in Italy four years later and played superbly to draw 1-1 with Holland. A 0-0 draw with Ireland gave them a chance to progress to the second round but they lost their final match 1-0 to England and were eliminated.

Injuries sustained in a car crash robbed Abdel Rasoul of a place in Egypt's 1990 World Cup squad after he had finished as their leading scorer in the qualifying stages.

EGYPT

Formed: *1921*
Joined FIFA: *1923*
Honours: *Nil*
Clubs: *247*
Players: *19,735*
Division I clubs: *12*
Season: *September-June*
Colours: *Red shirts, white shorts, black stockings*
Manager: *Mahmoud El Gohary*
Highest World Cup win: *7-1 v Palestine 1934 qualifying*

WORLD CUP RECORD

1930	Did not enter
1934	First Round
1938	Withdrew
1950	Did not enter
1954	Did not qualify
1958	Withdrew
1962	Withdrew
1966	Withdrew
1970	Did not enter
1974	Did not qualify
1978	Did not qualify
1982	Did not qualify
1986	Did not qualify
1990	First Round

ENGLAND

England's World Cup triumph in 1966 was achieved by discovering their best eleven during the competition. This was also the case with their best achievement on foreign soil, 4th place in 1990, when after being pilloried for their tactical naivety in their first match of the finals, they recovered to play superbly in the semi-final.

But though England had withdrawn from FIFA by the time of the first World Cup in 1930, such was the desire to entice them back to the fold, that they were invited to play in the 1938 finals when Austria was annexed by Germany. However it was not until 1950 that England were able to enter legitimately. It proved to be an embarrassing disaster. Despite beating Chile 2-0 in the opening game, they were stunned by the USA in Belo Horizonte and then lost 1-0 to Spain.

In 1954 they gave an improved performance after a shaky start which saw them held 4-4 by Belgium after extra time. A 2-0 win over Switzerland put them in the quarter-finals where they were not disgraced in losing 4-2 to Uruguay. The Munich air disaster robbed England of key players in 1958 but they drew 2-2 with the USSR, 0-0 with Brazil and 2-2 with Austria before losing to the Soviets 1-0 in a play-off. In 1962 England again reached the last eight before losing 3-1 to Brazil.

With home advantage in 1966 England began weakly, held 0-0 by Uruguay. They beat Mexico 2-0 and France by the same score. Ten-man Argentina were also defeated 1-0 and Portugal 2-1 in the semi-final before the dramatic win over West Germany 4-2 in extra time.

The Germans gained revenge in the quarter-finals in 1970 beating England 3-2 and there was no qualification again until 1982 when they failed to score in both second round games. They were thus eliminated despite being unbeaten in five matches. Then in 1986 they improved after a wretched opening two matches before being knocked out by Argentina 2-1 in the quarter-finals.

ENGLAND

Formed: *1863*
Joined FIFA: *1905-1920; 1924-1928; 1946*
Honours: *Winners 1966; 4th 1990*
Clubs: *41,000*
Players: *2,250,000*
Division I clubs: *20*
Season: *August-June*
Colours: *White shirts, royal blue shorts, white stockings*
Manager: *Bobby Robson*
Highest World Cup win: *9-0 v Luxembourg 1962 qualifying*

WORLD CUP RECORD

1930	*Not eligible*
1934	*Not eligible*
1938	*Not eligible*
1950	*First Round*
1954	*Quarter-finals*
1958	*First Round*
1962	*Quarter-finals*
1966	*Winners*
1970	*Quarter-finals*
1974	*Did not qualify*
1978	*Did not qualify*
1982	*Second Round*
1986	*Quarter-finals*
1990	*4th*

Billy Wright leads the England team out at the start of their first test of World Cup football in 1950.
(POPPERFOTO)

HOLLAND

Holland finished runners-up in successive finals in the 1970s when they were arguably the best team in Europe. But the 1990 finals perhaps came two years too late; the European Champions of 1988 were hugely disappointing.

There was a swift exit in 1934 when they lost 3-2 to Switzerland and though they forced extra time against Czechoslovakia four years later, they conceded three goals without reply. Holland did not enter in either 1950 or 1954 and failed to qualify in 1958. It was a similar story in 1962 and 1966 when the preliminaries proved too much for this still-then-emerging football country.

Still, there was a noticeable improvement in the 1970 qualifying competition, as they finished two places but only two points behind Bulgaria. But in 1974 there was an outstanding transformation. Holland qualified — if only just — on a vastly superior goal difference over neighbours Belgium, with both teams just dropping points to each other in goalless draws.

In the finals in West Germany they beat Uruguay 2-0, drew 0-0 with Sweden and then defeated Bulgaria 4-1. In the second round they took four goals off Argentina without reply, beat East Germany 2-0 and Brazil by the same score. In fact the only goal conceded had been by one of their own players. Alas the 2-1 final defeat by the West Germans was a huge anti-climax.

They were equally determined in 1978 beating Iran 3-0 and drawing 0-0 with Peru. But they were slack against Scotland and lost 3-2, although it did not prevent them reaching the second round where they beat Austria 5-1 and drew 2-2 with West Germany. Then a 2-1 success over Italy put them in the final where they lost again, this time 3-1 to Argentina after extra time.

Johan Neeskens (left, horizontal) one of the stars of the great Dutch side of 1974, in an aerial battle with Sweden's Ove Grahn in the 0-0 draw in Dortmund.

HOLLAND

Formed: *1889*
Joined FIFA: *1904*
Honours: *Runners-up 1974, 1978*
Clubs: *7912*
Players: *978,324*
Division I clubs: *18*
Season: *August-June*
Colours: *Orange shirts, white shorts, orange stockings*
Manager: *Leo Beenhakker*
Highest World Cup win: *9-0 v Norway 1974 Qualifying*

WORLD CUP RECORD

1930	*Did not enter*
1934	*First Round*
1938	*First Round*
1950	*Did not enter*
1954	*Did not enter*
1958	*Did not qualify*
1962	*Did not qualify*
1966	*Did not qualify*
1970	*Did not qualify*
1974	*Runners-up*
1978	*Runners-up*
1982	*Did not qualify*
1986	*Did not qualify*
1990	*Second Round*

REPUBLIC OF IRELAND

The Republic of Ireland have been keen supporters of the World Cup but had never previously succeeded in reaching the finals until the 1990 tournament.

Their first attempt was in 1934 and they began by drawing 4-4 with Belgium in Dublin. But a 5-2 defeat in Holland ruled them out. In 1938 they lost 3-2 in Oslo to Norway and were held 3-3 in the return game.

In 1950 they had Scandinavian opposition in Sweden and Finland and after losing 3-1 in Stockholm to the former they beat Finland 3-0 in Dublin to record their first win in the tournament. They also drew 1-1 in Helsinki before losing 3-1 at home to Sweden.

In 1954 home and away wins against Luxembourg were cancelled out by losing twice to France. Four years later they put up a determined challenge beating Denmark 2-1 at home and 2-0 away, but lost 5-1 to England away and were held by them 1-1 in Dublin.

But 1962 was definitely a non-vintage performance. They failed to take a point against either Scotland or Czechoslovakia, yet forced Spain to a play-off in 1966 before losing that game 1-0 in Paris. In 1970 they were undistinguished in the company of Hungary, Czechoslovakia and Denmark and managed three points in 1974 when faced with the USSR and France, from whom they retrieved the trio. Moreover it was France who

stood in their way in 1978, though they had the satisfaction of beating them 1-0 in Dublin.

Incredibly it was France again who barred their way in 1982, but for the Republic it was unquestionably their best performance to date, finishing above Holland and losing out to France only on goal difference. They were disappointing in 1986 but reached the finals comfortably in 1990. In Italy they drew all three group matches, then defeated Rumania on penalties to reach the quarter-finals where they gave the host nation a fright despite losing 1-0, crowning a highly satisfactory debut in the finals.

REPUBLIC OF IRELAND

Formed: *1921*
Joined FIFA: *1923*
Honours: *Nil*
Clubs: *3503*
Players: *33,028*
Division I clubs: *12*
Season: *August-May*
Colours: *Green shirts, white shorts, green stockings*
Manager: *Jack Charlton*
Highest World Cup win: *4-0 v Luxembourg 1954 qualifying*

WORLD CUP RECORD

1930	*Did not enter*
1934	*Did not qualify*
1938	*Did not qualify*
1950	*Did not qualify*
1954	*Did not qualify*
1958	*Did not qualify*
1962	*Did not qualify*
1966	*Did not qualify*
1970	*Did not qualify*
1974	*Did not qualify*
1978	*Did not qualify*
1982	*Did not qualify*
1986	*Did not qualify*
1990	*Quarter-finals*

Tony Cascarino takes a determined swipe at the ball for the Republic of Ireland in their last World Cup qualifying game of the 1990 series against Malta. A 2-0 win clinched their place in the finals for the first time.

WORLD CUP RECORDS

COUNTRY BY COUNTRY RECORDS IN THE FINALS
1930-1990

	P	W	D	L	F	A
Brazil	66	44	11	11	148	65
*West Germany	68	39	15	14	145	90
Italy	54	31	12	11	89	54
Argentina	48	24	9	15	82	59
England	41	18	12	11	55	38
Uruguay	37	15	8	14	61	52
USSR	31	15	6	10	53	34
France	34	15	5	14	71	56
Yugoslavia	33	15	5	13	55	42
Hungary	32	15	3	14	87	57
Spain	32	13	7	12	43	38
Poland	25	13	5	7	39	29
Sweden	31	11	6	14	51	52
Czechoslovakia	30	11	5	14	44	45
Austria	26	12	2	12	40	43
Holland	20	8	6	6	35	23
Belgium	25	7	4	14	33	49
Mexico	29	6	6	17	27	64
Chile	21	7	3	11	26	32
Scotland	20	4	6	10	23	35
Portugal	9	6	0	3	19	12
Switzerland	18	5	2	11	28	44
Northern Ireland	13	3	5	5	13	23
Peru	15	4	3	8	19	31
Paraguay	11	3	4	4	16	25
Rumania	12	3	3	6	16	20
Cameroon	8	3	3	2	8	10
Denmark	4	3	0	1	10	6
East Germany	6	2	2	2	5	5
USA	10	3	0	7	14	29

	P	W	D	L	F	A
Bulgaria	16	0	6	10	11	35
Wales	5	1	3	1	4	4
Algeria	6	2	1	3	6	10
Morocco	7	1	3	3	5	8
Republic of Ireland	5	0	4	1	2	3
Costa Rica	4	2	0	2	4	6
Colombia	7	1	2	4	9	15
Tunisia	3	1	1	1	3	2
North Korea	4	1	1	2	5	9
Cuba	3	1	1	1	5	12
Turkey	3	1	0	2	10	11
Honduras	3	0	2	1	2	3
Israel	3	1	0	2	1	3
Egypt	4	0	2	2	3	6
Kuwait	3	0	1	2	2	6
Australia	3	0	1	2	0	5
Iran	3	0	1	2	2	8
South Korea	8	0	1	7	5	29
Norway	1	0	0	1	1	2
Dutch East Indies	1	0	0	1	0	6
Iraq	3	0	0	3	1	4
Canada	3	0	0	3	0	5
United Arab Emirates	3	0	0	3	2	11
New Zealand	3	0	0	3	2	12
Haiti	3	0	0	3	2	14
Zaire	3	0	0	3	0	14
Bolivia	3	0	0	3	0	16
El Salvador	6	0	0	6	1	22

*includes Germany 1930-38

Matches decided by penalty kicks are shown as drawn games

GOALS

GAMES	GOALS	AVERAGE	YEAR	LEADING GOALSCORER	GOALS
18	70	3.88	1930	Guillermo Stabile (Argentina)	8
17	70	4.11	1934	Angelo Schiavio (Italy)	
				Oldrich Nejedly (Czechoslovakia)	
				Edmund Cohen (Germany)	4
18	84	4.66	1938	Leonidas da Silva (Brazil)	8
22	88	4.00	1950	Ademir (Brazil)	9
26	140	5.38	1954	Sandor Kocsis (Hungary)	11
35	126	3.60	1958	Just Fontaine (France)	13
32	89	2.78	1962	Drazen Jerkovic (Yugoslavia)	5
32	89	2.78	1966	Eusebio (Portugal)	9
32	95	2.96	1970	Gerd Muller (West Germany)	10
38	97	2.55	1974	Grzegorz Lato (Poland)	7
38	102	2.68	1978	Mario Kempes (Argentina)	6
52	146	2.81	1982	Paolo Rossi (Italy)	6
52	132	2.53	1986	Gary Lineker (England)	6
52	115	2.21	1990	Salvatore Schillaci (Italy)	6

Six goals in Mexico made England's Gary Lineker (below) the 1986 tournament's top scorer.

Mario Zagalo, the serious Brazilian manager who managed one successful World Cup winning team after playing in two others. (SYNDICATION INTERNATIONAL)

BOSSES

YEAR	WINNERS	MANAGER
1930	Uruguay	Alberto Supicci
1934	Italy	Vittorio Pozzo
1938	Italy	Vittorio Pozzo
1950	Uruguay	Juan Lopez
1954	West Germany	Sepp Herberger
1958	Brazil	Vicente Feola
1962	Brazil	Aymore Moreira
1966	England	Alf Ramsey
1970	Brazil	Mario Zagalo
1974	West Germany	Helmut Schoen
1978	Argentina	Cesar Luis Menotti
1982	Italy	Enzo Bearzot
1986	Argentina	Carlos Bilardo
1990	West Germany	Franz Beckenbauer

CROWDS

YEAR	VENUE	AGGREGATE ATTENDANCE	AVERAGE ATTENDANCE	GAMES
1930	Uruguay	434,500	24,139	18
1934	Italy	395,000	23,235	17
1938	France	483,000	26,833	18
1950	Brazil	1,337,000	60,772	22
1954	Switzerland	943,000	36,270	26
1958	Sweden	868,000	24,800	35
1962	Chile	776,000	24,250	32
1966	England	1,614,677	50,458	32
1970	Mexico	1,673,975	52,312	32
1974	West Germany	1,774,022	46,685	38
1978	Argentina	1,610,215	42,374	38
1982	Spain	1,766,277	33,967	52
1986	Mexico	2,401,480	46,182	52
1990	Italy	2,510,686 (prov.)	48,282	52

WORLD CUP FINAL ATTENDANCES

YEAR	RESULT	VENUE	ATTENDANCE
1930	Uruguay 4 Argentina 2	Montevideo	90,000
1934	Italy 2 Czechoslovakia 1	Rome	50,000
1938	Italy 4 Hungary 2	Paris	45,000
1950	Uruguay 2 Brazil 1	Rio de Janeiro	199,854
1954	West Germany 3 Hungary 2	Berne	60,000
1958	Brazil 5 Sweden 2	Stockholm	49,737
1962	Brazil 3 Czechoslovakia 1	Santiago	68,679
1966	England 4 West Germany 2	Wembley	93,802
1970	Brazil 4 Italy 1	Mexico City	107,412
1974	West Germany 2 Holland 1	Munich	77,833
1978	Argentina 3 Holland 1	Buenos Aires	77,000
1982	Italy 3 West Germany 1	Madrid	90,080
1986	Argentina 3 West Germany 2	Mexico City	114,580
1990	West Germany 1 Argentina 0	Rome	73,603

WORLD CUP TRIVIA

The **record margin** of victory in a World Cup final tournament is nine goals: Hungary 10 El Salvador 1 (1982), Hungary 9 South Korea 0 (1954), Yugoslavia 9 Zaire 0 (1974). **Highest aggregate**: Austria 7 Switzerland 5 (1954). The **record scoreline** in any World Cup match is New Zealand 13 Fiji 0 in a qualifying match on 15 August 1981.

Just Fontaine (France) scored a **record 13 goals** in six matches of the 1958 World Cup finals. Jairzinho (Brazil) scored **seven in six games** in 1970. The only other player to score in **every match in a final series** is Alcide Ghiggia (Uruguay) with four goals in four games in 1950. Gerd Muller (West Germany) scored 10 goals in 1970 and four in 1974 for the **highest aggregate** of 14 goals. Muller scored 19 goals in the 1970 competition as a whole, including nine in six qualifying games.

Pele is third highest scorer in World Cup final tournaments after Muller and Fontaine, having registered 12 goals: 1958 (6), 1962 (1), 1966 (1), 1970 (4).

Geoff Hurst (England) is the only player to have scored a **hat-trick in a World Cup Final**; he got three of his team's goals in their 4 - 2 win over West Germany in 1966.

The first player to score as many as **four goals in any World Cup match** was Paddy Moore who claimed all the Republic of Ireland's goals in the 4 - 4 draw with Belgium in Dublin during a World Cup qualifying match on 25 February 1934.

Robbie Rensenbrink (Holland) scored the **1000th goal** in World Cup finals when he converted a penalty against Scotland in the 1978 tournament.

The **first goal scored** in the World Cup was credited to Louis Laurent for France against Mexico on 13 July 1930 in Montevideo. France won 4 - 1. With the time difference, the news reached France on Bastille Day, 14 July.

The **fastest goal scored** in the World Cup finals came after 27 seconds, scored by Bryan Robson of England against France on 16 June 1982, exactly 44 years to the day after Olle Nyberg of Sweden had scored in 30 seconds against Hungary in Paris. Bernard Lacombe scored for France against Italy after 31 seconds during the 1978 tournament.

West Germany achieved the **highest scoring rate** for a winning World Cup side when in 1954 they scored 25 goals in six matches for an average of 4.16 per game. But the 14 goals they conceded was also a record!

Highest individual scorers in one match Finals- 4 goals:
Gustav Wetterstrom (Sweden v Cuba, 1938)
Leonidas da Silva (Brazil v Poland, 1938)
Ernest Willimowski (Poland v Brazil, 1938)
Ademir (Brazil v Sweden, 1950)
Juan Schiaffino (Uruguay v Bolivia, 1950)
Sandor Kocsis (Hungary v West Germany, 1954)
Just Fontaine (France v West Germany, 1958)
Eusebio (Portugal v North Korea, 1966)
Emilio Butragueno (Spain v Denmark, 1986)

The lowest attendance for a match in the World Cup finals was probably 300 for the Rumania v Peru game on 14 July 1930 in Montevideo, Uruguay. **The highest**: 205,000 for Brazil v Uruguay on 16 July 1950 in Rio de Janeiro, Brazil. Of this estimated figure 199,854 were officially recorded, 173,830 paid to enter.

The **first substitute** used in the World Cup finals was the Soviet player Anatoly Puzach at the beginning of the second half of the USSR v Mexico game in 1970. But on 11 October 1953 West Germany had used a substitute in a qualifying game with Saar, Horst Eckel replacing Richard Gottinger, and again in the return game on 28 March 1954 when Ottmar Walter took over from his brother Fritz.

The Brazilians were **unbeaten in 13 consecutive World Cup matches** between 1958 and 1966, winning 11 and drawing two. The run ended with a 3 - 1 defeat by Hungary at Goodison Park.

Brazil used **only 12 players** in the 1962 World Cup finals. Their one change came through injury to Pele, who was replaced by Amarildo after the second match.

Dino Zoff (Italy) became the **oldest player to win a World Cup winners medal** when he captained his country to their 1982 success at the age of 40. Apart from Zoff, only one other goalkeeper had captained a World Cup winning side. He was Giampiero Combi, the Italian goalkeeper in 1934.

Norman Whiteside (Northern Ireland) became the **youngest player**, at 17, to appear in the World Cup finals in 1982. His first team experience for Manchester United had consisted of just two appearances in their Division One side, one of them as substitute. He was 17 years 42 days old when he appeared against Yugoslavia on 17 June. Pele had been 17 years 237 days old in Sweden in 1958.

Quickest dismissal in a World Cup final tournament was directed at Uruguay's Jose Batista after 55 seconds of the match with Scotland in Mexico on 13 June 1986.

Pele is the only player to have played with **three World Cup winning teams,** though he missed the final in 1962 through injury. His 14 appearances came from: 1958 (4), 1962 (2), 1966 (2) and 1970 (6).

Vava (real name Edwaldo Isidio Neto) of Brazil is the only player to have **scored in successive World Cup Finals.** He did so against Sweden in 1958 (scoring twice) and against Czechoslovakia in 1962. Pele (Brazil) and Paul Breitner (West Germany) are the only others to have scored in two Finals. Pele scored two goals in 1958 and one in 1970; Breitner a penalty in 1974 and a goal in 1982.

Antonio Carbajal (Mexico) is the only player to have appeared in **five World Cup final tournaments.** He kept goal for Mexico in 1950, 1954, 1958, 1962 and 1966, with eleven appearances in all.

Only two men have **won a World Cup winners medal and managed a World Cup winning team.** Mario Zagalo played in the 1958 and 1962 World Cup winning teams of Brazil and was manager when they achieved their third success in 1970. Franz Beckenbauer led West Germany to victory as a player in 1974 and as manager in 1990. He was also a losing finalist both as a player in 1966 and as a manager in 1986.

Uwe Seeler (West Germany) established a record in World Cup final tournaments by making a total of **21 appearances.** This was equalled by Wladyslaw Zmuda (Poland). Seeler played in 1958, 1962, 1966 and 1970; Zmuda in 1974, 1978, 1982 and 1986.

The longest period that a **goalkeeper has remained unbeaten** in World Cup finals matches is 517 minutes. In 1990 Walter Zenga (Italy) did not concede a goal in three first round group matches against Austria, the United States and Czechoslovakia, and remained unbeaten throughout the second round match with Uruguay and the quarter-final against the Republic of Ireland. He was finally beaten in the 67th minute of the semi-final against Argentina by a header from Claudio Caniggia. Ironically he then conceded four from the penalty spot in the shoot-out which saw the Italians beaten 4-3 and knocked out of the competition. Previously the record had stood at 501 minutes, set by Peter Shilton (England) over two tournaments in 1982 and 1986. Shilton also played in the 1990 finals, where his longest unbeaten period was 381 minutes.

New Zealand established a record in the 1982 qualifying tournament by playing **15 matches.** During this period goalkeeper Richard Wilson completed 15 hours 20 minutes without conceding a goal.

Edmond Delfour and Etienne Mattler (both Frenchmen) and the Belgian Bernard Voorhof, were the **first players to appear in three successive finals**: 1930, 1934 and 1938. Luisito Monti played in the 1930 tournament for Argentina and the 1934 series for Italy. Ferenc Puskas was in the Hungarian team during the 1954 finals and Spain's for the 1962 competition.

One factual analysis of the **1966 World Cup final** in which England beat West Germany 4 - 2 after extra time revealed the following statistics:
Goal attempts:
England 45 (four goals, one hit post, ten saved, six blocked, three deflected, 21 high or wide)
West Germany 37 (two goals, nine saved, nine blocked, five deflected, 12 high or wide)
Corners:
England 6
West Germany 12
Fouls:
England 22 (including three for hands)
West Germany 16 (including three for hands)
Offside:
England 1
West Germany 4
Goal-kicks:
England 16
West Germany 24
Throw-ins:
England 36
West Germany 19

In December 1983 a motion before FIFA's conference from the USA to equip goalkeepers with **helmets** was turned down.

Two managers have taken **different teams to World Cup final tournaments**. Rudolf Vytlacil, a Czechoslovakian, was in charge of his own country when they finished runners-up to Brazil in 1962 and four years later led Bulgaria in the competition. Blagoje Vidinic was the coach of Morocco in 1970 and Zaire in 1974. He was a Yugoslavian.

The opening match of the 1966 finals at Wembley between England and Uruguay was nearly called off by Hungarian referee Istvan Zsolt. He discovered that seven England players had left their identity cards in the team hotel. Zsolt said: **No cards, no game.** A police motor cyclist was despatched to collect them.

The original **Jules Rimet trophy** had an eventful life. After being successfully hidden during World War Two, it was stolen while on display in a London stamp exhibition before the 1966 finals. It was discovered by a mongrel dog called Pickles, owned by David Corbett, a Norwood lighterman, from under a garden hedge. Handed to Brazil for permanent retainment in 1970 it was again stolen from a display box in Rio and never recovered.

Zaire became the **first black African country to reach the finals** in 1974. The country's president promised each member of the squad a house, car and free holiday for their families. The team lost all three games, failed to score a goal and conceded 14. The offer was withdrawn.

Friction which had existed throughout the post-war period between Honduras and El Salvador gradually became more intense in the late 1960s. The two countries met in a World Cup qualifying tie in June 1969. The first leg in Honduras on June 8 produced little or no trouble on the pitch, but the frustrations which had built up off it finally burst during the return game in San Salvador on June 15. Since both teams had won their home games, a third and deciding match was scheduled for Mexico City on June 27. Relations had deteriorated into open hostility, and **all-out war** lasted two weeks. Mercifully the play-off passed without any animosity between the players.

The first player banned by FIFA for **drug-taking** in a final series was the Haitian, Ernest Jean-Joseph in 1974. But his manager refused to send him home and he was extradited by security men sent from Haiti; he never played again. In 1978, Willie Johnston of Scotland was also sent home in disgrace after taking an illegal drug for medicinal purposes.

Pat Jennings (above) made his 119th appearance for Northern Ireland against Brazil during the 1986 World Cup, on his 41st birthday.

Mo Johnston (above) set up a record for one of the four Home International countries by **scoring in each of five successive World Cup qualifying matches** in 1988-89; Norway (1 goal), Yugoslavia (1), Cyprus (1), France (2), Cyprus (1).

Brazil is the only country to have **appeared in all World Cup final tournaments**. They have also won the competition three times, a record shared with Italy and West Germany.

Before departing to Brazil to compete in the 1950 series, the England players **trained at Ascot**. Unfortunately they finished as also-rans.

The 1982 finals produced a number of **records**: the first hat-trick by a substitute, Laszlo Kiss (Hungary) v El Salvador; the fastest goal, in 27 seconds by Bryan Robson (England); the first penalty miss in Final, by Antonio Cabrini (Italy); a record score by one team, Hungary 10 El Salvador 1; and the first match to be decided by penalty kicks, West Germany beating France 5 - 4 after a 3 - 3 draw.

A total of **12.8 billion** television viewers watched the 1986 finals in Mexico. The final between Argentina and West Germany was seen by 580 million people in 160 countries.

Ernesto Mascheroni, the **last survivor** of the Uruguayan team which won the 1930 World Cup, died on 3 July 1984 at the age of 76.

Scotland's manager Andy Beattie **resigned** after the 1 - 0 defeat by Austria in the 1954 World Cup. Uruguay then beat the Scots 7 - 0.

Dino Zoff (Italy) was able to celebrate his 100th international appearance with a **goalless draw** against Poland in the 1982 tournament. But Polish international **Kazimierz Deyna** was not so fortunate on his 100th game in 1978. He **missed a penalty** against Argentina and the Poles lost 2 - 0.

A special **World Cup stamp**, approved by the Post Office and the Football Association, showing the flags of the 16 nations in the 1966 finals was banned by the Foreign Office because the British government did not recognise North Korea. The special commemorative issue was quickly changed to reveal footballers in action and became the first British stamps to feature sportsmen.

When Northern Ireland qualified for the 1958 finals in Sweden, their players were **ordered by the Irish FA not to play** in two of their three group matches as they fell on Sundays. But the team ignored the ruling.

The United States trainer ran on to the field to attend to one of his injured players in the semi-final against Argentina in 1930. He tripped, fell and broke a bottle of chloroform. The trainer was **carried off unconscious** while the player recovered without treatment.

The Argentine journalist Osvaldo Ardizzone established a **communication record** after his team qualified for the 1966 quarter-finals. His cable to Buenos Aires was 20,246 words long and took 5 hours and 40 minutes to transmit.

Refereeing can be a **monstrous undertaking**. In 1934 and 1937, two World Cup qualifying matches involving Hungary and Bulgaria and Lithuania and Latvia respectively, were controlled by Herr Frankenstein of Austria.

Sharp-eyed English referee Jack Taylor delayed the start of the 1974 World Cup Final between West Germany and Holland when he noticed that all the **flag-posts in midfield and at the corners were missing.**

Neither Argentina nor Uruguay could decide on **which ball to use** in the 1930 final. Belgian referee John Langenus decided to toss a coin. Argentina won and used their ball in the first half after which they led 2 - 1. Uruguay used theirs after the interval, and won 4 - 2.

Uruguay's goalkeeper in 1930 was Antonio Mazzali. He had played in the country's successful 1924 and 1928 Olympic teams but was destined not to appear in the first World Cup. The Uruguayan team had been isolated for almost eight weeks in a Montevideo hotel. One night Mazzali **sneaked out** to visit his family and was caught upon his return. He was sent home for good.

The two players with the **shortest last names** to have appeared in a World Cup final tournament are Cayetano Re (Paraguay) in 1958 and Francisco Sa (Argentina) in 1974.

FIFA AFFILIATED COUNTRIES

Country	Colours	Founded	Affiliated	Country	Colours	Founded	Affiliated
AFGHANISTAN	White, red trim	1933	1948	DENMARK	Red, white	1889	1904
ALBANIA	All red	1930	1932	DOMINICAN REPUBLIC	Navy blue, white	1953	1958
ALGERIA	Green, white, red	1962	1963	ECUADOR	Yellow, blue, red	1925	1926
ANGOLA	Red, black	1979	1980	EGYPT	Red, white, black	1921	1923
ANTIGUA	Gold, black	1928	1970	ENGLAND	White, navy blue	1863	1905
ARGENTINA	Light blue/white	1893	1912	EQUATORIAL GUINEA	All red	*—	1986
ARUBA	Yellow, blue	1932	1988	ETHIOPIA	Green/yellow, red	1943	1953
AUSTRALIA	Gold, green trim	1961	1963	FAROE ISLANDS	White, blue, red	1979	1988
AUSTRIA	White, black	1904	1905	FIJI	White, black	1938	1963
BAHAMAS	Yellow, black	1967	1968	FINLAND	White, blue	1907	1908
BAHRAIN	White, red	1957	1966	FRANCE	Blue, white, red	1919	1904
BANGLADESH	Orange, white	1972	1974	GABON	Green,yellow, blue	1962	1953
BARBADOS	Royal blue/gold	1910	1968	GAMBIA	White	1952	1966
BELGIUM	All red	1895	1904	GERMANY East	White, blue	1948	1952
BELIZE	Blue, red/white	1980	1986	GERMANY West	White, black	1900	1904
BENIN	Green	1962	1962	GHANA	All white	1957	1958
BERMUDA	Royal blue, white	1928	1962	GREECE	White, blue	1926	1927
BOLIVIA	Green, white trim	1925	1926	GRENADA	Green/yellow, red	1924	1976
BOTSWANA	Blue, white	1970	1976	GUATEMALA	White	*—	1945
BRAZIL	Yellow, green trim	1914	1923	GUINEA	Red, yellow, green	1959	1961
BRUNEI	Gold, black	1959	1969	GUINEA-BISSAU	All green	1974	1986
BULGARIA	White, green, red	1923	1924	GUYANA	Green, yellow	1904	1968
BURKINA FASO	Red, green	1960	1964	HAITI	Black/red	1904	1933
BURMA	Red, white	1947	1947	HONDURAS	White, blue	1951	1951
BURUNDI	Red, white, green	1948	1972	HONG KONG	Red, white	1914	1954
CAMEROON	Green, red, yellow	1959	1962	HUNGARY	Red, white, green	1901	1906
CANADA	All red	1912	1912	ICELAND	Blue, white	1947	1929
CAPE VERDE ISLANDS	All green	1982	1986	INDIA	White, sky blue	1937	1948
CENTRAL AFRICA	Grey-blue, white	1937	1963	INDONESIA	Red, white	1930	1952
CHAD	*—	*—	1988	IRAN	Green, white, red	1920	1945
CHILE	Red, white, blue	1895	1912	IRAQ	All white	1948	1950
CHINA PR	Red, white	1924	1931	IRELAND Northern	Green, white	1880	1911
CHINESE TAIPEI	Blue, white, red	1936	1954	IRELAND Republic	Green, white	1921	1923
COLOMBIA	Red, blue	1924	1936	ISRAEL	Blue, white	*—	*—
CONGO	All red	1962	1962	ITALY	Blue, white	1898	1905
COSTA RICA	Red, blue, white	1921	1921	IVORY COAST	Orange,white, green	1960	1960
CUBA	White, blue	1924	1932	JAMAICA	Green, black, gold	1910	1962
CYPRUS	Blue, white	1934	1948	JAPAN	White, red	1921	1929
CZECHOSLOVAKIA	Red, white, blue	1901	1906	JORDAN	White, red	1949	1958

Country	Colours	Founded	Affiliated	Country	Colours	Founded	Affiliated
KAMPUCHEA	Blue, red, white	1933	1953	RWANDA	Red/green/yellow	1972	1976
KENYA	Red, green, white	1960	1960	EL SALVADOR	All blue	1935	1938
KOREA North (DPR)	All white	1945	1958	SAN MARINO	All light blue	1931	1988
KOREA South (Republic)	All red	1928	1948	SAO TOME & PRINCIPE	Green/yellow	1985	1986
KUWAIT	Blue, white	1952	1962	SAUDI ARABIA	White/green	1959	1959
LAOS	Red, white, blue	1951	1952	SCOTLAND	Dark blue, white, red	1873	1910
LEBANON	Red/white	1933	1935	SENEGAL	Green, yellow, red	1960	1962
LESOTHO	Blue, white	1932	1964	SEYCHELLES	Red, white	1979	1986
LIBERIA	Red, white	1962	1962	SIERRA LEONE	Green, white, blue	1967	1967
LIBYA	Green, white	1963	1963	SINGAPORE	All white	1892	1952
LIECHTENSTEIN	Blue, red	1933	1974	SOLOMON ISLANDS	*—	*—	1988
LUXEMBOURG	Red, white, blue	1908	1910	SOMALIA	Sky blue, white	1951	1960
MACAO	Red, green	1939	1976	SPAIN	Red, blue, black	1913	1913
MADAGASCAR	Red, white, green	1961	1962	SRI LANKA	Maroon/gold, white	1939	1950
MALAWI	All red	1966	1967	ST LUCIA	Blue/white, black	*—	1988
MALAYSIA	Yellow/black	1933	1956	ST VINCENT/GRENADINES	*—	*—	1988
MALDIVES REPUBLIC	Green, white, red	1982	1986	SUDAN	Green, white	1936	1948
MALI	Green, yellow, red	1960	1962	SURINAM	Red, green, white	1920	1929
MALTA	Red, white	1900	1959	SWAZILAND	Blue/gold, white	*—	1976
MAURITANIA	Green/yellow, blue	1961	1964	SWEDEN	Yellow, blue	1904	1904
MAURITIUS	Red, white	1952	1962	SWITZERLAND	Red, white	1895	1904
MEXICO	Green, red/white	1927	1929	SYRIA	All white	1936	1937
MOROCCO	All red	1955	1956	TANZANIA	Yellow/black	1930	1964
MOZAMBIQUE	Red, black	1978	1978	THAILAND	All red	1916	1925
NEPAL	All red	1951	1970	TOGO	White, green	1960	1962
NETHERLANDS (Holland)	Orange, white	1889	1904	TRINIDAD & TOBAGO	White, black, red	1908	1963
NETHERLANDS ANTILLES	White, red/blue	1921	1932	TUNISIA	Red, white	1956	1960
NEW ZEALAND	White, black trim	1891	1948	TURKEY	White	1923	1923
NICARAGUA	Blue/white	1931	1950	UGANDA	Yellow/black	1924	1959
NIGER	Orange, white, green	1967	1967	UNITED ARAB EMIRATES	All white	1971	1972
NIGERIA	Green, white	1945	1959	URUGUAY	Sky blue, white	1900	1923
NORWAY	Red, white, blue	1902	1908	USA	White, blue	1913	1913
OMAN	Red, white trim	1978	1980	USSR	Red, white	1912	1946
PAKISTAN	Green, white	1948	1948	VANATU	*—	*—	1988
PANAMA	Red/white, blue	1937	1938	VENEZUALA	Dark red, white	1926	1952
PAPUA NEW GUINEA	Red, black	1962	1963	VIETNAM	Red, white	1962	1964
PARAGUAY	Red/white, blue	1906	1921	WALES	All red	1876	1910
PERU	White, red trim	1922	1924	WESTERN SAMOA	Royal blue, white	1968	1986
PHILIPPINES	Blue/red, white	1907	1928	YEMEN North	All green	1962	1980
POLAND	White, red	1919	1923	YEMEN South	Light blue, white	1940	1967
PORTUGAL	Red, green	1914	1926	YUGOSLAVIA	Blue, white	1919	1919
PUERTO RICO	Red/white, blue	1940	1960	ZAIRE	Green, yellow	1919	1962
QATAR	White, maroon	1960	1970	ZAMBIA	Green/copper	1929	1964
RUMANIA	Yellow, blue, red	1908	1930	ZIMBABWE	Green, gold	*—	1965

*Accurate information not available

LOOKING AHEAD

USA 1994

The 1994 World Cup finals will be held in the USA. The FIFA Executive Committee made their decision on American Independence Day, 4 July 1988. After abstentions by Joao Havelange, FIFA's President, and Abilio d'Almeida, the Brazilian member of the Executive Committee, the USA received ten votes, Morocco seven and Brazil two. As a Brazilian, and with Brazil as one of the candidates, Havelange refrained from presiding over the meeting. Senior Vice-President Harry H. Cavan presided instead.

The main reason for the Executive Committee's decision was the well-structured presentation that the United States Soccer Federation (USSF) made, under the presidency of Werner Fricker. The FIFA inspection group had more than enough evidence as to the feasibility of a World Cup finals competition being organised in the USA without inordinate financial costs.

There are enough modern stadia, even though the dimensions of the pitches of some of them will have to be extended to FIFA standards. Neither does FIFA expect any obstacles as regards transport and tele-communications. The USA should make a success of staging the finals; support for big names in soccer has never been a problem there. The North American Soccer League (NASL) collapsed largely because there were insufficient numbers of star players. When Pele retired, followed by Franz Beckenbauer, there was a rapid decline of interest. Conversely, there is a grassroots revival of considerable proportions among several million young players of the game.

The 1984 Olympic Games football tournament in the US was a pronounced success. It attracted 1,421,627 paying spectators to the 32 matches and was the best attended sporting discipline in the entire Games. The problem will not be finding fans, but producing a strong team.

Even for the Los Angeles Olympics there were astonishing problems in this area. According to official FIFA reports, for incomprehensible reasons, the United States team changed its formation three weeks ahead of the competition itself. But then the playing side has been a constant source of concern, throughout the country's history.

Origins of the game in the USA point to some form of football being played there early in the 19th century. By the middle of the century a dribbling code was adhered to and historians claim that the Oneida Football Club founded in Boston in 1859 is the second oldest in the World. Just how valid this claim is might be measured from the fact that teams of 20 and 25-a-side were frequent.

There is a record that Yale played a team of Old Etonians in New Haven in 1873 using only 11. However in 1884 the American Football Association was formed and the following year the first attempt at an international took place in Newark where the USA lost 1 - 0 to Canada. In 1891 a combined USA/Canada team toured the British Isles and after the turn of the century there were tours first by the appropriately named Pilgrims and then by the Corinthians, from these shores to the USA.

The AFA became affiliated to the Football Association in London, but there was another body emerging in the States, called the American Amateur FA and the continual fragmentation of the game retarded any progress it may have made. Ethnic and local considerations always took preference over any national organisation. FIFA was not interested in two bodies vying with each other, but when the United States Football Association was formed on 5 April 1913, they changed their opinion and admitted USA at the FIFA Congress.

That season a National Challenge Cup had been

launched in the US and in 1916 the national team played two games in Scandinavia, beating Sweden 3-2 and drawing 1-1 with Norway. They competed in the 1924 Olympics beating Estonia 1-0 before losing 3-0 to the eventual winners Uruguay. On the way home, the Americans stopped off in Warsaw to beat Poland 3-2, but lost in Dublin 3-1 to the Irish Free State.

The USA competed in the first World Cup in 1930 but two years later the lack of development at home was underlined by the fact that no football tournament was scheduled for the Olympic Games held in the country. Two years on and they played in the second World Cup in Italy. They also sent a team to the 1936 Olympics in Berlin.

After the Second World War came the sensational performance in the World Cup in Belo Horizonte, Brazil. The hotch-potch American team beat the cream of England's professionals 1-0 in arguably the biggest upset in the history of the competition. Yet it did nothing to popularise the game in the USA.

In the 1960s the introduction of top foreign teams in tournaments proved to the liking of a wider audience and this was followed at the end of the decade by the formation of a fully professional competition, the NASL. This folded when the stars drifted away. Since then schools and colleges have taken greater interest and the future looks slightly brighter, at least at this level.

The US did qualify for the World Cup finals in 1990, and in Italy the team showed an encouraging willingness to learn from the elementary mistakes it made during the first match, a 5-1 defeat against Czechoslovakia in which the Americans had a player sent off. They defended in depth against the Italians and embarrassed them on the break on more than one occasion. This single goal defeat was followed by their losing 2-1 to the Austrians.

Not having to qualify for the 1994 tournament will at least afford the opportunity of developing the game at national level through the institution of a comprehensive national league which is likely to be formed in the short term. This is essential for the growth of the game at the highest level.

The notion that FIFA president Joao Havelange is thinking along the lines of a game of four quarters will also please the Americans, who will be one of the few countries to appreciate the use of penalty shoot-outs to decide the outcome of tied games, even if the concept of sudden death 'overtime' has not yet been given FIFA's blessing.

No fewer than 31 different stadia in 27 cities of varying size are interested in staging the tournament. The final selection will probably leave 12 venues and the final decision to be made on naming them could well be taken in June 1991.

The Joe Robbie Stadium, Miami, home of the Miami Dolphins and a possible venue for the 1994 World Cup Final.

INDEX

Entries in *italic* indicate photographs

Ademir 22, 116, 179
Aitken, Roy *160*
Albert, Florian 38
Albertosi, Enrico 146
Amarildo, 38, 179
Andrade, Jose 9, *9*
Andrade, Rodriguez 22, *24*
Antognoni, Giancarlo 79
Ardiles, Ossie 70
Armfield, Jimmy 131
Aston, Ken 37

Bahr, Walter 22
Baggio, Roberto 97
Ball, Alan 107
Banks, Gordon 46, *107*
Barassi, Ottorino 19
Barbosa *21*, 22
Baresi, Franco 97
Batista, Jose 179
Battiston, Patrick *78*, 79
Bauer *24-25*, 138
Beardsley, Peter 126
Bearzot, Enzo 77, *152*
Beattie, Andy 182
Beckenbauer, Franz 46, 53, 61, 96, *109*, 124, 179, 186
Beenhakker, Leo 98
Bell, Colin 53
Bergmark, Orvar *161*
Bertin, Ebwere *154*
Bertoni, Daniel 70
Blaut, Bernard 164
Bliss, Brian *153*
Bonhof, Rainer 61, 63
Boninsegna, Roberto *53*, 53, 54

Boszik, Joszef 26
Brandts, Emy 70
Brehme, Andreas 96, *99*
Breitner, Paul 63, 179
Bremner, Billy *60-61*
Brown, Luis *88*
Burgnich, Tarcisio 53
Burruchaga, Jorge 90
Butragueno, Emilio *167*, 179
Byrne, Roger 29

Cabrera, Wilmar *160*
Cabrini, Antonio 71, *182*
Caligaris, Umberto 11
Caniggia, Claudio 98
Carbajal, Antonio 179
Carlos 89
Carlos Alberto 54, 139, *159*
Cascarino, Tony *173*
Castilho *24-25*
Castro, Hector 9
Cavan, Harry 186
Cea, Pedro *8*, 9
Cervato, Sergio 119
Charles, John 29
Charlton, Bobby 46, 53, 108, *111*
Charlton, Jackie 110, *111*
Claesen, Nico *156*
Clarke, Allan 106
Clodoaldo 51, 54
Colaussi, Luigi 18
Coluna, Mario 44
Combi, Giampiero 179
Cruyff, Johan 63, 70, 98, *113*, 127
Cubilla, Luis 54
Cubillas, Teofilo 69
Czibor, Zoltan 26

d'Almeida, Abilio 186
da Guia, Domingos 18
da Silva, Leonidas 179
Dalglish, Kenny *115*
Dasayev, Rinat *156*
David, Mario 37
Delaunay, Henri 6
Delfour, Edmond 180
Deyna, Kazimierz 69, 182
Dezotti, Gustavo 96
Di Stefano, Alfredo 117
Dickinson, Jimmy 122
Didi *24-25*, 29, *117*
Dirceu 144
Doherty, Peter 29
Donadoni, Roberto 97
Donaghy, Mal 77
Dorado, Pablo 9

Eckel, Horst 179
Edstrom, Ralf *125*
Edwards, Duncan 29
Elkjaer, Preben *86-87*
Ellis, Arthur 26
Eusebio *44*, 44, 46, 106, 179

Facchetti, Giacinto *118*
Falcao 78, 89
Felix 51, 54
Feola, Vicente 31, 139
Ferguson, Bobby 130
Fernandez, Lorenzo *8*, 9
Ferrari, Giovanni 17
Ferreyra, Bernabe *10*
Ferrini, Giorgio 37
Finney, Jim 46
Finney, Tom *24*
Foni, Alfredo *18*
Fontaine, Just 29, *121*, 136, 178, 179
Forster, Karl-Heinz *86-87*
Francescoli, Enzo 98
Friaca 22
Fricker, Werner 186

Gaetjens, Larry *20-21*, 22
Gallovich, Tibor 122
Garrincha 29, 31, *36-37*, 38, 43
Gascoigne, Paul 98
Gazamiga, Silvio 7
Gentile, Claudio *79*
Gento 117
Gerson 51, 54
Gestido, Alvaro 9
Ghiggia, Alcide 'Chico' 22, 140, 178
Giannini, Giuseppe 97
Giresse, Alain 78
Gomez, Walter 140
Gorgon, Jerzy 62
Gottinger, Richard 179

Goycochea, Sergio 96
Grabowski, Jurgen 53, 132
Grahn, Ove *172*
Graziani, Francesco 79
Greenwood, Ron 130
Gren, Gunnar 31
Griffiths, Mervyn 26
Grosics, Gyula 26
Guaita, Enrico 14
Gullit, Ruud 98
Gylmar *31*, *32*

Hagi, Gheorghe 98
Haller, Helmut 46
Hamrin, Kurt 31
Hateley, Mark 126
Havelange, Joao 186-187
Hay, David *60-61*
Haynes, Johnny *31*
Held, Siggi 46
Hellstrom, Ronnie *58-59*
Herberger, Sepp 25, 109, 142
Herrera, Helenio 118
Hidegkuti, Nandor *24-25*, *123*
Higuita, Rene 98
Hoeness, Uli 61, *62*
Holzenbein, Bernd 63
Humberto 26
Hurst, Geoff 43, 44, *44-45*, 46, 107, 178

Iriarte, Santos 9

Jair 116
Jairzinho 51, 52, 54, 61, 106, 178
Jansen, Wim 63
Jean-Joseph, Ernest 181
Jennings, Pat *181*
Jeppson, Hans *21*
Johnston, Harry 122
Johnston, Mo *182*
Johnston, Willie 70, 181
Jongbloed, Jan *61*
Jonquet, Robert 121
Jordan, Joe *62*
Junior 78, 89
Juskowiak, Erich 31

Keegan, Kevin 114
Kempes, Mario *70*, 70
Kiss, Laszlo 182
Klinsmann, Jurgen 96
Kocsis, Sandor 26, 122, 179
Koeman, Ronald 98
Kohler, Jurgen 96
Kopa, Raymond 29, *32*, 117, 120
Kovacs, Stefan 112
Kreitlein, Rudolf 44
Krol, Rudi *125*

189

Lacatus, Marius *156*
Lacombe, Bernard 178
Lafleur, Abel 7
Langenus, John *10*, 183
Lato, Grzegorz 61
Laurent, Louis 178
Law, Denis 114, 115
Lee Hoe-Taik *169*
Libregts, Thijs 98
Liedholm, Nils 31
Lineker, Gary *88-89*, 89, 98, *127*, *175*
Ling, Bill 26
Linzmaier, Manfred *150*
Lofthouse, Nat *24*
Logofet, Gennadi *52*
Lopez, Horatio *52*

Machado 17
Maier, Sepp 63, 132, 180
Manicera, Jorge *45*
Manuel, Carlos 180
Maradona, Diego 78, 87, 89, 90, 96, 98, *129*
Mascheroni, Ernesto 182
Maschio, Humberto 37
Masopust, Josef 38, 151
Maspoli, Roque *24*
Matthews, Stanley *24*
Mattler, Etienne 180
Mauro, Francesco 19
Mauro, Giovanni 19
Mazzali, Antonio 183
McDonald, Colin 29, *32*
Meazza, Guisseppe 14, 17, 18
Menotti, Luis Cesar 128
Merrick, Gil 122
Michel, Miguel 89, 98
Michels, Rinus 112, 113
Milburn, Jackie 110
Milla, Roger 98
Monti, Luisito 9, 180
Monzon, Pedro 96
Moore, Booby 46, *131*
Moore, Paddy 178
Morais, 44
Moreira, Zeze 116
Morlock, Max 26
Muller, Gerd 52, *53*, 53, *58-59*, 61, 63, *133*, *165*, 178
Mullery, Alan 53

Nanninga, Dirk 70
Nasazzi, Jose *10*
Neeskens, Johan 63, *172*
Nejedly, Oldrich 17
Nerz, Otto 109
Netzer, Gunter 132
Nyberg, Olle 178

Orsi, Raimondo 14

Pak Doo Ik 44
Passarella, Daniel 70
Pearce, Stuart 98
Pele 29, 31, 38, 43, 44, *50-51*, 51, 52, 54, 61, *105*, 116, 124, 128, *135*, *139*, 178, 179, 186
Peters, Martin *42-43*, 44, 46, 53
Peucelle, Carlos 9
Piola, Silvio 18
Planicka, Frantisek 13, 17
Platini, Michel 78, *89*, 90, *137*
Platt, David *97*, 98
Pluskal, Svatopluk 38
Popluhar, Jan 38
Pozzo, Vittorio 13, *14*, *17*
Procopio, 17
Puskas, Ferenc 25, 26, 117, 120, 122, *143*, 180
Puzach, Anatoly *179*

Radakovic 38
Rahn, Helmut 26, 29
Ramsey, Alf 53, 130
Ramzi, Hany 97
Rasoul, Abdel *170*
Rattin, Antonio 43, 44, *155*
Raynor, George 22, 29
Re, Cayetano 182
Rego, Almeida 9
Reilly, Jack *133*
Rensenbrink, Robbie 178
Riha 17
Rijkaard, Frank 98
Rimet, Jules 6, 7, *7*, 17
Riva, Luigi *52-53*, 53
Rivelino 51, 54, *135*
Rivera, Gianni 53
Robson, Bobby 89, 126
Robson, Bryan 77, 89, 178, 182
Rojas, Eladio 38
Rossi, Paolo 70, *78-79*, 78, *152*
Ruggeri, Oscar 96
Rummenigge, Karl-Heinz *71*, 79

Sa, Francisco 183
Saldanha, Joao 51
Salvadore, Sandro 146
Sanchez, Leonel 37, 38
Santos, Djalma *139*
Santos, Nilton 26, 138
Saucedo, Ulysses 9
Scherer 38
Schiaffino, Juan Alberto 22, *141*, 179
Schiavio, Angelo 14
Schillaci, Salvatore *97*
Schnellinger, Karl-Heinz 46, 53
Schoen, Helmut 53, 61, 108, *109*, 179
Schricker, Ivo 19
Schroif, Wilhelm 38
Schumacher, Harald *78*, 79, 90
Scifo, Enzo 98

Sebes, Gustav 26
Seeler, Uwe, *45*, 52, 53, 180
Sensini, Robert 96
Shilton, Peter 89, 96, 106, 180
Simonsson, Agne 31
Skuhravy, Tomas 98
Skoglund, Nacka 139
Socrates 78, 89
Sosa, Ruben 98
Sparwasser, Jurgen 59
Springett, Ron 106
Stabile, Guillermo 9
Stiles, Nobby 46, *107*
Stojkovic, Dragan 98
Szepan, Fritz 109
Szusza, Ferenc 122

Taylor, Jack 63, 183
Taylor, Tommy 29, 110
Thomas, Clive *70*, 70, 144
Tigana, Jean 78
Tilkowski, Hans *44-45*
Tomaszewski, Jan 61
Torres, Jose 44
Tostao 51, *135*
Tresor, Marius *76-77*, 78
Turek, Toni 26

Vaccaro, Giorgio 19
Valderrama, Carlos *163*
Valdomiro 63
Van Basten, Marco 98
Van de Kerkhof, Rene 69
Van Moer, Wilfried *166*
Varela, Obdulio 22
Vava *30-31*, 31, 38, 179
Venables, Terry 127
Vicente 44
Vidinic, Blagoje 18
Voller, Rudi 96, 98
Voorhof, Bernard 180
Vytlacil, Rudolf 180

Walter, Fritz 109, *143*, 179
Walter, Ottmar 179
Weber, Wolfgang 46
Wetterstrom, Gustav 18, 179
Whiteside, Norman 179
Wilkins, Ray 89, *147*
Williams, Bert *20-21*, 22
Willimowkski, Ernest 179
Wilson, Ray *36-37*, 46
Wilson, Richard 180
Wright, Billy 122, *171*

Yashin, Lev 38

Zagalo, Mario 31, 38, 51, 61, 164, *175*, 179
Zamora, Ricardo 13

Zenga, Walter 180
Zico 70, 78, 89, *145*
Zito 38, *139*
Zizinho 116
Zmuda, Wladyslaw 180
Zoff, Dino *79*, 79, *147*, 179, 182
Zsolt, Istvan 180

191